Family Maps
of
Perry County, Mississippi
Deluxe Edition

With Homesteads, Roads, Waterways, Towns, Cemeteries, Railroads, and More

Family Maps
of
Perry County, Mississippi
Deluxe Edition

With Homesteads, Roads, Waterways, Towns, Cemeteries, Railroads, and More

by Gregory A. Boyd, J.D.

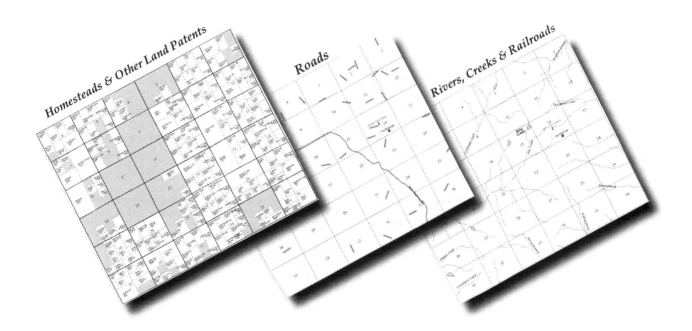

Featuring 3 *Maps Per Township...*

Arphax Publishing Co.
www.arphax.com

Family Maps of Perry County, Mississippi, Deluxe Edition: With Homesteads, Roads, Waterways, Towns, Cemeteries, Railroads, and More.
by Gregory A. Boyd, J.D.

ISBN 1-4203-1234-0

Printed in the United States of America

Published by Arphax Publishing Co., 2210 Research Park Blvd., Norman, Oklahoma, USA 73069
www.arphax.com

First Edition

ATTENTION HISTORICAL & GENEALOGICAL SOCIETIES, UNIVERSITIES, COLLEGES, CORPORATIONS, FAMILY REUNION COORDINATORS, AND PROFESSIONAL ORGANIZATIONS: Quantity discounts are available on bulk purchases of this book. For information, please contact Arphax Publishing Co., at the address listed above, or at (405) 366-6181, or visit our web-site at www.arphax.com and contact us through the "Bulk Sales" link.

—LEGAL—

The contents of this book rely on data published by the United States Government and its various agencies and departments, including but not limited to the General Land Office–Bureau of Land Management, the Department of the Interior, and the U.S. Census Bureau. The author has relied on said government agencies or re-sellers of its data, but makes no guarantee of the data's accuracy or of its representation herein, neither in its text nor maps. Said maps have been proportioned and scaled in a manner reflecting the author's primary goal—to make patentee names readable. This book will assist in the discovery of possible relationships between people, places, locales, rivers, streams, cemeteries, etc., but "proving" those relationships or exact geographic locations of any of the elements contained in the maps will require the use of other source material, which could include, but not be limited to: land patents, surveys, the patentees' applications, professionally drawn road-maps, etc.

Neither the author nor publisher makes any claim that the contents herein represent a complete or accurate record of the data it presents and disclaims any liability for reader's use of the book's contents. Many circumstances exist where human, computer, or data delivery errors could cause records to have been missed or to be inaccurately represented herein. Neither the author nor publisher shall assume any liability whatsoever for errors, inaccuracies, omissions or other inconsistencies herein.

This book is dedicated to my wonderful family:

Vicki, Jordan, & Amy Boyd

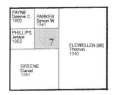

Contents

- Part I -

The Big Picture

- Part II -

Township Map Groups

(each Map Group contains a Patent Index, Patent Map, Road Map, & Historical Map)

Appendices

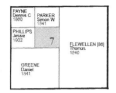

Preface

The quest for the discovery of my ancestors' origins, migrations, beliefs, and life-ways has brought me rewards that I could never have imagined. The *Family Maps* series of books is my first effort to share with historical and genealogical researchers, some of the tools that I have developed to achieve my research goals. I firmly believe that this effort will allow many people to reap the same sorts of treasures that I have.

Our Federal government's General Land Office of the Bureau of Land Management (the "GLO") has given genealogists and historians an incredible gift by virtue of its enormous database housed on its web-site at glorecords.blm.gov. Here, you can search for and find millions of parcels of land purchased by our ancestors in about thirty states.

This GLO web-site is one of the best FREE on-line tools available to family researchers. But, it is not for the faint of heart, nor is it for those unwilling or unable to to sift through and analyze the thousands of records that exist for most counties.

My immediate goal with this series is to spare you the hundreds of hours of work that it would take you to map the Land Patents for this county. Every Perry County homestead or land patent that I have gleaned from public GLO databases is mapped here. Consequently, I can usually show you in an instant, where your ancestor's land is located, as well as the names of nearby land-owners.

Originally, that was my primary goal. But after speaking to other genealogists, it became clear that there was much more that they wanted. Taking their advice set me back almost a full year, but I think you will agree it was worth the wait. Because now, you can learn so much more.

Now, this book answers these sorts of questions:

- Are there any variant spellings for surnames that I have missed in searching GLO records?
- Where is my family's traditional home-place?
- What cemeteries are near Grandma's house?
- My Granddad used to swim in such-and-such-Creek—where is that?
- How close is this little community to that one?
- Are there any other people with the same surname who bought land in the county?
- How about cousins and in-laws—did they buy land in the area?

And these are just for starters!

The rules for using the *Family Maps* books are simple, but the strategies for success are many. Some techniques are apparent on first use, but many are gained with time and experience. Please take the time to notice the roads, cemeteries, creek-names, family names, and unique first-names throughout the whole county. You cannot imagine what YOU might be the first to discover.

I hope to learn that many of you have answered age-old research questions within these pages or that you have discovered relationships previously not even considered. When these sorts of things happen to you, will you please let me hear about it? I would like nothing better. My contact information can always be found at www.arphax.com.

One more thing: please read the "How To Use This Book" chapter; it starts on the next page. This will give you the very best chance to find the treasures that lie within these pages.

My family and I wish you the very best of luck, both in life, and in your research.   Greg Boyd

How to Use This Book - A Graphical Summary

Part I
"The Big Picture"

Map A ▸ *Counties in the State*

Map B ▸ *Surrounding Counties*

Map C ▸ *Congressional Townships (Map Groups) in the County*

Map D ▸ *Cities & Towns in the County*

Map E ▸ *Cemeteries in the County*

Surnames in the County ▸ *Number of Land-Parcels for Each Surname*

Surname/Township Index ▸ *Directs you to Township Map Groups in Part II*

The <u>Surname/Township Index</u> *can direct you to any number of* **Township Map Groups**

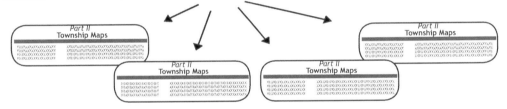

Part II
Township Map Groups
(1 for each Township in the County)

Each Township Map Group contains all four of of the following tools . . .

Land Patent Index ▸ *Every-name Index of Patents Mapped in this Township*

Land Patent Map ▸ *Map of Patents as listed in above Index*

Road Map ▸ *Map of Roads, City-centers, and Cemeteries in the Township*

Historical Map ▸ *Map of Railroads, Lakes, Rivers, Creeks, City-Centers, and Cemeteries*

Appendices

Appendix A ▸ *Congressional Authority enabling Patents within our Maps*

Appendix B ▸ *Section-Parts / Aliquot Parts (a comprehensive list)*

Appendix C ▸ *Multi-patentee Groups (Individuals within Buying Groups)*

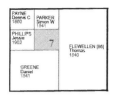

How to Use This Book

The two "Parts" of this *Family Maps* volume seek to answer two different types of questions. Part I deals with broad questions like: what counties surround Perry County, are there any ASHCRAFTs in Perry County, and if so, in which Townships or Maps can I find them? Ultimately, though, Part I should point you to a particular Township Map Group in Part II.

Part II concerns itself with details like: where exactly is this family's land, who else bought land in the area, and what roads and streams run through the land, or are located nearby. The Chart on the opposite page, and the remainder of this chapter attempt to convey to you the particulars of these two "parts", as well as how best to use them to achieve your research goals.

Part I
"The Big Picture"

Within Part I, you will find five "Big Picture" maps and two county-wide surname tools.

These include:

- Map A - Where Perry County lies within the state
- Map B - Counties that surround Perry County
- Map C - Congressional Townships of Perry County (+ Map Group Numbers)
- Map D - Cities & Towns of Perry County (with Index)
- Map E - Cemeteries of Perry County (with Index)
- Surnames in Perry County Patents (with Parcel-counts for each surname)
- Surname/Township Index (with Parcel-counts for each surname by Township)

The five "Big-Picture" Maps are fairly self-

explanatory, yet should not be overlooked. This is particularly true of Maps "C", "D", and "E", all of which show Perry County and its Congressional Townships (and their assigned Map Group Numbers).

Let me briefly explain this concept of Map Group Numbers. These are a device completely of our own invention. They were created to help you quickly locate maps without having to remember the full legal name of the various Congressional Townships. It is simply easier to remember "Map Group 1" than a legal name like: "Township 9-North Range 6-West, 5th Principal Meridian." But the fact is that the TRUE legal name for these Townships IS terribly important. These are the designations that others will be familiar with and you will need to accurately record them in your notes. This is why both Map Group numbers AND legal descriptions of Townships are almost always displayed together.

Map "C" will be your first intoduction to "Map Group Numbers", and that is all it contains: legal Township descriptions and their assigned Map Group Numbers. Once you get further into your research, and more immersed in the details, you will likely want to refer back to Map "C" from time to time, in order to regain your bearings on just where in the county you are researching.

Remember, township boundaries are a completely artificial device, created to standardize land descriptions. But do not let them become a boundary in your mind when choosing which townships to research. Your relative's in-laws, children, cousins, siblings, and mamas and papas, might just as easily have lived in the township next to the one your grandfather lived in—rather than in the one where he actually lived. So Map "C" can be your guide to which other Townships/Map Groups you likewise ought to analyze.

Of course, the same holds true for County lines; this is the purpose behind Map "B". It shows you surrounding counties that you may want to consider for further reserarch.

Map "D", the Cities and Towns map, is the first map with an index. Map "E" is the second (Cemeteries). Both, Maps "D" and "E" give you broad views of City (or Cemetery) locations in the County. But they go much further by pointing you toward pertinent Township Map Groups so you can locate the patents, roads, and waterways located near a particular city or cemetery.

Once you are familiar with these *Family Maps* volumes and the county you are researching, the "Surnames In Perry County" chapter (or its sister chapter in other volumes) is where you'll likely start your future research sessions. Here, you can quickly scan its few pages and see if anyone in the county possesses the surnames you are researching. The "Surnames in Perry County" list shows only two things: surnames and the number of parcels of land we have located for that surname in Perry County. But whether or not you immediately locate the surnames you are researching, please do not go any further without taking a few moments to scan ALL the surnames in these very few pages.

You cannot imagine how many lost ancestors are waiting to be found by someone willing to take just a little longer to scan the "Surnames In Perry County" list. Misspellings and typographical errors abound in most any index of this sort. Don't miss out on finding your Kinard that was written Rynard or Cox that was written Lox. If it looks funny or wrong, it very often is. And one of those little errors may well be your relative.

Now, armed with a surname and the knowledge that it has one or more entries in this book, you are ready for the "Surname/Township Index." Unlike the "Surnames In Perry County", which has only one line per Surname, the "Surname/Township Index" contains one line-item for each Township Map Group in which each surname is found. In other words, each line represents a different Township Map Group that you will need to review.

Specifically, each line of the Surname/Township Index contains the following four columns of information:

1. Surname
2. Township Map Group Number (these Map Groups are found in Part II)
3. Parcels of Land (number of them with the given Surname within the Township)
4. Meridian/Township/Range (the legal description for this Township Map Group)

The key column here is that of the Township Map Group Number. While you should definitely record the Meridian, Township, and Range, you can do that later. Right now, you need to dig a little deeper. That Map Group Number tells you where in Part II that you need to start digging.

But before you leave the "Surname/Township Index", do the same thing that you did with the "Surnames in Perry County" list: take a moment to scan the pages of the Index and see if there are similarly spelled or misspelled surnames that deserve your attention. Here again, is an easy opportunity to discover grossly misspelled family names with very little effort. Now you are ready to turn to . . .

Part II
"Township Map Groups"

You will normally arrive here in Part II after being directed to do so by one or more "Map Group Numbers" in the Surname/Township Index of Part I.

Each Map Group represents a set of four tools dedicated to a single Congressional Township that is either wholly or partially within the county. If you are trying to learn all that you can about a particular family or their land, then these tools should usually be viewed in the order they are presented.

These four tools include:

1. a Land Patent Index
2. a Land Patent Map
3. a Road Map, and
4. an Historical Map

As I mentioned earlier, each grouping of this sort is assigned a Map Group Number. So, let's now move on to a discussion of the four tools that make up one of these Township Map Groups.

Land Patent Index

Each Township Map Group's Index begins with a title, something along these lines:

MAP GROUP 1: Index to Land Patents
Township 16-North Range 5-West (2ⁿᵈ PM)

The Index contains seven (7) columns. They are:

1. ID (a unique ID number for this Individual and a corresponding Parcel of land in this Township)
2. Individual in Patent (name)
3. Sec. (Section), and
4. Sec. Part (Section Part, or Aliquot Part)
5. Date Issued (Patent)
6. Other Counties (often means multiple counties were mentioned in GLO records, or the section lies within multiple counties).
7. For More Info . . . (points to other places within this index or elsewhere in the book where you can find more information)

While most of the seven columns are self-explanatory, I will take a few moments to explain the "Sec. Part." and "For More Info" columns.

The "Sec. Part" column refers to what surveryors and other land professionals refer to as an Aliquot Part. The origins and use of such a term mean little to a non-surveyor, and I have chosen to simply call these sub-sections of land what they are: a "Section Part". No matter what we call them, what we are referring to are things like a quarter-section or half-section or quarter-quarter-section. See Appendix "B" for most of the "Section Parts" you will come across (and many you will not) and what size land-parcel they represent.

The "For More Info" column of the Index may seem like a small appendage to each line, but please

recognize quickly that this is not so. And to understand the various items you might find here, you need to become familiar with the Legend that appears at the top of each Land Patent Index.

Here is a sample of the Legend . . .

LEGEND

"For More Info . . . " column

A = Authority (Legislative Act, See Appendix "A")

B = Block or Lot (location in Section unknown)

C = Cancelled Patent

F = Fractional Section

G = Group (Multi-Patentee Patent, see Appendix "C")

V = Overlaps another Parcel

R = Re-Issued (Parcel patented more than once)

Most parcels of land will have only one or two of these items in their "For More Info" columns, but when that is not the case, there is often some valuable information to be gained from further investigation. Below, I will explain what each of these items means to you you as a researcher.

A = Authority
(Legislative Act, See Appendix "A")

All Federal Land Patents were issued because some branch of our government (usually the U.S. Congress) passed a law making such a transfer of title possible. And therefore every patent within these pages will have an "A" item next to it in the index. The number after the "A" indicates which item in Appendix "A" holds the citation to the particular law which authorized the transfer of land to the public. As it stands, most of the Public Land data compiled and released by our government, and which serves as the basis for the patents mapped here, concerns itself with "Cash Sale" homesteads. So in some Counties, the law which authorized cash sales will be the primary, if not the only, entry in the Appendix.

B = Block or Lot (location in Section unknown)
A "B" designation in the Index is a tip-off that the EXACT location of the patent within the map is not apparent from the legal description. This Patent will nonetheless be noted within the proper

Section along with any other Lots purchased in the Section. Given the scope of this project (many states and many Counties are being mapped), trying to locate all relevant plats for Lots (if they even exist) and accurately mapping them would have taken one person several lifetimes. But since our primary goal from the onset has been to establish relationships between neighbors and families, very little is lost to this goal since we can still observe who all lived in which Section.

C = Cancelled Patent

A Cancelled Patent is just that: cancelled. Whether the original Patentee forfeited his or her patent due to fraud, a technicality, non-payment, or whatever, the fact remains that it is significant to know who received patents for what parcels and when. A cancellation may be evidence that the Patentee never physically re-located to the land, but does not in itself prove that point. Further evidence would be required to prove that. *See also*, Re-issued Patents, *below*.

F = Fractional Section

A Fractional Section is one that contains less than 640 acres, almost always because of a body of water. The exact size and shape of land-parcels contained in such sections may not be ascertainable, but we map them nonetheless. Just keep in mind that we are not mapping an actual parcel to scale in such instances. Another point to consider is that we have located some fractional sections that are not so designated by the Bureau of Land Management in their data. This means that not all fractional sections have been so identified in our indexes.

G = Group
(Multi-Patentee Patent, see Appendix "C")

A "G" designation means that the Patent was issued to a GROUP of people (Multi-patentees). The "G" will always be followed by a number. Some such groups were quite large and it was impractical if not impossible to display each individual in our maps without unduly affecting readability. EACH person in the group is named in the Index, but they won't all be found on the Map. You will find the name of the first person in such a Group

on the map with the Group number next to it, enclosed in [square brackets].

To find all the members of the Group you can either scan the Index for all people with the same Group Number or you can simply refer to Appendix "C" where all members of the Group are listed next to their number.

O = Overlaps another Parcel

An Overlap is one where PART of a parcel of land gets issued on more than one patent. For genealogical purposes, both transfers of title are important and both Patentees are mapped. If the ENTIRE parcel of land is re-issued, that is what we call it, a Re-Issued Patent (*see below*). The number after the "O" indicates the ID for the overlapping Patent(s) contained within the same Index. Like Re-Issued and Cancelled Patents, Overlaps may cause a map-reader to be confused at first, but for genealogical purposes, all of these parties' relationships to the underlying land is important, and therefore, we map them.

R = Re-Issued (Parcel patented more than once)

The label, "Re-issued Patent" describes Patents which were issued more than once for land with the EXACT SAME LEGAL DESCRIPTION. Whether the original patent was cancelled or not, there were a good many parcels which were patented more than once. The number after the "R" indicates the ID for the other Patent contained within the same Index that was for the same land. A quick glance at the map itself within the relevant Section will be the quickest way to find the other Patentee to whom the Parcel was transferred. They should both be mapped in the same general area.

I have gone to some length describing all sorts of anomalies either in the underlying data or in their representation on the maps and indexes in this book. Most of this will bore the most ardent reseracher, but I do this with all due respect to those researchers who will inevitably (and rightfully) ask: *"Why isn't so-and-so's name on the exact spot that the index says it should be?"*

In most cases it will be due to the existence of a Multi-Patentee Patent, a Re-issued Patent, a Cancelled Patent, or Overlapping Parcels named in separate Patents. I don't pretend that this discussion will answer every question along these lines, but I hope it will at least convince you of the complexity of the subject.

Not to despair, this book's companion web-site will offer a way to further explain "odd-ball" or errant data. Each book (County) will have its own web-page or pages to discuss such situations. You can go to www.arphax.com to find the relevant web-page for Perry County.

Land Patent Map

On the first two-page spread following each Township's Index to Land Patents, you'll find the corresponding Land Patent Map. And here lies the real heart of our work. For the first time anywhere, researchers will be able to observe and analyze, on a grand scale, most of the original land-owners for an area AND see them mapped in proximity to each one another.

We encourage you to make vigorous use of the accompanying Index described above, but then later, to abandon it, and just stare at these maps for a while. This is a great way to catch misspellings or to find collateral kin you'd not known were in the area.

Each Land Patent Map represents one Congressional Township containing approximately 36-square miles. Each of these square miles is labeled by an accompanying Section Number (1 through 36, in most cases). Keep in mind, that this book concerns itself solely with Perry County's patents. Townships which creep into one or more other counties will not be shown in their entirety in any one book. You will need to consult other books, as they become available, in order to view other countys' patents, cities, cemeteries, etc.

But getting back to Perry County: each Land Patent Map contains a Statistical Chart that looks like the following:

Township Statistics

Parcels Mapped	:	173
Number of Patents	:	163
Number of Individuals	:	152
Patentees Identified	:	151
Number of Surnames	:	137
Multi-Patentee Parcels	:	4
Oldest Patent Date	:	11/27/1820
Most Recent Patent	:	9/28/1917
Block/Lot Parcels	:	0
Parcels Re-Issued	:	3
Parcels that Overlap	:	8
Cities and Towns	:	6
Cemeteries	:	6

This information may be of more use to a social statistician or historian than a genealogist, but I think all three will find it interesting.

Most of the statistics are self-explanatory, and what is not, was described in the above discussion of the Index's Legend, but I do want to mention a few of them that may affect your understanding of the Land Patent Maps.

First of all, Patents often contain more than one Parcel of land, so it is common for there to be more Parcels than Patents. Also, the Number of Individuals will more often than not, not match the number of Patentees. A Patentee is literally the person or PERSONS named in a patent. So, a Patent may have a multi-person Patentee or a single-person patentee. Nonetheless, we account for all these individuals in our indexes.

On the lower-righthand side of the Patent Map is a Legend which describes various features in the map, including Section Boundaries, Patent (land) Boundaries, Lots (numbered), and Multi-Patentee Group Numbers. You'll also find a "Helpful Hints" Box that will assist you.

One important note: though the vast majority of Patents mapped in this series will prove to be reasonably accurate representations of their actual locations, we cannot claim this for patents lying along state and county lines, or waterways, or that have been platted (lots).

Shifting boundaries and sparse legal descriptions in the GLO data make this a reality that we have nonetheless tried to overcome by estimating these patents' locations the best that we can.

Road Map

On the two-page spread following each Patent Map you will find a Road Map covering the exact same area (the same Congressional Township).

For me, fully exploring the past means that every once in a while I must leave the library and travel to the actual locations where my ancestors once walked and worked the land. Our Township Road Maps are a great place to begin such a quest.

Keep in mind that the scaling and proportion of these maps was chosen in order to squeeze hundreds of people-names, road-names, and place-names into tinier spaces than you would traditionally see. These are not professional road-maps, and like any secondary genealogical source, should be looked upon as an entry-way to original sources—in this case, original patents and applications, professionally produced maps and surveys, etc.

Both our Road Maps and Historical Maps contain cemeteries and city-centers, along with a listing of these on the left-hand side of the map. I should note that I am showing you city center-points, rather than city-limit boundaries, because in many instances, this will represent a place where settlement began. This may be a good time to mention that many cemeteries are located on private property, Always check with a local historical or genealogical society to see if aa particular cemetery is publicly accessible (if it is not obviously so). As a final point, look for your surnames among the road-names. You will often be surprised by what you find.

Historical Map

The third and final map in each Map Group is our attempt to display what each Township might have looked like before the advent of modern roads. In frontier times, people were usually more determined to settle near rivers and creeks than

they were near roads, which were often few and far between. As was the case with the Road Map, we've included the same cemeteries and city-centers. We've also included railroads, many of which came along before most roads.

While some may claim "Historical Map" to be a bit of a misnomer for this tool, we settled for this label simply because it was almost as accurate as saying "Railroads, Lakes, Rivers, Cities, and Cemeteries," and it is much easier to remember.

In Closing . . .

By way of example, here is *A Really Good Way to Use a Township Map Group.* First, find the person you are researching in the Township's Index to Land Patents, which will direct you to the proper Section and parcel on the Patent Map. But before leaving the Index, scan all the patents within it, looking for other names of interest. Now, turn to the Patent Map and locate your parcels of land. Pay special attention to the names of patent-holders who own land surrounding your person of interest. Next, turn the page and look at the same Section(s) on the Road Map. Note which roads are closest to your parcels and also the names of nearby towns and cemeteries. Using other resources, you may be able to learn of kin who have been buried here, plus, you may choose to visit these cemeteries the next time you are in the area.

Finally, turn to the Historical Map. Look once more at the same Sections where you found your research subject's land. Note the nearby streams, creeks, and other geographical features. You may be surprised to find family names were used to name them, or you may see a name you haven't heard mentioned in years and years—and a new research possibility is born.

Many more techniques for using these *Family Maps* volumes will no doubt be discovered. If from time to time, you will navigate to Perry County's web-page at www.arphax.com (use the "Research" link), you can learn new tricks as they become known (or you can share ones you have employed). But for now, you are ready to get started. So, go, and good luck.

– Part I –

The Big Picture

Map A - Where Perry County, Mississippi Lies Within the State

Legend

━━━ State Boundary

─── County Boundaries

▨ Perry County, Mississippi

Helpful Hints

1 We start with Map "A" which simply shows us where within the State this county lies.

2 Map "B" zooms in further to help us more easily identify surrounding Counties.

3 Map "C" zooms in even further to reveal the Congressional Townships that either lie within or intersect Perry County.

Map B - Perry County, Mississippi and Surrounding Counties

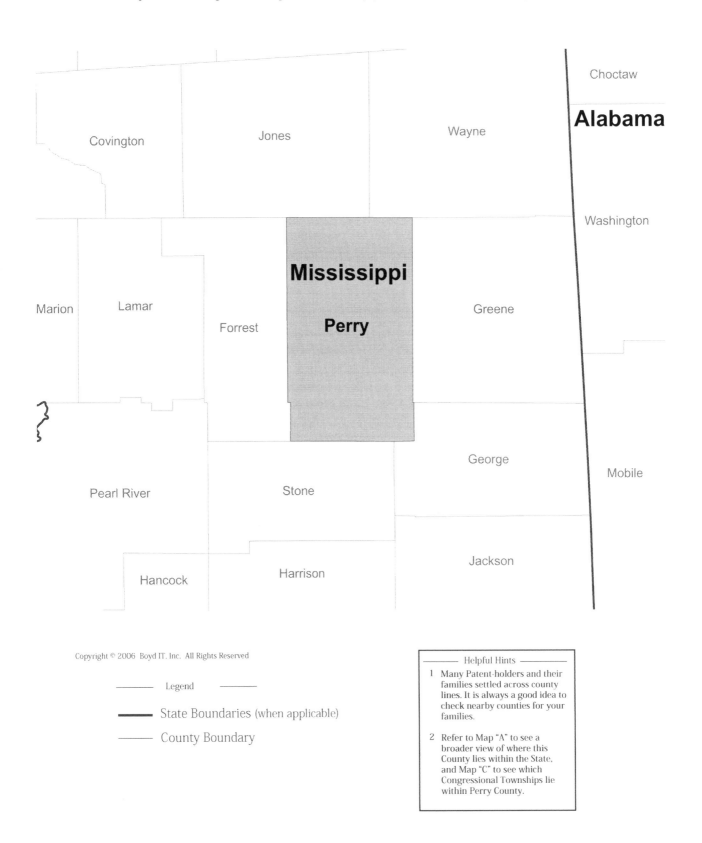

Copyright © 2006 Boyd IT. Inc. All Rights Reserved

——— Legend ———

━━━ State Boundaries (when applicable)

——— County Boundary

——— Helpful Hints ———

1 Many Patent-holders and their families settled across county lines. It is always a good idea to check nearby counties for your families.

2 Refer to Map "A" to see a broader view of where this County lies within the State, and Map "C" to see which Congressional Townships lie within Perry County.

Map C - Congressional Townships of Perry County, Mississippi

Map Group 1 Township 5-N Range 11-W	**Map Group 2** Township 5-N Range 10-W	**Map Group 3** Township 5-N Range 9-W
Map Group 4 Township 4-N Range 11-W	**Map Group 5** Township 4-N Range 10-W	**Map Group 6** Township 4-N Range 9-W
Map Group 7 Township 3-N Range 11-W	**Map Group 8** Township 3-N Range 10-W	**Map Group 9** Township 3-N Range 9-W
Map Group 10 Township 2-N Range 11-W	**Map Group 11** Township 2-N Range 10-W	**Map Group 12** Township 2-N Range 9-W
Map Group 13 Township 1-N Range 11-W	**Map Group 14** Township 1-N Range 10-W	**Map Group 15** Township 1-N Range 9-W
Map Group 16 Township 1-S Range 11-W	**Map Group 17** Township 1-S Range 10-W	**Map Group 18** Township 1-S Range 9-W

——————— Legend ———————

Perry County, Mississippi

Congressional Townships

——————— Helpful Hints ———————

1 Many Patent-holders and their families settled across county lines. It is always a good idea to check nearby counties for your families (See Map "B").

2 Refer to Map "A" to see a broader view of where this county lies within the State, and Map "B" for a view of the counties surrounding Perry County.

Map D Index: Cities & Towns of Perry County, Mississippi

The following represents the Cities and Towns of Perry County, along with the corresponding Map Group in which each is found. Cities and Towns are displayed in both the Road and Historical maps in the Group.

City/Town	Map Group No.
Barbara	17
Batt Place	17
Beaumont	12
Belleville	7
Benmore	9
Brewer	3
Corinth	4
Deep Creek	18
East Side	3
Ferguson	8
Good Hope	2
Hercules Station	9
Hintonville	6
Indian Springs	4
Janice	14
Kittrell	9
Little Creek	12
Mahned	7
McSwain	5
New Augusta	8
Oak Grove	14
Progress	15
Redhill	10
Rhodes	2
Richton	3
Runnelstown	1
Tallahala	1
Wingate	8

Map D - Cities & Towns of Perry County, Mississippi

Map Group 1
Township 5-N Range 11-W
● Tallahala
● Runnelstown

Rhodes ●

Good Hope ●

Map Group 2
Township 5-N Range 10-W

Map Group 3
Township 5-N Range 9-W
● Brewer
● East Side
● Richton

● Corinth

Map Group 4
Township 4-N Range 11-W
● Indian Springs

● McSwain

Map Group 5
Township 4-N Range 10-W

Map Group 6
Township 4-N Range 9-W

● Hintonville

Map Group 7
Township 3-N Range 11-W
● Belleville   ● Mahned

Map Group 8
Township 3-N Range 10-W
New Augusta ●
● Wingate
● Ferguson

● Benmore

Map Group 9
Township 3-N Range 9-W
● Kittrell

● Hercules Station

● Beaumont

Map Group 10
Township 2-N Range 11-W
Redhill ●

Map Group 11
Township 2-N Range 10-W

Map Group 12
Township 2-N Range 9-W
Little Creek ●

Progress ●

Map Group 13
Township 1-N Range 11-W

Map Group 14
Township 1-N Range 10-W
Oak Grove ●
● Janice

Map Group 15
Township 1-N Range 9-W

● Barbara
● Batt Place

Map Group 16
Township 1-S Range 11-W

Map Group 17
Township 1-S Range 10-W

Map Group 18
Township 1-S Range 9-W
● Deep Creek

——— Legend ———

Perry County, Mississippi

Congressional Townships

——— Helpful Hints ———

1 Cities and towns are marked only at their center-points as published by the USGS and/or NationalAtlas.gov. This often enables us to more closely approximate where these might have existed when first settled.

2 To see more specifically where these Cities & Towns are located within the county, refer to both the Road and Historical maps in the Map-Group referred to above. See also, the Map "D" Index on the opposite page.

Map E Index: Cemeteries of Perry County, Mississippi

The following represents many of the Cemeteries of Perry County, along with the corresponding Township Map Group in which each is found. Cemeteries are displayed in both the Road and Historical maps in the Map Groups referred to below.

Cemetery	Map Group No.
Belton Cem.	12
Breland Cem.	14
Browns Cem.	2
Burch Cem.	2
Carter Hill Cem.	8
Cochran Cem.	17
Courthey Cem.	4
Denham Cem.	7
Edwards Cem.	3
Fairley Cem.	17
Ferguson Cem.	7
Frisco Cem.	3
Garraway Cem.	7
Herring Cem.	11
Hinton Cem.	8
Hinton Cem.	8
Hinton Cem.	9
Hinton Cem.	11
Hollimon Cem.	7
Howard-Breland Cem.	17
Isaiah Hinton Cem.	6
James Cem.	4
Lott Cem.	9
McGilvary Cem.	4
McKenzie Cem.	7
McSwain Cem.	5
McSwain Cem.	7
Mixon Cem.	13
New Augusta Cem.	8
New York Cem.	16
Nichols Cem.	7
Prospect Cem.	4
Riley Cem.	15
Sims Cem.	16
Stevens Cem.	7
Sunset Cem.	6
Sweetwater Cem.	11
Sylvester Cem.	9
Sylvester Cem.	9
Taylor Cem.	16
Thomas Cem.	17
Wade Cem.	7
Woodard Cem.	2

Map E - Cemeteries of Perry County, Mississippi

Map Group 1 Township 5-N Range 11-W	⊕ Woodard Cem. **Map Group 2** Township 5-N Range 10-W Browns Cem. ⊕ ⊕ Burch Cem.	⊕ Edwards Cem. **Map Group 3** Township 5-N Range 9-W Frisco Cem. ⊕
McGilvary Cem. ⊕ **Map Group 4** Township 4-N Range 11-W Prospect Cem. ⊕ Courthey Cem. ⊕ James Cem. ⊕	⊕ Sunset Cem. ⊕ McSwain Cem. **Map Group 5** Township 4-N Range 10-W	⊕ Isaiah Hinton Cem. **Map Group 6** Township 4-N Range 9-W
Nichols Cem. ⊕ ⊕ Hollimon Wade Ferguson⊕ ⊕ Cem. Cem. Cem. McKenzie ⊕ Stevens Cem.⊕ Cem. McSwain Cem.⊕ Denham Cem.⊕ ⊕ Garraway Cem. **Map Group 7** Township 3-N Range 11-W	⊕ Hinton Cem. ⊕ Hinton Cem. **Map Group 8** Township 3-N Range 10-W Carter Hill Cem. ⊕ New Augusta Cem. ⊕	⊕ Hinton Cem. **Map Group 9** Township 3-N Range 9-W Sylvester Cem.⊕ Lott Cem.⊕ Sylvester Cem.⊕
Map Group 10 Township 2-N Range 11-W	⊕ Sweetwater Cem. **Map Group 11** Township 2-N Range 10-W Hinton Cem. ⊕ Herring Cem. ⊕	⊕ Belton Cem. **Map Group 12** Township 2-N Range 9-W
⊕ Mixon Cem. **Map Group 13** Township 1-N Range 11-W	Breland Cem.⊕ **Map Group 14** Township 1-N Range 10-W	**Map Group 15** Township 1-N Range 9-W ⊕ Riley Cem.
New York Cem. ⊕ **Map Group 16** Township 1-S Range 11-W ⊕ Sims Cem. ⊕ Taylor Cem.	⊕ Thomas Cem. ⊕ Howard-Breland Cem. **Map Group 17** Township 1-S Range 10-W Fairley Cem. ⊕ Cochran Cem. ⊕	**Map Group 18** Township 1-S Range 9-W

———— Legend ————

☐ Perry County, Mississippi

☐ Congressional Townships

———— Helpful Hints ————

1 Cemeteries are marked at locations as published by the USGS and/or NationalAtlas.gov.

2 To see more specifically where these Cemeteries are located, refer to the Road & Historical maps in the Map Group referred to above. See also, the Map "E" Index on the opposite page to make sure you don't miss any of the Cemeteries located within this Congressional township.

Surnames in Perry County, Mississippi Patents

The following list represents the surnames that we have located in Perry County, Mississippi Patents and the number of parcels that we have mapped for each one. Here is a quick way to determine the existence (or not) of Patents to be found in the subsequent indexes and maps of this volume.

Surname	# of Land Parcels	Surname	# of Land Parcels	Surname	# of Land Parcels	Surname	# of Land Parcels
ALBRITTON	7	CLARK	14	FORD	5	JOHNSON	37
ALDRIDGE	1	CLARKE	1	FOWLER	1	JONES	8
ALEXANDER	5	CLIFTON	6	FREEMAN	11	JORDAN	7
ALFRED	3	COACHMAN	2	FULLILOVE	2	KENNEDY	19
ALLEN	6	COATS	1	GAINES	6	KENT	14
ANDERSON	1	COCHRAN	14	GAMMILL	1	KILPATRICK	2
ANDREW	9	COLEMAN	1	GARAWAY	17	KIRKLAND	10
ANDREWS	7	COLLINS	3	GARDNER	3	KITTRELL	49
BACKSTROM	3	COMPANY	2	GARRAWAY	25	KNIGHT	4
BAGENT	2	CONKLIN	37	GAVIN	1	LAMBERT	6
BANG	1	CONN	1	GEORGE	1	LANDRUM	1
BARLOW	1	CONWAY	7	GIBSON	3	LANGLERY	1
BARNES	3	COOK	4	GILLINDER	3	LANTRIP	2
BARNETT	3	COOLEY	2	GILLIS	5	LAURENDINE	3
BARRON	1	COTTON	2	GILMER	1	LAURWENCE	1
BATCHELOR	1	COURTNEY	12	GODFREY	1	LAWRENCE	1
BATSON	2	COURTWRIGHT	1	GRANTHAM	4	LEATHERBURY	4
BATTE	1	COVINGTON	1	GREEN	2	LEE	1
BAZOR	1	COWART	3	GRIFFIN	195	LEWIS	4
BEARDSLEY	6	COX	1	GRIMBSLEY	3	LOPER	1
BEER	43	CREEL	3	GUINN	2	LOTT	17
BENJAMIN	4	CRONK	1	HAIRSTON	2	LUCAS	3
BENNETT	1	CROSBY	3	HARLSFIELD	1	MAINOR	1
BILBO	3	DANTZLER	24	HARRIS	5	MAMAN	1
BIRKETT	50	DAUGHTREY	2	HARTFIELD	23	MANNING	2
BIVINS	3	DAVIS	15	HARTLEY	5	MARTIN	13
BLACK	1	DEAKEL	2	HARTSFIELD	3	MASON	2
BLODGETT	36	DEARMAN	6	HARVISON	3	MATHESON	6
BOLTON	1	DEASE	1	HATHORN	9	MAXWELL	8
BOND	8	DENHAM	12	HATHORNE	1	MAYO	2
BONNER	5	DENNIS	8	HAVENS	1	MCCALLUM	5
BOOTH	3	DEVENPORT	2	HEMPHILL	4	MCCARDEL	1
BOULTON	52	DICKEY	3	HENDRY	2	MCCARDLE	20
BOWDEN	1	DIETZ	2	HENSAILING	1	MCCOLLUM	3
BOYKIN	1	DIKES	1	HENSARLING	4	MCCOY	1
BRADFORD	3	DILLARD	3	HERRING	9	MCDONALD	47
BRADLEY	40	DIXON	3	HESTLE	1	MCDOWELL	9
BRADLY	4	DOSSETT	1	HIDE	1	MCGAHA	1
BRANOM	1	DOUGLASS	1	HIGHTOWER	1	MCGILBERRY	6
BREELAND	9	DRAUGHN	40	HILLS	238	MCGILLVERRY	1
BRELAND	106	DUNIGAN	2	HINTON	163	MCGILRANY	3
BREWER	6	DUNLAP	1	HOGAN	9	MCGILVARY	1
BRIGHTMAN	2	DUNNAM	6	HOLDER	6	MCGILVRAY	13
BROADUS	1	DUNNAVANT	3	HOLLIMAN	9	MCHENRY	1
BRODLEY	2	DURDEN	2	HOLLIMON	35	MCINNIS	7
BROOKS	3	DYKES	8	HOLLINGSWORTH	7	MCKENZIE	9
BROWN	16	EASTERLING	11	HOLLINSWORTH	4	MCLAUGHLIN	2
BUCKALEW	1	EDWARDS	24	HOLLOMON	2	MCLEAN	3
BUCKHALTER	4	ELLIOTT	2	HORN	2	MCLEMORE	3
BULLOCK	6	ELLSWORTH	6	HOTEN	1	MCLEOD	5
BUNN	2	EPHRAM	2	HOTIN	1	MCLOUD	2
BURNETT	7	EVANS	2	HOTON	2	MCPHERSON	132
BURNNETT	3	EZELL	1	HOUSLEY	6	MCQUAGGE	1
BYNUM	2	FACEN	1	HOWARD	2	MCSWAIN	47
BYRD	7	FAIRLEY	100	HOWZE	11	MEADOWS	5
CARNES	2	FAIRLY	30	HUDSON	2	MERRETT	1
CARPENTER	11	FARMER	3	HUFF	2	MERRITT	16
CARROLL	1	FERGUSON	3	HUGGINS	10	MILES	6
CARTER	63	FERRELL	2	HUTSON	2	MISSISSIPPI	4
CEPHUS	3	FILINGIM	3	JACKSON	4	MIXON	25
CESAR	3	FILLINGAME	1	JAMES	22	MONTAGUE	35
CHAPPEL	1	FILLINGINE	3	JEFCOAT	1	MOODY	8

Surname	# of Land Parcels	Surname	# of Land Parcels
MOORE	41	SLOAN	1
MORGAN	17	SMITH	47
MORROW	1	SOWELL	4
MYERS	10	SPINKS	2
MYRICK	12	STAFFORD	18
NEAL	3	STALLWORTH	1
NEWELL	12	STEAN	1
NICHOLS	6	STEVENS	47
NIX	2	STOKLEY	1
NIXON	1	STRICKLAND	6
NOWELL	1	STRONG	3
ODOM	25	STUTTS	1
ONEAL	2	SULLIVAN	3
OVERSTREET	6	SUMMERS	5
OWENS	2	SWAYINGIN	3
PALMER	11	SYLVESTER	5
PARDUE	5	TANNER	2
PARKER	1	TAYLOR	8
PATTERSON	9	TERRELL	1
PATTON	3	THOMAS	44
PAYNE	2	THOMSON	3
PAYTON	3	TILLIS	1
PEARCE	32	TILLMAN	1
PERKINS	39	TINGLE	6
PHILIPS	2	TISDALE	9
PITTMAN	3	TOUCHSTONE	3
PITTS	1	TRAVIS	5
PORTER	1	TUCKER	1
PREISING	1	TURK	2
PRENTISS	2	VAUGHAN	31
PRIER	3	WADE	8
PRINE	2	WAGAR	87
PRYOR	2	WAGNER	20
PUGH	2	WALEY	2
RAMSEY	1	WALKER	3
RANSDELL	416	WALLEY	31
RAYBORN	5	WALTERS	2
RAYBURN	3	WALTMAN	3
READY	2	WARD	1
REVETTE	2	WARE	23
REYNOLDS	5	WARREN	2
RHODES	2	WATSON	151
RICH	58	WELDAY	1
RIGGS	2	WELLS	87
RILEY	6	WENTWORTH	3
ROBERTS	3	WEST	20
ROSS	1	WHATLEY	6
RUNNELLS	3	WHEELER	1
RUNNELS	10	WHITE	11
SAFFOLD	1	WHITTINGTON	1
SAGE	4	WHITTLE	3
SAMUEL	3	WILLIAMS	5
SAPP	4	WILLIAMSON	5
SAPPE	1	WILLINGHAM	4
SAVAGE	1	WOOD	2
SAWYER	32	WOODARD	5
SCARBOROUGH	2	WOODS	4
SCHILLING	1	WOODWARD	2
SCOTT	8	YARBROUGH	1
SEAL	3	YATES	1
SELLIVAN	3	YELVERTON	4
SHATTLES	2	YOUNG	4
SHAW	3		
SHEPARD	1		
SHORES	2		
SIMMONS	2		
SIMMS	2		
SIMS	2		
SINGLETON	1		
SINGLEY	2		

Surname/Township Index

This Index allows you to determine which *Township Map Group(s)* contain individuals with the following surnames. Each *Map Group* has a corresponding full-name index of all individuals who obtained patents for land within its Congressional township's borders. After each index you will find the Patent Map to which it refers, and just thereafter, you can view the township's Road Map and Historical Map, with the latter map displaying streams, railroads, and more.

So, once you find your Surname here, proceed to the Index at the beginning of the **Map Group** indicated below.

Surname	Map Group	Parcels of Land	Meridian/Township/Range		
ALBRITTON	9	3	St Stephens	3-N	9-W
" "	5	2	St Stephens	4-N	10-W
" "	4	2	St Stephens	4-N	11-W
ALDRIDGE	13	1	St Stephens	1-N	11-W
ALEXANDER	5	3	St Stephens	4-N	10-W
" "	10	1	St Stephens	2-N	11-W
" "	4	1	St Stephens	4-N	11-W
ALFRED	14	1	St Stephens	1-N	10-W
" "	13	1	St Stephens	1-N	11-W
" "	16	1	St Stephens	1-S	11-W
ALLEN	4	5	St Stephens	4-N	11-W
" "	7	1	St Stephens	3-N	11-W
ANDERSON	13	1	St Stephens	1-N	11-W
ANDREW	13	7	St Stephens	1-N	11-W
" "	16	2	St Stephens	1-S	11-W
ANDREWS	13	4	St Stephens	1-N	11-W
" "	16	1	St Stephens	1-S	11-W
" "	9	1	St Stephens	3-N	9-W
" "	4	1	St Stephens	4-N	11-W
BACKSTROM	6	2	St Stephens	4-N	9-W
" "	9	1	St Stephens	3-N	9-W
BAGENT	5	2	St Stephens	4-N	10-W
BANG	12	1	St Stephens	2-N	9-W
BARLOW	4	1	St Stephens	4-N	11-W
BARNES	4	3	St Stephens	4-N	11-W
BARNETT	7	3	St Stephens	3-N	11-W
BARRON	7	1	St Stephens	3-N	11-W
BATCHELOR	7	1	St Stephens	3-N	11-W
BATSON	16	2	St Stephens	1-S	11-W
BATTE	17	1	St Stephens	1-S	10-W
BAZOR	3	1	St Stephens	5-N	9-W
BEARDSLEY	12	3	St Stephens	2-N	9-W
" "	6	2	St Stephens	4-N	9-W
" "	3	1	St Stephens	5-N	9-W
BEER	1	29	St Stephens	5-N	11-W
" "	4	14	St Stephens	4-N	11-W
BENJAMIN	13	3	St Stephens	1-N	11-W
" "	16	1	St Stephens	1-S	11-W
BENNETT	17	1	St Stephens	1-S	10-W
BILBO	17	3	St Stephens	1-S	10-W
BIRKETT	1	33	St Stephens	5-N	11-W
" "	14	13	St Stephens	1-N	10-W
" "	11	3	St Stephens	2-N	10-W
" "	2	1	St Stephens	5-N	10-W

Surname	Map Group	Parcels of Land	Meridian/Township/Range		
BIVINS	**13**	3	St Stephens	1-N	11-W
BLACK	**2**	1	St Stephens	5-N	10-W
BLODGETT	**2**	23	St Stephens	5-N	10-W
" "	**3**	13	St Stephens	5-N	9-W
BOLTON	**12**	1	St Stephens	2-N	9-W
BOND	**17**	4	St Stephens	1-S	10-W
" "	**18**	4	St Stephens	1-S	9-W
BONNER	**7**	3	St Stephens	3-N	11-W
" "	**8**	2	St Stephens	3-N	10-W
BOOTH	**13**	3	St Stephens	1-N	11-W
BOULTON	**12**	40	St Stephens	2-N	9-W
" "	**16**	5	St Stephens	1-S	11-W
" "	**8**	3	St Stephens	3-N	10-W
" "	**13**	2	St Stephens	1-N	11-W
" "	**9**	2	St Stephens	3-N	9-W
BOWDEN	**3**	1	St Stephens	5-N	9-W
BOYKIN	**14**	1	St Stephens	1-N	10-W
BRADFORD	**12**	2	St Stephens	2-N	9-W
" "	**8**	1	St Stephens	3-N	10-W
BRADLEY	**8**	16	St Stephens	3-N	10-W
" "	**9**	15	St Stephens	3-N	9-W
" "	**5**	6	St Stephens	4-N	10-W
" "	**4**	3	St Stephens	4-N	11-W
BRADLY	**9**	4	St Stephens	3-N	9-W
BRANOM	**2**	1	St Stephens	5-N	10-W
BREELAND	**14**	5	St Stephens	1-N	10-W
" "	**16**	2	St Stephens	1-S	11-W
" "	**18**	2	St Stephens	1-S	9-W
BRELAND	**16**	32	St Stephens	1-S	11-W
" "	**13**	20	St Stephens	1-N	11-W
" "	**14**	15	St Stephens	1-N	10-W
" "	**17**	13	St Stephens	1-S	10-W
" "	**12**	10	St Stephens	2-N	9-W
" "	**9**	9	St Stephens	3-N	9-W
" "	**15**	3	St Stephens	1-N	9-W
" "	**18**	3	St Stephens	1-S	9-W
" "	**11**	1	St Stephens	2-N	10-W
BREWER	**3**	4	St Stephens	5-N	9-W
" "	**5**	1	St Stephens	4-N	10-W
" "	**2**	1	St Stephens	5-N	10-W
BRIGHTMAN	**14**	2	St Stephens	1-N	10-W
BROADUS	**13**	1	St Stephens	1-N	11-W
BRODLEY	**5**	2	St Stephens	4-N	10-W
BROOKS	**3**	3	St Stephens	5-N	9-W
BROWN	**4**	11	St Stephens	4-N	11-W
" "	**1**	2	St Stephens	5-N	11-W
" "	**13**	1	St Stephens	1-N	11-W
" "	**16**	1	St Stephens	1-S	11-W
" "	**7**	1	St Stephens	3-N	11-W
BUCKALEW	**3**	1	St Stephens	5-N	9-W
BUCKHALTER	**13**	4	St Stephens	1-N	11-W
BULLOCK	**4**	6	St Stephens	4-N	11-W
BUNN	**16**	2	St Stephens	1-S	11-W
BURNETT	**3**	7	St Stephens	5-N	9-W
BURNNETT	**3**	3	St Stephens	5-N	9-W
BYNUM	**7**	2	St Stephens	3-N	11-W
BYRD	**13**	2	St Stephens	1-N	11-W
" "	**9**	2	St Stephens	3-N	9-W
" "	**3**	2	St Stephens	5-N	9-W
" "	**14**	1	St Stephens	1-N	10-W

Surname	Map Group	Parcels of Land	Meridian/Township/Range		
CARNES	**2**	2	St Stephens	5-N	10-W
CARPENTER	**11**	6	St Stephens	2-N	10-W
" "	**8**	3	St Stephens	3-N	10-W
" "	**7**	1	St Stephens	3-N	11-W
" "	**4**	1	St Stephens	4-N	11-W
CARROLL	**2**	1	St Stephens	5-N	10-W
CARTER	**4**	23	St Stephens	4-N	11-W
" "	**7**	14	St Stephens	3-N	11-W
" "	**10**	8	St Stephens	2-N	11-W
" "	**8**	8	St Stephens	3-N	10-W
" "	**11**	5	St Stephens	2-N	10-W
" "	**14**	2	St Stephens	1-N	10-W
" "	**16**	2	St Stephens	1-S	11-W
" "	**15**	1	St Stephens	1-N	9-W
CEPHUS	**1**	3	St Stephens	5-N	11-W
CESAR	**13**	3	St Stephens	1-N	11-W
CHAPPEL	**1**	1	St Stephens	5-N	11-W
CLARK	**5**	10	St Stephens	4-N	10-W
" "	**8**	3	St Stephens	3-N	10-W
" "	**9**	1	St Stephens	3-N	9-W
CLARKE	**2**	1	St Stephens	5-N	10-W
CLIFTON	**8**	4	St Stephens	3-N	10-W
" "	**2**	2	St Stephens	5-N	10-W
COACHMAN	**16**	2	St Stephens	1-S	11-W
COATS	**3**	1	St Stephens	5-N	9-W
COCHRAN	**17**	5	St Stephens	1-S	10-W
" "	**6**	5	St Stephens	4-N	9-W
" "	**2**	4	St Stephens	5-N	10-W
COLEMAN	**8**	1	St Stephens	3-N	10-W
COLLINS	**7**	2	St Stephens	3-N	11-W
" "	**14**	1	St Stephens	1-N	10-W
COMPANY	**9**	2	St Stephens	3-N	9-W
CONKLIN	**17**	37	St Stephens	1-S	10-W
CONN	**17**	1	St Stephens	1-S	10-W
CONWAY	**4**	4	St Stephens	4-N	11-W
" "	**18**	3	St Stephens	1-S	9-W
COOK	**4**	3	St Stephens	4-N	11-W
" "	**7**	1	St Stephens	3-N	11-W
COOLEY	**14**	2	St Stephens	1-N	10-W
COTTON	**8**	2	St Stephens	3-N	10-W
COURTNEY	**4**	9	St Stephens	4-N	11-W
" "	**14**	1	St Stephens	1-N	10-W
" "	**11**	1	St Stephens	2-N	10-W
" "	**1**	1	St Stephens	5-N	11-W
COURTWRIGHT	**5**	1	St Stephens	4-N	10-W
COVINGTON	**1**	1	St Stephens	5-N	11-W
COWART	**15**	3	St Stephens	1-N	9-W
COX	**9**	1	St Stephens	3-N	9-W
CREEL	**2**	3	St Stephens	5-N	10-W
CRONK	**17**	1	St Stephens	1-S	10-W
CROSBY	**13**	2	St Stephens	1-N	11-W
" "	**16**	1	St Stephens	1-S	11-W
DANTZLER	**13**	12	St Stephens	1-N	11-W
" "	**16**	4	St Stephens	1-S	11-W
" "	**14**	3	St Stephens	1-N	10-W
" "	**17**	3	St Stephens	1-S	10-W
" "	**12**	1	St Stephens	2-N	9-W
" "	**7**	1	St Stephens	3-N	11-W
DAUGHTREY	**4**	2	St Stephens	4-N	11-W
DAVIS	**13**	5	St Stephens	1-N	11-W

Surname	Map Group	Parcels of Land	Meridian/Township/Range		
DAVIS (Cont'd)	7	4	St Stephens	3-N	11-W
" "	4	4	St Stephens	4-N	11-W
" "	14	1	St Stephens	1-N	10-W
" "	12	1	St Stephens	2-N	9-W
DEAKEL	13	2	St Stephens	1-N	11-W
DEARMAN	16	3	St Stephens	1-S	11-W
" "	7	3	St Stephens	3-N	11-W
DEASE	7	1	St Stephens	3-N	11-W
DENHAM	7	7	St Stephens	3-N	11-W
" "	10	3	St Stephens	2-N	11-W
" "	16	2	St Stephens	1-S	11-W
DENNIS	8	7	St Stephens	3-N	10-W
" "	5	1	St Stephens	4-N	10-W
DEVENPORT	9	2	St Stephens	3-N	9-W
DICKEY	7	3	St Stephens	3-N	11-W
DIETZ	7	2	St Stephens	3-N	11-W
DIKES	5	1	St Stephens	4-N	10-W
DILLARD	4	3	St Stephens	4-N	11-W
DIXON	4	3	St Stephens	4-N	11-W
DOSSETT	12	1	St Stephens	2-N	9-W
DOUGLASS	5	1	St Stephens	4-N	10-W
DRAUGHN	4	25	St Stephens	4-N	11-W
" "	7	5	St Stephens	3-N	11-W
" "	1	5	St Stephens	5-N	11-W
" "	8	3	St Stephens	3-N	10-W
" "	2	2	St Stephens	5-N	10-W
DUNIGAN	4	2	St Stephens	4-N	11-W
DUNLAP	16	1	St Stephens	1-S	11-W
DUNNAM	3	5	St Stephens	5-N	9-W
" "	2	1	St Stephens	5-N	10-W
DUNNAVANT	7	3	St Stephens	3-N	11-W
DURDEN	10	2	St Stephens	2-N	11-W
DYKES	3	8	St Stephens	5-N	9-W
EASTERLING	1	4	St Stephens	5-N	11-W
" "	4	3	St Stephens	4-N	11-W
" "	3	3	St Stephens	5-N	9-W
" "	2	1	St Stephens	5-N	10-W
EDWARDS	3	12	St Stephens	5-N	9-W
" "	2	7	St Stephens	5-N	10-W
" "	5	5	St Stephens	4-N	10-W
ELLIOTT	9	2	St Stephens	3-N	9-W
ELLSWORTH	1	6	St Stephens	5-N	11-W
EPHRAM	12	2	St Stephens	2-N	9-W
EVANS	7	2	St Stephens	3-N	11-W
EZELL	4	1	St Stephens	4-N	11-W
FACEN	12	1	St Stephens	2-N	9-W
FAIRLEY	17	46	St Stephens	1-S	10-W
" "	13	17	St Stephens	1-N	11-W
" "	16	17	St Stephens	1-S	11-W
" "	14	9	St Stephens	1-N	10-W
" "	18	6	St Stephens	1-S	9-W
" "	8	5	St Stephens	3-N	10-W
FAIRLY	17	23	St Stephens	1-S	10-W
" "	18	3	St Stephens	1-S	9-W
" "	15	2	St Stephens	1-N	9-W
" "	12	2	St Stephens	2-N	9-W
FARMER	5	3	St Stephens	4-N	10-W
FERGUSON	7	3	St Stephens	3-N	11-W
FERRELL	4	2	St Stephens	4-N	11-W
FILINGIM	13	3	St Stephens	1-N	11-W

Surname	Map Group	Parcels of Land	Meridian/Township/Range		
FILLINGAME	**10**	1	St Stephens	2-N	11-W
FILLINGINE	**13**	3	St Stephens	1-N	11-W
FORD	**4**	5	St Stephens	4-N	11-W
FOWLER	**9**	1	St Stephens	3-N	9-W
FREEMAN	**8**	3	St Stephens	3-N	10-W
" "	**9**	3	St Stephens	3-N	9-W
" "	**3**	3	St Stephens	5-N	9-W
" "	**12**	1	St Stephens	2-N	9-W
" "	**4**	1	St Stephens	4-N	11-W
FULLILOVE	**7**	2	St Stephens	3-N	11-W
GAINES	**12**	4	St Stephens	2-N	9-W
" "	**6**	2	St Stephens	4-N	9-W
GAMMILL	**13**	1	St Stephens	1-N	11-W
GARAWAY	**13**	8	St Stephens	1-N	11-W
" "	**11**	4	St Stephens	2-N	10-W
" "	**14**	2	St Stephens	1-N	10-W
" "	**10**	2	St Stephens	2-N	11-W
" "	**7**	1	St Stephens	3-N	11-W
GARDNER	**5**	2	St Stephens	4-N	10-W
" "	**8**	1	St Stephens	3-N	10-W
GARRAWAY	**7**	11	St Stephens	3-N	11-W
" "	**14**	9	St Stephens	1-N	10-W
" "	**13**	5	St Stephens	1-N	11-W
GAVIN	**12**	1	St Stephens	2-N	9-W
GEORGE	**4**	1	St Stephens	4-N	11-W
GIBSON	**16**	3	St Stephens	1-S	11-W
GILLINDER	**7**	3	St Stephens	3-N	11-W
GILLIS	**7**	5	St Stephens	3-N	11-W
GILMER	**9**	1	St Stephens	3-N	9-W
GODFREY	**16**	1	St Stephens	1-S	11-W
GRANTHAM	**4**	3	St Stephens	4-N	11-W
" "	**1**	1	St Stephens	5-N	11-W
GREEN	**15**	1	St Stephens	1-N	9-W
" "	**12**	1	St Stephens	2-N	9-W
GRIFFIN	**13**	92	St Stephens	1-N	11-W
" "	**14**	46	St Stephens	1-N	10-W
" "	**16**	24	St Stephens	1-S	11-W
" "	**17**	20	St Stephens	1-S	10-W
" "	**12**	6	St Stephens	2-N	9-W
" "	**10**	5	St Stephens	2-N	11-W
" "	**7**	2	St Stephens	3-N	11-W
GRIMBSLEY	**4**	3	St Stephens	4-N	11-W
GUINN	**8**	2	St Stephens	3-N	10-W
HAIRSTON	**8**	2	St Stephens	3-N	10-W
HARLSFIELD	**12**	1	St Stephens	2-N	9-W
HARRIS	**13**	4	St Stephens	1-N	11-W
" "	**9**	1	St Stephens	3-N	9-W
HARTFIELD	**12**	13	St Stephens	2-N	9-W
" "	**17**	6	St Stephens	1-S	10-W
" "	**13**	3	St Stephens	1-N	11-W
" "	**14**	1	St Stephens	1-N	10-W
HARTLEY	**4**	3	St Stephens	4-N	11-W
" "	**5**	2	St Stephens	4-N	10-W
HARTSFIELD	**12**	3	St Stephens	2-N	9-W
HARVISON	**9**	3	St Stephens	3-N	9-W
HATHORN	**4**	9	St Stephens	4-N	11-W
HATHORNE	**4**	1	St Stephens	4-N	11-W
HAVENS	**8**	1	St Stephens	3-N	10-W
HEMPHILL	**12**	2	St Stephens	2-N	9-W
" "	**2**	2	St Stephens	5-N	10-W

Surname	Map Group	Parcels of Land	Meridian/Township/Range		
HENDRY	8	2	St Stephens	3-N	10-W
HENSAILING	1	1	St Stephens	5-N	11-W
HENSARLING	4	3	St Stephens	4-N	11-W
" "	1	1	St Stephens	5-N	11-W
HERRING	11	3	St Stephens	2-N	10-W
" "	9	3	St Stephens	3-N	9-W
" "	15	2	St Stephens	1-N	9-W
" "	13	1	St Stephens	1-N	11-W
HESTLE	7	1	St Stephens	3-N	11-W
HIDE	7	1	St Stephens	3-N	11-W
HIGHTOWER	5	1	St Stephens	4-N	10-W
HILLS	11	62	St Stephens	2-N	10-W
" "	18	59	St Stephens	1-S	9-W
" "	12	57	St Stephens	2-N	9-W
" "	15	53	St Stephens	1-N	9-W
" "	8	7	St Stephens	3-N	10-W
HINTON	6	50	St Stephens	4-N	9-W
" "	5	38	St Stephens	4-N	10-W
" "	8	32	St Stephens	3-N	10-W
" "	9	15	St Stephens	3-N	9-W
" "	3	9	St Stephens	5-N	9-W
" "	11	7	St Stephens	2-N	10-W
" "	1	5	St Stephens	5-N	11-W
" "	2	3	St Stephens	5-N	10-W
" "	14	2	St Stephens	1-N	10-W
" "	4	2	St Stephens	4-N	11-W
HOGAN	13	8	St Stephens	1-N	11-W
" "	15	1	St Stephens	1-N	9-W
HOLDER	13	3	St Stephens	1-N	11-W
" "	7	2	St Stephens	3-N	11-W
" "	5	1	St Stephens	4-N	10-W
HOLLIMAN	4	3	St Stephens	4-N	11-W
" "	2	3	St Stephens	5-N	10-W
" "	5	2	St Stephens	4-N	10-W
" "	7	1	St Stephens	3-N	11-W
HOLLIMON	4	13	St Stephens	4-N	11-W
" "	7	10	St Stephens	3-N	11-W
" "	14	3	St Stephens	1-N	10-W
" "	16	3	St Stephens	1-S	11-W
" "	17	2	St Stephens	1-S	10-W
" "	2	2	St Stephens	5-N	10-W
" "	1	2	St Stephens	5-N	11-W
HOLLINGSWORTH	4	4	St Stephens	4-N	11-W
" "	9	3	St Stephens	3-N	9-W
HOLLINSWORTH	9	3	St Stephens	3-N	9-W
" "	12	1	St Stephens	2-N	9-W
HOLLOMON	4	2	St Stephens	4-N	11-W
HORN	5	2	St Stephens	4-N	10-W
HOTEN	16	1	St Stephens	1-S	11-W
HOTIN	13	1	St Stephens	1-N	11-W
HOTON	13	2	St Stephens	1-N	11-W
HOUSLEY	16	3	St Stephens	1-S	11-W
" "	12	3	St Stephens	2-N	9-W
HOWARD	11	2	St Stephens	2-N	10-W
HOWZE	14	6	St Stephens	1-N	10-W
" "	17	5	St Stephens	1-S	10-W
HUDSON	3	2	St Stephens	5-N	9-W
HUFF	9	2	St Stephens	3-N	9-W
HUGGINS	9	4	St Stephens	3-N	9-W
" "	5	3	St Stephens	4-N	10-W

Surname	Map Group	Parcels of Land	Meridian/Township/Range		
HUGGINS (Cont'd)	8	2	St Stephens	3-N	10-W
" "	4	1	St Stephens	4-N	11-W
HUTSON	4	2	St Stephens	4-N	11-W
JACKSON	16	2	St Stephens	1-S	11-W
" "	13	1	St Stephens	1-N	11-W
" "	5	1	St Stephens	4-N	10-W
JAMES	4	16	St Stephens	4-N	11-W
" "	13	4	St Stephens	1-N	11-W
" "	7	2	St Stephens	3-N	11-W
JEFCOAT	6	1	St Stephens	4-N	9-W
JOHNSON	5	32	St Stephens	4-N	10-W
" "	16	4	St Stephens	1-S	11-W
" "	17	1	St Stephens	1-S	10-W
JONES	4	3	St Stephens	4-N	11-W
" "	18	2	St Stephens	1-S	9-W
" "	14	1	St Stephens	1-N	10-W
" "	13	1	St Stephens	1-N	11-W
" "	17	1	St Stephens	1-S	10-W
JORDAN	9	7	St Stephens	3-N	9-W
KENNEDY	7	8	St Stephens	3-N	11-W
" "	4	4	St Stephens	4-N	11-W
" "	14	2	St Stephens	1-N	10-W
" "	13	2	St Stephens	1-N	11-W
" "	8	2	St Stephens	3-N	10-W
" "	1	1	St Stephens	5-N	11-W
KENT	3	14	St Stephens	5-N	9-W
KILPATRICK	12	2	St Stephens	2-N	9-W
KIRKLAND	9	4	St Stephens	3-N	9-W
" "	5	3	St Stephens	4-N	10-W
" "	8	2	St Stephens	3-N	10-W
" "	4	1	St Stephens	4-N	11-W
KITTRELL	8	30	St Stephens	3-N	10-W
" "	9	11	St Stephens	3-N	9-W
" "	6	6	St Stephens	4-N	9-W
" "	12	2	St Stephens	2-N	9-W
KNIGHT	16	4	St Stephens	1-S	11-W
LAMBERT	13	3	St Stephens	1-N	11-W
" "	11	3	St Stephens	2-N	10-W
LANDRUM	2	1	St Stephens	5-N	10-W
LANGLERY	4	1	St Stephens	4-N	11-W
LANTRIP	14	1	St Stephens	1-N	10-W
" "	17	1	St Stephens	1-S	10-W
LAURENDINE	2	3	St Stephens	5-N	10-W
LAURWENCE	9	1	St Stephens	3-N	9-W
LAWRENCE	9	1	St Stephens	3-N	9-W
LEATHERBURY	18	4	St Stephens	1-S	9-W
LEE	9	1	St Stephens	3-N	9-W
LEWIS	13	4	St Stephens	1-N	11-W
LOPER	2	1	St Stephens	5-N	10-W
LOTT	9	11	St Stephens	3-N	9-W
" "	16	3	St Stephens	1-S	11-W
" "	4	2	St Stephens	4-N	11-W
" "	5	1	St Stephens	4-N	10-W
LUCAS	3	3	St Stephens	5-N	9-W
MAINOR	15	1	St Stephens	1-N	9-W
MAMAN	12	1	St Stephens	2-N	9-W
MANNING	6	2	St Stephens	4-N	9-W
MARTIN	13	6	St Stephens	1-N	11-W
" "	12	4	St Stephens	2-N	9-W
" "	10	2	St Stephens	2-N	11-W

Surname	Map Group	Parcels of Land	Meridian/Township/Range		
MARTIN (Cont'd)	11	1	St Stephens	2-N	10-W
MASON	3	2	St Stephens	5-N	9-W
MATHESON	17	4	St Stephens	1-S	10-W
" "	14	2	St Stephens	1-N	10-W
MAXWELL	16	5	St Stephens	1-S	11-W
" "	13	3	St Stephens	1-N	11-W
MAYO	3	2	St Stephens	5-N	9-W
MCCALLUM	7	4	St Stephens	3-N	11-W
" "	8	1	St Stephens	3-N	10-W
MCCARDEL	4	1	St Stephens	4-N	11-W
MCCARDLE	4	10	St Stephens	4-N	11-W
" "	13	5	St Stephens	1-N	11-W
" "	1	5	St Stephens	5-N	11-W
MCCOLLUM	7	3	St Stephens	3-N	11-W
MCCOY	8	1	St Stephens	3-N	10-W
MCDONALD	9	16	St Stephens	3-N	9-W
" "	1	9	St Stephens	5-N	11-W
" "	3	9	St Stephens	5-N	9-W
" "	8	8	St Stephens	3-N	10-W
" "	6	5	St Stephens	4-N	9-W
MCDOWELL	16	7	St Stephens	1-S	11-W
" "	15	2	St Stephens	1-N	9-W
MCGAHA	4	1	St Stephens	4-N	11-W
MCGILBERRY	4	6	St Stephens	4-N	11-W
MCGILLVERRY	4	1	St Stephens	4-N	11-W
MCGILRANY	4	2	St Stephens	4-N	11-W
" "	1	1	St Stephens	5-N	11-W
MCGILVARY	7	1	St Stephens	3-N	11-W
MCGILVRAY	4	10	St Stephens	4-N	11-W
" "	1	3	St Stephens	5-N	11-W
MCHENRY	4	1	St Stephens	4-N	11-W
MCINNIS	13	4	St Stephens	1-N	11-W
" "	17	3	St Stephens	1-S	10-W
MCKENZIE	9	4	St Stephens	3-N	9-W
" "	12	2	St Stephens	2-N	9-W
" "	7	2	St Stephens	3-N	11-W
" "	4	1	St Stephens	4-N	11-W
MCLAUGHLIN	7	2	St Stephens	3-N	11-W
MCLEAN	7	3	St Stephens	3-N	11-W
MCLEMORE	8	2	St Stephens	3-N	10-W
" "	7	1	St Stephens	3-N	11-W
MCLEOD	16	3	St Stephens	1-S	11-W
" "	14	2	St Stephens	1-N	10-W
MCLOUD	13	2	St Stephens	1-N	11-W
MCPHERSON	1	85	St Stephens	5-N	11-W
" "	2	23	St Stephens	5-N	10-W
" "	5	13	St Stephens	4-N	10-W
" "	12	6	St Stephens	2-N	9-W
" "	11	5	St Stephens	2-N	10-W
MCQUAGGE	17	1	St Stephens	1-S	10-W
MCSWAIN	8	24	St Stephens	3-N	10-W
" "	5	12	St Stephens	4-N	10-W
" "	7	11	St Stephens	3-N	11-W
MEADOWS	3	4	St Stephens	5-N	9-W
" "	6	1	St Stephens	4-N	9-W
MERRETT	9	1	St Stephens	3-N	9-W
MERRITT	8	5	St Stephens	3-N	10-W
" "	9	5	St Stephens	3-N	9-W
" "	14	2	St Stephens	1-N	10-W
" "	12	2	St Stephens	2-N	9-W

Surname	Map Group	Parcels of Land	Meridian/Township/Range
MERRITT (Cont'd)	15	1	St Stephens 1-N 9-W
" "	5	1	St Stephens 4-N 10-W
MILES	17	5	St Stephens 1-S 10-W
" "	3	1	St Stephens 5-N 9-W
MISSISSIPPI	10	2	St Stephens 2-N 11-W
" "	14	1	St Stephens 1-N 10-W
" "	13	1	St Stephens 1-N 11-W
MIXON	10	10	St Stephens 2-N 11-W
" "	7	8	St Stephens 3-N 11-W
" "	13	4	St Stephens 1-N 11-W
" "	4	3	St Stephens 4-N 11-W
MONTAGUE	16	16	St Stephens 1-S 11-W
" "	17	10	St Stephens 1-S 10-W
" "	10	9	St Stephens 2-N 11-W
MOODY	12	5	St Stephens 2-N 9-W
" "	13	3	St Stephens 1-N 11-W
MOORE	2	32	St Stephens 5-N 10-W
" "	5	7	St Stephens 4-N 10-W
" "	17	1	St Stephens 1-S 10-W
" "	9	1	St Stephens 3-N 9-W
MORGAN	1	8	St Stephens 5-N 11-W
" "	4	5	St Stephens 4-N 11-W
" "	16	2	St Stephens 1-S 11-W
" "	12	1	St Stephens 2-N 9-W
" "	5	1	St Stephens 4-N 10-W
MORROW	15	1	St Stephens 1-N 9-W
MYERS	7	5	St Stephens 3-N 11-W
" "	5	2	St Stephens 4-N 10-W
" "	2	2	St Stephens 5-N 10-W
" "	4	1	St Stephens 4-N 11-W
MYRICK	4	7	St Stephens 4-N 11-W
" "	5	5	St Stephens 4-N 10-W
NEAL	10	3	St Stephens 2-N 11-W
NEWELL	3	5	St Stephens 5-N 9-W
" "	6	3	St Stephens 4-N 9-W
" "	1	2	St Stephens 5-N 11-W
" "	8	1	St Stephens 3-N 10-W
" "	2	1	St Stephens 5-N 10-W
NICHOLS	7	6	St Stephens 3-N 11-W
NIX	7	2	St Stephens 3-N 11-W
NIXON	13	1	St Stephens 1-N 11-W
NOWELL	5	1	St Stephens 4-N 10-W
ODOM	1	13	St Stephens 5-N 11-W
" "	2	6	St Stephens 5-N 10-W
" "	5	4	St Stephens 4-N 10-W
" "	3	2	St Stephens 5-N 9-W
ONEAL	18	2	St Stephens 1-S 9-W
OVERSTREET	6	4	St Stephens 4-N 9-W
" "	3	2	St Stephens 5-N 9-W
OWENS	16	2	St Stephens 1-S 11-W
PALMER	5	8	St Stephens 4-N 10-W
" "	2	3	St Stephens 5-N 10-W
PARDUE	4	5	St Stephens 4-N 11-W
PARKER	1	1	St Stephens 5-N 11-W
PATTERSON	14	4	St Stephens 1-N 10-W
" "	15	4	St Stephens 1-N 9-W
" "	12	1	St Stephens 2-N 9-W
PATTON	8	3	St Stephens 3-N 10-W
PAYNE	17	2	St Stephens 1-S 10-W
PAYTON	16	3	St Stephens 1-S 11-W

Surname	Map Group	Parcels of Land	Meridian/Township/Range		
PEARCE	13	16	St Stephens	1-N	11-W
" "	10	6	St Stephens	2-N	11-W
" "	11	5	St Stephens	2-N	10-W
" "	14	3	St Stephens	1-N	10-W
" "	17	2	St Stephens	1-S	10-W
PERKINS	13	25	St Stephens	1-N	11-W
" "	14	5	St Stephens	1-N	10-W
" "	17	5	St Stephens	1-S	10-W
" "	10	3	St Stephens	2-N	11-W
" "	5	1	St Stephens	4-N	10-W
PHILIPS	8	2	St Stephens	3-N	10-W
PITTMAN	5	2	St Stephens	4-N	10-W
" "	4	1	St Stephens	4-N	11-W
PITTS	2	1	St Stephens	5-N	10-W
PORTER	16	1	St Stephens	1-S	11-W
PREISING	6	1	St Stephens	4-N	9-W
PRENTISS	9	2	St Stephens	3-N	9-W
PRIER	5	3	St Stephens	4-N	10-W
PRINE	5	1	St Stephens	4-N	10-W
" "	4	1	St Stephens	4-N	11-W
PRYOR	8	2	St Stephens	3-N	10-W
PUGH	2	2	St Stephens	5-N	10-W
RAMSEY	13	1	St Stephens	1-N	11-W
RANSDELL	10	165	St Stephens	2-N	11-W
" "	14	94	St Stephens	1-N	10-W
" "	16	73	St Stephens	1-S	11-W
" "	11	41	St Stephens	2-N	10-W
" "	13	25	St Stephens	1-N	11-W
" "	7	18	St Stephens	3-N	11-W
RAYBORN	13	3	St Stephens	1-N	11-W
" "	16	2	St Stephens	1-S	11-W
RAYBURN	16	2	St Stephens	1-S	11-W
" "	17	1	St Stephens	1-S	10-W
READY	5	2	St Stephens	4-N	10-W
REVETTE	5	2	St Stephens	4-N	10-W
REYNOLDS	4	4	St Stephens	4-N	11-W
" "	1	1	St Stephens	5-N	11-W
RHODES	7	2	St Stephens	3-N	11-W
RICH	6	33	St Stephens	4-N	9-W
" "	3	13	St Stephens	5-N	9-W
" "	9	10	St Stephens	3-N	9-W
" "	2	2	St Stephens	5-N	10-W
RIGGS	5	2	St Stephens	4-N	10-W
RILEY	14	2	St Stephens	1-N	10-W
" "	15	2	St Stephens	1-N	9-W
" "	17	2	St Stephens	1-S	10-W
ROBERTS	12	2	St Stephens	2-N	9-W
" "	6	1	St Stephens	4-N	9-W
ROSS	4	1	St Stephens	4-N	11-W
RUNNELLS	1	3	St Stephens	5-N	11-W
RUNNELS	1	8	St Stephens	5-N	11-W
" "	4	1	St Stephens	4-N	11-W
" "	2	1	St Stephens	5-N	10-W
SAFFOLD	2	1	St Stephens	5-N	10-W
SAGE	3	4	St Stephens	5-N	9-W
SAMUEL	17	2	St Stephens	1-S	10-W
" "	14	1	St Stephens	1-N	10-W
SAPP	4	2	St Stephens	4-N	11-W
" "	1	2	St Stephens	5-N	11-W
SAPPE	1	1	St Stephens	5-N	11-W

Surname	Map Group	Parcels of Land	Meridian/Township/Range		
SAVAGE	1	1	St Stephens	5-N	11-W
SAWYER	18	13	St Stephens	1-S	9-W
" "	8	11	St Stephens	3-N	10-W
" "	11	8	St Stephens	2-N	10-W
SCARBOROUGH	16	1	St Stephens	1-S	11-W
" "	3	1	St Stephens	5-N	9-W
SCHILLING	8	1	St Stephens	3-N	10-W
SCOTT	5	4	St Stephens	4-N	10-W
" "	7	3	St Stephens	3-N	11-W
" "	4	1	St Stephens	4-N	11-W
SEAL	16	3	St Stephens	1-S	11-W
SELLIVAN	14	3	St Stephens	1-N	10-W
SHATTLES	13	2	St Stephens	1-N	11-W
SHAW	4	2	St Stephens	4-N	11-W
" "	5	1	St Stephens	4-N	10-W
SHEPARD	6	1	St Stephens	4-N	9-W
SHORES	4	2	St Stephens	4-N	11-W
SIMMONS	13	2	St Stephens	1-N	11-W
SIMMS	16	2	St Stephens	1-S	11-W
SIMS	16	2	St Stephens	1-S	11-W
SINGLETON	8	1	St Stephens	3-N	10-W
SINGLEY	13	2	St Stephens	1-N	11-W
SLOAN	13	1	St Stephens	1-N	11-W
SMITH	2	24	St Stephens	5-N	10-W
" "	14	5	St Stephens	1-N	10-W
" "	13	4	St Stephens	1-N	11-W
" "	16	4	St Stephens	1-S	11-W
" "	4	4	St Stephens	4-N	11-W
" "	10	3	St Stephens	2-N	11-W
" "	12	1	St Stephens	2-N	9-W
" "	8	1	St Stephens	3-N	10-W
" "	3	1	St Stephens	5-N	9-W
SOWELL	4	3	St Stephens	4-N	11-W
" "	9	1	St Stephens	3-N	9-W
SPINKS	1	2	St Stephens	5-N	11-W
STAFFORD	13	9	St Stephens	1-N	11-W
" "	11	3	St Stephens	2-N	10-W
" "	9	3	St Stephens	3-N	9-W
" "	12	2	St Stephens	2-N	9-W
" "	14	1	St Stephens	1-N	10-W
STALLWORTH	1	1	St Stephens	5-N	11-W
STEAN	8	1	St Stephens	3-N	10-W
STEVENS	5	20	St Stephens	4-N	10-W
" "	4	13	St Stephens	4-N	11-W
" "	8	8	St Stephens	3-N	10-W
" "	7	4	St Stephens	3-N	11-W
" "	2	2	St Stephens	5-N	10-W
STOKLEY	1	1	St Stephens	5-N	11-W
STRICKLAND	3	4	St Stephens	5-N	9-W
" "	11	2	St Stephens	2-N	10-W
STRONG	8	3	St Stephens	3-N	10-W
STUTTS	4	1	St Stephens	4-N	11-W
SULLIVAN	14	3	St Stephens	1-N	10-W
SUMMERS	6	3	St Stephens	4-N	9-W
" "	3	2	St Stephens	5-N	9-W
SWAYINGIN	2	2	St Stephens	5-N	10-W
" "	5	1	St Stephens	4-N	10-W
SYLVESTER	9	5	St Stephens	3-N	9-W
TANNER	9	2	St Stephens	3-N	9-W
TAYLOR	16	7	St Stephens	1-S	11-W

31

Surname	Map Group	Parcels of Land	Meridian/Township/Range		
TAYLOR (Cont'd)	6	1	St Stephens	4-N	9-W
TERRELL	7	1	St Stephens	3-N	11-W
THOMAS	17	25	St Stephens	1-S	10-W
" "	14	14	St Stephens	1-N	10-W
" "	16	2	St Stephens	1-S	11-W
" "	11	2	St Stephens	2-N	10-W
" "	15	1	St Stephens	1-N	9-W
THOMSON	8	3	St Stephens	3-N	10-W
TILLIS	14	1	St Stephens	1-N	10-W
TILLMAN	7	1	St Stephens	3-N	11-W
TINGLE	10	6	St Stephens	2-N	11-W
TISDALE	14	6	St Stephens	1-N	10-W
" "	2	3	St Stephens	5-N	10-W
TOUCHSTONE	5	2	St Stephens	4-N	10-W
" "	2	1	St Stephens	5-N	10-W
TRAVIS	4	4	St Stephens	4-N	11-W
" "	7	1	St Stephens	3-N	11-W
TUCKER	2	1	St Stephens	5-N	10-W
TURK	14	2	St Stephens	1-N	10-W
VAUGHAN	5	31	St Stephens	4-N	10-W
WADE	7	8	St Stephens	3-N	11-W
WAGAR	15	46	St Stephens	1-N	9-W
" "	18	33	St Stephens	1-S	9-W
" "	12	6	St Stephens	2-N	9-W
" "	11	2	St Stephens	2-N	10-W
WAGNER	2	20	St Stephens	5-N	10-W
WALEY	3	2	St Stephens	5-N	9-W
WALKER	16	2	St Stephens	1-S	11-W
" "	8	1	St Stephens	3-N	10-W
WALLEY	3	26	St Stephens	5-N	9-W
" "	2	4	St Stephens	5-N	10-W
" "	6	1	St Stephens	4-N	9-W
WALTERS	2	2	St Stephens	5-N	10-W
WALTMAN	2	2	St Stephens	5-N	10-W
" "	3	1	St Stephens	5-N	9-W
WARD	3	1	St Stephens	5-N	9-W
WARE	2	23	St Stephens	5-N	10-W
WARREN	7	2	St Stephens	3-N	11-W
WATSON	3	40	St Stephens	5-N	9-W
" "	6	36	St Stephens	4-N	9-W
" "	9	27	St Stephens	3-N	9-W
" "	1	25	St Stephens	5-N	11-W
" "	5	12	St Stephens	4-N	10-W
" "	4	10	St Stephens	4-N	11-W
" "	8	1	St Stephens	3-N	10-W
WELDAY	11	1	St Stephens	2-N	10-W
WELLS	15	46	St Stephens	1-N	9-W
" "	18	33	St Stephens	1-S	9-W
" "	12	6	St Stephens	2-N	9-W
" "	11	2	St Stephens	2-N	10-W
WENTWORTH	7	3	St Stephens	3-N	11-W
WEST	8	12	St Stephens	3-N	10-W
" "	7	5	St Stephens	3-N	11-W
" "	13	2	St Stephens	1-N	11-W
" "	10	1	St Stephens	2-N	11-W
WHATLEY	11	6	St Stephens	2-N	10-W
WHEELER	1	1	St Stephens	5-N	11-W
WHITE	2	5	St Stephens	5-N	10-W
" "	4	2	St Stephens	4-N	11-W
" "	6	2	St Stephens	4-N	9-W

Surname	Map Group	Parcels of Land	Meridian/Township/Range		
WHITE (Cont'd)	**13**	1	St Stephens	1-N	11-W
" "	**9**	1	St Stephens	3-N	9-W
WHITTINGTON	**9**	1	St Stephens	3-N	9-W
WHITTLE	**5**	3	St Stephens	4-N	10-W
WILLIAMS	**5**	3	St Stephens	4-N	10-W
" "	**12**	1	St Stephens	2-N	9-W
" "	**7**	1	St Stephens	3-N	11-W
WILLIAMSON	**15**	3	St Stephens	1-N	9-W
" "	**13**	2	St Stephens	1-N	11-W
WILLINGHAM	**6**	3	St Stephens	4-N	9-W
" "	**3**	1	St Stephens	5-N	9-W
WOOD	**17**	2	St Stephens	1-S	10-W
WOODARD	**2**	5	St Stephens	5-N	10-W
WOODS	**17**	3	St Stephens	1-S	10-W
" "	**14**	1	St Stephens	1-N	10-W
WOODWARD	**1**	2	St Stephens	5-N	11-W
YARBROUGH	**4**	1	St Stephens	4-N	11-W
YATES	**8**	1	St Stephens	3-N	10-W
YELVERTON	**17**	4	St Stephens	1-S	10-W
YOUNG	**14**	4	St Stephens	1-N	10-W

– Part II –

Township Map Groups

Map Group 1: Index to Land Patents

Township 5-North Range 11-West (St Stephens)

After you locate an individual in this Index, take note of the Section and Section Part then proceed to the Land Patent map on the pages immediately following. You should have no difficulty locating the corresponding parcel of land.

The "For More Info" Column will lead you to more information about the underlying Patents. See the *Legend* at right, and the "How to Use this Book" chapter, for more information.

ID	Individual in Patent	Sec.	Sec. Part	Date Issued	Other Counties	For More Info . . .
110	BEER, Henry	14	E½SW	1889-11-29		A1
111	" "	15	E½SE	1889-11-29		A1
112	" "	15	SWNE	1889-11-29		A1
113	" "	17	E½SE	1889-11-29		A1
114	" "	17	NENE	1889-11-29		A1
115	" "	21	E½NW	1889-11-29		A1
116	" "	21	NESE	1889-11-29		A1
117	" "	21	S½NE	1889-11-29		A1
118	" "	22	SESE	1889-11-29		A1
119	" "	22	SW	1889-11-29		A1
120	" "	23	N½SW	1889-11-29		A1 V121
121	" "	23	NWSW	1889-11-29		A1 V120
122	" "	23	SE	1889-11-29		A1 V139, 175
123	" "	23	SWNE	1889-11-29		A1
124	" "	24	N½SE	1889-11-29		A1
125	" "	24	NESW	1889-11-29		A1
126	" "	26	NENE	1889-11-29		A1
127	" "	26	SWNW	1889-11-29		A1
128	" "	27	NESW	1889-11-29		A1
129	" "	27	NWNW	1889-11-29		A1
130	" "	27	SE	1889-11-29		A1
131	" "	27	W½NE	1889-11-29		A1
132	" "	34	E½	1889-11-29		A1
133	" "	5	NESW	1889-11-29		A1
134	" "	5	NWSE	1889-11-29		A1
135	" "	5	SWNW	1889-11-29		A1
136	" "	8	NWNE	1889-11-29		A1
137	" "	8	SESE	1889-11-29		A1
138	" "	8	W½SE	1889-11-29		A1
194	BIRKETT, Thomas	11	NENE	1884-12-30		A1 G7
195	" "	11	NESE	1884-12-30		A1 G7
196	" "	11	NESW	1884-12-30		A1 G7
197	" "	11	NW	1884-12-30		A1 G7
198	" "	11	NWSW	1884-12-30		A1 G7
199	" "	11	S½SW	1884-12-30		A1 G7
200	" "	11	SESE	1884-12-30		A1 G7
201	" "	11	W½NE	1884-12-30		A1 G7
202	" "	11	W½SE	1884-12-30		A1 G7
203	" "	12	E½SW	1884-12-30		A1 G7
204	" "	12	S½NE	1884-12-30		A1 G7
205	" "	12	S½NW	1884-12-30		A1 G7
206	" "	12	SE	1884-12-30		A1 G7
207	" "	12	W½SW	1884-12-30		A1 G7
208	" "	13	N½NW	1884-12-30		A1 G7
219	" "	13	NENE	1884-12-30		A1 G8
220	" "	13	NWSE	1884-12-30		A1 G8

ID	Individual in Patent	Sec.	Sec. Part	Date Issued	Other Counties	For More Info . . .
209	BIRKETT, Thomas (Cont'd)	13	SENE	1884-12-30		A1 G7
210	" "	13	SENW	1884-12-30		A1 G7
211	" "	13	SESE	1884-12-30		A1 G7
221	" "	13	SWNW	1884-12-30		A1 G8
212	" "	13	SWSW	1884-12-30		A1 G7
222	" "	14	N½NE	1884-12-30		A1 G8
223	" "	14	NENW	1884-12-30		A1 G8
213	" "	2	E½NW	1884-12-30		A1 G7
214	" "	2	W½NW	1884-12-30		A1 G7
224	" "	24	N½NW	1884-12-30		A1 G8
215	" "	24	NWNE	1884-12-30		A1 G7
225	" "	24	SWNW	1884-12-30		A1 G8
216	" "	3	E½SE	1884-12-30		A1 G7
217	" "	3	NENE	1884-12-30		A1 G7
218	" "	3	SENE	1884-12-30		A1 G7
226	" "	31	SWNW	1884-12-30		A1 G8
178	BROWN, Mark	1	NENW	1861-05-01		A1
183	BROWN, Robert	1	S½SW	1901-06-25		A4
191	CEPHUS, Stephen	23	S½SW	1901-04-22		A4
192	" "	26	NWNW	1901-04-22		A4
193	" "	27	NENE	1901-04-22		A4
87	CHAPPEL, Christopher	18	W½SE	1841-01-05		A1
72	COURTNEY, Andrew F	8	E½NW	1913-06-16		A4
86	COVINGTON, Catherine F	6	NWSW	1919-10-20		A4
154	DRAUGHN, Jesse W	21	SESE	1914-05-22		A1
155	"	28	N½NE	1914-05-22		A1
168	DRAUGHN, John L	28	NENW	1895-01-17		A4
169	" "	28	S½NW	1895-01-17		A4
170	" "	28	SWNE	1895-01-17		A4
97	EASTERLING, Elizabeth	20	SWNW	1859-05-02		A1
165	EASTERLING, John	19	NWNE	1841-01-05		A1
166	"	19	SENE	1841-01-05		A1
164	"	19	E½SE	1846-09-01		A1
158	ELLSWORTH, John C	26	S½SW	1889-04-10		A1 G30
159	" "	26	SWSE	1889-04-10		A1 G30
160	" "	35	N½	1889-04-10		A1 G30
161	" "	35	NESE	1889-04-10		A1 G30
162	" "	35	SW	1889-04-10		A1 G30
163	" "	35	W½SE	1889-04-10		A1 G30
167	GRANTHAM, John	19	SWNE	1841-01-05		A1
177	HENSAILING, Louis	31	NWNW	1883-09-15		A1
180	HENSARLING, Nelley E	31	NENW	1889-05-06		A1
85	HINTON, Blake	30	NENE	1841-01-05		A1
83	" "	29	E½NW	1846-09-01		A1
84	" "	29	NWNW	1846-09-01		A1
150	HINTON, Jefferson D	17	E½SW	1894-12-17		A4
151	"	17	W½SE	1894-12-17		A4
181	HOLLIMON, Riley	1	S½SE	1891-05-20		A4
182	"	12	N½NE	1891-05-20		A4
152	KENNEDY, Jesse A	17	SENE	1889-04-23		A1
95	MCCARDLE, Duncan	17	E½NW	1890-08-16		A4
96	"	17	W½NE	1890-08-16		A4
145	MCCARDLE, James	31	W½SW	1890-08-16		A4
173	MCCARDLE, Joseph	31	E½SW	1891-05-20		A4
174	"	31	W½SE	1891-05-20		A4
74	MCDONALD, Angus M	6	N½NE	1896-12-14		A4
75	" "	6	NENW	1896-12-14		A4
76	" "	6	SENE	1896-12-14		A4
91	MCDONALD, Daniel	6	NESW	1896-12-14		A4
92	" "	6	NWSE	1896-12-14		A4
93	" "	6	SENW	1896-12-14		A4
94	" "	6	SWNE	1896-12-14		A4
230	MCDONALD, William H	6	E½SE	1896-12-18		A4
231	"	6	SWSE	1896-12-18		A4
77	MCGILRANY, Angus	33	SESE	1890-02-21		A4
88	MCGILVRAY, Daniel G	27	SESW	1906-08-10		A4
89	" "	27	W½SW	1906-08-10		A4
90	" "	28	NESE	1906-08-10		A4
194	MCPHERSON, Alexander	11	NENE	1884-12-30		A1 G7
195	" "	11	NESE	1884-12-30		A1 G7
196	" "	11	NESW	1884-12-30		A1 G7
197	" "	11	NW	1884-12-30		A1 G7
198	" "	11	NWSW	1884-12-30		A1 G7

ID	Individual in Patent	Sec.	Sec. Part	Date Issued	Other Counties	For More Info . . .
199	MCPHERSON, Alexander (Cont'd)	11	S½SW	1884-12-30		A1 G7
200	" "	11	SESE	1884-12-30		A1 G7
201	" "	11	W½NE	1884-12-30		A1 G7
202	" "	11	W½SE	1884-12-30		A1 G7
203	" "	12	E½SW	1884-12-30		A1 G7
204	" "	12	S½NE	1884-12-30		A1 G7
205	" "	12	S½NW	1884-12-30		A1 G7
206	" "	12	SE	1884-12-30		A1 G7
207	" "	12	W½SW	1884-12-30		A1 G7
208	" "	13	N½NW	1884-12-30		A1 G7
219	" "	13	NENE	1884-12-30		A1 G8
220	" "	13	NWSE	1884-12-30		A1 G8
209	" "	13	SENE	1884-12-30		A1 G7
210	" "	13	SENW	1884-12-30		A1 G7
211	" "	13	SESE	1884-12-30		A1 G7
221	" "	13	SWNW	1884-12-30		A1 G8
212	" "	13	SWSW	1884-12-30		A1 G7
222	" "	14	N½NE	1884-12-30		A1 G8
223	" "	14	NENW	1884-12-30		A1 G8
213	" "	2	E½NW	1884-12-30		A1 G7
214	" "	2	W½NW	1884-12-30		A1 G7
224	" "	24	N½NW	1884-12-30		A1 G8
215	" "	24	NWNE	1884-12-30		A1 G7
225	" "	24	SWNW	1884-12-30		A1 G8
216	" "	3	E½SE	1884-12-30		A1 G7
217	" "	3	NENE	1884-12-30		A1 G7
218	" "	3	SENE	1884-12-30		A1 G7
226	" "	31	SWNW	1884-12-30		A1 G8
1	" "	10	N½SW	1889-04-23		A1 G62
3	" "	10	SWNW	1889-04-23		A1 G62
13	" "	14	SWSE	1889-04-23		A1 G62
14	" "	14	W½SW	1889-04-23		A1 G62
15	" "	15	N½NW	1889-04-23		A1 G62
16	" "	15	NWNE	1889-04-23		A1 G62
17	" "	15	SENE	1889-04-23		A1 G62
18	" "	15	SENW	1889-04-23		A1 G62
19	" "	15	SWSW	1889-04-23		A1 G62
20	" "	15	W½SE	1889-04-23		A1 G62
21	" "	21	N½NE	1889-04-23		A1 G62
22	" "	21	NWNW	1889-04-23		A1 G62
23	" "	22	E½NE	1889-04-23		A1 G62
24	" "	22	S½NW	1889-04-23		A1 G62
29	" "	26	E½NW	1889-04-23		A1 G62
30	" "	26	N½SW	1889-04-23		A1 G62
31	" "	26	NWNE	1889-04-23		A1 G62
32	" "	26	NWSE	1889-04-23		A1 G62
33	" "	26	S½NE	1889-04-23		A1 G62
34	" "	3	N½NW	1889-04-23		A1 G62
35	" "	3	NWNE	1889-04-23		A1 G62
36	" "	3	S½SW	1889-04-23		A1 G62
37	" "	4	N½SE	1889-04-23		A1 G62
39	" "	4	NWNE	1889-04-23		A1 G62
40	" "	4	NWSW	1889-04-23		A1 G62
41	" "	4	S½NE	1889-04-23		A1 G62
42	" "	4	S½NW	1889-04-23		A1 G62
44	" "	4	SWSE	1889-04-23		A1 G62
45	" "	9	N½NW	1889-04-23		A1 G62 V68
46	" "	9	NENE	1889-04-23		A1 G62
2	" "	10	SESE	1889-11-29		A1 G62
4	" "	11	SENE	1889-11-29		A1 G62
5	" "	12	N½NW	1889-11-29		A1 G62
6	" "	13	E½SW	1889-11-29		A1 G62
7	" "	13	NESE	1889-11-29		A1 G62
8	" "	13	NWSW	1889-11-29		A1 G62
9	" "	13	SWSE	1889-11-29		A1 G62
10	" "	13	W½NE	1889-11-29		A1 G62
11	" "	14	E½SE	1889-11-29		A1 G62
12	" "	14	NWNW	1889-11-29		A1 G62
25	" "	23	E½NE	1889-11-29		A1 G62
26	" "	24	E½NE	1889-11-29		A1 G62
27	" "	24	SENW	1889-11-29		A1 G62
28	" "	24	SWNE	1889-11-29		A1 G62
38	" "	4	NENE	1889-11-29		A1 G62

ID	Individual in Patent		Sec.	Sec. Part	Date Issued	Other Counties	For More Info . . .
43	MCPHERSON, Alexander (Cont'd)	(Cont'd)	4	SESE	1889-11-29		A1 G62
194	MCPHERSON, Edward		11	NENE	1884-12-30		A1 G7
195	"	"	11	NESE	1884-12-30		A1 G7
196	"	"	11	NESW	1884-12-30		A1 G7
197	"	"	11	NW	1884-12-30		A1 G7
198	"	"	11	NWSW	1884-12-30		A1 G7
199	"	"	11	S½SW	1884-12-30		A1 G7
200	"	"	11	SESE	1884-12-30		A1 G7
201	"	"	11	W½NE	1884-12-30		A1 G7
202	"	"	11	W½SE	1884-12-30		A1 G7
203	"	"	12	E½SW	1884-12-30		A1 G7
204	"	"	12	S½NE	1884-12-30		A1 G7
205	"	"	12	S½NW	1884-12-30		A1 G7
206	"	"	12	SE	1884-12-30		A1 G7
207	"	"	12	W½SW	1884-12-30		A1 G7
208	"	"	13	N½NW	1884-12-30		A1 G7
209	"	"	13	SENE	1884-12-30		A1 G7
210	"	"	13	SENW	1884-12-30		A1 G7
211	"	"	13	SESE	1884-12-30		A1 G7
212	"	"	13	SWSW	1884-12-30		A1 G7
213	"	"	2	E½NW	1884-12-30		A1 G7
214	"	"	2	W½NW	1884-12-30		A1 G7
215	"	"	24	NWNE	1884-12-30		A1 G7
216	"	"	3	E½SE	1884-12-30		A1 G7
217	"	"	3	NENE	1884-12-30		A1 G7
218	"	"	3	SENE	1884-12-30		A1 G7
1	MCPHERSON, Edward G		10	N½SW	1889-04-23		A1 G62
3	"	"	10	SWNW	1889-04-23		A1 G62
13	"	"	14	SWSE	1889-04-23		A1 G62
14	"	"	14	W½SW	1889-04-23		A1 G62
15	"	"	15	N½NW	1889-04-23		A1 G62
16	"	"	15	NWNE	1889-04-23		A1 G62
17	"	"	15	SENE	1889-04-23		A1 G62
18	"	"	15	SENW	1889-04-23		A1 G62
19	"	"	15	SWSW	1889-04-23		A1 G62
20	"	"	15	W½SE	1889-04-23		A1 G62
21	"	"	21	N½NE	1889-04-23		A1 G62
22	"	"	21	NWNW	1889-04-23		A1 G62
23	"	"	22	E½NE	1889-04-23		A1 G62
24	"	"	22	S½NW	1889-04-23		A1 G62
29	"	"	26	E½NW	1889-04-23		A1 G62
30	"	"	26	N½SW	1889-04-23		A1 G62
31	"	"	26	NWNE	1889-04-23		A1 G62
32	"	"	26	NWSE	1889-04-23		A1 G62
33	"	"	26	S½NE	1889-04-23		A1 G62
34	"	"	3	N½NW	1889-04-23		A1 G62
35	"	"	3	NWNE	1889-04-23		A1 G62
36	"	"	3	S½SW	1889-04-23		A1 G62
37	"	"	4	N½SE	1889-04-23		A1 G62
39	"	"	4	NWNE	1889-04-23		A1 G62
40	"	"	4	NWSW	1889-04-23		A1 G62
41	"	"	4	S½NE	1889-04-23		A1 G62
42	"	"	4	S½NW	1889-04-23		A1 G62
44	"	"	4	SWSE	1889-04-23		A1 G62
45	"	"	9	N½NW	1889-04-23		A1 G62 V68
46	"	"	9	NENE	1889-04-23		A1 G62
2	"	"	10	SESE	1889-11-29		A1 G62
4	"	"	11	SENE	1889-11-29		A1 G62
5	"	"	12	N½NW	1889-11-29		A1 G62
6	"	"	13	E½SW	1889-11-29		A1 G62
7	"	"	13	NESE	1889-11-29		A1 G62
8	"	"	13	NWSW	1889-11-29		A1 G62
9	"	"	13	SWSE	1889-11-29		A1 G62
10	"	"	13	W½NE	1889-11-29		A1 G62
11	"	"	14	E½SE	1889-11-29		A1 G62
12	"	"	14	NWNW	1889-11-29		A1 G62
25	"	"	23	E½NE	1889-11-29		A1 G62
26	"	"	24	E½NE	1889-11-29		A1 G62
27	"	"	24	SENW	1889-11-29		A1 G62
28	"	"	24	SWNE	1889-11-29		A1 G62
38	"	"	4	NENE	1889-11-29		A1 G62
43	"	"	4	SESE	1889-11-29		A1 G62
158	MCPHERSON, Hugh A		26	S½SW	1889-04-10		A1 G30

ID	Individual in Patent	Sec.	Sec. Part	Date Issued	Other Counties	For More Info . . .
159	MCPHERSON, Hugh A (Cont'd)	26	SWSE	1889-04-10		A1 G30
160	" "	35	N½	1889-04-10		A1 G30
161	" "	35	NESE	1889-04-10		A1 G30
162	" "	35	SW	1889-04-10		A1 G30
163	" "	35	W½SE	1889-04-10		A1 G30
194	MCPHERSON, Martin	11	NENE	1884-12-30		A1 G7
195	" "	11	NESE	1884-12-30		A1 G7
196	" "	11	NESW	1884-12-30		A1 G7
197	" "	11	NW	1884-12-30		A1 G7
198	" "	11	NWSW	1884-12-30		A1 G7
199	" "	11	S½SW	1884-12-30		A1 G7
200	" "	11	SESE	1884-12-30		A1 G7
201	" "	11	W½NE	1884-12-30		A1 G7
202	" "	11	W½SE	1884-12-30		A1 G7
203	" "	12	E½SW	1884-12-30		A1 G7
204	" "	12	S½NE	1884-12-30		A1 G7
205	" "	12	S½NW	1884-12-30		A1 G7
206	" "	12	SE	1884-12-30		A1 G7
207	" "	12	W½SW	1884-12-30		A1 G7
208	" "	13	N½NW	1884-12-30		A1 G7
219	" "	13	NENE	1884-12-30		A1 G8
220	" "	13	NWSE	1884-12-30		A1 G8
209	" "	13	SENE	1884-12-30		A1 G7
210	" "	13	SENW	1884-12-30		A1 G7
211	" "	13	SESE	1884-12-30		A1 G7
221	" "	13	SWNW	1884-12-30		A1 G8
212	" "	13	SWSW	1884-12-30		A1 G7
222	" "	14	N½NE	1884-12-30		A1 G8
223	" "	14	NENW	1884-12-30		A1 G8
213	" "	2	E½NW	1884-12-30		A1 G7
214	" "	2	W½NW	1884-12-30		A1 G7
224	" "	24	N½NW	1884-12-30		A1 G8
215	" "	24	NWNE	1884-12-30		A1 G7
225	" "	24	SWNW	1884-12-30		A1 G8
216	" "	3	E½SE	1884-12-30		A1 G7
217	" "	3	NENE	1884-12-30		A1 G7
218	" "	3	SENE	1884-12-30		A1 G7
226	" "	31	SWNW	1884-12-30		A1 G8
1	MCPHERSON, Martin J	10	N½SW	1889-04-23		A1 G62
3	" "	10	SWNW	1889-04-23		A1 G62
13	" "	14	SWSE	1889-04-23		A1 G62
14	" "	14	W½SW	1889-04-23		A1 G62
15	" "	15	N½NW	1889-04-23		A1 G62
16	" "	15	NWNE	1889-04-23		A1 G62
17	" "	15	SENE	1889-04-23		A1 G62
18	" "	15	SENW	1889-04-23		A1 G62
19	" "	15	SWSW	1889-04-23		A1 G62
20	" "	15	W½SE	1889-04-23		A1 G62
21	" "	21	N½NE	1889-04-23		A1 G62
22	" "	21	NWNW	1889-04-23		A1 G62
23	" "	22	E½NE	1889-04-23		A1 G62
24	" "	22	S½NW	1889-04-23		A1 G62
29	" "	26	E½NW	1889-04-23		A1 G62
30	" "	26	N½SW	1889-04-23		A1 G62
31	" "	26	NWNE	1889-04-23		A1 G62
32	" "	26	NWSE	1889-04-23		A1 G62
33	" "	26	S½NE	1889-04-23		A1 G62
34	" "	3	N½NW	1889-04-23		A1 G62
35	" "	3	NWNE	1889-04-23		A1 G62
36	" "	3	S½SW	1889-04-23		A1 G62
37	" "	4	N½SE	1889-04-23		A1 G62
39	" "	4	NWNE	1889-04-23		A1 G62
40	" "	4	NWSW	1889-04-23		A1 G62
41	" "	4	S½NE	1889-04-23		A1 G62
42	" "	4	S½NW	1889-04-23		A1 G62
44	" "	4	SWSE	1889-04-23		A1 G62
45	" "	9	N½NW	1889-04-23		A1 G62 V68
46	" "	9	NENE	1889-04-23		A1 G62
2	" "	10	SESE	1889-11-29		A1 G62
4	" "	11	SENE	1889-11-29		A1 G62
5	" "	12	N½NW	1889-11-29		A1 G62
6	" "	13	E½SW	1889-11-29		A1 G62
7	" "	13	NESE	1889-11-29		A1 G62

ID	Individual in Patent	Sec.	Sec. Part	Date Issued	Other Counties	For More Info . . .
8	MCPHERSON, Martin J (Cont'd)	13	NWSW	1889-11-29		A1 G62
9	" "	13	SWSE	1889-11-29		A1 G62
10	" "	13	W½NE	1889-11-29		A1 G62
11	" "	14	E½SE	1889-11-29		A1 G62
12	" "	14	NWNW	1889-11-29		A1 G62
25	" "	23	E½NE	1889-11-29		A1 G62
26	" "	24	E½NE	1889-11-29		A1 G62
27	" "	24	SENW	1889-11-29		A1 G62
28	" "	24	SWNE	1889-11-29		A1 G62
38	" "	4	NENE	1889-11-29		A1 G62
43	" "	4	SESE	1889-11-29		A1 G62
194	MCPHERSON, William	11	NENE	1884-12-30		A1 G7
195	" "	11	NESE	1884-12-30		A1 G7
196	" "	11	NESW	1884-12-30		A1 G7
197	" "	11	NW	1884-12-30		A1 G7
198	" "	11	NWSW	1884-12-30		A1 G7
199	" "	11	S½SW	1884-12-30		A1 G7
200	" "	11	SESE	1884-12-30		A1 G7
201	" "	11	W½NE	1884-12-30		A1 G7
202	" "	11	W½SE	1884-12-30		A1 G7
203	" "	12	E½SW	1884-12-30		A1 G7
204	" "	12	S½NE	1884-12-30		A1 G7
205	" "	12	S½NW	1884-12-30		A1 G7
206	" "	12	SE	1884-12-30		A1 G7
207	" "	12	W½SW	1884-12-30		A1 G7
208	" "	13	N½NW	1884-12-30		A1 G7
219	" "	13	NENE	1884-12-30		A1 G8
220	" "	13	NWSE	1884-12-30		A1 G8
209	" "	13	SENE	1884-12-30		A1 G7
210	" "	13	SENW	1884-12-30		A1 G7
211	" "	13	SESE	1884-12-30		A1 G7
221	" "	13	SWNW	1884-12-30		A1 G8
212	" "	13	SWSW	1884-12-30		A1 G7
222	" "	14	N½NE	1884-12-30		A1 G8
223	" "	14	NENW	1884-12-30		A1 G8
213	" "	2	E½NW	1884-12-30		A1 G7
214	" "	2	W½NW	1884-12-30		A1 G7
224	" "	24	N½NW	1884-12-30		A1 G8
215	" "	24	NWNE	1884-12-30		A1 G7
225	" "	24	SWNW	1884-12-30		A1 G8
216	" "	3	E½SE	1884-12-30		A1 G7
217	" "	3	NENE	1884-12-30		A1 G7
218	" "	3	SENE	1884-12-30		A1 G7
226	" "	31	SWNW	1884-12-30		A1 G8
1	" "	10	N½SW	1889-04-23		A1 G62
3	" "	10	SWNW	1889-04-23		A1 G62
13	" "	14	SWSE	1889-04-23		A1 G62
14	" "	14	W½SW	1889-04-23		A1 G62
15	" "	15	N½NW	1889-04-23		A1 G62
16	" "	15	NWNE	1889-04-23		A1 G62
17	" "	15	SENE	1889-04-23		A1 G62
18	" "	15	SENW	1889-04-23		A1 G62
19	" "	15	SWSW	1889-04-23		A1 G62
20	" "	15	W½SE	1889-04-23		A1 G62
21	" "	21	N½NE	1889-04-23		A1 G62
22	" "	21	NWNW	1889-04-23		A1 G62
23	" "	22	E½NE	1889-04-23		A1 G62
24	" "	22	S½NW	1889-04-23		A1 G62
29	" "	26	E½NW	1889-04-23		A1 G62
30	" "	26	N½SW	1889-04-23		A1 G62
31	" "	26	NWNE	1889-04-23		A1 G62
32	" "	26	NWSE	1889-04-23		A1 G62
33	" "	26	S½NE	1889-04-23		A1 G62
34	" "	3	N½NW	1889-04-23		A1 G62
35	" "	3	NWNE	1889-04-23		A1 G62
36	" "	3	S½SW	1889-04-23		A1 G62
37	" "	4	N½SE	1889-04-23		A1 G62
39	" "	4	NWNE	1889-04-23		A1 G62
40	" "	4	NWSW	1889-04-23		A1 G62
41	" "	4	S½NE	1889-04-23		A1 G62
42	" "	4	S½NW	1889-04-23		A1 G62
44	" "	4	SWSE	1889-04-23		A1 G62
45	" "	9	N½NW	1889-04-23		A1 G62 V68

ID	Individual in Patent	Sec.	Sec. Part	Date Issued	Other Counties	For More Info . . .
46	MCPHERSON, William (Cont'd)	9	NENE	1889-04-23		A1 G62
2	" "	10	SESE	1889-11-29		A1 G62
4	" "	11	SENE	1889-11-29		A1 G62
5	" "	12	N½NW	1889-11-29		A1 G62
6	" "	13	E½SW	1889-11-29		A1 G62
7	" "	13	NESE	1889-11-29		A1 G62
8	" "	13	NWSW	1889-11-29		A1 G62
9	" "	13	SWSE	1889-11-29		A1 G62
10	" "	13	W½NE	1889-11-29		A1 G62
11	" "	14	E½SE	1889-11-29		A1 G62
12	" "	14	NWNW	1889-11-29		A1 G62
25	" "	23	E½NE	1889-11-29		A1 G62
26	" "	24	E½NE	1889-11-29		A1 G62
27	" "	24	SENW	1889-11-29		A1 G62
28	" "	24	SWNE	1889-11-29		A1 G62
38	" "	4	NENE	1889-11-29		A1 G62
43	" "	4	SESE	1889-11-29		A1 G62
78	MORGAN, Arther T	27	E½NW	1898-02-24		A4
79	" "	27	SWNW	1898-02-24		A4
80	" "	28	SENE	1898-02-24		A4
100	MORGAN, Gaines J	31	SENW	1906-06-21		A4
101	"	31	SWNE	1906-06-21		A4
227	MORGAN, William B	22	NESE	1895-11-11		A4
228	" "	22	SWNE	1895-11-11		A4
229	" "	22	W½SE	1895-11-11		A4
105	NEWELL, Grape	15	NWSW	1914-08-25		A1
106	"	15	SWNW	1914-08-25		A1
102	ODOM, George L	10	NWNE	1901-11-08		A4
103	" "	3	SWNE	1901-11-08		A4
104	" "	3	W½SE	1901-11-08		A4
139	ODOM, Hiram D	23	NWSE	1909-11-26		A4 V122
140	ODOM, Hugh	3	N½SW	1906-06-26		A4
141	" "	3	S½NW	1906-06-26		A4
179	ODOM, Michael	14	SWNW	1882-03-30		A4
186	ODOM, Sidney A	14	NWSE	1892-05-16		A4
187	" "	14	S½NE	1892-05-16		A4
188	" "	14	SENW	1892-05-16		A4
189	ODOM, Simeon	10	E½NE	1891-05-20		A4
190	" "	10	N½SE	1891-05-20		A4
232	ODOM, William Harmon	15	NENE	1912-08-01		A1
81	PARKER, Asa R	8	SW	1900-11-28		A4
148	REYNOLDS, Jason	32	SWNE	1846-09-01		A1
107	RUNNELLS, Hanson C	20	NESE	1884-12-30		A4
108	" "	20	S½NE	1884-12-30		A4
109	" "	21	SWNW	1884-12-30		A4
73	RUNNELS, Andrew J	20	N½NE	1899-02-25		A4
143	RUNNELS, Jacob	32	SWNW	1859-05-02		A1
146	RUNNELS, James P	21	E½SW	1895-01-17		A4
147	" "	21	W½SE	1895-01-17		A4
153	RUNNELS, Jesse	28	E½SW	1844-04-10		A1 G71
172	RUNNELS, Joseph L	31	NWNE	1914-06-23		A4
175	RUNNELS, Joseph N	23	E½SE	1911-06-29		A4 V122
176	" "	24	W½SW	1911-06-29		A4
153	RUNNELS, Lewis	28	E½SW	1844-04-10		A1 G71
142	SAPP, Jackson P	35	SESE	1890-08-16		A4
149	SAPP, Jason	29	NENE	1846-09-01		A1
144	SAPPE, Jake L	23	NWNE	1906-05-01		A4
82	SAVAGE, Benjamin F	26	E½SE	1914-04-13		A4
156	SPINKS, Joe	10	SENW	1912-06-14		A4
157	" "	10	SWNE	1912-06-14		A4
171	STALLWORTH, John W	9	SWNE	1905-03-11		A1
99	STOKLEY, Felix M	27	SENE	1917-08-09		A1
48	WATSON, Amasa B	10	S½SW	1883-02-03		A1 V49
55	" "	4	E½SW	1883-02-03		A1
56	" "	4	N½NW	1883-02-03		A1
57	" "	4	SWSW	1883-02-03		A1
58	" "	5	E½NW	1883-02-03		A1
59	" "	5	E½SE	1883-02-03		A1
60	" "	5	NE	1883-02-03		A1
61	" "	5	NWNW	1883-02-03		A1
62	" "	5	SESW	1883-02-03		A1
63	" "	5	SWSE	1883-02-03		A1
64	" "	8	E½NE	1883-02-03		A1

ID	Individual in Patent	Sec.	Sec. Part	Date Issued	Other Counties	For More Info . . .
65	WATSON, Amasa B (Cont'd)	8	NESE	1883-02-03		A1
66	"	8	SWNE	1883-02-03		A1
67	"	8	W½NW	1883-02-03		A1
68	"	9	NW	1883-02-03		A1 V45
69	"	9	NWNE	1883-02-03		A1
70	"	9	S½	1883-02-03		A1
71	"	9	SENE	1883-02-03		A1
47	"	1	NWNW	1883-09-15		A1
49	"	10	SWSW	1883-09-15		A1 V48
50	"	15	E½SW	1883-09-15		A1
51	"	2	E½	1883-09-15		A1
52	"	2	SW	1883-09-15		A1
53	"	22	N½NW	1883-09-15		A1
54	"	22	NWNE	1883-09-15		A1
98	WHEELER, Ellis	17	SWSW	1841-01-05		A1
184	WOODWARD, Samuel W	1	N½SW	1892-03-23		A4
185	"	1	S½NW	1892-03-23		A4

Patent Map

T5-N R11-W
St Stephens Meridian

Map Group 1

Township Statistics

Parcels Mapped	:	232
Number of Patents	:	93
Number of Individuals	:	66
Patentees Identified	:	60
Number of Surnames	:	37
Multi-Patentee Parcels	:	86
Oldest Patent Date	:	1/5/1841
Most Recent Patent	:	10/20/1919
Block/Lot Parcels	:	0
Parcels Re-Issued	:	0
Parcels that Overlap	:	9
Cities and Towns	:	2
Cemeteries	:	0

Copyright 2006 Boyd IT. Inc. All Rights Reserved

Section 6: MCDONALD Angus M 1896; MCDONALD Daniel 1896; MCDONALD Daniel 1896; MCDONALD Daniel 1896; MCDONALD William H 1896; MCDONALD Angus M 1896; MCDONALD Angus M 1896; MCDONALD William H 1896; MCDONALD Daniel 1896; COVINGTON Catherine F 1919

Section 5: WATSON Amasa B 1883; WATSON Amasa B 1883; WATSON Amasa B 1883; BEER Henry 1889; WATSON Amasa B 1883; BEER Henry 1889; BEER Henry 1889; WATSON Amasa B 1883; WATSON Amasa B 1883

Section 4: WATSON Amasa B 1883; MCPHERSON [62] Alexander 1889; MCPHERSON [62] Alexander 1889; MCPHERSON [62] Alexander 1889; MCPHERSON [62] Alexander 1889; MCPHERSON [62] Alexander 1889; MCPHERSON [62] Alexander 1889; WATSON Amasa B 1883; WATSON Amasa B 1883; MCPHERSON [62] Alexander 1889; MCPHERSON [62] Alexander 1889

Section 7

Section 8: WATSON Amasa B 1883; COURTNEY Andrew F 1913; BEER Henry 1889; WATSON Amasa B 1883; WATSON Amasa B 1883; PARKER Asa R 1900; BEER Henry 1889; WATSON Amasa B 1883; BEER Henry 1889

Section 9: MCPHERSON [62] Alexander 1889; MCPHERSON [62] Alexander 1889; WATSON Amasa B 1883; WATSON Amasa B 1883; STALLWORTH John W 1905; WATSON Amasa B 1883; WATSON Amasa B 1883

Section 18

Section 17: MCCARDLE Duncan 1890; MCCARDLE Duncan 1890; BEER Henry 1889; KENNEDY Jesse A 1889; HINTON Jefferson D 1894; WHEELER Ellis 1841; HINTON Jefferson D 1894; BEER Henry 1889; CHAPPEL Christopher 1841

Section 16

Section 19: EASTERLING John 1841; GRANTHAM John 1841; EASTERLING John 1841; EASTERLING John 1846

Section 20: EASTERLING Elizabeth 1859; RUNNELS Andrew J 1899; RUNNELLS Hanson C 1884; RUNNELLS Hanson C 1884

Section 21: MCPHERSON [62] Alexander 1889; MCPHERSON [62] Alexander 1889; RUNNELLS Hanson C 1884; BEER Henry 1889; BEER Henry 1889; RUNNELS James P 1895; BEER Henry 1889; RUNNELS James P 1895; DRAUGHN Jesse W 1914

Section 30: HINTON Blake 1841

Section 29: HINTON Blake 1846; HINTON Blake 1846; SAPP Jason 1846

Section 28: DRAUGHN John L 1895; DRAUGHN Jesse W 1914; DRAUGHN John L 1895; DRAUGHN John L 1895; MORGAN Arther T 1898; MCGILVRAY Daniel G 1906; RUNNELS [71] Jesse 1844

Section 31: HENSAILING Louis 1883; HENSARLING Nelley E 1889; RUNNELS Joseph L 1914; BIRKETT [8] Thomas 1884; MORGAN Gaines J 1906; MORGAN Gaines J 1906; MCCARDLE James 1890; MCCARDLE Joseph 1891; MCCARDLE Joseph 1891

Section 32: RUNNELS Jacob 1859; REYNOLDS Jason 1846

Section 33: MCGILRANY Angus 1890

44

Section 3
MCPHERSON [62] Alexander 1889
MCPHERSON [62] Alexander 1889
BIRKETT [7] Thomas 1884
ODOM Hugh 1906
ODOM George L 1901
BIRKETT [7] Thomas 1884
ODOM Hugh 1906
ODOM George L 1901
BIRKETT [7] Thomas 1884
MCPHERSON [62] Alexander 1889

Section 2
BIRKETT [7] Thomas 1884
BIRKETT [7] Thomas 1884
BIRKETT [7] Thomas 1884
WATSON Amasa B 1883
WATSON Amasa B 1883

Section 1
WATSON Amasa B 1883
BROWN Mark 1861
WOODWARD Samuel W 1892
WOODWARD Samuel W 1892
BROWN Robert 1901
HOLLIMON Riley 1891

Section 10
MCPHERSON [62] Alexander 1889
ODOM George L 1901
SPINKS Joe 1912
SPINKS Joe 1912
ODOM Simeon 1891
MCPHERSON [62] Alexander 1889
ODOM Simeon 1891
WATSON Amasa B 1883
WATSON Amasa B 1883
MCPHERSON [62] Alexander 1889

Section 11
BIRKETT [7] Thomas 1884
BIRKETT [7] Thomas 1884
BIRKETT [7] Thomas 1884
MCPHERSON [62] Alexander 1889
BIRKETT [7] Thomas 1884
BIRKETT [7] Thomas 1884
BIRKETT [7] Thomas 1884
BIRKETT [7] Thomas 1884
BIRKETT [7] Thomas 1884

Section 12
MCPHERSON [62] Alexander 1889
HOLLIMON Riley 1891
BIRKETT [7] Thomas 1884
BIRKETT [7] Thomas 1884
BIRKETT [7] Thomas 1884
BIRKETT [7] Thomas 1884

Section 15
MCPHERSON [62] Alexander 1889
MCPHERSON [62] Alexander 1889
ODOM William Harmon 1912
NEWELL Grape 1914
MCPHERSON [62] Alexander 1889
BEER Henry 1889
MCPHERSON [62] Alexander 1889
NEWELL Grape 1914
MCPHERSON [62] Alexander 1889
MCPHERSON [62] Alexander 1889
WATSON Amasa B 1883
BEER Henry 1889

Section 14
MCPHERSON [62] Alexander 1889
BIRKETT [8] Thomas 1884
BIRKETT [8] Thomas 1884
ODOM Michael 1882
ODOM Sidney A 1892
ODOM Sidney A 1892
MCPHERSON [62] Alexander 1889
ODOM Sidney A 1892
MCPHERSON [62] Alexander 1889
BEER Henry 1889
MCPHERSON [62] Alexander 1889

Section 13
BIRKETT [7] Thomas 1884
MCPHERSON [62] Alexander 1889
BIRKETT [8] Thomas 1884
BIRKETT [8] Thomas 1884
BIRKETT [7] Thomas 1884
BIRKETT [7] Thomas 1884
MCPHERSON [62] Alexander 1889
BIRKETT [8] Thomas 1884
MCPHERSON [62] Alexander 1889
MCPHERSON [62] Alexander 1889
BIRKETT [7] Thomas 1884
MCPHERSON [62] Alexander 1889
BIRKETT [7] Thomas 1884

Section 22
WATSON Amasa B 1883
WATSON Amasa B 1883
MCPHERSON [62] Alexander 1889
MCPHERSON [62] Alexander 1889
MORGAN William B 1895
MORGAN William B 1895
MORGAN William B 1895
BEER Henry 1889
BEER Henry 1889

Section 23
SAPPE Jake L 1906
MCPHERSON [62] Alexander 1889
BEER Henry 1889
BEER Henry 1889
BEER Henry 1889
ODOM Hiram D 1909
BEER Henry 1889
CEPHUS Stephen 1901
RUNNELS Joseph N 1911

Section 24
BIRKETT [8] Thomas 1884
BIRKETT [8] Thomas 1884
MCPHERSON [62] Alexander 1889
BIRKETT [8] Thomas 1884
MCPHERSON [62] Alexander 1889
RUNNELS Joseph N 1911
BEER Henry 1889
BEER Henry 1889

Section 27
BEER Henry 1889
BEER Henry 1889
CEPHUS Stephen 1901
MORGAN Arther T 1898
MORGAN Arther T 1898
STOKLEY Felix M 1917
MCGILVRAY Daniel G 1906
BEER Henry 1889
BEER Henry 1889
MCGILVRAY Daniel G 1906

Section 26
CEPHUS Stephen 1901
MCPHERSON [62] Alexander 1889
BEER Henry 1889
MCPHERSON [62] Alexander 1889
BEER Henry 1889
MCPHERSON [62] Alexander 1889
MCPHERSON [62] Alexander 1889
MCPHERSON [62] Alexander 1889
SAVAGE Benjamin F 1914
ELLSWORTH [30] John C 1889
ELLSWORTH [30] John C 1889

Section 25

Section 34

Section 35
BEER Henry 1889
ELLSWORTH [30] John C 1889
ELLSWORTH [30] John C 1889
ELLSWORTH [30] John C 1889
ELLSWORTH [30] John C 1889
SAPP Jackson P 1890

Section 36

Helpful Hints

1. This Map's INDEX can be found on the preceding pages.

2. Refer to Map "C" to see where this Township lies within Perry County, Mississippi.

3. Numbers within square brackets [ ] denote a multi-patentee land parcel (multi-owner). Refer to Appendix "C" for a full list of members in this group.

4. Areas that look to be crowded with Patentees usually indicate multiple sales of the same parcel (Re-issues) or Overlapping parcels. See this Township's Index for an explanation of these and other circumstances that might explain "odd" groupings of Patentees on this map.

Legend
——— Patent Boundary
▬▬▬ Section Boundary
No Patents Found (or Outside County)
1., 2., 3., ... Lot Numbers (when beside a name)
[ ] Group Number (see Appendix "C")

Scale: Section = 1 mile X 1 mile (generally, with some exceptions)

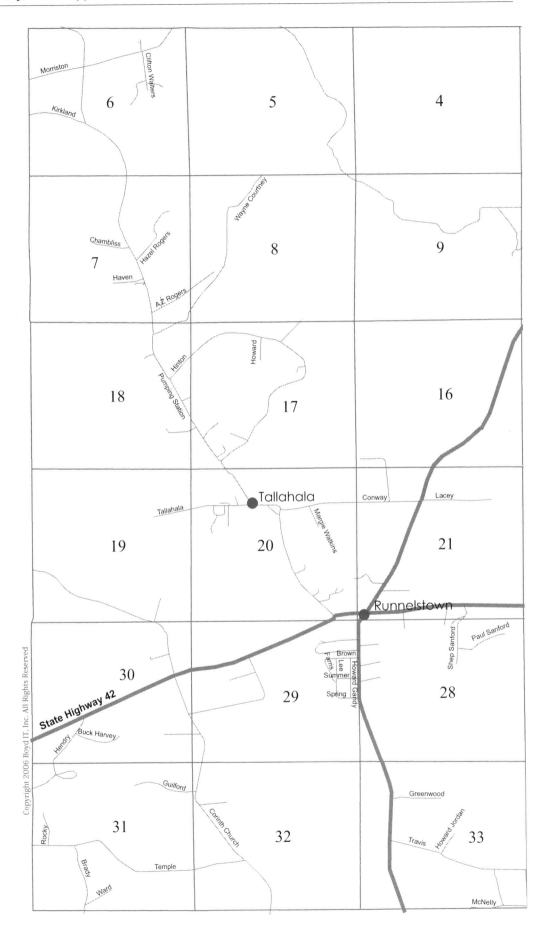

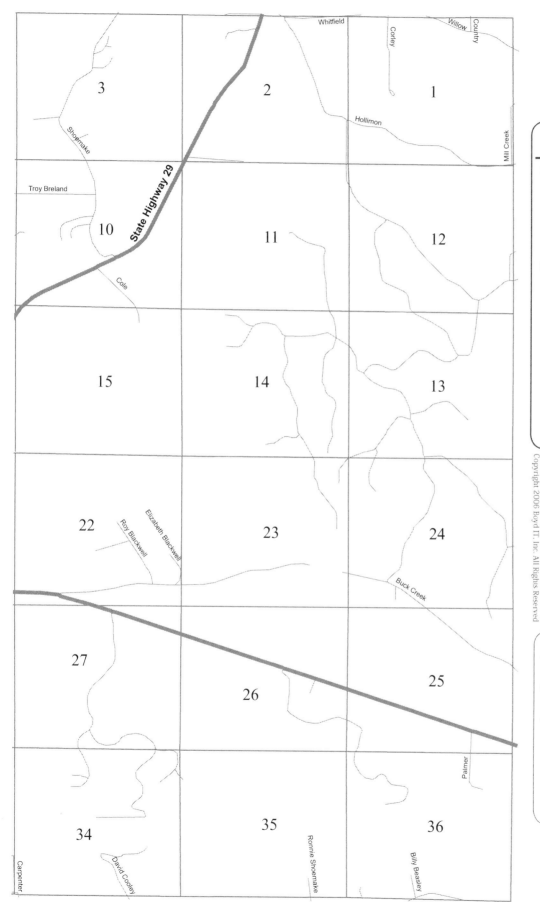

3

2

Whitfield

Corley

Willow

Country

1

Shoemake

Hollimon

Mill Creek

Troy Breland

State Highway 29

10

11

12

Cole

15

14

13

Elizabeth Blackwell

Roy Blackwell

22

23

24

Buck Creek

27

26

25

Palmer

34

35

36

Carpenter

David Cooley

Ronnie Shoemake

Billy Beasley

Helpful Hints

1. This road map has a number of uses, but primarily it is to help you: a) find the present location of land owned by your ancestors (at least the general area), b) find cemeteries and city-centers, and c) estimate the route/roads used by Census-takers & tax-assessors.

2. If you plan to travel to Perry County to locate cemeteries or land parcels, please pick up a modern travel map for the area before you do. Mapping old land parcels on modern maps is not as exact a science as you might think. Just the slightest variations in public land survey coordinates, estimates of parcel boundaries, or road-map deviations can greatly alter a map's representation of how a road either does or doesn't cross a particular parcel of land.

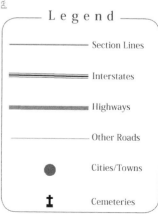

Legend

—————— Section Lines

══════ Interstates

━━━━━━ Highways

—————— Other Roads

● Cities/Towns

✝ Cemeteries

Scale: Section = 1 mile X 1 mile
(generally, with some exceptions)

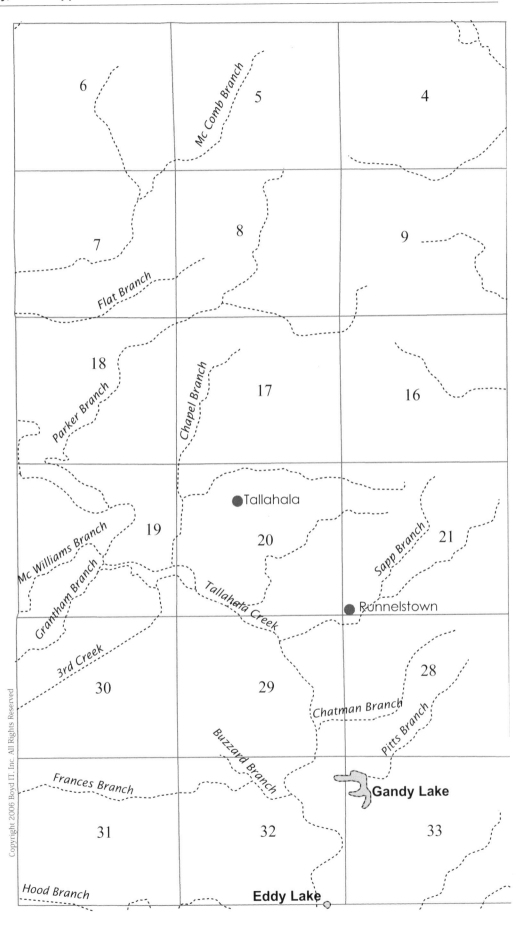

Historical Map

T5-N R11-W
St Stephens Meridian

Map Group 1

Cities & Towns
Runnelstown
Tallahala

Cemeteries
None

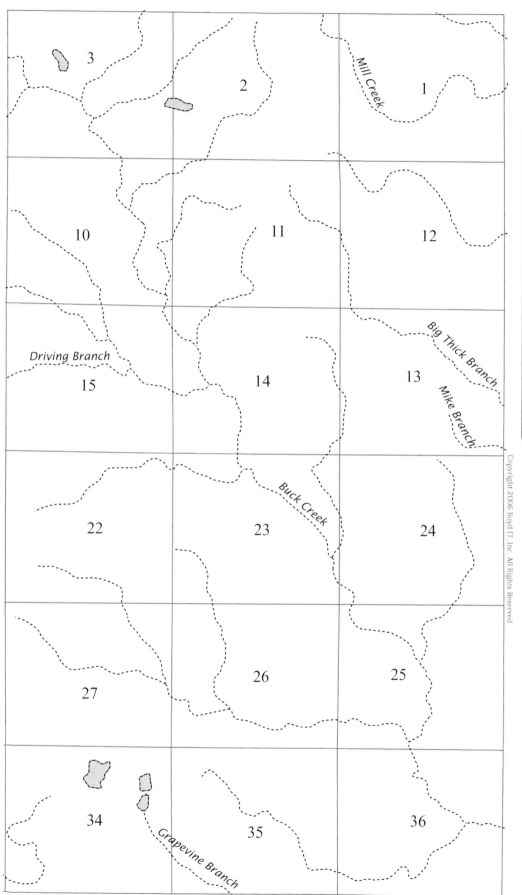

Helpful Hints

1. This Map takes a different look at the same Congressional Township displayed in the preceding two maps. It presents features that can help you better envision the historical development of the area: a) Water-bodies (lakes & ponds), b) Water-courses (rivers, streams, etc.), c) Railroads, d) City/town center-points (where they were oftentimes located when first settled), and e) Cemeteries.

2. Using this "Historical" map in tandem with this Township's Patent Map and Road Map, may lead you to some interesting discoveries. You will often find roads, towns, cemeteries, and waterways are named after nearby landowners: sometimes those names will be the ones you are researching. See how many of these research gems you can find here in Perry County.

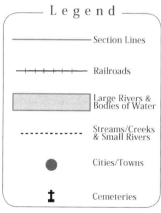

Legend

————	Section Lines
++++++	Railroads
▭	Large Rivers & Bodies of Water
- - - - -	Streams/Creeks & Small Rivers
●	Cities/Towns
♰	Cemeteries

Scale: Section = 1 mile X 1 mile
(there are some exceptions)

Map Group 2: Index to Land Patents

Township 5-North Range 10-West (St Stephens)

After you locate an individual in this Index, take note of the Section and Section Part then proceed to the Land Patent map on the pages immediately following. You should have no difficulty locating the corresponding parcel of land.

The "For More Info" Column will lead you to more information about the underlying Patents. See the *Legend* at right, and the "How to Use this Book" chapter, for more information.

```
                      LEGEND
              "For More Info . . . " column

A = Authority (Legislative Act, See Appendix "A")
B = Block or Lot (location in Section unknown)
C = Cancelled Patent
F = Fractional Section
G = Group  (Multi-Patentee Patent, see Appendix "C")
V = Overlaps another Parcel
R = Re-Issued (Parcel patented more than once)

(A & G items require you to look in the Appendixes referred
to above. All other Letter-designations followed by a number
require you to locate line-items in this index that possess
the ID number found after the letter).
```

ID	Individual in Patent	Sec.	Sec. Part	Date Issued	Other Counties	For More Info . . .
389	BIRKETT, Thomas	7	SWSW	1884-12-30		A1 G7
365	BLACK, Lewis C	1	SWSW	1909-12-09		A2
261	BLODGETT, Delos A	1	E½	1889-11-21		A1
262	" "	1	E½SW	1889-11-21		A1
263	" "	1	NW	1889-11-21		A1
264	" "	1	NWSW	1889-11-21		A1
265	" "	11	NENE	1889-11-21		A1
266	" "	11	SESE	1889-11-21		A1
267	" "	14	E½NE	1889-11-21		A1
268	" "	14	SE	1889-11-21		A1
269	" "	15	N½NW	1889-11-21		A1
270	" "	15	NWNE	1889-11-21		A1
271	" "	15	W½SE	1889-11-21		A1
272	" "	2	E½NE	1889-11-21		A1
273	" "	2	SE	1889-11-21		A1
274	" "	2	SWNE	1889-11-21		A1
275	" "	21	E½NE	1889-11-21		A1
276	" "	22	NE	1889-11-21		A1
277	" "	22	W½NW	1889-11-21		A1
278	" "	24	E½NE	1889-11-21		A1
279	" "	24	E½SE	1889-11-21		A1
280	" "	24	NESW	1889-11-21		A1
281	" "	24	SENW	1889-11-21		A1
282	" "	24	SWSE	1889-11-21		A1
283	" "	25	NENE	1889-11-21		A1
314	BRANOM, Henry Buford	23	NWSE	1921-06-24		A4
316	BREWER, Howel N	35	SENW	1915-09-27		A4
323	CARNES, John A	36	NENE	1859-05-02		A1
324	" "	36	SENE	1859-05-02		A1
319	CARROLL, James M	33	SENW	1916-02-14		A4
380	CLARKE, Samuel	17	W½NE	1841-01-05		A1
311	CLIFTON, George	36	N½SW	1901-06-25		A4
312	"	36	SENW	1901-06-25		A4
385	COCHRAN, Solomon	12	NESW	1889-01-05		A4
386	" "	12	NWSE	1889-01-05		A4
387	" "	12	SENW	1889-01-05		A4
388	" "	12	SWNE	1889-01-05		A4
253	CREEL, Daniel	30	W½SE	1841-01-05		A1 G24
325	CREEL, John	30	SW	1841-01-05		A1 G25
253	" "	30	W½SE	1841-01-05		A1 G24
377	CREEL, Reubin	31	SWNE	1841-01-05		A1
325	CREEL, Thomas	30	SW	1841-01-05		A1 G25
378	DRAUGHN, Rufus	20	SENE	1854-03-15		A1 G29
379	"	6	SESW	1859-05-02		A1 G29
313	DUNNAM, George R	35	SESE	1913-02-14		A4
390	EASTERLING, Thomas	36	S½SE	1906-05-01		A1

ID	Individual in Patent	Sec.	Sec. Part	Date Issued	Other Counties	For More Info . . .
234	EDWARDS, Albert L	12	SESW	1900-11-28		A4
235	" "	12	SWSE	1900-11-28		A4
236	" "	12	W½SW	1900-11-28		A4
315	EDWARDS, Henry	13	S½SW	1894-12-17		A4
368	EDWARDS, Martin	23	SENE	1890-08-16		A4
369	" "	24	N½NW	1890-08-16		A4
370	" "	24	SWNW	1890-08-16		A4
243	HEMPHILL, Brickley C	15	SW	1889-04-20		A1 G44
244	" "	15	SWNW	1889-04-20		A1 G44
243	HEMPHILL, Samuel H	15	SW	1889-04-20		A1 G44
244	" "	15	SWNW	1889-04-20		A1 G44
391	HINTON, Wiley M	33	N½SW	1884-11-20		A4
393	" "	33	W½NW	1884-11-20		A4
392	" "	33	NENW	1884-12-30		A1
258	HOLLIMAN, David	10	S½SW	1895-02-15		A4
259	" "	10	SWSE	1895-02-15		A4
260	" "	9	SESE	1895-02-15		A4
254	HOLLIMON, Darley A	7	NENW	1897-09-09		A4
255	" "	7	W½NW	1897-09-09		A4
371	LANDRUM, Mary	4	W½SW	1919-02-10		A1 G59
360	LAURENDINE, Joseph	32	SESE	1904-11-30		A1
361	" "	33	S½SW	1904-11-30		A1
367	LAURENDINE, Louis	34	N½SE	1906-11-02		A4
371	LOPER, Isaac	4	W½SW	1919-02-10		A1 G59
389	MCPHERSON, Alexander	7	SWSW	1884-12-30		A1 G7
237	" "	2	NW	1889-04-10		A1 G62
238	" "	2	NWNE	1889-04-10		A1 G62
389	MCPHERSON, Edward	7	SWSW	1884-12-30		A1 G7
237	MCPHERSON, Edward G	2	NW	1889-04-10		A1 G62
238	" "	2	NWNE	1889-04-10		A1 G62
389	MCPHERSON, Martin	7	SWSW	1884-12-30		A1 G7
237	MCPHERSON, Martin J	2	NW	1889-04-10		A1 G62
238	" "	2	NWNE	1889-04-10		A1 G62
389	MCPHERSON, William	7	SWSW	1884-12-30		A1 G7
237	" "	2	NW	1889-04-10		A1 G62
238	" "	2	NWNE	1889-04-10		A1 G62
396	" "	10	N½SE	1890-07-03		A1 G63
397	" "	10	N½SW	1890-07-03		A1 G63
398	" "	10	SESE	1890-07-03		A1 G63
399	" "	11	NWSE	1890-07-03		A1 G63
400	" "	11	W½NE	1890-07-03		A1 G63
401	" "	12	N½NW	1890-07-03		A1 G63
402	" "	15	NENE	1890-07-03		A1 G63
403	" "	15	SENW	1890-07-03		A1 G63
404	" "	15	SWNE	1890-07-03		A1 G63
405	" "	2	SW	1890-07-03		A1 G63
406	" "	21	S½NW	1890-07-03		A1 G63
407	" "	21	W½NE	1890-07-03		A1 G63
408	" "	22	E½NW	1890-07-03		A1 G63
409	" "	3	SESE	1890-07-03		A1 G63
410	" "	4	SE	1890-07-03		A1 G63
411	" "	9	E½SW	1890-12-04		A1 G63
412	" "	9	N½SE	1890-12-04		A1 G63
413	" "	9	NE	1890-12-04		A1 G63
414	" "	9	SENW	1890-12-04		A1 G63
415	" "	9	SWSE	1890-12-04		A1 G63
333	MOORE, Joseph B	13	N½	1889-11-21		A1
334	" "	13	N½SW	1889-11-21		A1
335	" "	13	S½SE	1889-11-21		A1
338	" "	23	NENE	1889-11-21		A1
340	" "	23	SENW	1889-11-21		A1
341	" "	23	SW	1889-11-21		A1
342	" "	23	SWSE	1889-11-21		A1
343	" "	23	W½NW	1889-11-21		A1
344	" "	24	NWSE	1889-11-21		A1
345	" "	24	W½NE	1889-11-21		A1
330	" "	12	E½NE	1889-11-29		A1
331	" "	12	E½SE	1889-11-29		A1
332	" "	12	NWNE	1889-11-29		A1
346	" "	25	SENW	1889-11-29		A1
349	" "	25	W½SE	1889-11-29		A1
352	" "	26	NWNE	1889-11-29		A1
354	" "	26	SENW	1889-11-29		A1

ID	Individual in Patent	Sec.	Sec. Part	Date Issued	Other Counties	For More Info . . .
359	MOORE, Joseph B (Cont'd)	36	N½NW	1889-11-29		A1
328	" "	10	N½	1890-04-25		A1
329	" "	11	W½	1890-04-25		A1
336	" "	14	S½SW	1890-07-03		A1
337	" "	14	W½NE	1890-07-03		A1
339	" "	23	NENW	1890-07-03		A1
347	" "	25	SESE	1890-07-03		A1
348	" "	25	W½NW	1890-07-03		A1 R242
350	" "	26	NENE	1890-07-03		A1
351	" "	26	NENW	1890-07-03		A1
353	" "	26	S½NE	1890-07-03		A1
355	" "	35	E½SW	1890-07-03		A1
356	" "	35	NESE	1890-07-03		A1
357	" "	35	NWSW	1890-07-03		A1
358	" "	35	W½SE	1890-07-03		A1
378	MYERS, John W	20	SENE	1854-03-15		A1 G29
379	" "	6	SESW	1859-05-02		A1 G29
378	MYERS, Levi	20	SENE	1854-03-15		A1 G29
379	" "	6	SESW	1859-05-02		A1 G29
416	NEWELL, William	13	N½SE	1906-03-05		A4
241	ODOM, Benjamin	23	NESE	1846-09-01		A1
257	ODOM, Darling	26	SE	1889-11-21		A1
256	" "	25	SW	1890-02-21		A4
310	ODOM, Ezekiel	17	NENE	1841-01-05		A1
318	ODOM, Jackson	36	S½SW	1884-11-20		A4
372	ODOM, Michael	35	NWNE	1859-05-02		A1
362	PALMER, Joseph S	35	E½NE	1900-11-28		A4
363	" "	35	SWNE	1900-11-28		A4
364	" "	36	SWNW	1900-11-28		A4
422	PITTS, William W	32	W½SE	1860-04-02		A1
326	PUGH, John R	27	NWNW	1912-06-14		A4
327	" "	28	NENE	1912-06-14		A4
394	RICH, William D	36	N½SE	1900-11-28		A4
395	" "	36	W½NE	1900-11-28		A4
366	RUNNELS, Lewis	32	SWNW	1841-01-05		A1
242	SAFFOLD, Bird	25	W½NW	1841-01-05		A1 C R348
247	SMITH, Charley H	11	NESE	1909-06-14		A4 R250
248	" "	11	SENE	1909-06-14		A4 R251
249	" "	12	SWNW	1909-06-14		A4 R252
250	SMITH, Charley N	11	NESE	1900-11-28		A4 C R247
251	" "	11	SENE	1900-11-28		A4 C R248
252	" "	12	SWNW	1900-11-28		A4 C R249
309	SMITH, Ervin A	5	SW	1908-11-23		A1 G72
396	SMITH, Frederick A	10	N½SE	1890-07-03		A1 G63
397	" "	10	N½SW	1890-07-03		A1 G63
398	" "	10	SESE	1890-07-03		A1 G63
399	" "	11	NWSE	1890-07-03		A1 G63
400	" "	11	W½NE	1890-07-03		A1 G63
401	" "	12	N½NW	1890-07-03		A1 G63
402	" "	15	NENE	1890-07-03		A1 G63
403	" "	15	SENW	1890-07-03		A1 G63
404	" "	15	SWNE	1890-07-03		A1 G63
405	" "	2	SW	1890-07-03		A1 G63
406	" "	21	S½NW	1890-07-03		A1 G63
407	" "	21	W½NE	1890-07-03		A1 G63
408	" "	22	E½NW	1890-07-03		A1 G63
409	" "	3	SESE	1890-07-03		A1 G63
410	" "	4	SE	1890-07-03		A1 G63
411	" "	9	E½SW	1890-12-04		A1 G63
412	" "	9	N½SE	1890-12-04		A1 G63
413	" "	9	NE	1890-12-04		A1 G63
414	" "	9	SENW	1890-12-04		A1 G63
415	" "	9	SWSE	1890-12-04		A1 G63
309	SMITH, John	5	SW	1908-11-23		A1 G72
378	STEVENS, William	20	SENE	1854-03-15		A1 G29
379	" "	6	SESW	1859-05-02		A1 G29
245	SWAYINGIN, Celia	34	S½SE	1898-12-01		A4
246	" "	35	SWSW	1898-12-01		A4
381	TISDALE, Seaborn	7	E½SW	1895-05-11		A4
382	" "	7	NWSW	1895-05-11		A4
383	" "	7	SENW	1895-05-11		A4
322	TOUCHSTONE, Jesse	7	NENE	1853-11-01		A1
233	TUCKER, Albert G	4	NESW	1859-06-01		A1

ID	Individual in Patent	Sec.	Sec. Part	Date Issued	Other Counties	For More Info . . .
396	WAGNER, Jacob K	10	N½SE	1890-07-03		A1 G63
397	" "	10	N½SW	1890-07-03		A1 G63
398	" "	10	SESE	1890-07-03		A1 G63
399	" "	11	NWSE	1890-07-03		A1 G63
400	" "	11	W½NE	1890-07-03		A1 G63
401	" "	12	N½NW	1890-07-03		A1 G63
402	" "	15	NENE	1890-07-03		A1 G63
403	" "	15	SENW	1890-07-03		A1 G63
404	" "	15	SWNE	1890-07-03		A1 G63
405	" "	2	SW	1890-07-03		A1 G63
406	" "	21	S½NW	1890-07-03		A1 G63
407	" "	21	W½NE	1890-07-03		A1 G63
408	" "	22	E½NW	1890-07-03		A1 G63
409	" "	3	SESE	1890-07-03		A1 G63
410	" "	4	SE	1890-07-03		A1 G63
411	" "	9	E½SW	1890-12-04		A1 G63
412	" "	9	N½SE	1890-12-04		A1 G63
413	" "	9	NE	1890-12-04		A1 G63
414	" "	9	SENW	1890-12-04		A1 G63
415	" "	9	SWSE	1890-12-04		A1 G63
285	WALLEY, Elizabeth E	22	NESW	1904-08-30		A4
320	WALLEY, James T	15	E½SE	1895-06-27		A4
321	" "	15	SENE	1895-06-27		A4
376	WALLEY, Pinkney	24	NWSW	1911-11-01		A1
284	WALTERS, Dory M	32	SWNE	1905-11-08		A4
317	WALTERS, Irvin W	21	SE	1898-09-28		A4
239	WALTMAN, Archie	14	E½NW	1902-01-17		A4
240	" "	14	NWNW	1902-01-17		A4
286	WARE, Emmor	22	SE	1882-12-30		A1
287	" "	22	SESW	1882-12-30		A1
288	" "	22	W½SW	1882-12-30		A1
289	" "	26	SW	1882-12-30		A1
290	" "	26	W½NW	1882-12-30		A1
291	" "	27	E½NW	1882-12-30		A1
292	" "	27	NE	1882-12-30		A1
293	" "	27	S½	1882-12-30		A1
294	" "	27	SWNW	1882-12-30		A1
295	" "	28	SE	1882-12-30		A1
296	" "	28	SENE	1882-12-30		A1
297	" "	28	W½NE	1882-12-30		A1
298	" "	3	N½	1882-12-30		A1
299	" "	3	NESE	1882-12-30		A1
300	" "	3	SW	1882-12-30		A1
301	" "	3	W½SE	1882-12-30		A1
302	" "	33	E½	1882-12-30		A1
303	" "	34	N½	1882-12-30		A1
304	" "	34	SW	1882-12-30		A1
305	" "	35	NENW	1882-12-30		A1
306	" "	35	W½NW	1882-12-30		A1
307	" "	4	NE	1882-12-30		A1
308	" "	4	NENW	1882-12-30		A1
373	WHITE, Nathan	32	N½NE	1895-11-11		A4
374	" "	32	NESE	1895-11-11		A4
375	" "	32	SENE	1895-11-11		A4
384	WHITE, Sidney	28	NW	1898-06-01		A4
423	WHITE, William	21	SW	1892-07-20		A4
419	WOODARD, William R	9	N½NW	1859-11-10		A1
420	" "	9	SWNW	1861-02-01		A1
421	" "	9	W½SW	1861-02-01		A1
417	" "	4	SENW	1897-05-05		A1
418	" "	4	SESW	1897-05-05		A1

Patent Map

T5-N R10-W
St Stephens Meridian

Map Group 2

Township Statistics

Parcels Mapped	:	191
Number of Patents	:	85
Number of Individuals	:	72
Patentees Identified	:	59
Number of Surnames	:	46
Multi-Patentee Parcels	:	31
Oldest Patent Date	:	1/5/1841
Most Recent Patent	:	6/24/1921
Block/Lot Parcels	:	0
Parcels Re - Issued	:	4
Parcels that Overlap	:	0
Cities and Towns	:	2
Cemeteries	:	3

6

5

WARE
Emmor
1882

WARE
Emmor
1882

WOODARD
William R
1897

SMITH [72]
Ervin A
1908

LANDRUM [59]
Mary
1919

TUCKER
Albert G
1859

4

MCPHERSON [63]
William
1890

WOODARD
William R
1897

DRAUGHN [29]
Rufus
1859

HOLLIMON
Darley A
1897

HOLLIMON
Darley A
1897

TOUCHSTONE
Jesse
1853

WOODARD
William R
1859

MCPHERSON [63]
William
1890

TISDALE
Seaborn
1895

7

8

WOODARD
William R
1861

MCPHERSON [63]
William
1890

TISDALE
Seaborn
1895

WOODARD
William R
1861

9

MCPHERSON [63]
William
1890

BIRKETT [7]
Thomas
1884

TISDALE
Seaborn
1895

MCPHERSON [63]
William
1890

MCPHERSON [63]
William
1890

HOLLIMAN
David
1895

CLARKE
Samuel
1841

ODOM
Ezekiel
1841

18

17

16

19

20

DRAUGHN [29]
Rufus
1854

MCPHERSON [63]
William
1890

MCPHERSON [63]
William
1890

BLODGETT
Delos A
1889

21

WHITE
William
1892

WALTERS
Irvin W
1898

30

29

WHITE
Sidney
1898

WARE
Emmor
1882

PUGH
John R
1912

28

WARE
Emmor
1882

CREEL [25]
John
1841

CREEL [24]
Daniel
1841

WARE
Emmor
1882

CREEL
Reubin
1841

RUNNELS
Lewis
1841

WHITE
Nathan
1895

HINTON
Wiley M
1884

HINTON
Wiley M
1884

WALTERS
Dory M
1905

WHITE
Nathan
1895

CARROLL
James M
1916

32

WARE
Emmor
1882

PITTS
William W
1860

WHITE
Nathan
1895

HINTON
Wiley M
1884

33

31

LAURENDINE
Joseph
1904

LAURENDINE
Joseph
1904

Helpful Hints

1. This Map's INDEX can be found on the preceding pages.

2. Refer to Map "C" to see where this Township lies within Perry County, Mississippi.

3. Numbers within square brackets [ ] denote a multi-patentee land parcel (multi-owner). Refer to Appendix "C" for a full list of members in this group.

4. Areas that look to be crowded with Patentees usually indicate multiple sales of the same parcel (Re-issues) or Overlapping parcels. See this Township's Index for an explanation of these and other circumstances that might explain "odd" groupings of Patentees on this map.

Legend

— Patent Boundary

— Section Boundary

No Patents Found (or Outside County)

1., 2., 3., ... Lot Numbers (when beside a name)

[ ] Group Number (see Appendix "C")

Scale: Section = 1 mile X 1 mile (generally, with some exceptions)

Section 3 — WARE Emmor 1882; WARE Emmor 1882; WARE Emmor 1882; WARE Emmor 1882; MCPHERSON [63] William 1890

Section 2 — MCPHERSON [62] Alexander 1889; MCPHERSON [62] Alexander 1889; BLODGETT Delos A 1889; BLODGETT Delos A 1889; MCPHERSON [63] William 1890; BLODGETT Delos A 1889

Section 1 — BLODGETT Delos A 1889; BLODGETT Delos A 1889; BLODGETT Delos A 1889; BLACK Lewis C 1909; BLODGETT Delos A 1889

Section 10 — MOORE Joseph B 1890; MCPHERSON [63] William 1890; MCPHERSON [63] William 1890; MCPHERSON [63] William 1890; HOLLIMAN David 1895; HOLLIMAN David 1895

Section 11 — MCPHERSON [63] William 1890; BLODGETT Delos A 1889; SMITH Charley H; SMITH Charley N 1909/1900; MOORE Joseph B 1890; MCPHERSON [63] William 1890; SMITH Charley N; SMITH Charley H 1909; BLODGETT Delos A 1889

Section 12 — MCPHERSON [63] William 1890; MOORE Joseph B 1889; SMITH Charley N 1900; COCHRAN Solomon 1889; SMITH Charley H 1909; COCHRAN Solomon 1889; MOORE Joseph B 1889; EDWARDS Albert L 1900; COCHRAN Solomon 1889; COCHRAN Solomon 1900; EDWARDS Henry 1894; EDWARDS Albert L 1900; MOORE Joseph B 1889

Section 15 — BLODGETT Delos A 1889; MCPHERSON [63] William 1890; BLODGETT Delos A 1889; MCPHERSON [63] William 1890; HEMPHILL [44] Brickley C 1889; MCPHERSON William 1890; MCPHERSON [63] William 1890; WALLEY James T 1895; BLODGETT Delos A 1889; HEMPHILL [44] Brickley C 1889; WALLEY James T 1895

Section 14 — WALTMAN Archie 1902; WALTMAN Archie 1902; MOORE Joseph B 1890; BLODGETT Delos A 1889; MOORE Joseph B 1890; BLODGETT Delos A 1889

Section 13 — MOORE Joseph B 1889; MOORE Joseph B 1889; NEWELL William 1906; EDWARDS Henry 1894; MOORE Joseph B 1889

Section 22 — MCPHERSON [63] William 1890; BLODGETT Delos A 1889; BLODGETT Delos A 1889; WARE Emmor 1882; WALLEY Elizabeth E 1904; WARE Emmor 1882; WARE Emmor 1882

Section 23 — MOORE Joseph B 1889; MOORE Joseph B 1890; MOORE Joseph B 1889; 23; EDWARDS Martin 1890; MOORE Joseph B 1889; BRANOM Henry Buford 1921; ODOM Benjamin 1846; MOORE Joseph B 1889

Section 24 — MOORE Joseph B 1889; EDWARDS Martin 1890; MOORE Joseph B 1889; EDWARDS Martin 1890; BLODGETT Delos A 1889; BLODGETT Delos A 1889; WALLEY Pinkney 1911; BLODGETT Delos A 1889; MOORE Joseph B 1889; BLODGETT Delos A 1889

Section 27 — PUGH John R 1912; WARE Emmor 1882; WARE Emmor 1882; WARE Emmor 1882; 27; WARE Emmor 1882

Section 26 — WARE Emmor 1882; MOORE Joseph B 1890; MOORE Joseph B 1889; MOORE Joseph B 1890; MOORE Joseph B 1889; MOORE Joseph B 1890; 26; WARE Emmor 1882; ODOM Darling 1889

Section 25 — MOORE Joseph B 1890; BLODGETT Delos A 1889; SAFFOLD Bird 1841; MOORE Joseph B 1889; 25; MOORE Joseph B 1889; ODOM Darling 1890; MOORE Joseph B 1890

Section 34 — WARE Emmor 1882; 34; WARE Emmor 1882; WARE Emmor 1882

Section 35 — WARE Emmor 1882; WARE Emmor 1882; ODOM Michael 1859; BREWER Howel N 1915; PALMER Joseph S 1900; PALMER Joseph S 1900; MOORE Joseph B 1890; 35; MOORE Joseph B 1890; MOORE Joseph B 1890; LAURENDINE Louis 1906; SWAYINGIN Celia 1898; SWAYINGIN Celia 1898; MOORE Joseph B 1890

Section 36 — MOORE Joseph B 1889; RICH William D 1900; CARNES John A 1859; PALMER Joseph S 1900; CLIFTON George 1901; 36; CARNES John A 1859; CLIFTON George 1901; RICH William D 1900; DUNNAM George R 1913; ODOM Jackson 1884; EASTERLING Thomas 1906

Copyright 2006 Boyd IT, Inc. All Rights Reserved

Road Map

T5-N R10-W
St Stephens Meridian

Map Group 2

Cities & Towns
Good Hope
Rhodes

Cemeteries
Browns Cemetery
Burch Cemetery
Woodard Cemetery

Copyright 2006 Boyd IT. Inc. All Rights Reserved

Eastside

Mill Creek

6

5

4

✝ Woodard Cem.

Hollimon

Willow

7

8

9

Mackie

Hancock

Gavins

Leonard Clark

18

17

16

19

20

21

Leonard Clark

30

29

28

Buck Creek

Backstrom

Dement

State Highway 42

Burch Cem. ✝

Wendell

Graham

32

31

Mick Cooley

Annie Hinton

33

Joseph Hinton

Shady

Carroll

Daughtry Hill

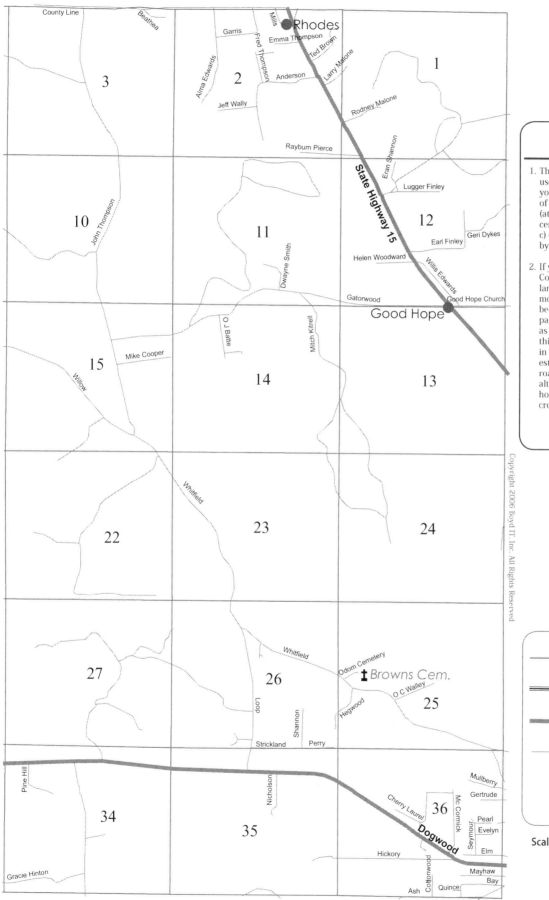

Helpful Hints

1. This road map has a number of uses, but primarily it is to help you: a) find the present location of land owned by your ancestors (at least the general area), b) find cemeteries and city-centers, and c) estimate the route/roads used by Census-takers & tax-assessors.

2. If you plan to travel to Perry County to locate cemeteries or land parcels, please pick up a modern travel map for the area before you do. Mapping old land parcels on modern maps is not as exact a science as you might think. Just the slightest variations in public land survey coordinates, estimates of parcel boundaries, or road-map deviations can greatly alter a map's representation of how a road either does or doesn't cross a particular parcel of land.

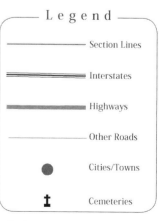

Legend

	Section Lines
	Interstates
	Highways
	Other Roads
●	Cities/Towns
✝	Cemeteries

Scale: Section = 1 mile X 1 mile
(generally, with some exceptions)

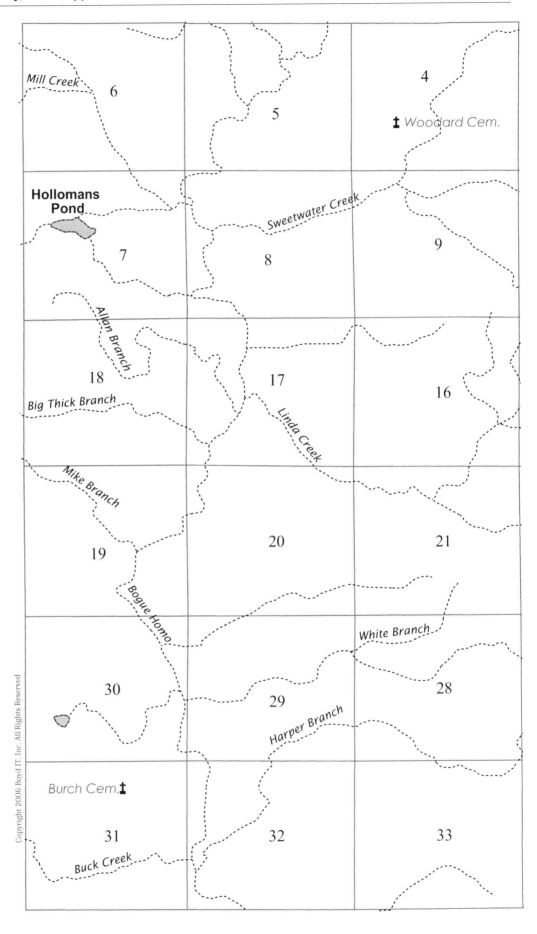

Historical Map

T5-N R10-W
St Stephens Meridian

Map Group 2

Cities & Towns
Good Hope
Rhodes

Cemeteries
Browns Cemetery
Burch Cemetery
Woodard Cemetery

Mill Creek

6

5

4

✝ Woodard Cem.

Hollomans Pond

Sweetwater Creek

7

8

9

Allan Branch

Big Thick Branch

18

17

16

Linda Creek

Mike Branch

19

20

21

Bogue Homo

White Branch

30

29

28

Harper Branch

Burch Cem. ✝

31

32

33

Buck Creek

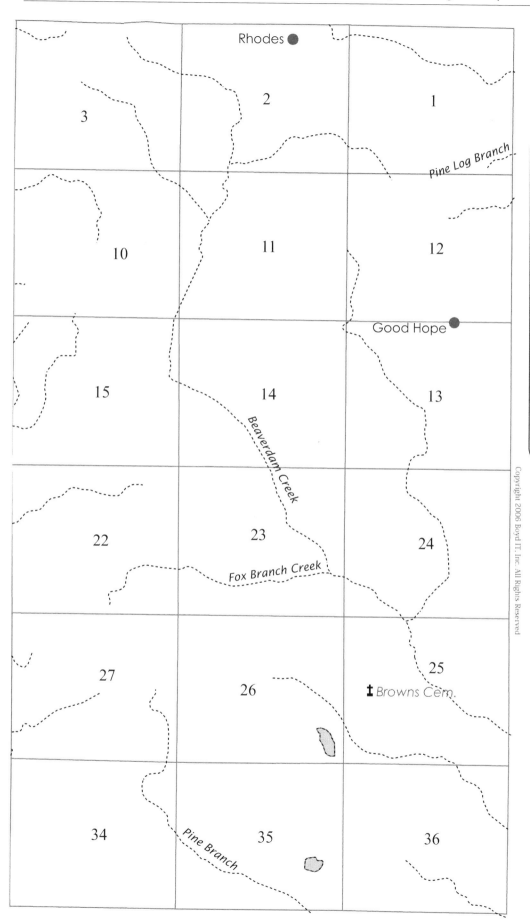

Rhodes ●

3

2

1

Pine Log Branch

10

11

12

Good Hope ●

15

14

13

Beaverdam Creek

22

23

24

Fox Branch Creek

27

26

25

‡ Browns Cem.

34

Pine Branch

35

36

Helpful Hints

1. This Map takes a different look at the same Congressional Township displayed in the preceding two maps. It presents features that can help you better envision the historical development of the area: a) Water-bodies (lakes & ponds), b) Water-courses (rivers, streams, etc.), c) Railroads, d) City/town center-points (where they were oftentimes located when first settled), and e) Cemeteries.

2. Using this "Historical" map in tandem with this Township's Patent Map and Road Map, may lead you to some interesting discoveries. You will often find roads, towns, cemeteries, and waterways are named after nearby landowners: sometimes those names will be the ones you are researching. See how many of these research gems you can find here in Perry County.

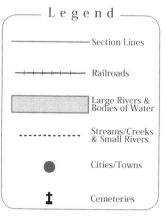

L e g e n d

——————— Section Lines

+++++++ Railroads

▭ Large Rivers & Bodies of Water

------- Streams/Creeks & Small Rivers

● Cities/Towns

‡ Cemeteries

Scale: Section = 1 mile X 1 mile
(there are some exceptions)

59

Map Group 3: Index to Land Patents

Township 5-North Range 9-West (St Stephens)

After you locate an individual in this Index, take note of the Section and Section Part then proceed to the Land Patent map on the pages immediately following. You should have no difficulty locating the corresponding parcel of land.

The "For More Info" Column will lead you to more information about the underlying Patents. See the *Legend* at right, and the "How to Use this Book" chapter, for more information.

```
                        LEGEND
              "For More Info . . . " column
A = Authority (Legislative Act, See Appendix "A")
B = Block or Lot (location in Section unknown)
C = Cancelled Patent
F = Fractional Section
G = Group  (Multi-Patentee Patent, see Appendix "C")
V = Overlaps another Parcel
R = Re-Issued (Parcel patented more than once)

(A & G items require you to look in the Appendixes referred
to above. All other Letter-designations followed by a number
require you to locate line-items in this index that possess
the ID number found after the letter).
```

ID	Individual in Patent	Sec.	Sec. Part	Date Issued	Other Counties	For More Info . . .
570	BAZOR, Jim	15	W½SW	1919-07-01		A4
606	BEARDSLEY, Scott	34	NW	1905-03-30		A4
506	BLODGETT, Delos A	5	N½SE	1889-11-21		A1
507	" "	5	NE	1889-11-21		A1
508	" "	5	S½SW	1889-11-21		A1
509	" "	6	NENE	1889-11-21		A1
510	" "	6	SESE	1889-11-21		A1
511	" "	6	W½	1889-11-21		A1
512	" "	6	W½NE	1889-11-21		A1
513	" "	6	W½SE	1889-11-21		A1
517	" "	8	E½NW	1889-11-21		A1
518	" "	8	NWNW	1889-11-21		A1
514	" "	7	E½SW	1890-07-03		A1
515	" "	7	S½NW	1890-07-03		A1
516	" "	7	SWSE	1890-07-03		A1
491	BOWDEN, Benjamin F	20	NW	1901-03-23		A4
608	BREWER, Sim	25	NWSW	1902-07-03		A4
609	" "	25	SWNW	1902-07-03		A4
610	" "	26	NESE	1902-07-03		A4
611	" "	26	SENE	1902-07-03		A4
580	BROOKS, John W	9	NESW	1912-02-01		A4
632	BROOKS, William A	9	NESE	1911-07-28		A4
633	" "	9	SENE	1911-07-28		A4
571	BUCKALEW, Joe	29	NESE	1906-06-30		A1
441	BURNETT, Alvin L	26	SWSW	1901-03-23		A4
442	" "	27	NESE	1901-03-23		A4
443	" "	27	S½SE	1901-03-23		A4
519	BURNETT, Dennis	22	SE	1901-03-23		A4
521	BURNETT, Duncan N	34	NWNE	1918-04-11		A4
586	BURNETT, Joseph E	36	NENE	1905-03-30		A4
637	BURNETT, William H	26	NWSW	1908-10-26		A4
583	BURNNETT, Joseph	25	SESW	1902-02-12		A4
584	" "	36	NENW	1902-02-12		A4
585	" "	36	NWNE	1902-02-12		A4
427	BYRD, Absalom B	35	S½NE	1902-02-12		A4
428	" "	35	S½NW	1902-02-12		A4
639	COATS, William P	33	NE	1904-10-28		A1
522	DUNNAM, Edward W	25	SENE	1914-01-23		A4
568	DUNNAM, James W	25	SENW	1911-01-05		A4
590	DUNNAM, Lewis	3	NWNW	1912-06-14		A4
591	" "	4	NENE	1912-06-14		A4
629	DUNNAM, Wiley	9	SWNE	1910-06-02		A4
489	DYKES, Barbry A	10	N½SE	1905-10-10		A4
490	" "	10	N½SW	1905-10-10		A4
528	DYKES, George	9	NWSE	1895-12-14		A4
529	" "	9	S½SE	1895-12-14		A4

ID	Individual in Patent	Sec.	Sec. Part	Date Issued	Other Counties	For More Info . . .
530	DYKES, George (Cont'd)	9	SESW	1895-12-14		A4
572	DYKES, John	10	NWNW	1911-07-28		A4
573	" "	3	SWSW	1911-07-28		A4
574	" "	9	NENE	1911-07-28		A4
577	EASTERLING, John S	5	N½NW	1901-03-23		A4
578	" "	5	NESW	1901-03-23		A4
579	" "	5	SENW	1901-03-23		A4
429	EDWARDS, Albert	18	E½SW	1890-02-21		A4
430	" "	18	SWSE	1890-02-21		A4
431	" "	19	NWNE	1890-02-21		A4
501	EDWARDS, Cornelius	18	E½NE	1892-04-29		A4
502	" "	18	E½SE	1892-04-29		A4
504	EDWARDS, David	19	NW	1888-04-05		A4
549	EDWARDS, Henry	32	E½NW	1859-05-02		A1
550	EDWARDS, Henry M	19	NWSW	1910-06-02		A4
558	EDWARDS, James G	7	N½SE	1904-08-30		A4
559	" "	7	SESE	1904-08-30		A4
641	EDWARDS, Willis O	19	E½NE	1912-06-27		A4
642	" "	19	SWNE	1912-06-27		A4
505	FREEMAN, David	33	SW	1898-05-16		A4
588	FREEMAN, Lawrence A	36	SWNW	1906-10-18		A1
589	" "	36	W½SW	1906-10-18		A1
496	HINTON, Bud	31	NWNE	1859-05-02		A1
498	" "	31	SENE	1859-05-02		A1
495	" "	31	N½SW	1859-06-01		A1
497	" "	31	NWSE	1859-06-01		A1
499	" "	31	SWNE	1859-06-01		A1
500	" "	31	SWSE	1859-11-10		A1
603	HINTON, Rufus	32	NESE	1904-09-28		A4
604	" "	32	SENE	1904-09-28		A4
605	" "	33	S½NW	1904-09-28		A4
592	HUDSON, Lorenza D	13	N½SW	1899-06-28		A4
593	" "	13	S½NW	1899-06-28		A4
531	KENT, George	1	NWSW	1887-05-27		A1
532	" "	1	SWNW	1887-05-27		A1
533	" "	10	NE	1887-05-27		A1
534	" "	10	NENW	1887-05-27		A1
535	" "	10	S½NW	1887-05-27		A1
536	" "	11	N½NE	1887-05-27		A1
537	" "	11	NW	1887-05-27		A1
538	" "	2	NESE	1887-05-27		A1
539	" "	2	SENE	1887-05-27		A1
540	" "	2	W½	1887-05-27		A1
541	" "	2	W½NE	1887-05-27		A1
542	" "	2	W½SE	1887-05-27		A1
543	" "	3	E½	1887-05-27		A1
544	" "	3	E½SW	1887-05-27		A1
634	LUCAS, William E	24	SESE	1899-05-05		A4
635	" "	25	N½NE	1899-05-05		A4
636	" "	25	SWNE	1899-05-05		A4
619	MASON, Thomas N	11	S½NE	1909-01-11		A4
620	MASON, Thomas P	13	NWNW	1920-09-10		A4
630	MAYO, Will S H	15	SENW	1918-07-05		A4
631	" "	15	SWNE	1918-07-05		A4
432	MCDONALD, Alexander	19	SE	1884-12-30		A1
433	" "	20	N½SW	1884-12-30		A1
434	" "	20	SESW	1884-12-30		A1
435	" "	20	W½SE	1884-12-30		A1
436	" "	21		1884-12-30		A1
437	" "	22	W½	1884-12-30		A1
438	" "	27	NWNW	1884-12-30		A1
439	" "	28	N½	1884-12-30		A1
440	" "	30	E½	1884-12-30		A1
484	MEADOWS, Andrew J	1	W½SE	1899-05-31		A4
485	" "	12	NWNE	1899-05-31		A4
486	" "	35	NWNE	1909-07-02		A4
598	MEADOWS, Micage	32	SWNE	1906-06-30		A1
638	MILES, William	31	SENW	1859-05-02		A1
520	NEWELL, Derrall T	1	E½SW	1859-11-10		A1
565	NEWELL, James T	18	S½NW	1888-04-05		A4
567	" "	18	W½SW	1888-04-05		A4
564	" "	18	N½NW	1892-05-26		A4
566	" "	18	W½NE	1892-05-26		A4

ID	Individual in Patent	Sec.	Sec. Part	Date Issued	Other Counties	For More Info . . .
562	ODOM, James P	19	SWSW	1894-08-14		A4
563	" "	30	W½NW	1894-08-14		A4
575	OVERSTREET, John J	12	E½SE	1859-05-02		A1
576	" "	13	E½NE	1859-05-02		A1
492	RICH, Berry	28	SWSW	1905-06-30		A4
493	" "	29	SESE	1905-06-30		A4
494	" "	32	N½NE	1905-06-30		A4
523	RICH, Edward W	23	SESE	1912-02-01		A4
524	" "	24	SWSW	1912-02-01		A4
555	RICH, Ida	30	NESW	1904-11-15		A4 G70
555	RICH, John	30	NESW	1904-11-15		A4 G70
612	RICH, Stephen C	13	E½SE	1859-11-10		A1
614	" "	24	NENE	1859-11-10		A1
613	" "	13	SWSW	1884-12-30		A4
615	" "	24	NWSW	1884-12-30		A4
616	" "	24	W½NW	1884-12-30		A4
617	RICH, Steven C	13	SESW	1911-04-05		A4
618	RICH, Stirling B	35	S½	1882-10-10		A1
551	SAGE, Henry W	24	W½SE	1890-07-03		A1
552	" "	33	SE	1890-07-03		A1
553	" "	34	E½SE	1890-07-03		A1
554	" "	34	W½SW	1890-07-03		A1
557	SCARBOROUGH, James A	7	N½NW	1904-09-28		A4
556	SMITH, Ira T	7	NE	1901-12-17		A4
594	STRICKLAND, Lucritia	5	NWSW	1889-01-05		A4
595	" "	5	SWNW	1889-01-05		A4
596	" "	6	NESE	1889-01-05		A4
597	" "	6	SENE	1889-01-05		A4
581	SUMMERS, John W	36	E½SW	1910-01-20		A4
582	" "	36	W½SE	1910-01-20		A4
621	WALEY, Thomas	4	S½NE	1860-07-02		A1
622	" "	9	NWNE	1860-07-02		A1
424	WALLEY, Abner B	36	NESE	1904-09-28		A4
425	" "	36	S½NE	1904-09-28		A4
426	" "	36	SENW	1904-09-28		A4
487	WALLEY, Asberry P	28	N½SE	1918-04-11		A4
488	" "	28	N½SW	1918-04-11		A4
525	WALLEY, General P	3	NENW	1901-02-27		A4
526	" "	3	NWSW	1901-02-27		A4
527	" "	3	S½NW	1901-02-27		A4
545	WALLEY, Gouldsbury	25	SWSW	1900-11-28		A4
546	" "	26	SESE	1900-11-28		A4
547	" "	35	NENE	1900-11-28		A4
548	" "	36	NWNW	1900-11-28		A4
560	WALLEY, James J	19	E½SW	1885-05-25		A4
561	" "	30	E½NW	1885-05-25		A4
599	WALLEY, Pinkney	8	SW	1891-05-20		A4
600	WALLEY, Priscella	5	SWSE	1905-03-30		A4
601	" "	8	NWSE	1905-03-30		A4
602	" "	8	W½NE	1905-03-30		A4
607	WALLEY, Sidney A J	33	NWNW	1908-07-30		A5
626	WALLEY, Thomas	4	SE	1859-05-02		A1
623	" "	25	NESW	1901-12-04		A4
624	" "	25	NWSE	1901-12-04		A4
625	" "	25	S½SE	1901-12-04		A4
627	WALLEY, Ulis	8	SWNW	1916-01-21		A4
628	WALLEY, Virginious	8	SWSE	1917-09-13		A4
640	WALLEY, Willis G	31	W½NW	1905-03-11		A1
587	WALTMAN, Joseph	7	W½SW	1906-06-30		A4
503	WARD, Daniel	13	W½NE	1860-04-02		A1
444	WATSON, Amasa B	1	E½NW	1883-09-15		A1
445	" "	1	E½SW	1883-09-15		A1
446	" "	1	NWNW	1883-09-15		A1
447	" "	1	SWSW	1883-09-15		A1
448	" "	1	W½NE	1883-09-15		A1
449	" "	10	S½SE	1883-09-15		A1
450	" "	10	S½SW	1883-09-15		A1
451	" "	11	S½	1883-09-15		A1
452	" "	12	W½	1883-09-15		A1
453	" "	13	NENW	1883-09-15		A1
454	" "	14		1883-09-15		A1
455	" "	15	E½NE	1883-09-15		A1
456	" "	15	E½SW	1883-09-15		A1

ID	Individual in Patent	Sec.	Sec. Part	Date Issued	Other Counties	For More Info . . .
457	WATSON, Amasa B (Cont'd)	15	NENW	1883-09-15		A1
458	"	15	NWNE	1883-09-15		A1
459	"	15	SE	1883-09-15		A1
460	"	15	W½NW	1883-09-15		A1
461	"	2	NENE	1883-09-15		A1
462	"	2	SESE	1883-09-15		A1
463	"	22	NE	1883-09-15		A1
464	"	23	N½	1883-09-15		A1
465	"	23	NESE	1883-09-15		A1
466	"	23	SW	1883-09-15		A1
467	"	23	W½SE	1883-09-15		A1
468	"	24	E½NW	1883-09-15		A1
469	"	24	E½SW	1883-09-15		A1
470	"	25	N½NW	1883-09-15		A1
471	"	26	E½SW	1883-09-15		A1
472	"	26	NENE	1883-09-15		A1
473	"	26	NW	1883-09-15		A1
474	"	26	W½NE	1883-09-15		A1
475	"	26	W½SE	1883-09-15		A1
476	"	27	E½NW	1883-09-15		A1
477	"	27	N½SW	1883-09-15		A1
478	"	27	NE	1883-09-15		A1
479	"	27	NWSE	1883-09-15		A1
480	"	27	SWNW	1883-09-15		A1
481	"	34	E½SW	1883-09-15		A1
482	"	34	SWNE	1883-09-15		A1
483	"	34	W½SE	1883-09-15		A1
569	WILLINGHAM, Jeremiah	31	S½SW	1859-11-10		A1

Patent Map

T5-N R9-W
St Stephens Meridian

Map Group 3

Township Statistics

Parcels Mapped	:	219
Number of Patents	:	96
Number of Individuals	:	78
Patentees Identified	:	77
Number of Surnames	:	40
Multi-Patentee Parcels	:	1
Oldest Patent Date	:	5/2/1859
Most Recent Patent	:	9/10/1920
Block/Lot Parcels	:	0
Parcels Re-Issued	:	0
Parcels that Overlap	:	0
Cities and Towns	:	3
Cemeteries	:	2

Section 6:
BLODGETT Delos A 1889
BLODGETT Delos A 1889
STRICKLAND Lucritia 1889
BLODGETT Delos A 1889
STRICKLAND Lucritia 1889
BLODGETT Delos A 1889
BLODGETT Delos A 1889

Section 5:
EASTERLING John S 1901
STRICKLAND Lucritia 1889
EASTERLING John S 1901
BLODGETT Delos A 1889
STRICKLAND Lucritia 1889
EASTERLING John S 1901
BLODGETT Delos A 1889
BLODGETT Delos A 1889
WALLEY Priscella 1905

Section 4:
DUNNAM Lewis 1912
WALEY Thomas 1860
WALLEY Thomas 1859

Section 7:
SCARBOROUGH James A 1904
SMITH Ira T 1901
BLODGETT Delos A 1890
WALTMAN Joseph 1906
EDWARDS James G 1904
BLODGETT Delos A 1890
BLODGETT Delos A 1890
EDWARDS James G 1904

Section 8:
BLODGETT Delos A 1889
WALLEY Priscella 1905
WALLEY Ulis 1916
BLODGETT Delos A 1889
WALLEY Priscella 1905
WALLEY Pinkney 1891
WALLEY Virginious 1917

Section 9:
WALEY Thomas 1860
DYKES John 1911
DUNNAM Wiley 1910
BROOKS William A 1911
BROOKS John W 1912
DYKES George 1895
BROOKS William A 1911
DYKES George 1895
DYKES George 1895

Section 18:
NEWELL James T 1892
NEWELL James T 1892
NEWELL James T 1888
EDWARDS Cornelius 1892
NEWELL James T 1888
EDWARDS Albert 1890
EDWARDS Albert 1890
EDWARDS Cornelius 1892

Section 17

Section 16

Section 19:
EDWARDS Albert 1890
EDWARDS David 1888
EDWARDS Willis O 1912
EDWARDS Willis O 1912
EDWARDS Henry M 1910
ODOM James P 1894
WALLEY James J 1885
MCDONALD Alexander 1884

Section 20:
BOWDEN Benjamin F 1901
MCDONALD Alexander 1884
MCDONALD Alexander 1884
MCDONALD Alexander 1884

Section 21:
MCDONALD Alexander 1884

Section 30:
ODOM James P 1894
WALLEY James J 1885
MCDONALD Alexander 1884
RICH [70] Ida 1904

Section 29

Section 28:
MCDONALD Alexander 1884
BUCKALEW Joe 1906
WALLEY Asberry P 1918
WALLEY Asberry P 1918
RICH Berry 1905
RICH Berry 1905

Section 31:
WALLEY Willis G 1905
HINTON Bud 1859
MILES William 1859
HINTON Bud 1859
HINTON Bud 1859
HINTON Bud 1859
HINTON Bud 1859
WILLINGHAM Jeremiah 1859
HINTON Bud 1859

Section 32:
EDWARDS Henry 1859
RICH Berry 1905
MEADOWS Micage 1906
HINTON Rufus 1904
HINTON Rufus 1904

Section 33:
WALLEY Sidney A J 1908
COATS William P 1904
HINTON Rufus 1904
FREEMAN David 1898
SAGE Henry W 1890

DUNNAM Lewis 1912	WALLEY General P 1901		KENT George 1887	WATSON Amasa B 1883	WATSON Amasa B 1883	WATSON Amasa B 1883

Section 3
DUNNAM Lewis 1912 / WALLEY General P 1901
WALLEY General P 1901
WALLEY General P 1901 / **3**
DYKES John 1911 / KENT George 1887
KENT George 1887

Section 2
2
KENT George 1887
KENT George 1887
KENT George 1887
KENT George 1887
WATSON Amasa B 1883

Section 1
KENT George 1887 / WATSON Amasa B 1883
WATSON Amasa B 1883
KENT George 1887 / WATSON Amasa B 1883
WATSON Amasa B 1883
KENT George 1887 / WATSON Amasa B 1883
1
NEWELL Derrall T 1859
MEADOWS Andrew J 1899

Section 10
DYKES John 1911 / KENT George 1887
KENT George 1887
KENT George 1887 / **10**
DYKES Barbry A 1905 / DYKES Barbry A 1905
WATSON Amasa B 1883 / WATSON Amasa B 1883

Section 11
KENT George 1887 / KENT George 1887
MASON Thomas N 1909
WATSON Amasa B 1883 / **11**

Section 12
MEADOWS Andrew J 1899
12
WATSON Amasa B 1883
OVERSTREET John J 1859

Section 15
WATSON Amasa B 1883 / WATSON Amasa B 1883 / WATSON Amasa B 1883
MAYO Will S H 1918 / MAYO Will S H 1918 / WATSON Amasa B 1883
BAZOR Jim 1919 / **15**
WATSON Amasa B 1883 / WATSON Amasa B 1883

Section 14
14
WATSON Amasa B 1883

Section 13
MASON Thomas P 1920 / WATSON Amasa B 1883 / WARD Daniel 1860
HUDSON Lorenza D 1899 / OVERSTREET John J 1859
13
HUDSON Lorenza D 1899
RICH Stephen C 1884 / RICH Steven C 1911 / RICH Stephen C 1859

Section 22
WATSON Amasa B 1883
22
MCDONALD Alexander 1884
BURNETT Dennis 1901

Section 23
23
WATSON Amasa B 1883
WATSON Amasa B 1883
WATSON Amasa B 1883 / WATSON Amasa B 1883
RICH Edward W 1912

Section 24
RICH Stephen C 1884 / RICH Stephen C 1859
WATSON Amasa B 1883
RICH Stephen C 1884 / **24** / SAGE Henry W 1890
RICH Edward W 1912 / WATSON Amasa B 1883 / LUCAS William E 1899

Section 27
MCDONALD Alexander 1884
WATSON Amasa B 1883
WATSON Amasa B 1883 / WATSON Amasa B 1883 / **27**
WATSON Amasa B 1883 / WATSON Amasa B 1883 / BURNETT Alvin L 1901
BURNETT Alvin L 1901

Section 26
WATSON Amasa B 1883
WATSON Amasa B 1883 / WATSON Amasa B 1883
BURNETT William H 1908 / **26** / WATSON Amasa B 1883
BURNETT Alvin L 1901 / WATSON Amasa B 1883
BREWER Sim 1902

Section 25
WATSON Amasa B 1883 / WATSON Amasa B 1883 / LUCAS William E 1899
BREWER Sim 1902 / DUNNAM James W 1911 / LUCAS William E 1899 / DUNNAM Edward W 1914
BREWER Sim 1902 / WALLEY Thomas 1901 / WALLEY Thomas 1901
WALLEY Gouldsbury 1900 / WALLEY Gouldsbury 1900 / BURNNETT Joseph 1902 / WALLEY Thomas 1901
25

Section 34
BURNETT Duncan N 1918
BEARDSLEY Scott 1905
WATSON Amasa B 1883
SAGE Henry W 1890 / **34** / WATSON Amasa B 1883
WATSON Amasa B 1883

Section 35
MEADOWS Andrew J 1909 / WALLEY Gouldsbury 1900
BYRD Absalom B 1902 / BYRD Absalom B 1902
RICH Stirling B 1882 / **35**
SAGE Henry W 1890

Section 36
WALLEY Gouldsbury 1900 / BURNNETT Joseph 1902 / BURNNETT Joseph 1902 / BURNETT Joseph E 1905
FREEMAN Lawrence A 1906 / WALLEY Abner B 1904 / WALLEY Abner B 1904
FREEMAN Lawrence A 1906 / **36** / SUMMERS John W 1910 / WALLEY Abner B 1904
SUMMERS John W 1910

Copyright 2006 Boyd IT, Inc. All Rights Reserved

Helpful Hints

1. This Map's INDEX can be found on the preceding pages.

2. Refer to Map "C" to see where this Township lies within Perry County, Mississippi.

3. Numbers within square brackets [ ] denote a multi-patentee land parcel (multi-owner). Refer to Appendix "C" for a full list of members in this group.

4. Areas that look to be crowded with Patentees usually indicate multiple sales of the same parcel (Re-issues) or Overlapping parcels. See this Township's Index for an explanation of these and other circumstances that might explain "odd" groupings of Patentees on this map.

Legend

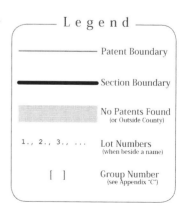

— Patent Boundary

— Section Boundary

No Patents Found (or Outside County)

1., 2., 3., ... Lot Numbers (when beside a name)

[ ] Group Number (see Appendix "C")

Scale: Section = 1 mile X 1 mile (generally, with some exceptions)

65

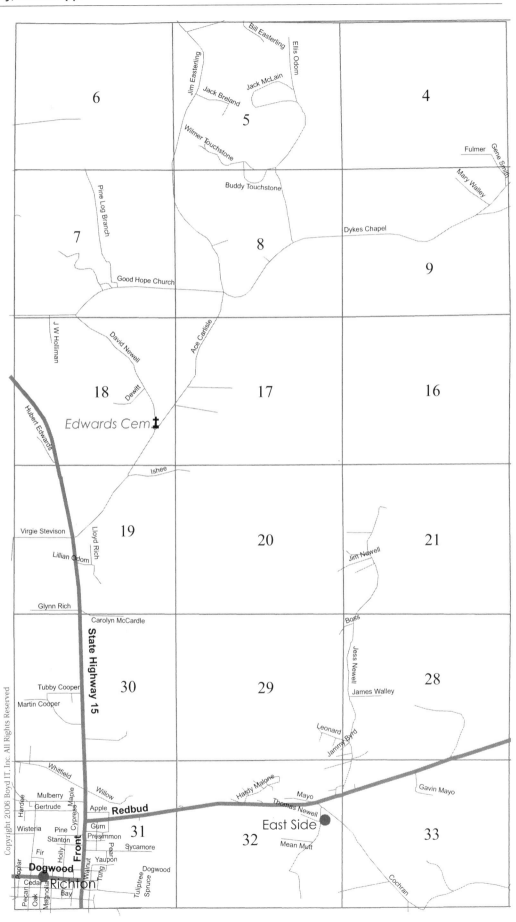

Road Map

T5-N R9-W
St Stephens Meridian

Map Group 3

Cities & Towns

Brewer
East Side
Richton

Cemeteries

Edwards Cemetery
Frisco Cemetery

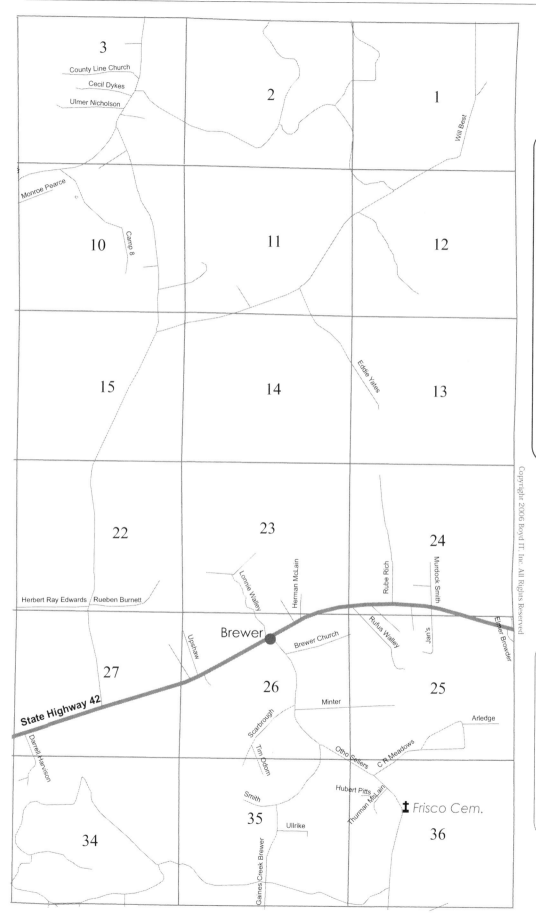

Helpful Hints

1. This road map has a number of uses, but primarily it is to help you: a) find the present location of land owned by your ancestors (at least the general area), b) find cemeteries and city-centers, and c) estimate the route/roads used by Census-takers & tax-assessors.

2. If you plan to travel to Perry County to locate cemeteries or land parcels, please pick up a modern travel map for the area before you do. Mapping old land parcels on modern maps is not as exact a science as you might think. Just the slightest variations in public land survey coordinates, estimates of parcel boundaries, or road-map deviations can greatly alter a map's representation of how a road either does or doesn't cross a particular parcel of land.

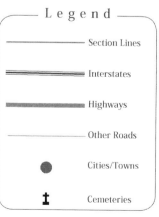

Legend

———————	Section Lines
════════	Interstates
▓▓▓▓▓▓▓	Highways
———————	Other Roads
●	Cities/Towns
✝	Cemeteries

Scale: Section = 1 mile X 1 mile
(generally, with some exceptions)

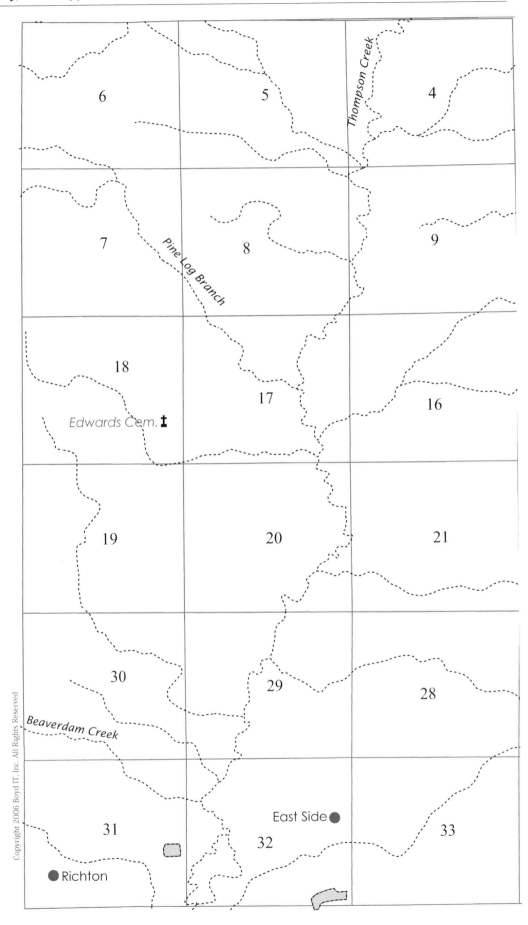

Historical Map

T5-N R9-W
St Stephens Meridian

Map Group 3

Cities & Towns

Brewer
East Side
Richton

Cemeteries

Edwards Cemetery
Frisco Cemetery

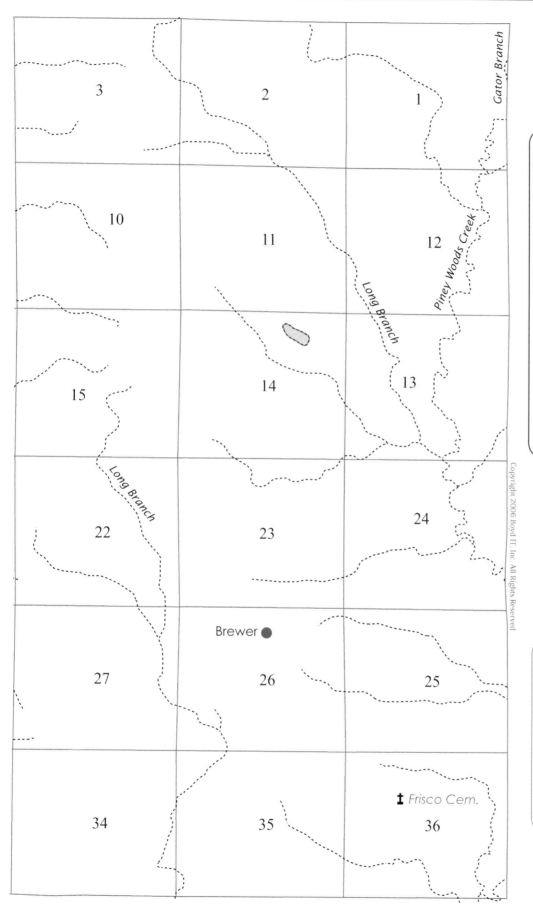

3

2

1

Gator Branch

10

11

12

Piney Woods Creek

15

14

Long Branch

13

Long Branch

22

23

24

Brewer ●

27

26

25

34

35

✝ *Frisco Cem.*

36

Helpful Hints

1. This Map takes a different look at the same Congressional Township displayed in the preceding two maps. It presents features that can help you better envision the historical development of the area: a) Water-bodies (lakes & ponds), b) Water-courses (rivers, streams, etc.), c) Railroads, d) City/town center-points (where they were oftentimes located when first settled), and e) Cemeteries.

2. Using this "Historical" map in tandem with this Township's Patent Map and Road Map, may lead you to some interesting discoveries. You will often find roads, towns, cemeteries, and waterways are named after nearby landowners: sometimes those names will be the ones you are researching. See how many of these research gems you can find here in Perry County.

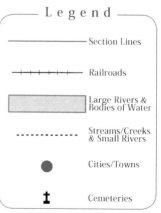

L e g e n d

———— Section Lines

┼┼┼┼┼┼ Railroads

▭ Large Rivers & Bodies of Water

------- Streams/Creeks & Small Rivers

● Cities/Towns

✝ Cemeteries

Scale: Section = 1 mile X 1 mile
(there are some exceptions)

Map Group 4: Index to Land Patents

Township 4-North Range 11-West (St Stephens)

After you locate an individual in this Index, take note of the Section and Section Part then proceed to the Land Patent map on the pages immediately following. You should have no difficulty locating the corresponding parcel of land.

The "For More Info" Column will lead you to more information about the underlying Patents. See the *Legend* at right, and the "How to Use this Book" chapter, for more information.

```
                        LEGEND
            "For More Info . . . " column
A = Authority (Legislative Act, See Appendix "A")
B = Block or Lot (location in Section unknown)
C = Cancelled Patent
F = Fractional Section
G = Group  (Multi-Patentee Patent, see Appendix "C")
V = Overlaps another Parcel
R = Re-Issued (Parcel patented more than once)

(A & G items require you to look in the Appendixes referred
to above. All other Letter-designations followed by a number
require you to locate line-items in this index that possess
the ID number found after the letter).
```

ID	Individual in Patent	Sec.	Sec. Part	Date Issued	Other Counties	For More Info . . .
894	ALBRITTON, Milton J	25	E½NW	1893-12-19		A4
895	" "	25	N½NE	1893-12-19		A4
896	ALEXANDER, Nancy	36	SESE	1896-07-11		A4 G1
881	ALLEN, Margaret	33	SESE	1859-05-02		A1
879	" "	32	SESE	1859-06-01		A1
880	" "	33	E½SW	1859-06-01		A1
882	" "	33	SWSE	1859-06-01		A1
883	" "	33	SWSW	1859-06-01		A1
718	ANDREWS, Charlie E	12	SENW	1923-01-04		A4
844	BARLOW, John	27	W½NE	1826-07-25		A1
917	BARNES, Richard C	17	E½SE	1904-08-30		A4
918	" "	17	NWSE	1904-08-30		A4
919	" "	20	NENE	1904-08-30		A4
772	BEER, Henry	1	S½SW	1889-11-29		A1
773	" "	1	SWSE	1889-11-29		A1
774	" "	11	E½NW	1889-11-29		A1
775	" "	11	NENE	1889-11-29		A1
776	" "	13	N½SW	1889-11-29		A1
777	" "	13	NENW	1889-11-29		A1
778	" "	13	NESE	1889-11-29		A1
779	" "	13	SENE	1889-11-29		A1
780	" "	13	W½NE	1889-11-29		A1
781	" "	13	W½SE	1889-11-29		A1
782	" "	2	N½NW	1889-11-29		A1
783	" "	23	SENE	1889-11-29		A1
784	" "	23	W½NE	1889-11-29		A1
785	" "	3	NENE	1889-11-29		A1
703	BRADLEY, Caladonia S	20	S½NE	1905-03-30		A4 G12
749	BRADLEY, Flora C	12	SESE	1895-06-27		A4 G13
750	" "	13	NENE	1895-06-27		A4 G13
749	BRADLEY, Leonedes C	12	SESE	1895-06-27		A4 G13
750	" "	13	NENE	1895-06-27		A4 G13
660	BROWN, Alfred G	14	SWSW	1884-12-30		A4
661	" "	15	SESE	1884-12-30		A4
662	" "	22	NENE	1884-12-30		A4
664	" "	23	NWNW	1884-12-30		A4
663	" "	22	NENW	1897-08-09		A1
707	BROWN, Carroll E	17	NWSW	1905-05-09		A4
708	" "	17	S½NW	1905-05-09		A4
874	BROWN, Joseph	1	N½SW	1900-10-04		A4
907	BROWN, Phillip M	14	SESW	1901-03-23		A4
908	" "	23	NENW	1901-03-23		A4
909	" "	23	S½NW	1901-03-23		A4
709	BULLOCK, Charley H	14	N½SE	1895-05-11		A4
710	" "	14	N½SW	1895-05-11		A4
830	BULLOCK, Jane	30	NESW	1890-08-16		A4 G19

ID	Individual in Patent	Sec.	Sec. Part	Date Issued	Other Counties	For More Info . . .
831	BULLOCK, Jane (Cont'd)	30	NWSE	1890-08-16		A4 G19
832	" "	30	SENW	1890-08-16		A4 G19
833	" "	30	SWNE	1890-08-16		A4 G19
830	BULLOCK, Joshua	30	NESW	1890-08-16		A4 G19
831	" "	30	NWSE	1890-08-16		A4 G19
832	" "	30	SENW	1890-08-16		A4 G19
833	" "	30	SWNE	1890-08-16		A4 G19
845	CARPENTER, John	2	SE	1899-06-28		A4
643	CARTER, Abner U	8	N½NE	1889-12-19		A4
644	" "	8	SENW	1889-12-19		A4
645	" "	8	SWNE	1889-12-19		A4
656	CARTER, Alex	31	S½SE	1890-06-25		A4
683	CARTER, Asa	9	SWNW	1859-05-02		A1
735	CARTER, Daniel W	17	N½NW	1901-12-17		A4
736	" "	8	W½SW	1901-12-17		A4
915	CARTER, Reuben W	5	S½NW	1890-12-31		A4
914	" "	5	NWSW	1892-04-16		A4
916	" "	6	SENE	1892-04-16		A4
924	CARTER, Sarah P	19	E½NW	1900-11-28		A4
925	" "	19	NWNW	1900-11-28		A4
933	CARTER, William	4	W½SE	1846-09-01		A1
937	" "	9	E½NW	1846-09-01		A1
938	" "	9	SENE	1846-09-01		A1
939	" "	9	W½NE	1846-09-01		A1
940	" "	9	W½SW	1846-09-01		A1
935	" "	8	SESE	1859-05-02		A1
932	" "	17	W½NE	1882-05-10		A1
936	" "	8	W½SE	1882-05-10		A1
931	" "	17	E½NE	1896-05-16		A1
934	" "	8	NESE	1896-05-16		A1
949	CARTER, William L	17	SWSE	1883-09-15		A1
786	CONWAY, Henry	12	NESE	1916-05-31		A4
823	CONWAY, James	1	SWNW	1909-03-11		A4
824	" "	2	NWNE	1909-03-11		A4
825	" "	2	S½NE	1909-03-11		A4
887	COOK, Martin V	35	NESW	1894-02-01		A4
888	" "	35	SWNW	1894-02-01		A4
889	" "	35	W½SW	1894-02-01		A4
696	COURTNEY, Benjamin T	31	N½SE	1885-12-19		A4
697	" "	31	S½NE	1885-12-19		A4
752	COURTNEY, Francis	24	N½SW	1895-01-17		A4
753	" "	24	S½NW	1895-01-17		A4
805	COURTNEY, Isaac P	20	N½NW	1901-11-08		A4
860	COURTNEY, John J	24	S½SE	1891-05-20		A4
861	" "	24	S½SW	1891-05-20		A4
892	COURTNEY, Micagia E	31	NW	1861-02-01		A1
893	COURTNEY, Micajah E	31	NWSW	1885-06-12		A4
729	DAUGHTREY, Daniel M	2	N½SW	1898-12-27		A4
730	" "	2	S½NW	1898-12-27		A4
826	DAVIS, James	11	W½NE	1901-07-09		A4
866	DAVIS, John P	33	E½NW	1897-11-22		A4
867	" "	33	NWSW	1897-11-22		A4
868	" "	33	SWNW	1897-11-22		A4
920	DILLARD, Robert	26	NWSE	1901-08-12		A4
921	" "	26	SENE	1901-08-12		A4
922	" "	26	W½NE	1901-08-12		A4
841	DIXON, Jesse V	29	NWNW	1900-11-28		A4
842	" "	30	E½NE	1900-11-28		A4
843	" "	30	NESE	1900-11-28		A4
653	DRAUGHN, Albert S	32	SWSE	1882-10-10		A1
650	" "	32	NESW	1884-12-30		A1
652	" "	32	SESW	1884-12-30		A1
654	" "	33	NWNW	1884-12-30		A1
649	" "	32	N½SE	1885-04-04		A4
651	" "	32	S½NE	1885-04-04		A4
747	DRAUGHN, Felix	18	N½SE	1901-03-23		A4
748	" "	18	S½NE	1901-03-23		A4
760	DRAUGHN, Gabriel D	15	SESW	1884-12-30		A4
761	" "	15	SWSE	1884-12-30		A4
762	" "	22	W½NE	1884-12-30		A4
764	DRAUGHN, George W	20	SE	1907-05-09		A4
765	DRAUGHN, Griffin S	26	NWSW	1881-09-17		A4
767	" "	26	SWNW	1881-09-17		A4

ID	Individual in Patent	Sec.	Sec. Part	Date Issued	Other Counties	For More Info . . .
768	DRAUGHN, Griffin S (Cont'd)	27	NESE	1881-09-17		A4
769	" "	27	SENE	1881-09-17		A4
766	" "	26	SENW	1883-02-03		A1
847	DRAUGHN, John D	29	NESE	1884-12-30		A1
849	" "	29	SESW	1884-12-30		A1
850	" "	29	SWSW	1889-04-10		A1
846	" "	28	SWSW	1890-03-28		A4
848	" "	29	S½SE	1890-03-28		A4
851	" "	32	NENE	1890-03-28		A4
955	DRAUGHN, Wyatt J	28	NWNW	1851-10-01		A1
956	" "	33	NESE	1851-10-01		A1
821	DUNIGAN, James C	30	W½NW	1901-06-08		A4
822	" "	30	W½SW	1901-06-08		A4
682	EASTERLING, Asa B	22	SENW	1859-05-02		A1
681	" "	21	NESE	1859-11-10		A1
787	EASTERLING, Henry	22	W½SE	1826-07-25		A1
703	EZELL, Caladonia S	20	S½NE	1905-03-30		A4 G12
855	FERRELL, John	25	N½SW	1901-08-12		A4
856	" "	25	SESW	1901-08-12		A4
744	FORD, Elias	19	NESW	1892-05-16		A4
745	" "	19	NWSE	1892-05-16		A4
746	" "	19	W½NE	1892-05-16		A4
803	FORD, Isaac	19	SWNW	1898-12-12		A4
804	" "	19	W½SW	1898-12-12		A4
725	FREEMAN, Cornelius	21	NENE	1841-01-05		A1
788	GEORGE, Henry	29	NENW	1913-04-22		A4
798	GRANTHAM, Howel	6	N½NW	1891-05-20		A4
799	" "	6	W½NE	1891-05-20		A4
944	GRANTHAM, William	14	NW	1895-11-11		A4
812	GRIMBSLEY, Jacob	30	S½SE	1890-08-16		A4
813	" "	30	SESW	1890-08-16		A4
814	" "	31	NENE	1890-08-16		A4
657	HARTLEY, Alex	25	NWNW	1901-11-08		A4
658	" "	26	NENE	1901-11-08		A4
923	HARTLEY, Samuel H	12	SWNE	1905-05-09		A4
737	HATHORN, Davis	21	SESW	1886-07-20		A1
758	HATHORN, Franklin D	20	NWNE	1882-10-10		A1
757	" "	18	SWSE	1883-09-15		A1
754	" "	17	E½SW	1888-03-29		A4
755	" "	17	SWSW	1888-03-29		A4
756	" "	18	SESE	1888-03-29		A4
941	HATHORN, William E	18	SESW	1898-08-15		A4
942	" "	18	SWNW	1898-08-15		A4
943	" "	18	W½SW	1898-08-15		A4
759	HATHORNE, Franklin D	19	NENE	1884-12-30		A1
862	HENSARLING, John L	6	NESW	1901-02-27		A4
863	" "	6	SWNW	1901-02-27		A4
864	" "	6	W½SW	1901-02-27		A4
912	HINTON, Rachael	24	N½SE	1895-02-21		A4
913	" "	24	S½NE	1895-02-21		A4
698	HOLLIMAN, Boke	36	N½SE	1894-02-10		A4
699	" "	36	NESW	1894-02-10		A4
700	" "	36	SWSE	1894-02-10		A4
704	HOLLIMON, Caroline	26	SWSE	1883-05-25		A4
705	" "	35	NWSE	1883-05-25		A4
706	" "	35	W½NE	1883-05-25		A4
719	HOLLIMON, Charlotte	36	SESW	1890-06-25		A4
720	" "	36	SWNW	1890-06-25		A4
721	" "	36	W½SW	1890-06-25		A4
859	HOLLIMON, John	9	SE	1841-01-05		A1 G54
858	" "	9	NESW	1846-09-01		A1
857	" "	35	SESW	1890-08-16		A4
875	HOLLIMON, Luke	35	E½SE	1890-08-16		A4
876	" "	35	SENE	1890-08-16		A4
877	" "	35	SWSE	1890-08-16		A4
928	HOLLIMON, Thad D	34	E½SE	1913-02-25		A4
815	HOLLINGSWORTH, Jacob H	13	SWSW	1861-05-01		A1
816	" "	14	SESE	1861-05-01		A1
817	" "	23	NENE	1861-05-01		A1
818	" "	24	NWNW	1861-05-01		A1
885	HOLLOMON, Martha	26	E½SW	1894-04-14		A4
886	" "	35	E½NW	1894-04-14		A4
878	HUGGINS, Manlius	14	SWSE	1854-03-15		A1 G56

ID	Individual in Patent	Sec.	Sec. Part	Date Issued	Other Counties	For More Info . . .
701	HUTSON, Burrel	24	NENW	1881-09-17		A4
702	" "	24	NWNE	1881-09-17		A4
666	JAMES, Alvin	28	NWSW	1910-03-17		A4
667	" "	28	SWNW	1910-03-17		A4
711	JAMES, Charley	19	S½SE	1901-03-23		A4
712	" "	19	SESW	1901-03-23		A4
713	" "	30	NWNE	1901-03-23		A4
793	JAMES, Henry T	23	SESW	1883-02-03		A1
794	" "	23	SWSW	1883-02-03		A1
792	" "	22	SESE	1894-02-01		A4
795	" "	26	N½NW	1894-02-01		A4
796	" "	27	NENE	1894-02-01		A4
806	JAMES, Isaac W	19	NESE	1891-05-20		A4
807	" "	19	SENE	1891-05-20		A4
808	" "	20	NWSW	1891-05-20		A4
809	" "	20	SWNW	1891-05-20		A4
905	JAMES, Phillip C	7	N½SW	1905-05-12		A1
906	" "	7	S½NW	1905-05-12		A1
945	JONES, William J	1	E½NE	1901-03-23		A4
946	" "	1	NWSE	1901-03-23		A4
947	" "	1	SWNE	1901-03-23		A4
770	KENNEDY, Hampton	32	NW	1893-12-21		A4
835	KENNEDY, Jesse A	29	NWNE	1882-10-10		A1
836	" "	29	S½NW	1882-10-10		A1
834	" "	29	N½SW	1884-12-30		A1
878	KIRKLAND, Rebecca	14	SWSE	1854-03-15		A1 G56
665	LANGLERY, Alice N	31	NESW	1905-05-02		A4
723	LOTT, Columbus	25	N½SE	1890-08-16		A4
724	" "	25	S½NE	1890-08-16		A4
929	MCCARDEL, Thomas	5	NESW	1859-05-02		A1
646	MCCARDLE, Ada	18	N½NW	1901-02-27		A4
647	" "	18	NESW	1901-02-27		A4
648	" "	18	SENW	1901-02-27		A4
789	MCCARDLE, Henry	8	NENW	1860-04-02		A1
827	MCCARDLE, James M	5	S½SW	1890-08-16		A4
828	" "	6	E½SE	1890-08-16		A4
869	MCCARDLE, John R	18	NWNE	1910-09-06		A4
870	" "	7	S½SE	1910-09-06		A4
871	" "	7	SESW	1910-09-06		A4
930	MCCARDLE, Thomas	5	NENW	1859-06-01		A1
859	MCGAHA, Tabitha	9	SE	1841-01-05		A1 G54
659	MCGILBERRY, Alexander	4	NESE	1841-01-05		A1
731	MCGILBERRY, Daniel	3	E½SE	1859-05-02		A1
732	" "	3	NWSE	1859-11-10		A1
733	" "	3	NWSW	1879-05-06		A4
734	" "	3	SWNW	1879-05-06		A4
865	MCGILBERRY, John	4	NENW	1846-09-01		A1
950	MCGILLVERRY, William	4	W½NE	1859-11-10		A1
678	MCGILRANY, Angus	3	NWNW	1890-02-21		A4
679	" "	4	E½NE	1890-02-21		A4
727	MCGILVRAY, Daniel A	2	S½SW	1900-11-28		A4
728	" "	3	S½SE	1900-11-28		A4
738	MCGILVRAY, Duncan	3	NESE	1901-07-09		A4
739	" "	3	NWNE	1901-07-09		A4
740	" "	3	S½NE	1901-07-09		A4
800	MCGILVRAY, Hugh A	10	NENE	1895-02-21		A4
801	" "	11	NWSW	1895-02-21		A4
802	" "	11	W½NW	1895-02-21		A4
910	MCGILVRAY, Pompy	10	S½SW	1892-02-12		A4
911	" "	10	W½SE	1892-02-12		A4
763	MCHENRY, George A	7	NE	1895-11-11		A4 V819, 927
904	MCKENZIE, Peter	8	E½SW	1882-12-30		A1
852	MIXON, John F	29	NENE	1894-07-24		A4
853	" "	29	NWSE	1894-07-24		A4
854	" "	29	S½NE	1894-07-24		A4
655	MORGAN, Albert W	13	SESW	1898-12-12		A4
680	MORGAN, Arthur A	12	S½SW	1915-04-12		A4
726	MORGAN, D Gaines	24	NENE	1910-05-17		A1
926	MORGAN, Sarah P	7	N½SE	1901-06-25		A4
927	" "	7	S½NE	1901-06-25		A4 V763
872	MYERS, John W	21	SWSW	1854-03-15		A1 G65
872	MYERS, Levi	21	SWSW	1854-03-15		A1 G65
741	MYRICK, Eli	11	NESW	1898-07-18		A4

ID	Individual in Patent	Sec.	Sec. Part	Date Issued	Other Counties	For More Info . . .
742	MYRICK, Eli (Cont'd)	11	NWSE	1898-07-18		A4
743	" "	11	S½SW	1898-07-18		A4
790	MYRICK, Henry	10	NESE	1901-03-23		A4
791	" "	10	SENE	1901-03-23		A4
902	MYRICK, Peter M	11	SWSE	1901-03-23		A4
903	" "	14	W½NE	1901-03-23		A4
897	PARDUE, Napoleon B	15	W½NW	1892-05-31		A4
898	" "	15	W½SW	1892-05-31		A4
899	PARDUE, Pamela	26	SWSW	1860-04-02		A1
900	" "	27	SESE	1860-04-02		A1
901	" "	35	NWNW	1860-04-02		A1
751	PITTMAN, Floyed	1	NWNE	1911-09-18		A4
948	PRINE, William J	1	SENW	1916-11-01		A4
771	REYNOLDS, Henry B	7	NWNW	1905-12-13		A4
837	REYNOLDS, Jesse M	6	SESW	1904-09-28		A4
838	" "	6	W½SE	1904-09-28		A4
839	" "	7	NENW	1904-09-28		A4
840	ROSS, Jesse	22	W½SW	1841-01-05		A1
884	RUNNELS, Marion F	4	SENW	1859-05-02		A1
810	SAPP, Jackson P	1	N½NW	1890-08-16		A4
811	" "	2	NENE	1890-08-16		A4
896	SCOTT, Nancy	36	SESE	1896-07-11		A4 G1
890	SHAW, Mary A	1	E½SE	1896-10-10		A4
891	" "	12	NENE	1896-10-10		A4
717	SHORES, Charley R	30	NENW	1905-03-30		A4
873	SHORES, John W	7	SWSW	1902-12-30		A4
722	SMITH, Clayton	21	SENE	1846-09-01		A1
957	SMITH, Zachary	15	N½SE	1890-02-21		A4
958	" "	15	NESW	1890-02-21		A4
959	" "	15	SENE	1890-02-21		A4
714	SOWELL, Charley N	22	NESE	1896-10-10		A4
715	" "	22	SENE	1896-10-10		A4
716	" "	23	N½SW	1896-10-10		A4
685	STEVENS, Benjamin	25	SWNW	1889-04-10		A1
688	" "	26	NESE	1889-04-10		A1
690	" "	31	NWNE	1889-04-10		A1
692	" "	35	NENE	1889-04-10		A1
693	" "	36	N½NW	1889-04-10		A1
695	" "	36	SENW	1889-04-10		A1
686	" "	25	SWSE	1889-04-20		A1
687	" "	25	SWSW	1889-04-20		A1
689	" "	26	SESE	1889-04-20		A1
691	" "	31	S½SW	1889-04-20		A1
694	" "	36	NE	1889-04-20		A1
872	STEVENS, William	21	SWSW	1854-03-15		A1 G65
951	" "	12	SENE	1883-09-15		A1
829	STUTTS, James	6	SENW	1906-06-30		A4
797	TRAVIS, Horace	32	NWNE	1906-03-05		A1
952	TRAVIS, William	20	NESW	1897-08-05		A4
953	" "	20	S½SW	1897-08-05		A4
954	" "	20	SENW	1897-08-05		A4
668	WATSON, Amasa B	11	E½SE	1883-02-03		A1
669	" "	11	SENE	1883-02-03		A1
670	" "	12	N½SW	1883-02-03		A1
671	" "	12	NENW	1883-02-03		A1
672	" "	12	NWNE	1883-02-03		A1
673	" "	12	W½NW	1883-02-03		A1
674	" "	12	W½SE	1883-02-03		A1
675	" "	13	SENW	1883-02-03		A1
676	" "	13	W½NW	1883-02-03		A1
677	" "	14	E½NE	1883-02-03		A1
819	WHITE, Jacob	7	N½NE	1895-02-21		A4 V763
820	" "	8	W½NW	1895-02-21		A4
684	YARBROUGH, Benjamin F	8	SENE	1905-03-30		A4

Patent Map

T4-N R11-W
St Stephens Meridian

Map Group 4

Township Statistics

Parcels Mapped	:	317
Number of Patents	:	169
Number of Individuals	:	140
Patentees Identified	:	134
Number of Surnames	:	77
Multi-Patentee Parcels	:	11
Oldest Patent Date	:	7/25/1826
Most Recent Patent	:	1/4/1923
Block/Lot Parcels	:	0
Parcels Re - Issued	:	0
Parcels that Overlap	:	3
Cities and Towns	:	2
Cemeteries	:	4

Section 6
GRANTHAM Howel 1891
GRANTHAM Howel 1891
HENSARLING John L 1901
STUTTS James 1906
CARTER Reuben W 1892
HENSARLING John L 1901
REYNOLDS Jesse M 1904
HENSARLING John L 1901
REYNOLDS Jesse M 1904
MCCARDLE James M 1890

Section 5
MCCARDLE Thomas 1859
CARTER Reuben W 1890
CARTER Reuben W 1892
MCCARDEL Thomas 1859
MCCARDLE James M 1890

Section 4
MCGILBERRY John 1846
MCGILLVERRY William 1859
RUNNELS Marion F 1859
MCGILRANY Angus 1890
MCGILBERRY Alexander 1841
CARTER William 1846

Section 7
REYNOLDS Henry B 1905
REYNOLDS Jesse M 1904
WHITE Jacob 1895
MCHENRY George A 1895
JAMES Phillip C 1905
MORGAN Sarah P 1901
JAMES Phillip C 1905
MORGAN Sarah P 1901
SHORES John W 1902
MCCARDLE John R 1910
MCCARDLE John R 1910

Section 8
WHITE Jacob 1895
MCCARDLE Henry 1860
CARTER Abner U 1889
CARTER Abner U 1889
YARBROUGH Benjamin F 1905
CARTER Daniel W 1901
CARTER William 1882
CARTER William 1896
MCKENZIE Peter 1882
CARTER William 1859

Section 9
CARTER William 1846
CARTER Asa 1859
CARTER William 1846
CARTER William 1846
HOLLIMON John 1846
HOLLIMON [54] John 1841

Section 18
MCCARDLE Ada 1901
MCCARDLE John R 1910
HATHORN William E 1898
MCCARDLE Ada 1901
DRAUGHN Felix 1901
HATHORN William E 1898
MCCARDLE Ada 1901
DRAUGHN Felix 1901
HATHORN William E 1898
HATHORN Franklin D 1883
HATHORN Franklin D 1888

Section 17
CARTER Daniel W 1901
CARTER William 1882
BROWN Carroll E 1905
CARTER William 1896
BROWN Carroll E 1905
BARNES Richard C 1904
HATHORN Franklin D 1888
HATHORN Franklin D 1888
CARTER William L 1883
BARNES Richard C 1904

Section 16

Section 19
CARTER Sarah P 1900
FORD Elias 1892
HATHORNE Franklin D 1884
FORD Isaac 1898
CARTER Sarah P 1900
JAMES Isaac W 1891
FORD Isaac 1898
FORD Elias 1892
FORD Elias 1892
JAMES Isaac W 1891
JAMES Charley 1901
JAMES Charley 1901

Section 20
COURTNEY Isaac P 1901
HATHORN Franklin D 1882
BARNES Richard C 1904
JAMES Isaac W 1891
TRAVIS William 1897
BRADLEY [12] Caladonia S 1905
JAMES Isaac W 1891
TRAVIS William 1897
DRAUGHN George W 1907
TRAVIS William 1897

Section 21
FREEMAN Cornelius 1841
SMITH Clayton 1846
EASTERLING Asa B 1859
MYERS [65] John W 1854
HATHORN Davis 1886

Section 30
DUNIGAN James C 1901
SHORES Charley R 1905
JAMES Charley 1901
BULLOCK [19] Jane 1890
DIXON Jesse V 1900
BULLOCK [19] Jane 1890
BULLOCK [19] Jane 1890
BULLOCK [19] Jane 1890
DIXON Jesse V 1900
DUNIGAN James C 1901
GRIMBSLEY Jacob 1890
GRIMBSLEY Jacob 1890

Section 29
DIXON Jesse V 1900
GEORGE Henry 1913
KENNEDY Jesse A 1882
MIXON John F 1894
KENNEDY Jesse A 1882
MIXON John F 1894
KENNEDY Jesse A 1884
MIXON John F 1894
DRAUGHN John D 1884
DRAUGHN John D 1889
DRAUGHN John D 1884
DRAUGHN John D 1890

Section 28
DRAUGHN Wyatt J 1851
JAMES Alvin 1910
JAMES Alvin 1910
DRAUGHN John D 1890

Section 31
COURTNEY Micagia E 1861
STEVENS Benjamin 1889
GRIMBSLEY Jacob 1890
COURTNEY Benjamin T 1885
COURTNEY Micajah E 1885
LANGLERY Alice N 1905
COURTNEY Benjamin T 1885
STEVENS Benjamin 1889
CARTER Alex 1890

Section 32
KENNEDY Hampton 1893
TRAVIS Horace 1906
DRAUGHN John D 1890
DRAUGHN Albert S 1885
DRAUGHN Albert S 1884
DRAUGHN Albert S 1885
DRAUGHN Albert S 1884
DRAUGHN Albert S 1882
ALLEN Margaret 1859

Section 33
DRAUGHN Albert S 1884
DAVIS John P 1897
DAVIS John P 1897
DAVIS John P 1897
ALLEN Margaret 1859
ALLEN Margaret 1859
ALLEN Margaret 1859
DRAUGHN Wyatt J 1851
ALLEN Margaret 1859

Section 3
- MCGILRANY Angus 1890
- MCGILRAY Duncan 1901
- BEER Henry 1889
- MCGILBERRY Daniel 1879
- MCGILVRAY Duncan 1901
- MCGILBERRY Daniel 1879
- MCGILBERRY Daniel 1859
- MCGILVRAY Duncan 1901
- MCGILBERRY Daniel 1859
- MCGILVRAY Daniel A 1900

Section 2
- BEER Henry 1889
- CONWAY James 1909
- SAPP Jackson P 1890
- DAUGHTREY Daniel M 1898
- CONWAY James 1909
- DAUGHTREY Daniel M 1898
- CARPENTER John 1899
- MCGILVRAY Daniel A 1900

Section 1
- SAPP Jackson P 1890
- PITTMAN Floyed 1911
- CONWAY James 1909
- PRINE William J 1916
- JONES William J 1901
- JONES William J 1901
- BROWN Joseph 1900
- JONES William J 1901
- BEER Henry 1889
- BEER Henry 1889
- SHAW Mary A 1896

Section 10
- MCGILVRAY Hugh A 1895
- MCGILVRAY Hugh A 1895
- MYRICK Henry 1901
- MCGILVRAY Pompy 1892
- MYRICK Henry 1901
- MCGILVRAY Pompy 1892

Section 11
- DAVIS James 1901
- BEER Henry 1889
- BEER Henry 1889
- WATSON Amasa B 1883
- MCGILVRAY Hugh A 1895
- MYRICK Eli 1898
- MYRICK Eli 1898
- MYRICK Eli 1898
- MYRICK Peter M 1901
- MYRICK Eli 1898
- MYRICK Peter M 1901
- WATSON Amasa B 1883

Section 12
- WATSON Amasa B 1883
- WATSON Amasa B 1883
- WATSON Amasa B 1883
- SHAW Mary A 1896
- ANDREWS Charlie E 1923
- HARTLEY Samuel H 1905
- STEVENS William 1883
- WATSON Amasa B 1883
- WATSON Amasa B 1883
- CONWAY Henry 1916
- MORGAN Arthur A 1915
- BRADLEY [13] Flora C 1895

Section 15
- PARDUE Napoleon B 1892
- SMITH Zachary 1890
- SMITH Zachary 1890
- SMITH Zachary 1890
- PARDUE Napoleon B 1892

Section 14
- MYRICK Peter M 1901
- GRANTHAM William 1895
- WATSON Amasa B 1883
- WATSON Amasa B 1883
- BULLOCK Charley H 1895
- BULLOCK Charley H 1895

Section 13
- WATSON Amasa B 1883
- BEER Henry 1889
- BEER Henry 1889
- BRADLEY [13] Flora C 1895
- WATSON Amasa B 1883
- BEER Henry 1889
- BEER Henry 1889
- BEER Henry 1889
- BEER Henry 1889

Section 22
- DRAUGHN Gabriel D 1884
- DRAUGHN Gabriel D 1884
- BROWN Alfred G 1884
- BROWN Alfred G 1897
- DRAUGHN Gabriel D 1884
- BROWN Alfred G 1884
- EASTERLING Asa B 1859
- SOWELL Charley N 1896
- ROSS Jesse 1841
- SOWELL Charley N 1896
- EASTERLING Henry 1826
- JAMES Henry T 1894

Section 23
- BROWN Alfred G 1884
- BROWN Phillip M 1901
- HOLLINGSWORTH Manlius 1854
- HUGGINS [56]
- BROWN Alfred G 1884
- BROWN Phillip M 1901
- BEER Henry 1889
- BROWN Phillip M 1901
- BEER Henry 1889
- SOWELL Charley N 1896
- JAMES Henry T 1883
- JAMES Henry T 1883

Section 24
- HOLLINGSWORTH Jacob H 1861
- HOLLINGSWORTH Jacob H 1861
- HOLLINGSWORTH Jacob H 1861
- MORGAN Albert W 1898
- HOLLINGSWORTH Jacob H 1861
- HUTSON Burrel 1881
- HUTSON Burrel 1881
- MORGAN D Gaines 1910
- COURTNEY Francis 1895
- HINTON Rachael 1895
- COURTNEY Francis 1895
- HINTON Rachael 1895
- COURTNEY John J 1891
- COURTNEY John J 1891

Section 27
- BARLOW John 1826
- JAMES Henry T 1894
- DRAUGHN Griffin S 1881
- DRAUGHN Griffin S 1881
- PARDUE Pamela 1860

Section 26
- JAMES Henry T 1894
- DILLARD Robert 1901
- HARTLEY Alex 1901
- DRAUGHN Griffin S 1881
- DRAUGHN Griffin S 1883
- DILLARD Robert 1901
- DRAUGHN Griffin S 1881
- DILLARD Robert 1901
- STEVENS Benjamin 1889
- HOLLOMON Martha 1894
- PARDUE Pamela 1860
- HOLLIMON Caroline 1883
- STEVENS Benjamin 1889

Section 25
- HARTLEY Alex 1901
- ALBRITTON Milton J 1893
- ALBRITTON Milton J 1893
- STEVENS Benjamin 1889
- LOTT Columbus 1890
- FERRELL John 1901
- LOTT Columbus 1890
- STEVENS Benjamin 1889
- FERRELL John 1901
- STEVENS Benjamin 1889

Section 34
- HOLLIMON Thad D 1913

Section 35
- PARDUE Pamela 1860
- HOLLOMON Caroline 1883
- STEVENS Benjamin 1889
- COOK Martin V 1894
- HOLLOMON Martha 1894
- HOLLIMON Caroline 1883
- HOLLIMON Luke 1890
- COOK Martin V 1894
- COOK Martin V 1894
- HOLLIMON John 1890
- HOLLIMON Luke 1890
- HOLLIMON Luke 1890

Section 36
- STEVENS Benjamin 1889
- STEVENS Benjamin 1889
- HOLLIMON Charlotte 1890
- STEVENS Benjamin 1889
- HOLLIMON Charlotte 1890
- HOLLIMON Boke 1894
- HOLLIMAN Boke 1894
- HOLLIMON Charlotte 1890
- HOLLIMAN Boke 1894
- ALEXANDER [1] Nancy 1896

Helpful Hints

1. This Map's INDEX can be found on the preceding pages.

2. Refer to Map "C" to see where this Township lies within Perry County, Mississippi.

3. Numbers within square brackets [ ] denote a multi-patentee land parcel (multi-owner). Refer to Appendix "C" for a full list of members in this group.

4. Areas that look to be crowded with Patentees usually indicate multiple sales of the same parcel (Re-issues) or Overlapping parcels. See this Township's Index for an explanation of these and other circumstances that might explain "odd" groupings of Patentees on this map.

Legend
- —— Patent Boundary
- —— Section Boundary
- No Patents Found (or Outside County)
- 1., 2., 3., ... Lot Numbers (when beside a name)
- [ ] Group Number (see Appendix "C")

Scale: Section = 1 mile X 1 mile (generally, with some exceptions)

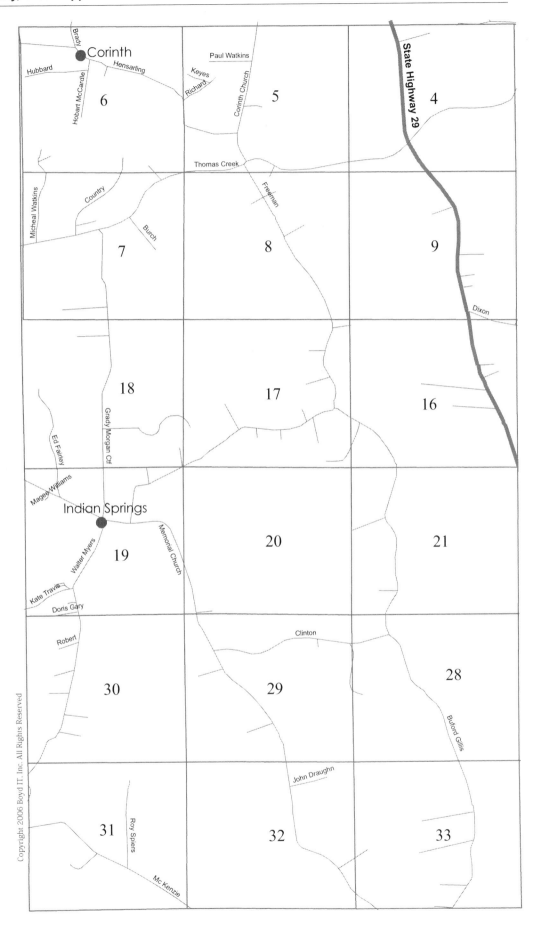

Road Map

T4-N R11-W
St Stephens Meridian

Map Group 4

Cities & Towns
Corinth
Indian Springs

Cemeteries
Courthey Cemetery
James Cemetery
McGilvary Cemetery
Prospect Cemetery

Copyright 2006 Boyd IT. Inc. All Rights Reserved

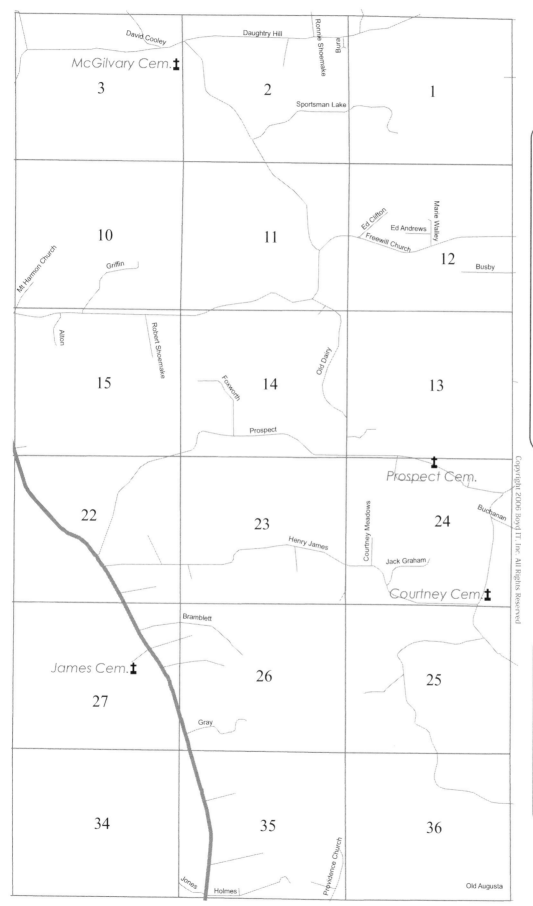

3

David Cooley

McGilvary Cem. ♱

Daughtry Hill

Ronnie Shoemake

Bura

2

Sportsman Lake

1

10

Mt Harmon Church

Griffin

11

Ed Clifton

Ed Andrews

Marie Walley

Freewill Church

12

Busby

15

Alton

Robert Shoemake

Foxworth

14

Old Dairy

13

Prospect

22

Prospect Cem. ♱

Courtney Meadows

23

Henry James

Jack Graham

24

Buchanan

Courtney Cem. ♱

Bramblett

James Cem. ♱

27

26

Gray

25

34

35

Providence Church

36

Jones

Holmes

Old Augusta

Helpful Hints

1. This road map has a number of uses, but primarily it is to help you: a) find the present location of land owned by your ancestors (at least the general area), b) find cemeteries and city-centers, and c) estimate the route/roads used by Census-takers & tax-assessors.

2. If you plan to travel to Perry County to locate cemeteries or land parcels, please pick up a modern travel map for the area before you do. Mapping old land parcels on modern maps is not as exact a science as you might think. Just the slightest variations in public land survey coordinates, estimates of parcel boundaries, or road-map deviations can greatly alter a map's representation of how a road either does or doesn't cross a particular parcel of land.

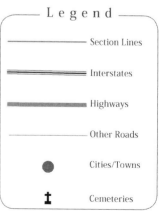

L e g e n d

———— Section Lines

════ Interstates

▓▓▓▓ Highways

———— Other Roads

● Cities/Towns

♱ Cemeteries

Scale: Section = 1 mile X 1 mile
(generally, with some exceptions)

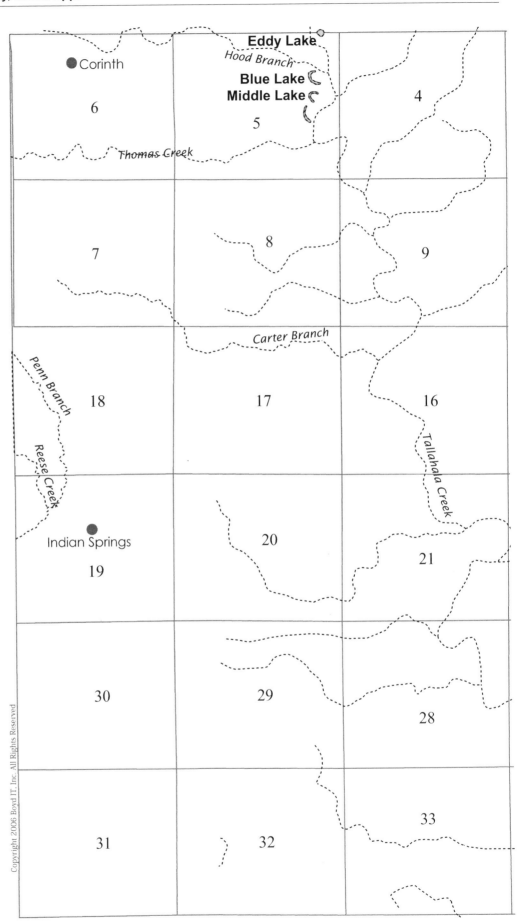

Historical Map

T4-N R11-W
St Stephens Meridian

Map Group 4

Cities & Towns
Corinth
Indian Springs

Cemeteries
Courthey Cemetery
James Cemetery
McGilvary Cemetery
Prospect Cemetery

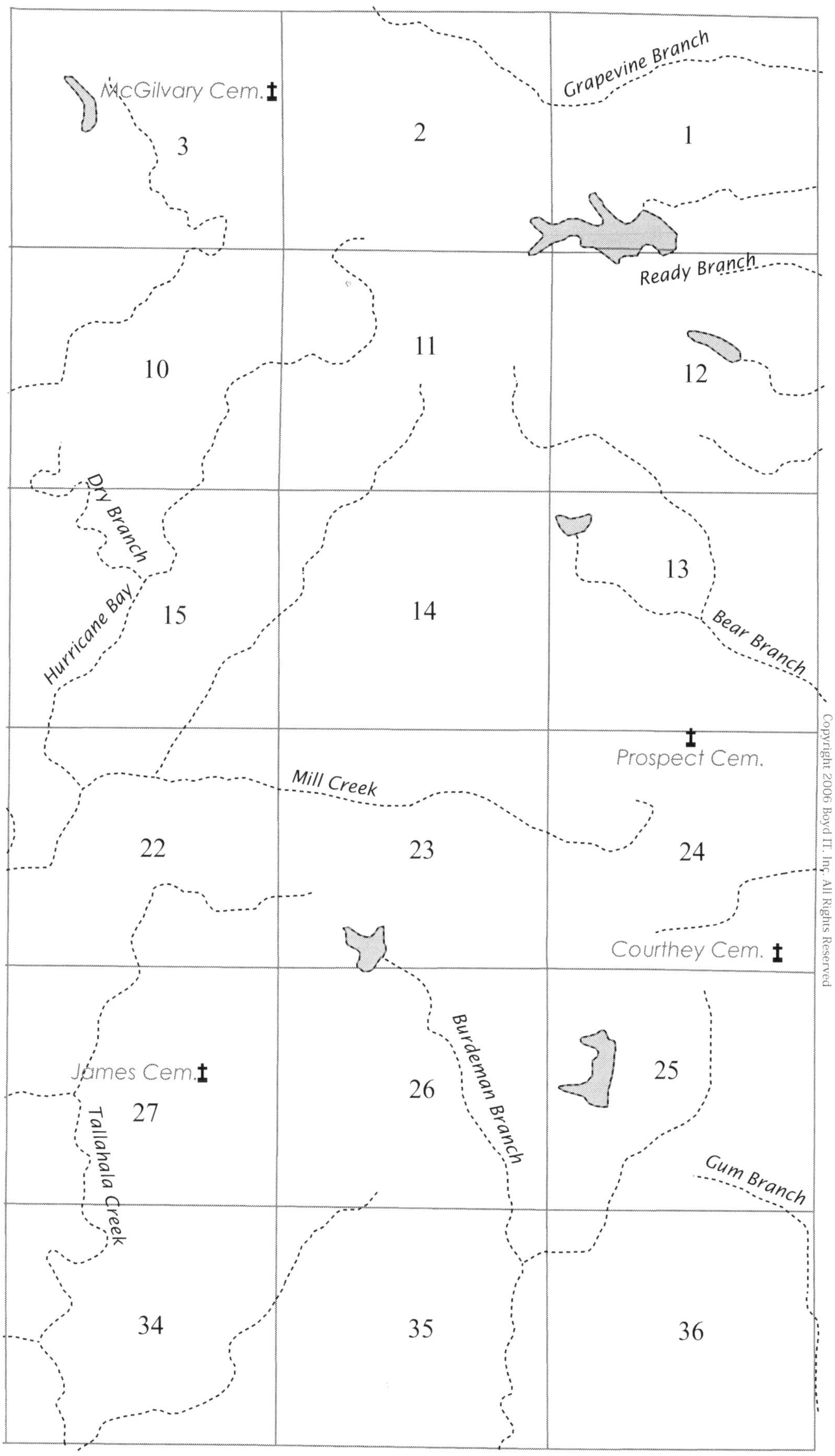

McGilvary Cem.
Grapevine Branch
Ready Branch
Dry Branch
Hurricane Bay
Bear Branch
Prospect Cem.
Mill Creek
Courthey Cem.
Burdeman Branch
James Cem.
Tallahala Creek
Gum Branch
3
2
1
10
11
12
15
14
13
22
23
24
27
26
25
34
35
36

Helpful Hints

1. This Map takes a different look at the same Congressional Township displayed in the preceding two maps. It presents features that can help you better envision the historical development of the area: a) Water-bodies (lakes & ponds), b) Water-courses (rivers, streams, etc.), c) Railroads, d) City/town center-points (where they were oftentimes located when first settled), and e) Cemeteries.
2. Using this "Historical" map in tandem with this Township's Patent Map and Road Map, may lead you to some interesting discoveries. You will often find roads, towns, cemeteries, and waterways are named after nearby landowners: sometimes those names will be the ones you are researching. See how many of these research gems you can find here in Perry County.

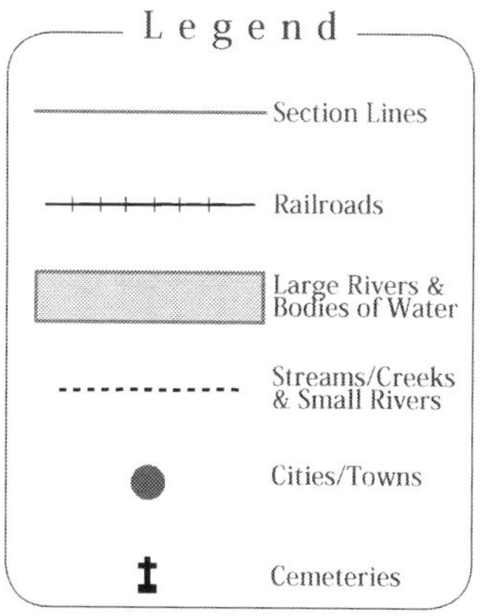

Legend
Section Lines
Railroads
Large Rivers & Bodies of Water
Streams/Creeks & Small Rivers
Cities/Towns
Cemeteries

Scale: Section = 1 mile X 1 mile
(there are some exceptions)

Map Group 5: Index to Land Patents

Township 4-North Range 10-West (St Stephens)

After you locate an individual in this Index, take note of the Section and Section Part then proceed to the Land Patent map on the pages immediately following. You should have no difficulty locating the corresponding parcel of land.

The "For More Info" Column will lead you to more information about the underlying Patents. See the *Legend* at right, and the "How to Use this Book" chapter, for more information.

```
                      LEGEND
            "For More Info . . . " column
A = Authority (Legislative Act, See Appendix "A")
B = Block or Lot (location in Section unknown)
C = Cancelled Patent
F = Fractional Section
G = Group (Multi-Patentee Patent, see Appendix "C")
V = Overlaps another Parcel
R = Re-Issued (Parcel patented more than once)

(A & G items require you to look in the Appendixes referred
to above. All other Letter-designations followed by a number
require you to locate line-items in this index that possess
the ID number found after the letter).
```

ID	Individual in Patent	Sec.	Sec. Part	Date Issued	Other Counties	For More Info . . .
1082	ALBRITTON, Josephine E	30	NWSW	1897-02-15		A4
1083	" "	30	W½NW	1897-02-15		A4
1031	ALEXANDER, General	21	NENE	1901-03-23		A4
1100	ALEXANDER, Nancy	31	SWNW	1896-07-11		A4 G1
1101	"	31	W½SW	1896-07-11		A4 G1
1109	BAGENT, Pink	4	E½NE	1921-04-27		A4
1110	" "	4	NWNE	1921-04-27		A4
960	BRADLEY, Adolphus D	27	NWSE	1894-06-28		A4 V1168
961	" "	27	S½NW	1894-06-28		A4
962	" "	27	SWNE	1894-06-28		A4
1027	BRADLEY, Flora C	18	W½NW	1895-06-27		A4 G13
1027	BRADLEY, Leonedes C	18	W½NW	1895-06-27		A4 G13
1121	BRADLEY, Rufus C	20	N½NE	1901-12-30		A4
1122	BRADLEY, Rufus P	30	NWSE	1889-04-23		A1
1065	BREWER, John	4	NWSW	1859-05-02		A1
1053	BRODLEY, James M	33	SENW	1859-11-10		A1
1054	" "	33	W½NW	1859-11-10		A1
1007	CLARK, Colon	23	NESE	1900-10-04		A4
1008	" "	23	S½SE	1900-10-04		A4
1017	CLARK, Elizabeth	30	NWNE	1892-07-20		A4
1018	" "	30	S½NE	1892-07-20		A4
1019	" "	30	SENW	1892-07-20		A4
1032	CLARK, General	27	NESE	1892-05-16		A4 V1168
1033	" "	27	S½SE	1892-05-16		A4
1034	" "	27	SENE	1892-05-16		A4
1046	CLARK, Hughie C	32	W½SE	1914-06-23		A4
1123	CLARK, Sallie	27	SW	1914-06-19		A4 G21
1012	COURTWRIGHT, Dora A	17	E½SW	1900-11-28		A4 G23
1028	DENNIS, Franklin	31	E½SE	1890-03-28		A4
1116	DIKES, Rebecca	32	NWNE	1859-06-01		A1
1123	DOUGLASS, Sallie	27	SW	1914-06-19		A4 G21
1023	EDWARDS, Emaline	22	NENE	1899-06-28		A4
1043	EDWARDS, Henry	9	NWNE	1859-05-02		A1
1141	EDWARDS, Wiley	3	N½SW	1898-07-18		A4
1142	" "	3	SENW	1898-07-18		A4
1143	" "	3	SWNE	1898-07-18		A4
963	FARMER, Agenton	32	S½NE	1899-07-15		A4
1039	FARMER, Gus	17	NENW	1910-06-02		A4
1132	FARMER, Thomas	20	SESE	1902-12-30		A4
1015	GARDNER, Elijah	7	E½SW	1906-05-01		A4
1016	" "	7	W½SE	1906-05-01		A4
1124	HARTLEY, Samuel	8	E½SW	1881-08-20		A4
1125	" "	8	SENW	1881-08-20		A4
1050	HIGHTOWER, James A	8	N½NW	1859-05-02		A1
1004	HINTON, Clarisa	15	SWSW	1889-12-19		A4 G47
1005	" "	22	SENW	1889-12-19		A4 G47

ID	Individual in Patent	Sec.	Sec. Part	Date Issued	Other Counties	For More Info . . .
1006	HINTON, Clarisa (Cont'd)	22	W½NW	1889-12-19		A4 G47
1020	HINTON, Ellis	11	NWNW	1898-09-28		A4
1021	" "	2	SESW	1898-09-28		A4
1022	" "	2	W½SW	1898-09-28		A4
1029	HINTON, Gabriel	15	E½SW	1892-03-23		A4
1030	" "	15	S½SE	1892-03-23		A4
1035	HINTON, George	17	W½NW	1883-09-15		A4
1036	" "	17	W½SW	1883-09-15		A4
1057	HINTON, James R	10	NESE	1901-04-22		A4
1058	" "	10	SENE	1901-04-22		A4
1059	" "	11	S½NW	1901-04-22		A4
1066	HINTON, John	3	S½SW	1915-06-16		A4
1067	" "	4	SESE	1915-06-16		A4
1068	" "	9	NENE	1915-06-16		A4
1084	HINTON, Logan	11	SESW	1894-04-14		A4
1085	" "	14	N½NE	1894-04-14		A4
1086	" "	14	NENW	1894-04-14		A4
1087	HINTON, Mahala	3	SE	1918-07-05		A4
1091	HINTON, Margaret I	3	N½NE	1911-06-29		A4
1092	" "	3	N½NW	1911-06-29		A4
1094	HINTON, Mary	11	SWSW	1905-03-30		A4 G49
1095	" "	14	NWNW	1905-03-30		A4 G49
1107	HINTON, Pheriba	14	W½SW	1893-04-12		A4 G50
1108	" "	15	N½SE	1893-04-12		A4 G50
1118	HINTON, Robert	20	SENE	1854-03-15		A1
1117	" "	20	N½SE	1890-06-25		A4
1119	" "	20	SWNE	1890-06-25		A4
1120	" "	20	SWSE	1890-06-25		A4
1094	HINTON, Sam A	11	SWSW	1905-03-30		A4 G49
1095	" "	14	NWNW	1905-03-30		A4 G49
1129	HINTON, Sandy	15	NWSW	1896-10-31		A4
1130	" "	15	SWNW	1896-10-31		A4
1133	HINTON, Thomas P	9	W½SE	1859-05-02		A1
1138	HINTON, Washington	22	N½SW	1906-06-26		A4
1139	" "	22	NWSE	1906-06-26		A4
1140	" "	22	SESW	1906-06-26		A4
1144	HINTON, Wiley	34	NESW	1914-07-17		A4
1145	HINTON, Wiley O	34	SESE	1908-08-10		A3
1062	HOLDER, Jerome B	6	NESW	1860-04-02		A1
1000	HOLLIMAN, Cary	17	W½NE	1885-07-27		A4
1001	" "	17	W½SE	1885-07-27		A4
1063	HORN, Joda	4	E½NW	1918-04-11		A4
1064	" "	4	E½SW	1918-04-11		A4
1088	HUGGINS, Manlius	19	SWSE	1854-03-15		A1 G55
1089	" "	20	SWNW	1854-03-15		A1 G56
1090	" "	34	NWSW	1854-03-15		A1 G56
1099	JACKSON, Millie L	3	SWNW	1918-04-11		A4
1080	JOHNSON, Joseph E	10	N½NE	1920-07-19		A1
1147	JOHNSON, William E	1	E½	1889-04-20		A1 G58
1148	" "	1	S½NW	1889-04-20		A1 G58
1149	" "	1	SW	1889-04-20		A1 G58
1150	" "	11	SE	1889-04-20		A1 G58
1151	" "	12		1889-04-20		A1 G58
1152	" "	13		1889-04-20		A1 G58
1153	" "	14	E½SW	1889-04-20		A1 G58
1154	" "	14	S½NE	1889-04-20		A1 G58
1155	" "	14	SE	1889-04-20		A1 G58
1156	" "	14	SENW	1889-04-20		A1 G58
1157	" "	22	E½SE	1889-04-20		A1 G58
1158	" "	22	NENW	1889-04-20		A1 G58
1159	" "	22	SENE	1889-04-20		A1 G58
1160	" "	22	SWSE	1889-04-20		A1 G58
1161	" "	22	W½NE	1889-04-20		A1 G58
1162	" "	23	NE	1889-04-20		A1 G58
1163	" "	23	NWSE	1889-04-20		A1 G58
1164	" "	23	W½	1889-04-20		A1 G58
1165	" "	24		1889-04-20		A1 G58
1166	" "	25		1889-04-20		A1 G58
1167	" "	26	NWNW	1889-04-20		A1 G58
1168	" "	27	N½SE	1889-04-20		A1 G58 V1032, 960
1169	" "	27	NENW	1889-04-20		A1 G58
1170	" "	34	N½NE	1889-11-21		A1 G58
1171	" "	34	SWNE	1889-11-21		A1 G58

ID	Individual in Patent	Sec.	Sec. Part	Date Issued	Other Counties	For More Info . . .
1172	JOHNSON, William E (Cont'd)	34	W½SE	1889-11-21		A1 G58
1173	" "	35	S½SW	1889-11-21		A1 G58
1174	" "	36	E½	1889-11-21		A1 G58
1175	" "	36	E½NW	1889-11-21		A1 G58
1176	" "	36	E½SW	1889-11-21		A1 G58
1177	" "	36	SWSW	1889-11-21		A1 G58
1088	KIRKLAND, Philemon	19	SWSE	1854-03-15		A1 G55
1088	KIRKLAND, Rebecca	19	SWSE	1854-03-15		A1 G55
1089	" "	20	SWNW	1854-03-15		A1 G56
1090	" "	34	NWSW	1854-03-15		A1 G56
1146	LOTT, William C	30	NENW	1889-11-21		A1
964	MCPHERSON, Alexander	26	E½NW	1889-04-23		A1 G62
965	" "	26	NENE	1889-04-23		A1 G62
966	" "	26	NWSE	1889-04-23		A1 G62
967	" "	26	S½SE	1889-04-23		A1 G62
968	" "	26	SW	1889-04-23		A1 G62
969	" "	26	SWNW	1889-04-23		A1 G62
970	" "	26	W½NE	1889-04-23		A1 G62
971	" "	34	NESE	1889-04-23		A1 G62
972	" "	34	SENE	1889-04-23		A1 G62
973	" "	35	N½SW	1889-04-23		A1 G62
974	" "	35	NENE	1889-04-23		A1 G62
975	" "	35	NW	1889-04-23		A1 G62
976	" "	35	W½NE	1889-04-23		A1 G62
964	MCPHERSON, Edward G	26	E½NW	1889-04-23		A1 G62
965	" "	26	NENE	1889-04-23		A1 G62
966	" "	26	NWSE	1889-04-23		A1 G62
967	" "	26	S½SE	1889-04-23		A1 G62
968	" "	26	SW	1889-04-23		A1 G62
969	" "	26	SWNW	1889-04-23		A1 G62
970	" "	26	W½NE	1889-04-23		A1 G62
971	" "	34	NESE	1889-04-23		A1 G62
972	" "	34	SENE	1889-04-23		A1 G62
973	" "	35	N½SW	1889-04-23		A1 G62
974	" "	35	NENE	1889-04-23		A1 G62
975	" "	35	NW	1889-04-23		A1 G62
976	" "	35	W½NE	1889-04-23		A1 G62
964	MCPHERSON, Martin J	26	E½NW	1889-04-23		A1 G62
965	" "	26	NENE	1889-04-23		A1 G62
966	" "	26	NWSE	1889-04-23		A1 G62
967	" "	26	S½SE	1889-04-23		A1 G62
968	" "	26	SW	1889-04-23		A1 G62
969	" "	26	SWNW	1889-04-23		A1 G62
970	" "	26	W½NE	1889-04-23		A1 G62
971	" "	34	NESE	1889-04-23		A1 G62
972	" "	34	SENE	1889-04-23		A1 G62
973	" "	35	N½SW	1889-04-23		A1 G62
974	" "	35	NENE	1889-04-23		A1 G62
975	" "	35	NW	1889-04-23		A1 G62
976	" "	35	W½NE	1889-04-23		A1 G62
964	MCPHERSON, William	26	E½NW	1889-04-23		A1 G62
965	" "	26	NENE	1889-04-23		A1 G62
966	" "	26	NWSE	1889-04-23		A1 G62
967	" "	26	S½SE	1889-04-23		A1 G62
968	" "	26	SW	1889-04-23		A1 G62
969	" "	26	SWNW	1889-04-23		A1 G62
970	" "	26	W½NE	1889-04-23		A1 G62
971	" "	34	NESE	1889-04-23		A1 G62
972	" "	34	SENE	1889-04-23		A1 G62
973	" "	35	N½SW	1889-04-23		A1 G62
974	" "	35	NENE	1889-04-23		A1 G62
975	" "	35	NW	1889-04-23		A1 G62
976	" "	35	W½NE	1889-04-23		A1 G62
1047	MCSWAIN, Jack	15	N½NE	1892-07-20		A4
1048	" "	15	N½NW	1892-07-20		A4
1055	MCSWAIN, James	33	NENW	1859-11-10		A1
1056	" "	34	W½NW	1859-11-10		A1
1104	MCSWAIN, Nathan	11	SENE	1910-06-02		A4
1107	MCSWAIN, Pheriba	14	W½SW	1893-04-12		A4 G50
1108	" "	15	N½SE	1893-04-12		A4 G50
1126	MCSWAIN, Samuel	14	SWNW	1892-03-17		A4
1127	" "	15	S½NE	1892-03-17		A4
1128	" "	15	SENW	1892-03-17		A4

ID	Individual in Patent	Sec.	Sec. Part	Date Issued	Other Counties	For More Info . . .
1180	MCSWAIN, William	10	S½SE	1904-08-26		A4
1181	" "	10	S½SW	1904-08-26		A4
1011	MERRITT, David S	34	NENW	1883-02-03		A1
1073	MOORE, Joseph B	2	E½NW	1889-11-21		A1
1074	" "	2	NENE	1889-11-21		A1
1075	" "	2	NESW	1889-11-21		A1
1076	" "	2	SE	1889-11-21		A1
1077	" "	2	SWNW	1889-11-21		A1
1078	" "	2	W½NE	1889-11-21		A1
1079	" "	3	SENE	1889-11-21		A1
1009	MORGAN, D Gaines	19	NWNW	1910-05-17		A1
1071	MYERS, John W	7	E½SE	1854-03-15		A1 G65
1072	" "	8	W½SW	1854-03-15		A1 G65
1071	MYERS, Levi	7	E½SE	1854-03-15		A1 G65
1072	" "	8	W½SW	1854-03-15		A1 G65
1044	MYRICK, Henry	21	NW	1841-01-05		A1
1045	" "	32	NENE	1846-09-01		A1 G67
1113	MYRICK, Print	11	N½NE	1896-10-31		A4
1114	" "	11	NENW	1896-10-31		A4
1115	" "	11	SWNE	1896-10-31		A4
1003	NOWELL, Charles E	9	SESE	1919-06-28		A1
1049	ODOM, Jackson	1	N½NW	1884-11-20		A4
1081	ODOM, Joseph	11	N½SW	1859-06-01		A1
1105	ODOM, Owen	4	NWNW	1859-06-01		A1
1106	" "	4	SWNW	1860-07-02		A1
1013	PALMER, Ed	26	NESE	1893-09-01		A4
1014	" "	26	SENE	1893-09-01		A4
1131	PALMER, Singleton L	36	NWNW	1905-03-11		A1
1134	PALMER, Thomas	35	NESE	1892-05-16		A4
1135	" "	35	SENE	1892-05-16		A4
1136	" "	36	NWSW	1892-05-16		A4
1137	" "	36	SWNW	1892-05-16		A4
1178	PALMER, William J	2	SENE	1911-06-29		A4
1182	PERKINS, William	32	E½SE	1909-01-21		A4
1037	PITTMAN, George W	6	NENW	1901-03-23		A4
1038	" "	6	S½NW	1901-03-23		A4
1004	PRIER, Clarisa	15	SWSW	1889-12-19		A4 G47
1005	" "	22	SENW	1889-12-19		A4 G47
1006	" "	22	W½NW	1889-12-19		A4 G47
1179	PRINE, William J	6	NWSW	1907-05-13		A4
1052	READY, James L	34	SENW	1905-02-13		A4
1051	" "	31	SWNE	1913-05-08		A4
1069	REVETTE, John	7	S½NW	1906-05-01		A4
1070	" "	7	W½SW	1906-05-01		A4
1111	RIGGS, Porter M	35	NWSE	1899-05-31		A4
1112	" "	35	S½SE	1899-05-31		A4
1060	SCOTT, James W	30	S½SW	1896-01-10		A4
1061	" "	31	N½NW	1896-01-10		A4
1100	SCOTT, Nancy	31	SWNW	1896-07-11		A4 G1
1101	" "	31	W½SW	1896-07-11		A4 G1
1093	SHAW, Mary A	6	SWSW	1896-10-10		A4
998	STEVENS, Benjamin	30	NESW	1887-05-27		A1
994	"	18	SESW	1889-04-10		A1
995	"	18	SWSE	1889-04-10		A1
996	"	19	SWSW	1889-04-10		A1
997	"	30	NESE	1889-04-23		A1
999	"	31	SENW	1889-04-23		A1
989	STEVENS, Benjamin S	18	NESE	1889-05-06		A1
990	"	18	NESW	1895-02-21		A4
991	"	18	NWSE	1895-02-21		A4
992	"	18	SENW	1895-02-21		A4
993	"	18	SWNE	1895-02-21		A4
1024	STEVENS, Emma	18	E½NE	1906-08-10		A4
1025	"	18	NENW	1906-08-10		A4
1026	"	18	NWNE	1906-08-10		A4
1096	STEVENS, Mary	6	SESW	1891-05-20		A4
1097	" "	7	N½NW	1891-05-20		A4
1098	" "	7	NWNE	1891-05-20		A4
1071	STEVENS, William	7	E½SE	1854-03-15		A1 G65
1072	" "	8	W½SW	1854-03-15		A1 G65
1183	STEVENS, William W	18	NWSW	1901-03-23		A4
1002	SWAYINGIN, Celia	2	NWNW	1898-12-01		A4
1010	TOUCHSTONE, Daniel	6	SE	1841-01-05		A1 G74

ID	Individual in Patent	Sec.	Sec. Part	Date Issued	Other Counties	For More Info . . .
1010	TOUCHSTONE, Jesse	6	SE	1841-01-05		A1 G74
1045	" "	32	NENE	1846-09-01		A1 G67
1147	VAUGHAN, Coleman C	1	E½	1889-04-20		A1 G58
1148	" "	1	S½NW	1889-04-20		A1 G58
1149	" "	1	SW	1889-04-20		A1 G58
1150	" "	11	SE	1889-04-20		A1 G58
1151	" "	12		1889-04-20		A1 G58
1152	" "	13		1889-04-20		A1 G58
1153	" "	14	E½SW	1889-04-20		A1 G58
1154	" "	14	S½NE	1889-04-20		A1 G58
1155	" "	14	SE	1889-04-20		A1 G58
1156	" "	14	SENW	1889-04-20		A1 G58
1157	" "	22	E½SE	1889-04-20		A1 G58
1158	" "	22	NENW	1889-04-20		A1 G58
1159	" "	22	SENE	1889-04-20		A1 G58
1160	" "	22	SWSE	1889-04-20		A1 G58
1161	" "	22	W½NE	1889-04-20		A1 G58
1162	" "	23	NE	1889-04-20		A1 G58
1163	" "	23	NWSE	1889-04-20		A1 G58
1164	" "	23	W½	1889-04-20		A1 G58
1165	" "	24		1889-04-20		A1 G58
1166	" "	25		1889-04-20		A1 G58
1167	" "	26	NWNW	1889-04-20		A1 G58
1168	" "	27	N½SE	1889-04-20		A1 G58 V1032, 960
1169	" "	27	NENW	1889-04-20		A1 G58
1170	" "	34	N½NE	1889-11-21		A1 G58
1171	" "	34	SWNE	1889-11-21		A1 G58
1172	" "	34	W½SE	1889-11-21		A1 G58
1173	" "	35	S½SW	1889-11-21		A1 G58
1174	" "	36	E½	1889-11-21		A1 G58
1175	" "	36	E½NW	1889-11-21		A1 G58
1176	" "	36	E½SW	1889-11-21		A1 G58
1177	" "	36	SWSW	1889-11-21		A1 G58
977	WATSON, Amasa B	18	SESE	1883-09-15		A1
978	" "	19	E½SE	1883-09-15		A1
979	" "	19	NE	1883-09-15		A1
980	" "	19	NENW	1883-09-15		A1
981	" "	19	NWSE	1883-09-15		A1
982	" "	19	SESW	1883-09-15		A1
983	" "	30	NENE	1883-09-15		A1
984	" "	30	S½SE	1883-09-15		A1
985	" "	31	E½SW	1883-09-15		A1
986	" "	31	NWNE	1883-09-15		A1
987	" "	31	SENE	1883-09-15		A1
988	" "	31	W½SE	1883-09-15		A1
1012	WHITTLE, Dora A	17	E½SW	1900-11-28		A4 G23
1102	WHITTLE, Napoleon	19	N½SW	1897-02-17		A1
1103	" "	19	S½NW	1897-02-17		A1
1040	WILLIAMS, Guss	4	N½SE	1918-04-11		A4
1041	" "	4	SWNE	1918-04-11		A4
1042	" "	4	SWSE	1918-04-11		A4

Patent Map

T4-N R10-W
St Stephens Meridian

Map Group 5

Township Statistics

Parcels Mapped	:	224
Number of Patents	:	108
Number of Individuals	:	106
Patentees Identified	:	92
Number of Surnames	:	51
Multi-Patentee Parcels	:	63
Oldest Patent Date	:	1/5/1841
Most Recent Patent	:	4/27/1921
Block/Lot Parcels	:	0
Parcels Re - Issued	:	0
Parcels that Overlap	:	3
Cities and Towns	:	1
Cemeteries	:	1

Section 6
PITTMAN George W 1901; PITTMAN George W 1901; PRINE William J 1907; HOLDER Jerome B 1860; TOUCHSTONE [74] Daniel 1841; SHAW Mary A 1896; STEVENS Mary 1891

Section 5

Section 4
ODOM Owen 1859; BAGENT Pink 1921; ODOM Owen 1860; HORN Joda 1918; WILLIAMS Guss 1918; BAGENT Pink 1921; BREWER John 1859; WILLIAMS Guss 1918; HORN Joda 1918; WILLIAMS Guss 1918; HINTON John 1915

Section 7
STEVENS Mary 1891; STEVENS Mary 1891; REVETTE John 1906; REVETTE John 1906; GARDNER Elijah 1906; GARDNER Elijah 1906; MYERS [65] John W 1854

Section 8
HIGHTOWER James A 1859; HARTLEY Samuel 1881; MYERS [65] John W 1854; HARTLEY Samuel 1881

Section 9
EDWARDS Henry 1859; HINTON John 1915; HINTON John 1915; HINTON Thomas P 1859; NOWELL Charles E 1919

Section 18
BRADLEY [13] Flora C 1895; STEVENS Emma 1906; STEVENS Emma 1906; STEVENS Benjamin S 1895; STEVENS Benjamin S 1895; STEVENS Emma 1906; STEVENS William W 1901; STEVENS Benjamin S 1895; STEVENS Benjamin S 1895; STEVENS Benjamin S 1889; STEVENS Benjamin 1889; STEVENS Benjamin 1889; WATSON Amasa B 1883

Section 17
HINTON George 1883; FARMER Gus 1910; HOLLIMAN Cary 1885; HINTON George 1883; HOLLIMAN Cary 1885; COURTWRIGHT [23] Dora A 1900

Section 16

Section 19
MORGAN D Gaines 1910; WATSON Amasa B 1883; WATSON Amasa B 1883; WHITTLE Napoleon 1897; WHITTLE Napoleon 1897; WATSON Amasa B 1883; WATSON Amasa B 1883; STEVENS Benjamin 1889; WATSON Amasa B 1883; HUGGINS [55] Manlius 1854

Section 20
HUGGINS [56] Manlius 1854

Section 21
BRADLEY Rufus C 1901; HINTON Robert 1890; HINTON Robert 1854; HINTON Robert 1890; HINTON Robert 1890; FARMER Thomas 1902; MYRICK Henry 1841; ALEXANDER General 1901

Section 30
LOTT William C 1889; CLARK Elizabeth 1892; WATSON Amasa B 1883; ALBRITTON Josephine E 1897; CLARK Elizabeth 1892; CLARK Elizabeth 1892; ALBRITTON Josephine E 1897; STEVENS Benjamin 1887; BRADLEY Rufus P 1889; STEVENS Benjamin 1889; SCOTT James W 1896; WATSON Amasa B 1883

Section 29

Section 28

Section 31
SCOTT James W 1896; WATSON Amasa B 1883; ALEXANDER [1] Nancy 1896; STEVENS Benjamin 1889; READY James L 1913; WATSON Amasa B 1883; ALEXANDER [1] Nancy 1896; WATSON Amasa B 1883; WATSON Amasa B 1883; DENNIS Franklin 1890

Section 32
DIKES Rebecca 1859; MYRICK [67] Henry 1846; FARMER Agenton 1899; CLARK Hughie C 1914; PERKINS William 1909

Section 33
BRODLEY James M 1859; MCSWAIN James 1859; BRODLEY James M 1859

88

Section 3
HINTON Margaret I 1911
HINTON Margaret I 1911
JACKSON Millie L 1918
EDWARDS Wiley 1898
EDWARDS Wiley 1898
MOORE Joseph B 1889
EDWARDS Wiley 1898
3
HINTON Mahala 1918
HINTON John 1915

Section 2
SWAYINGIN Celia 1898
MOORE Joseph B 1889
MOORE Joseph B 1889
MOORE Joseph B 1889
MOORE Joseph B 1889
2
PALMER William J 1911
HINTON Ellis 1898
MOORE Joseph B 1889
MOORE Joseph B 1889
HINTON Ellis 1898

Section 1
ODOM Jackson 1884
JOHNSON [58] William E 1889
1
JOHNSON [58] William E 1889
JOHNSON [58] William E 1889

Section 10
10

JOHNSON Joseph E 1920
HINTON James R 1901
HINTON James R 1901
MCSWAIN William 1904
MCSWAIN William 1904

Section 11
HINTON Ellis 1898
MYRICK Print 1896
MYRICK Print 1896
HINTON James R 1901
MYRICK Print 1896
MCSWAIN Nathan 1910
11
ODOM Joseph 1859
JOHNSON [58] William E 1889
HINTON [49] Mary 1905
HINTON Logan 1894

Section 12
JOHNSON [58] William E 1889
12

Section 15
MCSWAIN Jack 1892
MCSWAIN Jack 1892
HINTON Sandy 1896
MCSWAIN Samuel 1892
MCSWAIN Samuel 1892
HINTON Sandy 1896
15
MCSWAIN Samuel 1892
HINTON [50] Pheriba 1893
HINTON [47] Clarisa 1889
HINTON Gabriel 1892
HINTON Gabriel 1892

Section 14
HINTON [49] Mary 1905
HINTON Logan 1894
HINTON Logan 1894
JOHNSON [58] William E 1889
JOHNSON [58] William E 1889
HINTON [50] Pheriba 1893
14
JOHNSON [58] William E 1889
JOHNSON [58] William E 1889

Section 13
JOHNSON [58] William E 1889
13

Section 22
JOHNSON [58] William E 1889
EDWARDS Emaline 1899
HINTON [47] Clarisa 1889
JOHNSON [58] William E 1889
JOHNSON [58] William E 1889
HINTON [47] Clarisa 1889
22
HINTON Washington 1906
HINTON Washington 1906
JOHNSON [58] William E 1889
HINTON Washington 1906
JOHNSON [58] William E 1889

Section 23
JOHNSON [58] William E 1889
JOHNSON [58] William E 1889
23
JOHNSON [58] William E 1889
CLARK Colon 1900
CLARK Colon 1900

Section 24
JOHNSON [58] William E 1889
24

Section 27
JOHNSON [58] William E 1889
BRADLEY Adolphus D 1894
BRADLEY Adolphus D 1894
CLARK General 1892
BRADLEY Adolphus D 1894
JOHNSON [58] William E 1889
CLARK General 1892
27
CLARK [21] Sallie 1914
CLARK General 1892

Section 26
JOHNSON [58] William E 1889
MCPHERSON [62] Alexander 1889
MCPHERSON [62] Alexander 1889
MCPHERSON [62] Alexander 1889
MCPHERSON [62] Alexander 1889
PALMER Ed 1893
MCPHERSON [62] Alexander 1889
PALMER Ed 1893
26
MCPHERSON [62] Alexander 1889
MCPHERSON [62] Alexander 1889

Section 25
JOHNSON [58] William E 1889
25

Section 34
MCSWAIN James 1859
MERRITT David S 1883
JOHNSON [58] William E 1889
READY James L 1905
MCPHERSON [62] Alexander 1889
JOHNSON [58] William E 1889
34
HUGGINS [56] Manlius 1854
HINTON Wiley 1914
MCPHERSON [62] Alexander 1889
JOHNSON [58] William E 1889

Section 35
MCPHERSON [62] Alexander 1889
MCPHERSON [62] Alexander 1889
35
MCPHERSON [62] Alexander 1889
RIGGS Porter M 1899
PALMER Thomas 1892
HINTON Wiley O 1908
JOHNSON [58] William E 1889

Section 36
MCPHERSON [62] Alexander 1889
PALMER Singleton L 1905
PALMER Thomas 1892
JOHNSON [58] William E 1889
PALMER Thomas 1892
RIGGS Porter M 1899
PALMER Thomas 1892
36
JOHNSON [58] William E 1889
JOHNSON [58] William E 1889
JOHNSON [58] William E 1889

Helpful Hints

1. This Map's INDEX can be found on the preceding pages.

2. Refer to Map "C" to see where this Township lies within Perry County, Mississippi.

3. Numbers within square brackets [ ] denote a multi-patentee land parcel (multi-owner). Refer to Appendix "C" for a full list of members in this group.

4. Areas that look to be crowded with Patentees usually indicate multiple sales of the same parcel (Re-issues) or Overlapping parcels. See this Township's Index for an explanation of these and other circumstances that might explain "odd" groupings of Patentees on this map.

Legend

——————— Patent Boundary

━━━━━━━ Section Boundary

No Patents Found (or Outside County)

1., 2., 3., ... Lot Numbers (when beside a name)

[ ] Group Number (see Appendix "C")

Scale: Section = 1 mile X 1 mile (generally, with some exceptions)

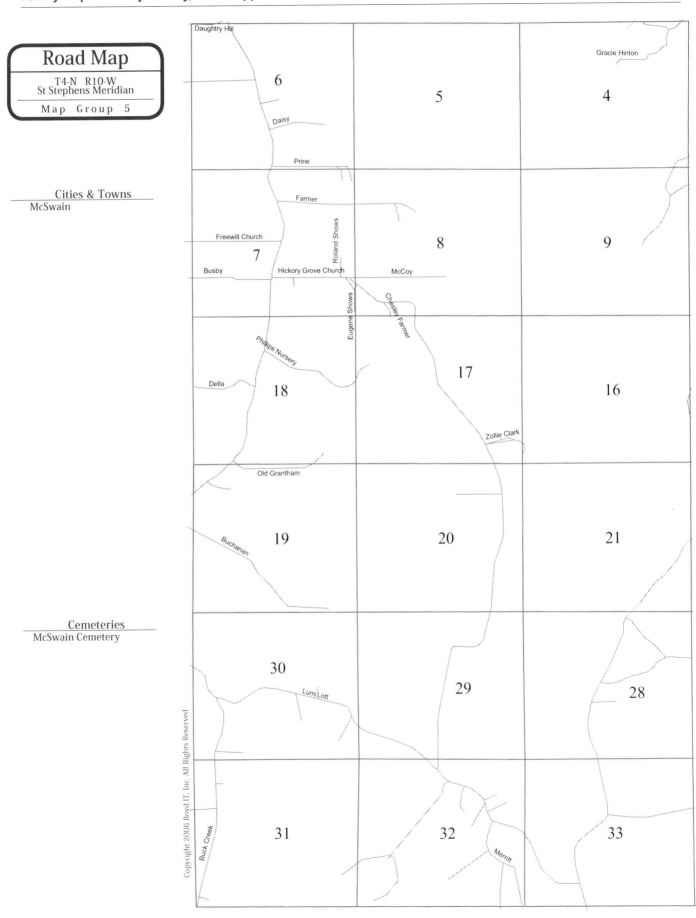

Road Map

T4-N R10-W
St Stephens Meridian

Map Group 5

Cities & Towns
McSwain

Cemeteries
McSwain Cemetery

Daughtry Hill

Gracie Hinton

6

5

4

Daisy

Prine

Farmer

Freewill Church

Roland Shows

8

9

7

Busby

Hickory Grove Church

McCoy

Eugene Shows

Chesley Farmer

Phillips Nursery

Della

18

17

16

Zollie Clark

Old Grantham

19

20

21

Buchanan

30

Lum Lott

29

28

31

32

33

Merritt

Buck Creek

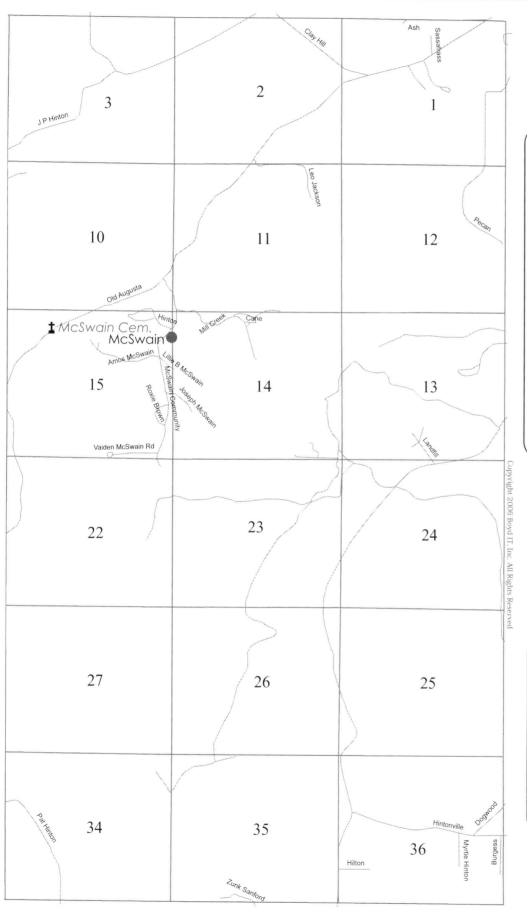

3

2

1

Clay Hill

Ash

Sassafras

J P Hinton

Leo Jackson

10

11

12

Pecan

Old Augusta

✝ McSwain Cem.
McSwain ●

Hinton

Mill Creek

Cane

Amos McSwain

Lillie B McSwain

McSwain Community

Roxie Brown

Joseph McSwain

15

14

13

Vaiden McSwain Rd

22

23

24

Landfill

27

26

25

Pat Hinton

34

35

36

Hintonville

Dogwood

Myrtle Hinton

Burgess

Hilton

Zunk Sanford

Helpful Hints

1. This road map has a number of uses, but primarily it is to help you: a) find the present location of land owned by your ancestors (at least the general area), b) find cemeteries and city-centers, and c) estimate the route/roads used by Census-takers & tax-assessors.

2. If you plan to travel to Perry County to locate cemeteries or land parcels, please pick up a modern travel map for the area before you do. Mapping old land parcels on modern maps is not as exact a science as you might think. Just the slightest variations in public land survey coordinates, estimates of parcel boundaries, or road-map deviations can greatly alter a map's representation of how a road either does or doesn't cross a particular parcel of land.

L e g e n d

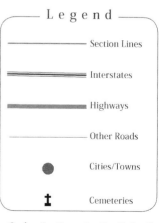

—————— Section Lines

━━━━━━ Interstates

▬▬▬▬▬▬ Highways

———— Other Roads

● Cities/Towns

✝ Cemeteries

Scale: Section = 1 mile X 1 mile
(generally, with some exceptions)

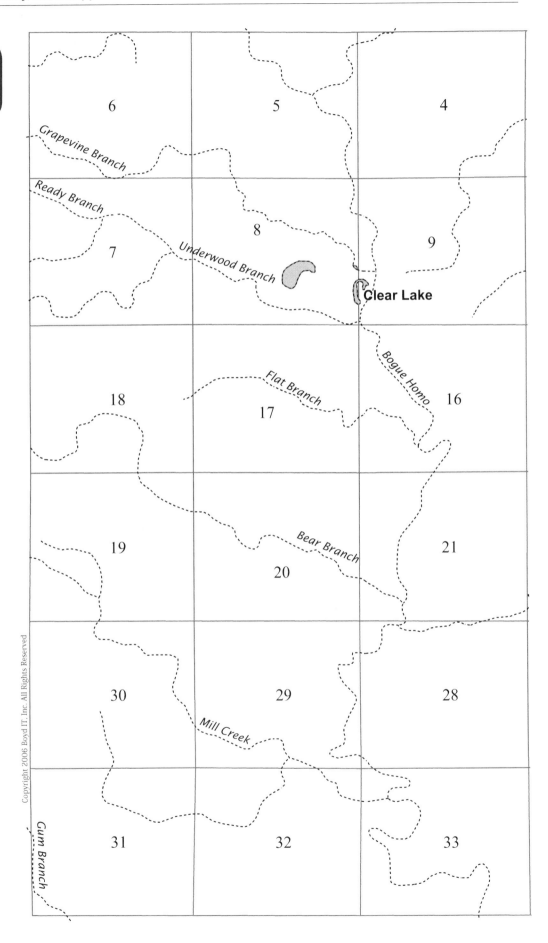

Historical Map

T4-N R10-W
St Stephens Meridian

Map Group 5

Cities & Towns
McSwain

Cemeteries
McSwain Cemetery

Copyright 2006 Boyd IT. Inc. All Rights Reserved

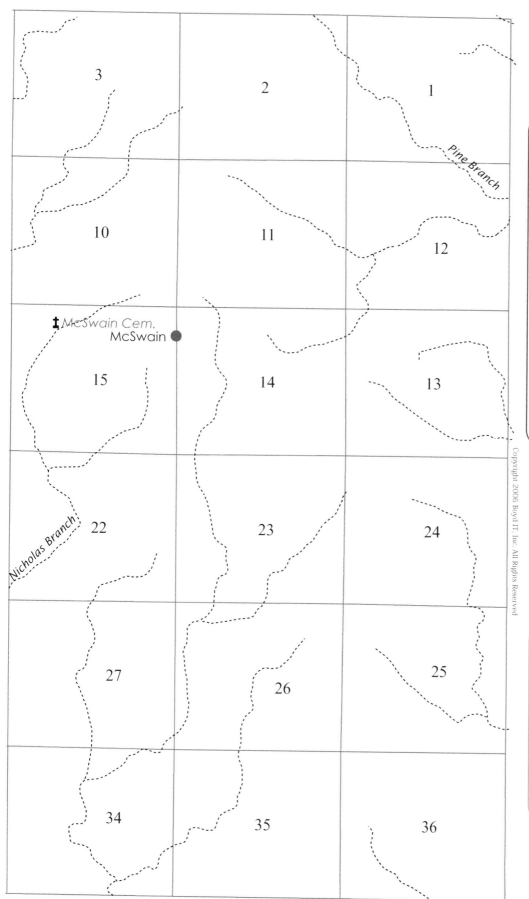

3

2

1

Pine Branch

10

11

12

✝ McSwain Cem.
McSwain ●

15

14

13

Nicholas Branch

22

23

24

27

26

25

34

35

36

Helpful Hints

1. This Map takes a different look at the same Congressional Township displayed in the preceding two maps. It presents features that can help you better envision the historical development of the area: a) Water-bodies (lakes & ponds), b) Water-courses (rivers, streams, etc.), c) Railroads, d) City/town center-points (where they were oftentimes located when first settled), and e) Cemeteries.

2. Using this "Historical" map in tandem with this Township's Patent Map and Road Map, may lead you to some interesting discoveries. You will often find roads, towns, cemeteries, and waterways are named after nearby landowners: sometimes those names will be the ones you are researching. See how many of these research gems you can find here in Perry County.

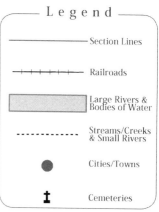

Legend

———————— Section Lines

+++++++ Railroads

▭ Large Rivers & Bodies of Water

- - - - - Streams/Creeks & Small Rivers

● Cities/Towns

✝ Cemeteries

Scale: Section = 1 mile X 1 mile
(there are some exceptions)

Map Group 6: Index to Land Patents

Township 4-North Range 9-West (St Stephens)

After you locate an individual in this Index, take note of the Section and Section Part then proceed to the Land Patent map on the pages immediately following. You should have no difficulty locating the corresponding parcel of land.

The "For More Info" Column will lead you to more information about the underlying Patents. See the *Legend* at right, and the "How to Use this Book" chapter, for more information.

```
                    LEGEND
          "For More Info . . . " column
A = Authority (Legislative Act, See Appendix "A")
B = Block or Lot (location in Section unknown)
C = Cancelled Patent
F = Fractional Section
G = Group  (Multi-Patentee Patent, see Appendix "C")
V = Overlaps another Parcel
R = Re-Issued (Parcel patented more than once)

(A & G items require you to look in the Appendixes referred
to above. All other Letter-designations followed by a number
require you to locate line-items in this index that possess
the ID number found after the letter).
```

ID	Individual in Patent	Sec.	Sec. Part	Date Issued	Other Counties	For More Info . . .
1269	BACKSTROM, John F	24	N½SW	1882-05-10		A1
1270	"	24	S½SE	1895-12-26		A4
1251	BEARDSLEY, Hellen	25	NWSW	1893-05-19		A4 G4
1252	"	25	W½NW	1893-05-19		A4 G4
1271	COCHRAN, John S	13	NWSW	1906-05-01		A4
1272	"	13	W½NW	1906-05-01		A4
1336	COCHRAN, William D	14	W½SW	1882-08-03		A1
1337	"	23	NENW	1906-06-30		A4
1338	"	23	NWNE	1906-06-30		A4
1249	GAINES, George S	14	NESW	1859-05-02		A1
1250	"	14	NWSE	1859-05-02		A1
1184	HINTON, Aaron	35	NESE	1890-08-16		A4
1185	"	35	SENE	1890-08-16		A4
1186	"	36	W½SW	1890-08-16		A4
1231	HINTON, Boss R	31	W½SW	1901-06-25		A4
1232	HINTON, Brutus	25	SWSW	1885-12-19		A4
1233	"	26	E½SE	1885-12-19		A4
1234	"	35	NENE	1885-12-19		A4
1235	HINTON, Cade M	29	SWNW	1889-12-19		A4
1236	"	29	W½SW	1889-12-19		A4
1237	"	32	NWNW	1889-12-19		A4
1241	HINTON, Eli	31	E½SW	1859-06-01		A1
1242	"	31	NWNE	1859-06-01		A1
1244	HINTON, Ellen V	33	W½NW	1907-05-13		A4
1246	HINTON, General	28	E½SW	1888-04-05		A4
1247	"	33	E½NW	1888-04-05		A4
1251	HINTON, Hellen	25	NWSW	1893-05-19		A4 G4
1252	"	25	W½NW	1893-05-19		A4 G4
1255	HINTON, Henry	23	SESE	1888-04-05		A4
1256	"	24	SWSW	1888-04-05		A4
1257	"	26	E½NE	1888-04-05		A4
1253	"	23	E½NE	1901-06-08		A4
1254	"	23	N½SE	1901-06-08		A4
1262	HINTON, Isaiah	20	NWNW	1889-04-20		A1
1261	"	18	SE	1890-02-21		A4
1260	"	17	NENE	1890-07-03		A1
1263	HINTON, Jephthah P	31	NWSE	1889-04-20		A1
1264	"	31	SWNE	1889-04-20		A1
1265	HINTON, Jepthah P	32	SWSW	1889-01-05		A4
1277	HINTON, Lorenzo D	6	W½NE	1905-02-04		A1
1279	HINTON, Martha	23	E½SW	1906-10-15		A4
1280	"	23	SENW	1906-10-15		A4
1281	"	23	SWSE	1906-10-15		A4
1282	HINTON, Martin V	19	SESE	1888-04-05		A4
1283	"	20	SWNW	1888-04-05		A4
1284	"	20	W½SW	1888-04-05		A4

ID	Individual in Patent	Sec.	Sec. Part	Date Issued	Other Counties	For More Info . . .
1286	HINTON, Queen V	32	W½SE	1905-03-30		A4 G51
1289	HINTON, Ransafer	28	NENW	1882-05-10		A1
1287	" "	21	SWNW	1888-04-05		A4
1288	" "	21	W½SW	1888-04-05		A4
1290	" "	28	NWNW	1888-04-05		A4
1291	HINTON, Richard	17	SENE	1914-05-28		A4
1292	HINTON, Samuel	26	NESW	1892-03-23		A4
1293	" "	26	S½SW	1892-03-23		A4
1334	HINTON, Timothy W	7	W½NE	1888-04-05		A4
1335	" "	7	W½SE	1888-04-05		A4
1339	HINTON, William	5	E½SW	1859-05-02		A1
1340	" "	5	W½SE	1859-05-02		A1
1341	" "	8	E½NW	1859-05-02		A1
1342	" "	8	W½NE	1859-05-02		A1
1345	HINTON, Winnie	34	NENE	1920-07-14		A4
1238	JEFCOAT, Carl	29	E½NW	1917-11-14		A4
1187	KITTRELL, Absalum B	1	SWSW	1882-05-10		A1
1188	" "	11	E½NE	1882-05-10		A1
1189	" "	11	NESE	1882-05-10		A1
1190	" "	12	W½NW	1882-05-10		A1
1191	" "	13	SWSE	1882-05-10		A1
1192	" "	2	SESE	1882-05-10		A1
1240	MANNING, Edmond	12	E½NE	1859-06-01		A1
1243	MANNING, Elizabeth	13	E½NW	1859-05-02		A1
1193	MCDONALD, Albert	34	E½SE	1910-04-11		A4
1248	MCDONALD, George P	29	NWNW	1889-04-20		A1
1258	MCDONALD, Hiram C	31	E½NE	1894-12-17		A4
1259	" "	32	S½NW	1894-12-17		A4
1286	MCDONALD, Queen V	32	W½SE	1905-03-30		A4 G51
1285	MEADOWS, Micage C	7	NENE	1919-06-28		A1
1273	NEWELL, Judia	31	NESE	1896-02-20		A1
1274	" "	31	S½SE	1896-02-20		A1
1275	" "	32	NWSW	1896-02-20		A1
1329	OVERSTREET, Thomas	1	NWSE	1859-06-01		A1
1331	" "	1	SWNE	1859-06-01		A1
1328	" "	1	E½SE	1859-11-10		A1
1330	" "	1	SENE	1859-11-10		A1
1245	PREISING, Ernest	13	SESW	1919-06-30		A4
1317	RICH, Stirling B	27		1882-06-01		A1
1318	" "	28	E½	1882-06-01		A1
1319	" "	28	S½NW	1882-06-01		A1
1320	" "	28	W½SW	1882-06-01		A1
1322	" "	34	W½	1882-06-01		A1
1323	" "	34	W½NE	1882-06-01		A1
1294	" "	11	NW	1882-08-03		A1
1295	" "	11	SESE	1882-08-03		A1
1297	" "	11	W½NE	1882-08-03		A1
1298	" "	11	W½SE	1882-08-03		A1
1299	" "	14	E½NW	1882-08-03		A1
1302	" "	2	NESE	1882-08-03		A1
1304	" "	2	SW	1882-08-03		A1
1305	" "	2	W½SE	1882-08-03		A1
1307	" "	21	E½NW	1882-08-03		A1
1308	" "	21	E½SW	1882-08-03		A1
1309	" "	21	NWNW	1882-08-03		A1
1310	" "	22	E½	1882-08-03		A1
1312	" "	25	E½	1882-08-03		A1
1313	" "	25	E½NW	1882-08-03		A1
1314	" "	25	E½SW	1882-08-03		A1
1315	" "	26	NW	1882-08-03		A1
1316	" "	26	NWSW	1882-08-03		A1
1324	" "	6	E½SW	1882-08-03		A1
1325	" "	6	SENW	1882-08-03		A1
1326	" "	6	W½SE	1882-08-03		A1
1296	" "	11	SW	1882-10-10		A1
1300	" "	15	S½	1882-10-10		A1
1301	" "	2	NE	1882-10-10		A1
1303	" "	2	NW	1882-10-10		A1
1306	" "	21	E½	1882-10-10		A1
1311	" "	22	W½	1882-10-10		A1
1321	" "	33	E½	1882-10-10		A1
1278	ROBERTS, Lorenzo D	23	W½NW	1882-08-03		A1
1239	SHEPARD, Cornelious	17	SWSW	1909-07-06		A1

ID	Individual in Patent	Sec.	Sec. Part	Date Issued	Other Counties	For More Info . . .
1230	SUMMERS, Amos C	1	NWSW	1917-08-15		A4
1343	SUMMERS, William W	1	E½SW	1907-05-09		A4
1344	" "	1	S½NW	1907-05-09		A4
1327	TAYLOR, Thomas B	1	NENE	1859-11-10		A1
1276	WALLEY, Layford	1	SWSE	1917-08-11		A4
1195	WATSON, Amasa B	12	SE	1882-10-10		A1
1196	" "	12	W½NE	1882-10-10		A1
1197	" "	12	W½SW	1882-10-10		A1
1198	" "	13	E½SE	1882-10-10		A1
1199	" "	13	NE	1882-10-10		A1
1200	" "	13	NWSE	1882-10-10		A1
1201	" "	14	NE	1882-10-10		A1
1202	" "	14	NESE	1882-10-10		A1
1203	" "	14	S½SE	1882-10-10		A1
1204	" "	14	SESW	1882-10-10		A1
1205	" "	14	W½NW	1882-10-10		A1
1207	" "	18	N½	1882-10-10		A1
1208	" "	18	SW	1882-10-10		A1
1209	" "	19	NE	1882-10-10		A1
1210	" "	19	NESE	1882-10-10		A1
1211	" "	19	W½SE	1882-10-10		A1
1212	" "	23	W½SW	1882-10-10		A1
1213	" "	24	N½	1882-10-10		A1
1214	" "	24	N½SE	1882-10-10		A1
1216	" "	30		1882-10-10		A1
1217	" "	35	W½	1882-10-10		A1
1218	" "	36	E½	1882-10-10		A1
1219	" "	36	E½SW	1882-10-10		A1
1220	" "	36	NW	1882-10-10		A1
1221	" "	4	N½	1882-10-10		A1
1222	" "	4	SE	1882-10-10		A1
1223	" "	4	SW	1882-10-10		A1
1226	" "	7	W½	1882-10-10		A1
1227	" "	8	E½NE	1882-10-10		A1
1228	" "	8	E½SE	1882-10-10		A1
1229	" "	9		1882-10-10		A1
1194	" "	10		1882-12-30		A1
1206	" "	15	N½	1882-12-30		A1
1215	" "	3		1882-12-30		A1
1224	" "	5	E½NE	1882-12-30		A1
1225	" "	5	E½SE	1882-12-30		A1
1332	WHITE, Thomas	34	SENE	1882-05-10		A1
1333	" "	34	W½SE	1882-05-10		A1
1266	WILLINGHAM, Jeremiah	6	NENW	1859-05-02		A1
1267	" "	6	W½NW	1859-11-10		A1
1268	" "	6	W½SW	1859-11-10		A1

Patent Map

T4-N R9-W
St Stephens Meridian

Map Group 6

Township Statistics

Parcels Mapped	:	162
Number of Patents	:	85
Number of Individuals	:	49
Patentees Identified	:	47
Number of Surnames	:	22
Multi-Patentee Parcels	:	3
Oldest Patent Date	:	5/2/1859
Most Recent Patent	:	7/14/1920
Block/Lot Parcels	:	0
Parcels Re - Issued	:	0
Parcels that Overlap	:	0
Cities and Towns	:	1
Cemeteries	:	2

Copyright 2006 Boyd IT. Inc. All Rights Reserved

WATSON
Amasa B
1882

3

RICH
Stirling B
1882

RICH
Stirling B
1882

2

RICH
Stirling B
1882

RICH
Stirling B
1882

RICH
Stirling B
1882

KITTRELL
Absalum B
1882

SUMMERS
William W
1907

SUMMERS
Amos C
1917

KITTRELL
Absalum B
1882

SUMMERS
William W
1907

TAYLOR
Thomas B
1859

OVERSTREET
Thomas
1859

OVERSTREET
Thomas
1859

1

OVERSTREET
Thomas
1859

OVERSTREET
Thomas
1859

WALLEY
Layford
1917

WATSON
Amasa B
1882

10

RICH
Stirling B
1882

11

RICH
Stirling B
1882

RICH
Stirling B
1882

RICH
Stirling B
1882

KITTRELL
Absalum B
1882

RICH
Stirling B
1882

KITTRELL
Absalum B
1882

KITTRELL
Absalum B
1882

WATSON
Amasa B
1882

KITTRELL
Absalum B
1882

WATSON
Amasa B
1882

12

WATSON
Amasa B
1882

MANNING
Edmond
1859

WATSON
Amasa B
1882

WATSON
Amasa B
1882

15

RICH
Stirling B
1882

WATSON
Amasa B
1882

RICH
Stirling B
1882

14

WATSON
Amasa B
1882

COCHRAN
William D
1882

GAINES
George S
1859

GAINES
George S
1859

WATSON
Amasa B
1882

WATSON
Amasa B
1882

WATSON
Amasa B
1882

COCHRAN
John S
1906

MANNING
Elizabeth
1859

COCHRAN
John S
1906

13

PREISING
Ernest
1919

WATSON
Amasa B
1882

WATSON
Amasa B
1882

KITTRELL
Absalum B
1882

WATSON
Amasa B
1882

RICH
Stirling B
1882

22

RICH
Stirling B
1882

ROBERTS
Lorenzo D
1882

COCHRAN
William D
1906

COCHRAN
William D
1906

HINTON
Martha
1906

23

HINTON
Henry
1901

WATSON
Amasa B
1882

HINTON
Henry
1901

HINTON
Martha
1906

HINTON
Martha
1906

HINTON
Henry
1888

WATSON
Amasa B
1882

24

BACKSTROM
John F
1882

HINTON
Henry
1888

WATSON
Amasa B
1882

BACKSTROM
John F
1895

RICH
Stirling B
1882

27

RICH
Stirling B
1882

26

RICH
Stirling B
1882

HINTON
Samuel
1892

HINTON
Samuel
1892

HINTON
Henry
1888

HINTON
Brutus
1885

BEARDSLEY [4]
Hellen
1893

RICH
Stirling B
1882

BEARDSLEY [4]
Hellen
1893

HINTON
Brutus
1885

RICH
Stirling B
1882

25

RICH
Stirling B
1882

RICH
Stirling B
1882

HINTON
Winnie
1920

34

HINTON
Winnie
1920

WHITE
Thomas
1882

RICH
Stirling B
1882

WHITE
Thomas
1882

MCDONALD
Albert
1910

WATSON
Amasa B
1882

35

HINTON
Brutus
1885

HINTON
Aaron
1890

HINTON
Aaron
1890

WATSON
Amasa B
1882

HINTON
Aaron
1890

36

WATSON
Amasa B
1882

WATSON
Amasa B
1882

Helpful Hints

1. This Map's INDEX can be found on the preceding pages.

2. Refer to Map "C" to see where this Township lies within Perry County, Mississippi.

3. Numbers within square brackets [ ] denote a multi-patentee land parcel (multi-owner). Refer to Appendix "C" for a full list of members in this group.

4. Areas that look to be crowded with Patentees usually indicate multiple sales of the same parcel (Re-issues) or Overlapping parcels. See this Township's Index for an explanation of these and other circumstances that might explain "odd" groupings of Patentees on this map.

Legend

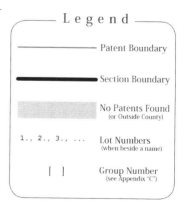

———— Patent Boundary

▬▬▬▬ Section Boundary

░░░░ No Patents Found
(or Outside County)

1., 2., 3., ... Lot Numbers
(when beside a name)

[ ] Group Number
(see Appendix "C")

Scale: Section = 1 mile X 1 mile
(generally, with some exceptions)

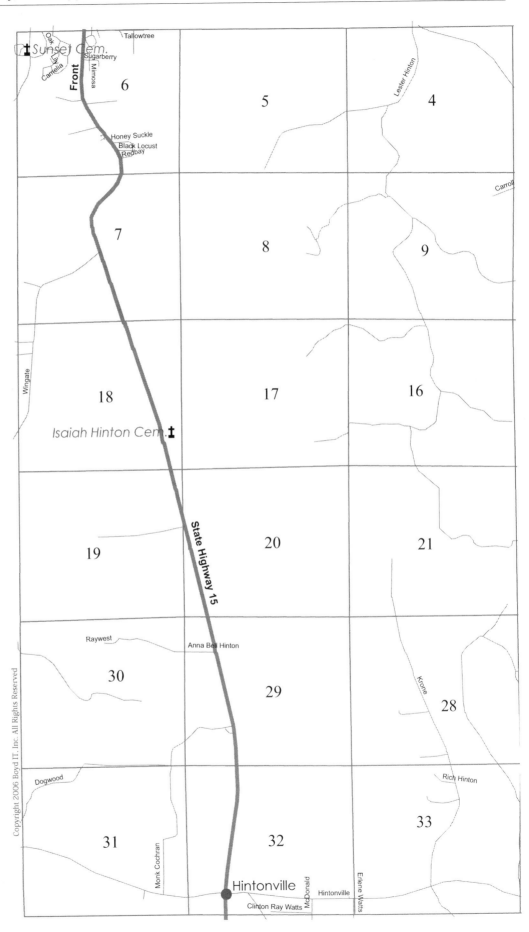

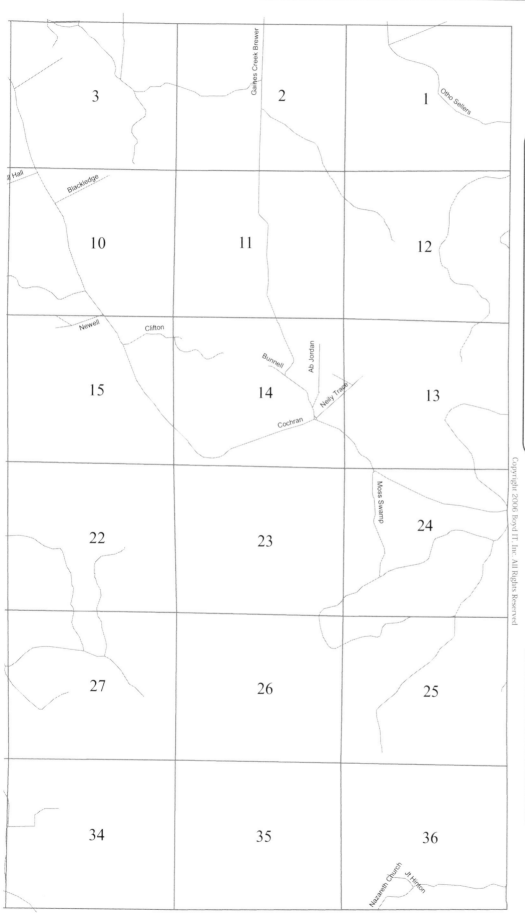

Helpful Hints

1. This road map has a number of uses, but primarily it is to help you: a) find the present location of land owned by your ancestors (at least the general area), b) find cemeteries and city-centers, and c) estimate the route/roads used by Census-takers & tax-assessors.

2. If you plan to travel to Perry County to locate cemeteries or land parcels, please pick up a modern travel map for the area before you do. Mapping old land parcels on modern maps is not as exact a science as you might think. Just the slightest variations in public land survey coordinates, estimates of parcel boundaries, or road-map deviations can greatly alter a map's representation of how a road either does or doesn't cross a particular parcel of land.

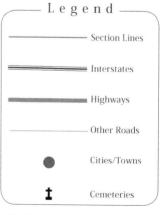

Legend

————	Section Lines
══════	Interstates
▬▬▬▬	Highways
————	Other Roads
●	Cities/Towns
✝	Cemeteries

Scale: Section = 1 mile X 1 mile
(generally, with some exceptions)

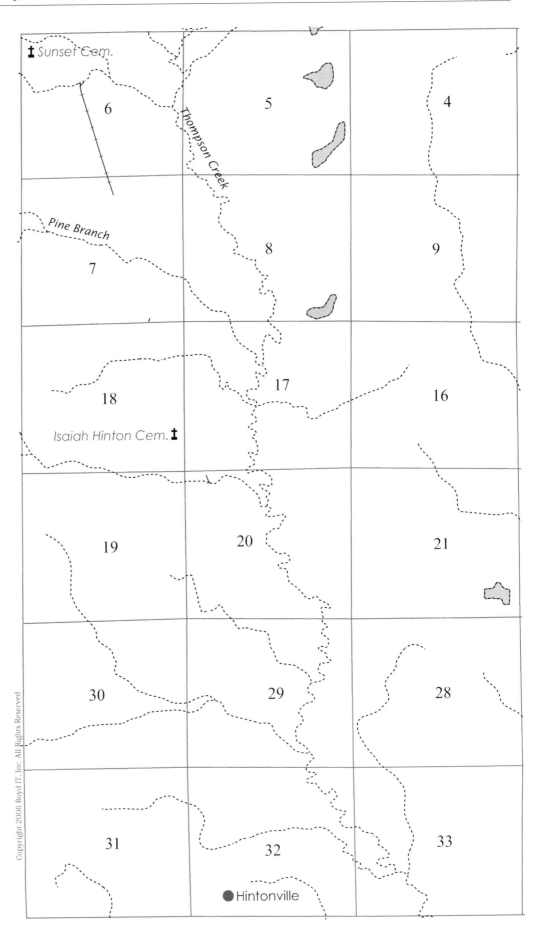

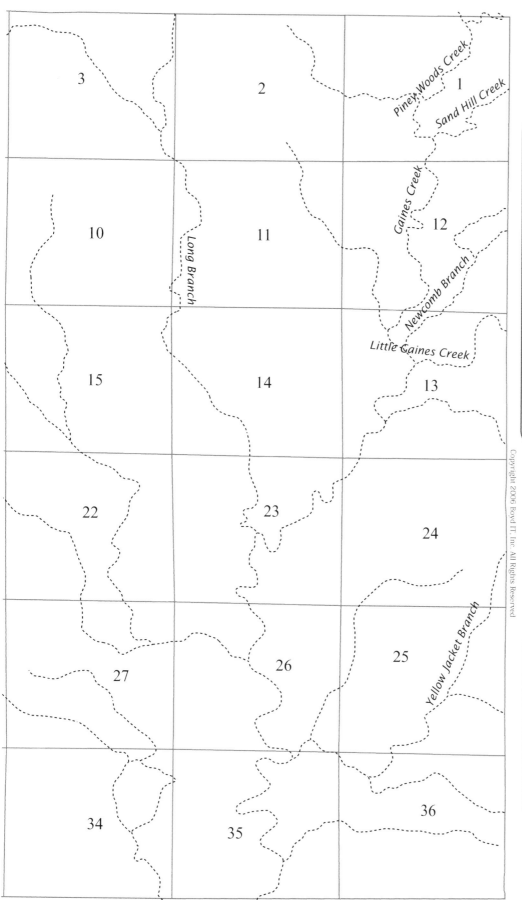

Helpful Hints

1. This Map takes a different look at the same Congressional Township displayed in the preceding two maps. It presents features that can help you better envision the historical development of the area: a) Water-bodies (lakes & ponds), b) Water-courses (rivers, streams, etc.), c) Railroads, d) City/town center-points (where they were oftentimes located when first settled), and e) Cemeteries.

2. Using this "Historical" map in tandem with this Township's Patent Map and Road Map, may lead you to some interesting discoveries. You will often find roads, towns, cemeteries, and waterways are named after nearby landowners: sometimes those names will be the ones you are researching. See how many of these research gems you can find here in Perry County.

Legend

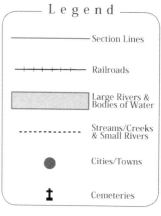

— Section Lines
+++ Railroads
▓ Large Rivers & Bodies of Water
---- Streams/Creeks & Small Rivers
● Cities/Towns
✝ Cemeteries

Scale: Section = 1 mile X 1 mile
(there are some exceptions)

Map Group 7: Index to Land Patents

Township 3-North Range 11-West (St Stephens)

After you locate an individual in this Index, take note of the Section and Section Part then proceed to the Land Patent map on the pages immediately following. You should have no difficulty locating the corresponding parcel of land.

The "For More Info" Column will lead you to more information about the underlying Patents. See the *Legend* at right, and the "How to Use this Book" chapter, for more information.

```
                            LEGEND
               "For More Info . . . " column
A = Authority (Legislative Act, See Appendix "A")
B = Block or Lot (location in Section unknown)
C = Cancelled Patent
F = Fractional Section
G = Group  (Multi-Patentee Patent, see Appendix "C")
V = Overlaps another Parcel
R = Re-Issued (Parcel patented more than once)

(A & G items require you to look in the Appendixes referred
to above. All other Letter-designations followed by a number
require you to locate line-items in this index that possess
the ID number found after the letter).
```

ID	Individual in Patent	Sec.	Sec. Part	Date Issued	Other Counties	For More Info . . .
1482	ALLEN, Margaret	4	N½NW	1859-06-01		A1
1352	BARNETT, Andrew J	23	N½7	1915-04-27		A4
1353	" "	23	S½7	1915-08-11		A4
1354	" "	23	S½8	1915-08-11		A4
1471	BARRON, Joseph O	20	W½SE	1907-05-10		A1
1397	BATCHELOR, Edward W	36	E½NE	1911-06-26		A1
1483	BONNER, Margaret	5	NWSW	1895-02-21		A4
1484	" "	6	E½SE	1895-02-21		A4
1485	" "	6	SWSE	1895-02-21		A4
1448	BROWN, Joe B	19	NESW	1915-06-09		A4 G17
1448	BROWN, Letha	19	NESW	1915-06-09		A4 G17
1395	BYNUM, Drury	13	1	1859-05-02		A1
1396	" "	13	2	1859-05-02		A1
1438	CARPENTER, James	24	N½5	1860-04-02		A1
1346	CARTER, Alex	5	NWNW	1890-06-25		A4
1347	" "	6	NENE	1890-06-25		A4
1432	CARTER, Isaac	1	NESE	1906-06-16		A4
1452	CARTER, John	36	S½SE	1906-09-14		A4
1472	CARTER, Lem	26	SESW	1890-08-16		A4
1473	" "	26	SWSE	1890-08-16		A4
1474	" "	35	N½NE	1890-08-16		A4
1493	CARTER, Nancy	36	NENW	1906-06-26		A4
1494	" "	36	W½NW	1906-06-26		A4
1505	CARTER, Peter	31	NESW	1906-05-01		A4
1534	CARTER, Stephen	23	6	1889-11-23		A4
1535	" "	26	N½NW	1889-11-23		A4
1539	CARTER, Washington W	27	NWSE	1860-10-01		A1
1540	" "	27	S½NE	1860-10-01		A1
1368	COLLINS, Charity	8	E½NW	1882-11-10		A4
1506	COLLINS, Peter	9	SWNE	1899-06-28		A4
1435	COOK, Isham H	12	SE	1891-05-20		A4
1457	DANTZLER, John Lewis	17		1908-11-23		A1 F
1398	DAVIS, Elijah	26	NE	1915-08-11		A4
1541	DAVIS, Wiley D	1	NENW	1894-04-06		A4
1542	" "	1	NWSE	1894-04-06		A4
1543	" "	1	W½NE	1894-04-06		A4 R1488
1439	DEARMAN, James E	7	N½SW	1889-01-05		A4
1440	" "	7	NWSE	1889-01-05		A4
1441	" "	7	SWNW	1889-01-05		A4
1436	DEASE, Jack	1	SW	1884-12-30		A4
1437	DENHAM, James A	21	NENE	1848-09-01		A1
1487	DENHAM, Mary	1	SWNW	1881-09-17		A4
1488	" "	1	W½NE	1881-09-17		A4 R1543
1489	" "	2	SENE	1881-09-17		A4
1516	DENHAM, Samuel	26	SWNW	1906-06-04		A4
1517	" "	26	W½SW	1906-06-04		A4

ID	Individual in Patent	Sec.	Sec. Part	Date Issued	Other Counties	For More Info . . .
1518	DENHAM, Samuel (Cont'd)	27	NESE	1906-06-04		A4
1363	DICKEY, Calvin	5	NESW	1890-02-21		A4
1364	" "	5	S½SW	1890-02-21		A4
1365	" "	8	NWNW	1890-02-21		A4
1537	DIETZ, Walter	22	E½NW	1906-06-04		A4
1538	"	22	E½SW	1906-06-04		A4
1348	DRAUGHN, Alpheus	4	SESW	1888-04-05		A4
1349	" "	4	SWSE	1888-04-05		A4
1350	" "	9	NENW	1888-04-05		A4
1351	" "	9	NWNE	1888-04-05		A4
1371	DRAUGHN, Cyrus	11	NE	1883-04-30		A4
1449	DUNNAVANT, John A	30	NESE	1911-02-23		A4
1450	" "	30	S½NE	1911-02-23		A4
1451	" "	30	SENW	1911-02-23		A4
1393	EVANS, David	29	NWNW	1859-05-02		A1
1394	" "	30	NENE	1859-05-02		A1
1508	FERGUSON, Randolph	3	SWSW	1892-04-29		A4
1509	" "	4	E½SE	1892-04-29		A4
1510	" "	4	SENE	1892-04-29		A4
1369	FULLILOVE, Charlie T	25	N½NE	1895-08-30		A4
1370	" "	25	NENW	1895-08-30		A4
1524	GARAWAY, Solomon T	29	NWNE	1854-03-15		A1
1358	GARRAWAY, Benjamin	27	NENE	1891-05-20		A4
1523	GARRAWAY, Sollomon T	29	SENE	1854-03-15		A1 G39
1525	GARRAWAY, Solomon T	19	E½NE	1859-05-02		A1
1532	" "	30	NWNE	1859-05-02		A1
1531	" "	30	N½NW	1859-05-02		A1
1533	" "	30	SWNW	1883-09-15		A1
1529	" "	19	SWSW	1885-05-25		A4
1527	" "	19	NWSW	1898-12-01		A4
1528	" "	19	S½NW	1898-12-01		A4
1526	" "	19	NENW	1904-10-17		A4
1530	" "	19	W½NE	1904-10-17		A4
1413	GILLINDER, Green	8	E½NE	1890-08-16		A4
1414	" "	8	SWNE	1890-08-16		A4
1415	" "	9	NWNW	1890-08-16		A4
1458	GILLIS, John M	4	NESW	1890-08-16		A4
1459	" "	4	NWSE	1890-08-16		A4
1460	" "	4	S½NW	1890-08-16		A4
1520	GILLIS, Sarah	5	N½NE	1907-05-13		A4
1521	" "	5	NENW	1907-05-13		A4
1445	GRIFFIN, James W	33	S½NW	1884-12-30		A1
1446	" "	33	SE	1884-12-30		A1
1407	HESTLE, Fred	26	SESE	1916-07-31		A4
1507	HIDE, Prentis	12	SW	1891-05-20		A4
1430	HOLDER, Hesperia J	29	SENW	1859-05-02		A1
1523	HOLDER, Willis	29	SENE	1854-03-15		A1 G39
1536	HOLLIMAN, Theodosia	25	SW	1911-07-20		A4 G53
1416	HOLLIMON, Griffin H	10	E½SE	1846-09-01		A1
1417	" "	14	N½1	1846-09-01		A1 F
1418	" "	14	N½2	1846-09-01		A1 F
1419	" "	2	E½SW	1859-05-02		A1
1420	" "	2	SE	1859-05-02		A1
1421	" "	2	SWNW	1859-05-02		A1
1422	" "	2	SWSW	1859-05-02		A1
1442	HOLLIMON, James Powell	1	SENW	1916-05-31		A4
1455	HOLLIMON, John	2	E½NW	1890-08-16		A4
1456	" "	2	NWNW	1890-08-16		A4
1433	JAMES, Isaac	5	S½NE	1890-08-16		A4
1434	" "	5	S½NW	1890-08-16		A4
1412	KENNEDY, George M	27	SESE	1889-11-29		A1
1409	" "	27	E½NW	1890-08-16		A4
1410	" "	27	NESW	1890-08-16		A4
1411	" "	27	NWNW	1890-08-16		A4
1447	KENNEDY, Jesse A	27	SWSE	1890-08-13		A1
1468	KENNEDY, Joseph B	34	E½NE	1898-08-27		A4
1469	" "	34	NESE	1898-08-27		A4
1470	" "	35	SWNW	1898-08-27		A4
1399	MCCALLUM, Eliza	33	N½NW	1884-12-30		A1
1400	"	28	SW	1899-06-28		A4 G60
1431	MCCALLUM, Hugh M	28	SE	1890-08-16		A4
1400	MCCALLUM, Malcolm	28	SW	1899-06-28		A4 G60
1479	MCCALLUM, Malcom	28	NE	1859-11-10		A1

ID	Individual in Patent	Sec.	Sec. Part	Date Issued	Other Counties	For More Info . . .
1476	MCCOLLUM, Malcolm	28	E½NW	1859-05-02		A1
1477	"	28	SWNW	1859-05-02		A1
1478	"	29	NENE	1859-05-02		A1
1536	MCGILVARY, Theodosia	25	SW	1911-07-20		A4 G53
1366	MCKENZIE, Catharine	8	N½SE	1884-12-30		A1
1367	MCKENZIE, Catherine	9	E½SE	1897-05-20		A4
1547	MCLAUGHLIN, William J	4	NENE	1900-02-02		A4
1548	"	4	W½NE	1900-02-02		A4
1404	MCLEAN, Frank	4	SWSW	1884-11-20		A4
1405	"	5	S½SE	1884-11-20		A4
1406	"	8	NWNE	1884-11-20		A4
1549	MCLEMORE, William	36	NESE	1897-05-07		A4
1355	MCSWAIN, Angus	9	S½NW	1860-04-02		A1
1356	"	9	SW	1860-04-02		A1
1357	"	9	W½SE	1860-04-02		A1
1480	MCSWAIN, Malcom	19	SE	1860-04-02		A1
1481	"	20	SW	1860-04-02		A1
1498	MCSWAIN, Ned	27	SESW	1890-08-16		A4
1499	"	34	N½NW	1890-08-16		A4
1500	"	34	NWNE	1890-08-16		A4
1502	MCSWAIN, Patsey	25	SESE	1897-06-07		A4 G64
1503	"	25	SWNE	1897-06-07		A4 G64
1504	"	25	W½SE	1897-06-07		A4 G64
1401	MIXON, Elizabeth	10	W½NW	1881-09-17		A4
1402	"	9	E½NE	1881-09-17		A4
1461	MIXON, John	22	NESE	1859-05-02		A1
1462	"	22	SENE	1859-05-02		A1
1463	"	22	SESE	1859-06-01		A1
1464	"	22	SWNE	1859-06-01		A1
1465	"	22	W½SE	1859-06-01		A1
1466	"	23	5	1859-06-01		A1
1408	MYERS, Frederick F	11	SE	1898-07-18		A4
1475	MYERS, Levi S	7	NESE	1859-05-02		A1 G66
1486	MYERS, Margaret P	13	3	1859-05-02		A1
1490	MYERS, Matilda	7	SENW	1890-12-31		A4
1491	"	7	SWNE	1890-12-31		A4
1475	NICHOLS, Daniel R	7	NESE	1859-05-02		A1 G66
1390	"	7	SENE	1882-05-10		A1
1391	"	8	SWNW	1882-12-30		A1
1544	NICHOLS, William H	4	NWSW	1859-05-02		A1
1545	"	5	NESE	1859-05-02		A1
1546	"	5	NWSE	1859-05-02		A1
1453	NIX, John D	27	NWSW	1859-05-02		A1
1454	"	27	SWNW	1859-05-02		A1
1372	RANSDELL, Daniel M	29	S½	1884-12-30		A1
1373	"	30	N½SW	1884-12-30		A1
1374	"	30	NWSE	1884-12-30		A1
1375	"	30	SESE	1884-12-30		A1
1376	"	31	N½	1884-12-30		A1
1377	"	31	N½SE	1884-12-30		A1
1378	"	31	SESW	1884-12-30		A1
1379	"	31	SWSE	1884-12-30		A1
1380	"	31	W½SW	1884-12-30		A1
1381	"	32	E½NW	1884-12-30		A1
1382	"	32	NESW	1884-12-30		A1
1383	"	32	NWNE	1884-12-30		A1
1384	"	32	NWNW	1884-12-30		A1
1385	"	32	SESE	1884-12-30		A1
1386	"	33	NE	1884-12-30		A1
1387	"	33	SW	1884-12-30		A1
1388	"	34	S½NW	1884-12-30		A1
1389	"	34	SW	1884-12-30		A1
1403	RHODES, Elizabeth	10	E½SW	1841-01-05		A1
1501	RHODES, Oliver C	10	W½SW	1841-01-05		A1
1443	SCOTT, James	6	SWSW	1895-07-08		A4
1444	"	7	NWNW	1895-07-08		A4
1467	SCOTT, John	6	N½SW	1881-05-10		A4
1359	STEVENS, Benjamin	1	E½NE	1889-04-10		A1
1360	"	1	NWNW	1889-04-10		A1
1361	"	1	SESE	1889-04-10		A1
1362	"	19	SESW	1889-04-10		A1
1495	TERRELL, Nancy	13	4	1846-09-01		A1 F
1429	TILLMAN, Henry	27	NWNE	1913-02-14		A4

ID	Individual in Patent	Sec.	Sec. Part	Date Issued	Other Counties	For More Info . . .
1392	TRAVIS, Daniel	22	W½NW	1907-05-13		A4
1423	WADE, Hamp	6	NWSE	1892-06-25		A4
1424	" "	6	SWNE	1892-06-25		A4
1425	WADE, Hampton	6	SENE	1882-08-03		A1
1426	WADE, Harriette	6	SESW	1882-03-30		A4
1427	" "	7	N½NE	1882-03-30		A4
1428	" "	7	NENW	1882-03-30		A4
1492	WADE, Michael	6	NW	1881-05-10		A4
1519	WADE, Samuel L	6	NWNE	1914-03-25		A4
1496	WARREN, Nathan T	30	S½SW	1912-06-27		A1
1497	" "	30	SWSE	1912-06-27		A1
1511	WENTWORTH, Robert G	26	N½SE	1906-10-18		A1
1512	" "	26	NESW	1906-10-18		A1
1513	" "	26	SENW	1906-10-18		A1
1502	WEST, Patsey	25	SESE	1897-06-07		A4 G64
1503	" "	25	SWNE	1897-06-07		A4 G64
1504	" "	25	W½SE	1897-06-07		A4 G64
1514	WEST, Sam	25	NESE	1881-08-20		A4
1515	" "	25	SENE	1881-08-20		A4
1522	WILLIAMS, Scott W	27	SWSW	1913-05-26		A4

Patent Map

T3-N R11-W
St Stephens Meridian

Map Group 7

Township Statistics

Parcels Mapped	:	204
Number of Patents	:	110
Number of Individuals	:	99
Patentees Identified	:	95
Number of Surnames	:	59
Multi-Patentee Parcels	:	8
Oldest Patent Date	:	1/5/1841
Most Recent Patent	:	7/31/1916
Block/Lot Parcels	:	12
Parcels Re - Issued	:	1
Parcels that Overlap	:	0
Cities and Towns	:	2
Cemeteries	:	9

Section 6
- WADE Michael 1881
- WADE Samuel L 1914
- CARTER Alex 1890
- WADE Hamp 1892
- WADE Hampton 1882
- SCOTT John 1881
- WADE Hamp 1892
- SCOTT James 1895
- WADE Harriette 1882
- BONNER Margaret 1895
- BONNER Margaret 1895

Section 5
- CARTER Alex 1890
- GILLIS Sarah 1907
- GILLIS Sarah 1907
- JAMES Isaac 1890
- JAMES Isaac 1890
- BONNER Margaret 1895
- DICKEY Calvin 1890
- NICHOLS William H 1859
- NICHOLS William H 1859
- DICKEY Calvin 1890
- MCLEAN Frank 1884

Section 4
- ALLEN Margaret 1859
- MCLAUGHLIN William J 1900
- MCLAUGHLIN William J 1900
- GILLIS John M 1890
- FERGUSON Randolph 1892
- NICHOLS William H 1859
- GILLIS John M 1890
- GILLIS John M 1890
- FERGUSON Randolph 1892
- MCLEAN Frank 1884
- DRAUGHN Alpheus 1888
- DRAUGHN Alpheus 1888

Section 7
- SCOTT James 1895
- WADE Harriette 1882
- WADE Harriette 1882
- DICKEY Calvin 1890
- MCLEAN Frank 1884
- GILLINDER Green 1890
- DRAUGHN Alpheus 1888
- DRAUGHN Alpheus 1888
- DEARMAN James E 1889
- MYERS Matilda 1890
- MYERS Matilda 1890
- NICHOLS Daniel R 1882
- NICHOLS Daniel R 1882
- COLLINS Charity 1882
- GILLINDER Green 1890
- GILLINDER Green 1890
- MCSWAIN Angus 1860
- COLLINS Peter 1899
- MIXON Elizabeth 1881
- DEARMAN James E 1889
- DEARMAN James E 1889
- MYERS [66] Levi S 1859

Section 8
- MCKENZIE Catharine 1884

Section 9
- MCSWAIN Angus 1860
- MCSWAIN Angus 1860
- MCSWAIN Angus 1860
- MCKENZIE Catherine 1897

Section 18
- (18)

Section 17
- DANTZLER John Lewis 1908

Section 16
- (16)

Section 19
- GARRAWAY Solomon T 1904
- GARRAWAY Solomon T 1904
- GARRAWAY Solomon T 1859
- GARRAWAY Solomon T 1898
- GARRAWAY Solomon T 1898
- BROWN [17] Joe B 1915
- MCSWAIN Malcom 1860
- GARRAWAY Solomon T 1885
- STEVENS Benjamin 1889

Section 20
- MCSWAIN Malcom 1860
- BARRON Joseph O 1907

Section 21
- DENHAM James A 1848

Section 30
- GARRAWAY Solomon T 1859
- GARRAWAY Solomon T 1859
- EVANS David 1859
- GARRAWAY Solomon T 1883
- DUNNAVANT John A 1911
- DUNNAVANT John A 1911
- DUNNAVANT John A 1911
- RANSDELL Daniel M 1884
- RANSDELL Daniel M 1884
- WARREN Nathan T 1912
- WARREN Nathan T 1912
- RANSDELL Daniel M 1884

Section 29
- EVANS David 1859
- GARAWAY Solomon T 1854
- MCCOLLUM Malcom 1859
- HOLDER Hesperia J 1859
- GARRAWAY [39] Sollomon T 1854
- MCCOLLUM Malcom 1859
- RANSDELL Daniel M 1884

Section 28
- MCCOLLUM Malcom 1859
- MCCALLUM Malcom 1859
- MCCALLUM Eliza 1899
- MCCALLUM Hugh M 1890

Section 31
- RANSDELL Daniel M 1884
- RANSDELL Daniel M 1884
- CARTER Peter 1906
- RANSDELL Daniel M 1884
- RANSDELL Daniel M 1884
- RANSDELL Daniel M 1884

Section 32
- RANSDELL Daniel M 1884
- RANSDELL Daniel M 1884
- RANSDELL Daniel M 1884
- RANSDELL Daniel M 1884
- RANSDELL Daniel M 1884
- RANSDELL Daniel M 1884

Section 33
- MCCALLUM Eliza 1884
- GRIFFIN James W 1884
- RANSDELL Daniel M 1884
- RANSDELL Daniel M 1884
- GRIFFIN James W 1884

3

HOLLIMON John 1890
HOLLIMON Griffin H 1859
HOLLIMON John 1890
DENHAM Mary 1881
2
HOLLIMON Griffin H 1859
HOLLIMON Griffin H 1859
HOLLIMON Griffin H 1859

STEVENS Benjamin 1889
DAVIS Wiley D 1894
DENHAM Mary 1881
DENHAM Mary 1881
HOLLIMON James Powell 1916
DAVIS Wiley D 1894
STEVENS Benjamin 1889
1
DEASE Jack 1884
DAVIS Wiley D 1894
CARTER Isaac 1906
STEVENS Benjamin 1889

FERGUSON Randolph 1892

MIXON Elizabeth 1881
10
RHODES Oliver C 1841
RHODES Elizabeth 1841
HOLLIMON Griffin H 1846

11
DRAUGHN Cyrus 1883
MYERS Frederick F 1898

12
HIDE Prentis 1891
COOK Isham H 1891

15

14
Lots-Sec. 14
4 HOLLIMON, Griffin H 1846
4 HOLLIMON, Griffin H 1846

13
Lots-Sec. 13
1 BYNUM, Drury 1859
2 BYNUM, Drury 1859
3 MYERS, Margaret P 1859
4 TERRELL, Nancy 1846

TRAVIS Daniel 1907
DIETZ Walter 1906
MIXON John 1859
MIXON John 1859
22
MIXON John 1859
MIXON John 1859
DIETZ Walter 1906
MIXON John 1859

23
Lots-Sec. 23
5 MIXON, John 1859
6 BARNETT, Andrew J 1915
6 BARNETT, Andrew J 1915
6 BARNETT, Andrew J 1915
6 CARTER, Stephen 1889

24
Lots-Sec. 24
6 CARPENTER, James 1860

KENNEDY George M 1890
TILLMAN Henry 1913
GARRAWAY Benjamin 1891
KENNEDY George M 1890
NIX John D 1859
27
CARTER Washington W 1860
NIX John D 1859
KENNEDY George M 1890
CARTER Washington W 1860
DENHAM Samuel 1906
WILLIAMS Scott W 1913
MCSWAIN Ned 1890
KENNEDY Jesse A 1890
KENNEDY George M 1889

CARTER Stephen 1889
DAVIS Elijah 1915
DENHAM Samuel 1906
WENTWORTH Robert G 1906
26
DENHAM Samuel 1906
WENTWORTH Robert G 1906
WENTWORTH Robert G 1906
CARTER Lem 1890
CARTER Lem 1890
HESTLE Fred 1916

FULLILOVE Charlie T 1895
FULLILOVE Charlie T 1895
MCSWAIN [64] Patsey 1897
WEST Sam 1881
25
MCSWAIN [64] Patsey 1897
WEST Sam 1881
HOLLIMAN [53] Theodosia 1911
MCSWAIN [64] Patsey 1897

MCSWAIN Ned 1890
MCSWAIN Ned 1890
RANSDELL Daniel M 1884
34
KENNEDY Joseph B 1898
KENNEDY Joseph B 1898
RANSDELL Daniel M 1884

KENNEDY Joseph B 1898
CARTER Lem 1890
35

CARTER Nancy 1906
CARTER Nancy 1906
36
BATCHELOR Edward W 1911
MCLEMORE William 1897
CARTER John 1906

Helpful Hints

1. This Map's INDEX can be found on the preceding pages.
2. Refer to Map "C" to see where this Township lies within Perry County, Mississippi.
3. Numbers within square brackets [ ] denote a multi-patentee land parcel (multi-owner). Refer to Appendix "C" for a full list of members in this group.
4. Areas that look to be crowded with Patentees usually indicate multiple sales of the same parcel (Re-issues) or Overlapping parcels. See this Township's Index for an explanation of these and other circumstances that might explain "odd" groupings of Patentees on this map.

L e g e n d

—— Patent Boundary
━━ Section Boundary
░ No Patents Found (or Outside County)
1., 2., 3., ... Lot Numbers (when beside a name)
[ ] Group Number (see Appendix "C")

Scale: Section = 1 mile X 1 mile (generally, with some exceptions)

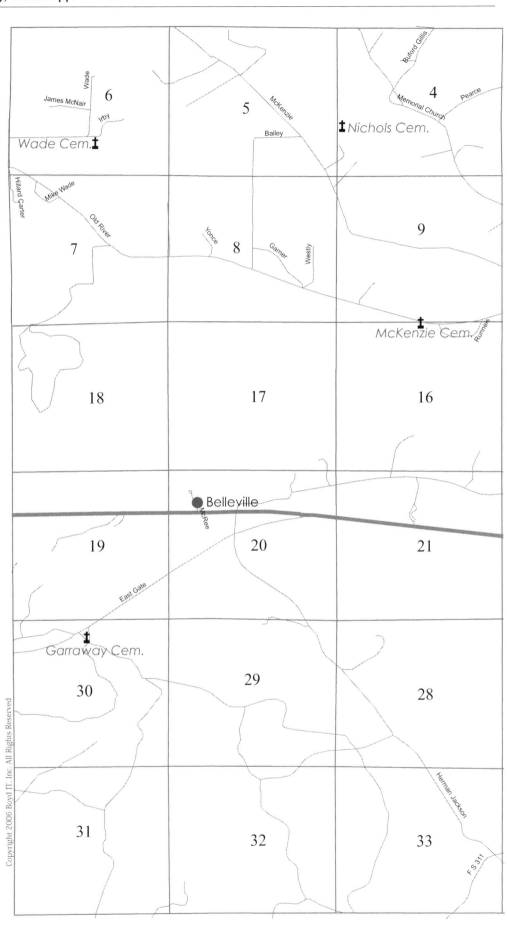

Road Map

T3-N R11-W
St Stephens Meridian

Map Group 7

Cities & Towns
Belleville
Mahned

Cemeteries
Denham Cemetery
Ferguson Cemetery
Garraway Cemetery
Hollimon Cemetery
McKenzie Cemetery
McSwain Cemetery
Nichols Cemetery
Stevens Cemetery
Wade Cemetery

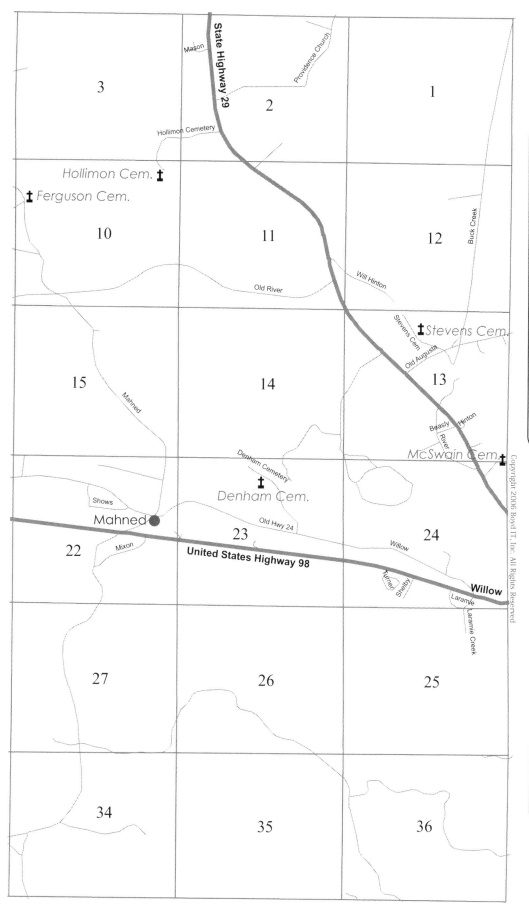

3

State Highway 29

Mason

2

Providence Church

1

Hollimon Cemetery

Hollimon Cem.

Ferguson Cem.

10

11

12

Buck Creek

Old River

Will Hinton

15

14

Mahned

Stevens Cem

Stevens Cem.

Old Augusta

13

Beasly   Hinton

River

McSwain Cem.

Denham Cemetery

Denham Cem.

Shows

Mahned

22

Mixon

23

Old Hwy 24

United States Highway 98

Willow

24

Turner
Shelby

Willow

Laramie

Laramie Creek

27

26

25

34

35

36

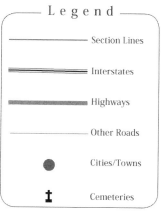

Legend

—————— Section Lines

══════ Interstates

▬▬▬▬▬ Highways

———— Other Roads

● Cities/Towns

✝ Cemeteries

Scale: Section = 1 mile X 1 mile
(generally, with some exceptions)

Historical Map

T3-N R11-W
St Stephens Meridian

Map Group 7

Cities & Towns
Belleville
Mahned

Cemeteries
Denham Cemetery
Ferguson Cemetery
Garraway Cemetery
Hollimon Cemetery
McKenzie Cemetery
McSwain Cemetery
Nichols Cemetery
Stevens Cemetery
Wade Cemetery

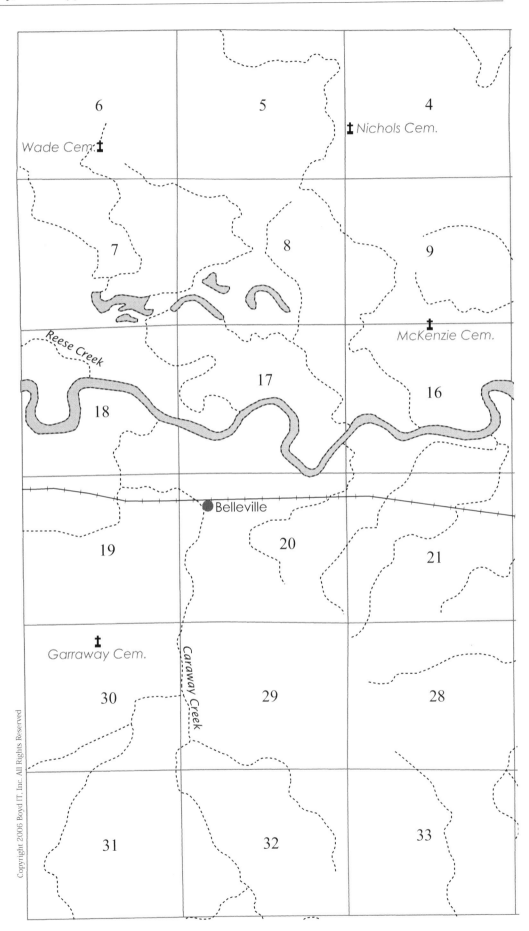

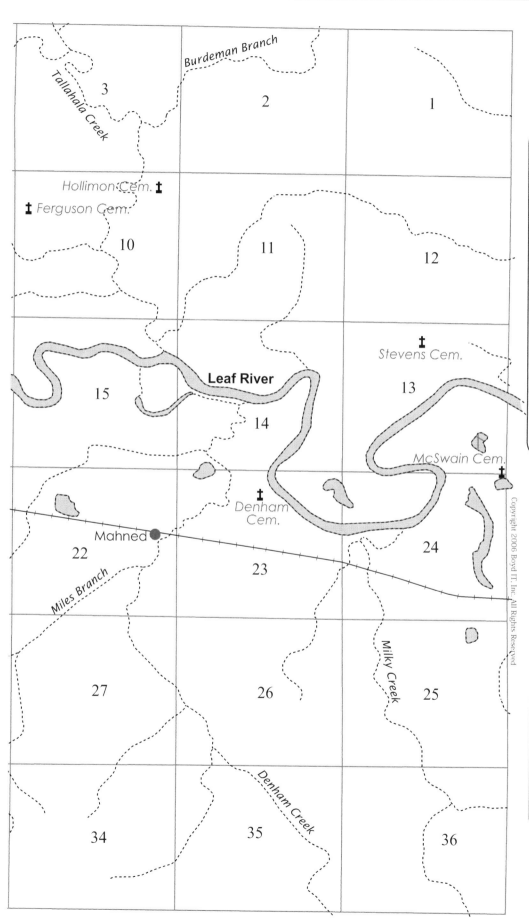

Burdeman Branch

Tallahala Creek

3

2

1

Hollimon Cem. ✝

✝ Ferguson Cem.

10

11

12

✝ Stevens Cem.

Leaf River

15

13

14

McSwain Cem. ✝

Denham Cem. ✝

22

Mahned ⬤

23

24

Miles Branch

Milky Creek

27

26

25

34

Denham Creek

35

36

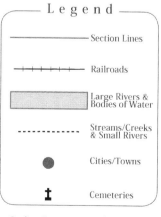

Helpful Hints

1. This Map takes a different look at the same Congressional Township displayed in the preceding two maps. It presents features that can help you better envision the historical development of the area: a) Water-bodies (lakes & ponds), b) Water-courses (rivers, streams, etc.), c) Railroads, d) City/town center-points (where they were oftentimes located when first settled), and e) Cemeteries.

2. Using this "Historical" map in tandem with this Township's Patent Map and Road Map, may lead you to some interesting discoveries. You will often find roads, towns, cemeteries, and waterways are named after nearby landowners: sometimes those names will be the ones you are researching. See how many of these research gems you can find here in Perry County.

Legend

———————— Section Lines

+++++++++ Railroads

▭ Large Rivers & Bodies of Water

- - - - - - Streams/Creeks & Small Rivers

⬤ Cities/Towns

✝ Cemeteries

Scale: Section = 1 mile X 1 mile
(there are some exceptions)

Map Group 8: Index to Land Patents

Township 3-North Range 10-West (St Stephens)

After you locate an individual in this Index, take note of the Section and Section Part then proceed to the Land Patent map on the pages immediately following. You should have no difficulty locating the corresponding parcel of land.

The "For More Info" Column will lead you to more information about the underlying Patents. See the *Legend* at right, and the "How to Use this Book" chapter, for more information.

ID	Individual in Patent	Sec.	Sec. Part	Date Issued	Other Counties	For More Info . . .
1646	BONNER, Eran	6	S½NE	1895-06-22		A1 G9
1647	" "	6	W½SE	1895-06-22		A1 G9
1633	BOULTON, Collin	12	S½SE	1907-05-09		A4
1695	BOULTON, John	27	N½SW	1895-02-21		A4
1696	"	27	S½NW	1895-02-21		A4
1616	BRADFORD, Catharine C	20	W½SE	1885-06-12		A1
1614	BRADLEY, Calvin	8	SWNW	1888-04-05		A4
1615	" "	8	W½SW	1888-04-05		A4
1613	" "	7	SENE	1892-07-25		A4
1656	BRADLEY, Henry	32	NW	1897-11-01		A4
1677	BRADLEY, James M	4	E½SW	1859-11-10		A1
1678	" "	4	SWSW	1859-11-10		A1
1679	" "	5	SESE	1859-11-10		A1
1682	" "	8	NENE	1859-11-10		A1
1683	" "	8	SENE	1859-11-10		A1
1684	" "	9	5	1859-11-10		A1
1680	" "	8	E½NW	1881-05-10		A4
1681	" "	8	E½SW	1881-05-10		A4
1735	BRADLEY, Rufus P	6	SESE	1882-10-10		A1
1736	" "	7	NWSW	1882-12-30		A1
1737	" "	3	NWSE	1889-04-10		A1 G14
1738	" "	3	SENE	1889-11-21		A1 G14
1663	CARPENTER, Henry S	34	NENW	1884-12-30		A1
1661	" "	27	S½SW	1890-06-25		A4
1662	" "	28	E½SE	1890-06-25		A4
1550	CARTER, Abner	21	E½SE	1841-01-05		A1
1588	CARTER, Alexander	26	E½SW	1882-03-30		A4
1589	" "	26	W½SE	1882-03-30		A4
1675	CARTER, Isaac	5	SENW	1896-01-25		A4
1676	CARTER, Isabella	18	9	1848-09-01		A1 F
1697	CARTER, John W	23	SE	1859-05-02		A1 F
1698	" "	26	E½NW	1859-05-02		A1
1699	" "	26	W½NE	1859-05-02		A1
1706	CLARK, Loyed	1	NESW	1894-12-17		A4
1707	" "	1	SENW	1894-12-17		A4
1708	" "	1	W½NW	1894-12-17		A4
1642	CLIFTON, Elias	1	N½NE	1895-02-21		A4
1643	" "	1	NENW	1895-02-21		A4
1644	" "	1	SWNE	1895-02-21		A4
1651	CLIFTON, Florence	14	SWNE	1915-11-04		A4
1741	COLEMAN, Samuel	20	E½SE	1919-11-18		A1 G22
1659	COTTON, Henry R	1	NESE	1914-05-28		A4
1660	"	1	SENE	1914-05-28		A4
1652	DENNIS, Franklin	6	N½NE	1890-03-28		A4
1688	DENNIS, James T	2	E½NW	1892-05-16		A4
1689	" "	2	NESW	1892-05-16		A4

ID	Individual in Patent	Sec.	Sec. Part	Date Issued	Other Counties	For More Info . . .
1690	DENNIS, James T (Cont'd)	2	SWNW	1892-05-16		A4
1752	DENNIS, Thomas	5	N½SW	1890-02-21		A4
1753	" "	5	NWSE	1890-02-21		A4
1754	" "	5	SWNE	1890-02-21		A4
1763	DRAUGHN, William	29	N½SE	1894-03-12		A4
1764	" "	29	NESW	1894-03-12		A4
1765	" "	29	SWSE	1894-03-12		A4
1612	FAIRLEY, Caesar	30	SWSW	1904-12-31		A4
1636	FAIRLEY, David	30	SESW	1893-04-12		A4
1637	" "	30	SWSE	1893-04-12		A4
1638	" "	31	NENW	1893-04-12		A4
1639	" "	31	NWNE	1893-04-12		A4
1725	FREEMAN, Perry K	34	N½NE	1883-02-03		A1
1726	" "	35	W½NW	1890-07-03		A1
1758	FREEMAN, Walter J	36	SE	1910-04-11		A4
1761	GARDNER, William A	27	SWSE	1918-04-11		A4
1755	GUINN, Thomas W	20	E½SW	1902-09-06		A4
1756	" "	20	W½SE	1902-09-06		A4
1634	HAIRSTON, David D	31	NESW	1905-05-12		A1
1635	" "	31	S½SW	1905-05-12		A1
1611	HAVENS, Bruno	30	W½NE	1898-02-18		A1
1586	HENDRY, Alex	28	E½NW	1895-12-14		A4
1587	" "	28	W½NE	1895-12-14		A4
1623	HILLS, Charles T	28	SWSE	1889-11-29		A1
1624	" "	33	NENE	1889-11-29		A1
1625	" "	34	E½SW	1889-11-29		A1
1626	" "	34	S½NE	1889-11-29		A1
1627	" "	34	SE	1889-11-29		A1
1628	" "	34	SENW	1889-11-29		A1
1629	" "	34	W½NW	1889-11-29		A1
1590	HINTON, Allen	25	S½4	1896-06-06		A1
1591	" "	26	E½SE	1896-06-06		A1
1592	" "	36	SW	1904-12-01		A4 G46
1600	HINTON, Annie L	8	W½SE	1905-02-13		A4
1592	HINTON, Catherine	36	SW	1904-12-01		A4 G46
1655	HINTON, Hardee	11	SESE	1915-09-03		A4
1703	HINTON, Joshua	26	NENE	1859-05-02		A1
1702	HINTON, Joshua A	28	E½SW	1882-10-10		A1
1701	" "	27	SENE	1897-08-05		A4
1713	HINTON, Mary F	27	NENW	1897-08-05		A4
1714	" "	27	NWSE	1897-08-05		A4
1715	" "	27	W½NE	1897-08-05		A4
1733	HINTON, Robert	26	W½NW	1860-07-02		A1
1734	" "	27	NENE	1860-07-02		A1
1742	HINTON, Samuel	1	W½SW	1896-12-14		A4
1743	" "	2	N½SE	1896-12-14		A4
1737	HINTON, Singleton	3	NWSE	1889-04-10		A1 G14
1738	" "	3	SENE	1889-11-21		A1 G14
1746	HINTON, Singleton L	2	NE	1888-04-05		A4
1747	" "	3	NESE	1890-07-03		A1
1759	HINTON, Wiley O	2	NWNW	1908-08-10		A3
1760	" "	3	NENE	1908-08-10		A3
1768	HINTON, William	21	SENE	1841-01-05		A1
1770	" "	21	SWNE	1859-05-02		A1
1771	" "	21	W½SE	1859-05-02		A1
1766	" "	21	N½SW	1860-04-02		A1
1767	" "	21	S½NW	1860-04-02		A1
1769	" "	21	SESW	1860-04-02		A1
1774	HINTON, William R	21	SWSW	1883-04-30		A4
1775	" "	28	W½NW	1883-04-30		A4
1776	" "	29	NENE	1883-04-30		A4
1777	" "	29	SENE	1884-12-30		A1
1778	HINTON, William T	8	NWNE	1915-05-18		A4
1711	HUGGINS, Manlius	27	NWNW	1854-03-15		A1 G56
1712	" "	8	SWNE	1854-03-15		A1 G56
1653	KENNEDY, George M	28	NWSW	1890-07-03		A1
1654	" "	29	SESE	1890-07-03		A1
1711	KIRKLAND, Rebecca	27	NWNW	1854-03-15		A1 G56
1712	" "	8	SWNE	1854-03-15		A1 G56
1554	KITTRELL, Absolom	10	N½NE	1882-12-30		A1
1555	" "	11	N½	1882-12-30		A1
1556	" "	11	N½SE	1882-12-30		A1
1557	" "	11	N½SW	1882-12-30		A1

ID	Individual in Patent	Sec.	Sec. Part	Date Issued	Other Counties	For More Info . . .
1558	KITTRELL, Absolom (Cont'd)	11	SESW	1882-12-30		A1
1559	"	11	SWSE	1882-12-30		A1
1563	" "	12	NWSW	1882-12-30		A1
1565	" "	12	SWNW	1882-12-30		A1
1568	"	13	E½NW	1882-12-30		A1
1569	" "	13	NESW	1882-12-30		A1
1571	" "	13	SESE	1882-12-30		A1
1573	" "	13	SWNE	1882-12-30		A1
1575	" "	13	W½SE	1882-12-30		A1
1579	" "	2	W½SW	1882-12-30		A1
1580	" "	3	SESE	1882-12-30		A1
1551	" "	1	NWSE	1883-09-15		A1
1552	" "	1	SESE	1883-09-15		A1
1553	" "	1	SESW	1883-09-15		A1
1560	" "	12	E½SW	1883-09-15		A1
1561	" "	12	N½SE	1883-09-15		A1
1562	" "	12	NWNW	1883-09-15		A1
1564	" "	12	SENW	1883-09-15		A1
1566	" "	12	SWSW	1883-09-15		A1
1567	" "	12	W½NE	1883-09-15		A1
1570	" "	13	NWSW	1883-09-15		A1
1572	" "	13	SESW	1883-09-15		A1
1574	" "	13	SWNW	1883-09-15		A1
1576	" "	14	E½NE	1883-09-15		A1
1577	" "	2	S½SE	1883-09-15		A1
1578	" "	2	SESW	1883-09-15		A1
1762	MCCALLUM, William A	1	SWSE	1906-06-30		A1
1705	MCCOY, Leonidas S	7	SWSW	1898-03-15		A4
1620	MCDONALD, Charles R	13	E½NE	1898-02-24		A4
1621	" "	13	NESE	1898-02-24		A4
1622	" "	13	NWNE	1898-02-24		A4
1720	MCDONALD, Norman	24	1	1860-04-02		A1
1721	"	24	2	1860-04-02		A1
1722	MCDONALD, Norman W	7	N½NE	1905-02-13		A4
1723	" "	7	NWSE	1905-02-13		A4
1724	" "	7	SWNE	1905-02-13		A4
1772	MCLEMORE, William	31	NWSW	1897-05-07		A4
1773	"	31	W½NW	1897-05-07		A4
1582	MCSWAIN, Albert H	19	SE	1890-02-21		A4
1595	MCSWAIN, Allen	3	W½SW	1859-05-02		A1
1593	" "	10	E½SW	1860-04-02		A1
1594	" "	10	NW	1860-04-02		A1
1597	MCSWAIN, Angus	35	E½SE	1897-11-01		A4
1598	" "	35	SESW	1897-11-01		A4
1599	" "	35	SWSE	1897-11-01		A4
1602	MCSWAIN, Austin	30	E½NE	1891-09-07		A4
1603	" "	30	N½SE	1891-09-07		A4
1630	MCSWAIN, Colin M	30	N½NW	1879-05-06		A4
1631	" "	30	NESW	1879-05-06		A4
1632	" "	30	SENW	1879-05-06		A4
1645	MCSWAIN, Emma R	29	NWNW	1904-11-15		A4
1657	MCSWAIN, Henry C	10	N½SE	1897-02-15		A4
1658	" "	10	S½NE	1897-02-15		A1
1727	MCSWAIN, Peter	10	S½SE	1859-05-02		A1
1728	" "	14	NWNW	1859-05-02		A1
1729	" "	14	W½SW	1859-05-02		A1
1731	MCSWAIN, Robert B	3	E½NW	1893-12-21		A4
1732	" "	3	W½NE	1893-12-21		A4
1748	MCSWAIN, Solomon	35	N½NE	1882-05-20		A4
1749	" "	35	NENW	1882-05-20		A4
1751	" "	36	NWNW	1882-05-20		A4
1750	" "	36	E½NW	1898-01-19		A4
1640	MERRITT, David S	4	N½NW	1891-11-09		A4
1641	" "	5	E½NE	1891-11-09		A4
1685	MERRITT, James P	4	NWSW	1890-12-31		A4
1686	" "	4	S½NW	1890-12-31		A4
1687	" "	5	NESE	1890-12-31		A4
1741	NEWELL, James	20	E½SE	1919-11-18		A1 G22
1691	PATTON, Jeff	29	SESW	1895-08-08		A4
1692	" "	29	SWNW	1895-08-08		A4
1693	" "	29	W½SW	1895-08-08		A4
1709	PHILIPS, Lucy	29	E½NW	1892-06-15		A4
1710	" "	29	W½NE	1892-06-15		A4

ID	Individual in Patent	Sec.	Sec. Part	Date Issued	Other Counties	For More Info . . .
1646	PRYOR, Eran	6	S½NE	1895-06-22		A1 G9
1647	" "	6	W½SE	1895-06-22		A1 G9
1664	SAWYER, Hiram W	30	SESE	1889-05-06		A1
1665	" "	31	E½NE	1889-05-06		A1
1666	" "	31	E½SE	1889-05-06		A1
1667	" "	32	E½	1889-05-06		A1
1668	" "	32	SW	1889-05-06		A1
1669	" "	33	N½SE	1889-05-06		A1
1670	" "	33	NWNE	1889-05-06		A1
1671	" "	33	S½NE	1889-05-06		A1
1672	" "	33	SWSE	1889-05-06		A1
1673	" "	33	W½	1889-05-06		A1
1674	" "	34	NWSW	1889-05-06		A1
1779	SCHILLING, Young M	11	SWSW	1901-03-23		A4
1581	SINGLETON, Ada	7	SWSE	1918-04-11		A4
1704	SMITH, Lee	28	SWSW	1919-01-24		A4
1716	STEAN, Milton	7	NW	1894-12-17		A4
1608	STEVENS, Benjamin	6	S½SW	1882-12-30		A1
1604	" "	5	SWNW	1884-12-30		A1
1606	" "	6	NESE	1884-12-30		A1
1605	" "	6	N½SW	1889-04-20		A1
1607	" "	6	NWNW	1889-04-20		A1
1609	" "	6	SENW	1889-04-20		A1
1610	" "	6	SWNW	1889-04-20		A1
1730	STEVENS, Richard	20	S½NW	1860-04-02		A1
1648	STRONG, Ezekiel	5	S½SW	1890-12-31		A4
1649	" "	5	SWSE	1890-12-31		A4
1650	" "	8	NWNW	1890-12-31		A4
1583	THOMSON, Albert H	14	E½NW	1901-03-23		A4
1584	" "	14	NWNE	1901-03-23		A4
1585	" "	14	SWNW	1901-03-23		A4
1694	WALKER, Joe	12	NENW	1919-05-26		A4
1596	WATSON, Amasa B	6	NENW	1883-09-15		A1
1601	WEST, Austin C	35	SWSW	1918-04-11		A4
1617	WEST, Cesar	31	SENW	1897-06-07		A4
1618	" "	31	SWNE	1897-06-07		A4
1619	" "	31	W½SE	1897-06-07		A4
1717	WEST, Ned	35	N½SW	1896-01-25		A4
1718	" "	35	NWSE	1896-01-25		A4
1719	" "	35	SENW	1896-01-25		A4
1739	WEST, Sam	30	NWSW	1881-08-20		A4
1740	" "	30	SWNW	1881-08-20		A4
1744	WEST, Samuel	35	SENE	1882-10-10		A1
1745	" "	36	SWNW	1882-10-10		A1
1757	WEST, Toney B	35	SWNE	1914-05-06		A4
1700	YATES, John	28	NWSE	1917-10-27		A4

Patent Map

T3-N R10-W
St Stephens Meridian

Map Group 8

Township Statistics

Parcels Mapped	:	230
Number of Patents	:	117
Number of Individuals	:	92
Patentees Identified	:	89
Number of Surnames	:	47
Multi-Patentee Parcels	:	8
Oldest Patent Date	:	1/5/1841
Most Recent Patent	:	11/18/1919
Block/Lot Parcels	:	5
Parcels Re - Issued	:	0
Parcels that Overlap	:	0
Cities and Towns	:	3
Cemeteries	:	4

Section 3
MCSWAIN Robert B 1893
MCSWAIN Robert B 1893
HINTON Wiley O 1908
BRADLEY [14] Rufus P 1889
MCSWAIN Allen 1859
3
BRADLEY [14] Rufus P 1889
HINTON Singleton L 1890
KITTRELL Absolom 1882

Section 2
HINTON Wiley O 1908
DENNIS James T 1892
DENNIS James T 1892
HINTON Singleton L 1888
2
DENNIS James T 1892
HINTON Samuel 1896
KITTRELL Absolom 1883
KITTRELL Absolom 1883

Section 1
CLARK Loyed 1894
CLIFTON Elias 1895
CLIFTON Elias 1895
CLARK Loyed 1894
CLIFTON Elias 1895
COTTON Henry R 1914
HINTON Samuel 1896
CLARK Loyed 1894
KITTRELL Absolom 1883
COTTON Henry R 1914
1
CLARK Loyed 1894
KITTRELL Absolom 1883
MCCALLUM William A 1906
KITTRELL Absolom 1883

Section 10
MCSWAIN Allen 1860
KITTRELL Absolom 1882
MCSWAIN Henry C 1897
10
MCSWAIN Henry C 1897
MCSWAIN Allen 1860
MCSWAIN Peter 1859

Section 11
KITTRELL Absolom 1882
11
KITTRELL Absolom 1882
KITTRELL Absolom 1882
SCHILLING Young M 1901
KITTRELL Absolom 1882
KITTRELL Absolom 1882
HINTON Hardee 1915

Section 12
KITTRELL Absolom 1883
WALKER Joe 1919
KITTRELL Absolom 1883
KITTRELL Absolom 1882
KITTRELL Absolom 1883
KITTRELL Absolom 1882
KITTRELL Absolom 1883
12
KITTRELL Absolom 1883
BOULTON Collin 1907

Section 15
15

Section 14
MCSWAIN Peter 1859
THOMSON Albert H 1901
THOMSON Albert H 1901
THOMSON Albert H 1901
CLIFTON Florence 1915
KITTRELL Absolom 1883
MCSWAIN Peter 1859
14

Section 13
MCDONALD Charles R 1898
MCDONALD Charles R 1898
KITTRELL Absolom 1883
KITTRELL Absolom 1882
KITTRELL Absolom 1882
KITTRELL Absolom 1883
KITTRELL Absolom 1882
13
MCDONALD Charles R 1898
KITTRELL Absolom 1883
KITTRELL Absolom 1882
KITTRELL Absolom 1882

Section 22
22

Section 23
23

Section 24
Lots-Sec. 24
----
1   MCDONALD, Norman   1860
2   MCDONALD, Norman   1860
CARTER John W 1859
24

Section 27
HUGGINS [56] Manlius 1854
HINTON Mary F 1897
HINTON Mary F 1897
HINTON Robert 1860
BOULTON John 1895
27
HINTON Joshua A 1897
BOULTON John 1895
HINTON Mary F 1897
CARPENTER Henry S 1890
GARDNER William A 1918

Section 26
HINTON Robert 1860
CARTER John W 1859
HINTON Joshua 1859
CARTER John W 1859
26
CARTER Alexander 1882
CARTER Alexander 1882
HINTON Allen 1896

Section 25
Lots-Sec. 25
----
2   HINTON, Allen   1896
25

Section 34
HILLS Charles T 1889
CARPENTER Henry S 1884
FREEMAN Perry K 1883
HILLS Charles T 1889
HILLS Charles T 1889
SAWYER Hiram W 1889
34
HILLS Charles T 1889
HILLS Charles T 1889

Section 35
FREEMAN Perry K 1890
MCSWAIN Solomon 1882
MCSWAIN Solomon 1882
WEST Ned 1896
WEST Toney B 1914
WEST Samuel 1882
WEST Ned 1896
35
WEST Ned 1896
WEST Austin C 1918
MCSWAIN Angus 1897
MCSWAIN Angus 1897

Section 36
MCSWAIN Solomon 1882
WEST Samuel 1882
MCSWAIN Solomon 1898
36
HINTON [46] Allen 1904
FREEMAN Walter J 1910

Helpful Hints

1. This Map's INDEX can be found on the preceding pages.

2. Refer to Map "C" to see where this Township lies within Perry County, Mississippi.

3. Numbers within square brackets [ ] denote a multi-patentee land parcel (multi-owner). Refer to Appendix "C" for a full list of members in this group.

4. Areas that look to be crowded with Patentees usually indicate multiple sales of the same parcel (Re-issues) or Overlapping parcels. See this Township's Index for an explanation of these and other circumstances that might explain "odd" groupings of Patentees on this map.

Legend
Patent Boundary
Section Boundary
No Patents Found (or Outside County)
1., 2., 3., ...   Lot Numbers (when beside a name)
[ ]   Group Number (see Appendix "C")

Scale: Section = 1 mile X 1 mile (generally, with some exceptions)

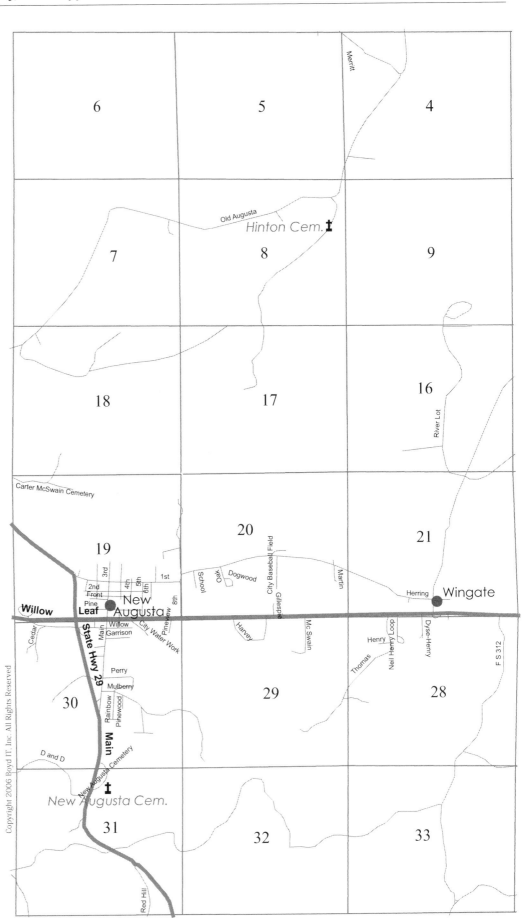

Road Map

T3-N R10-W
St Stephens Meridian

Map Group 8

Cities & Towns
Ferguson
New Augusta
Wingate

Cemeteries
Carter Hill Cemetery
Hinton Cemetery
Hinton Cemetery
New Augusta Cemetery

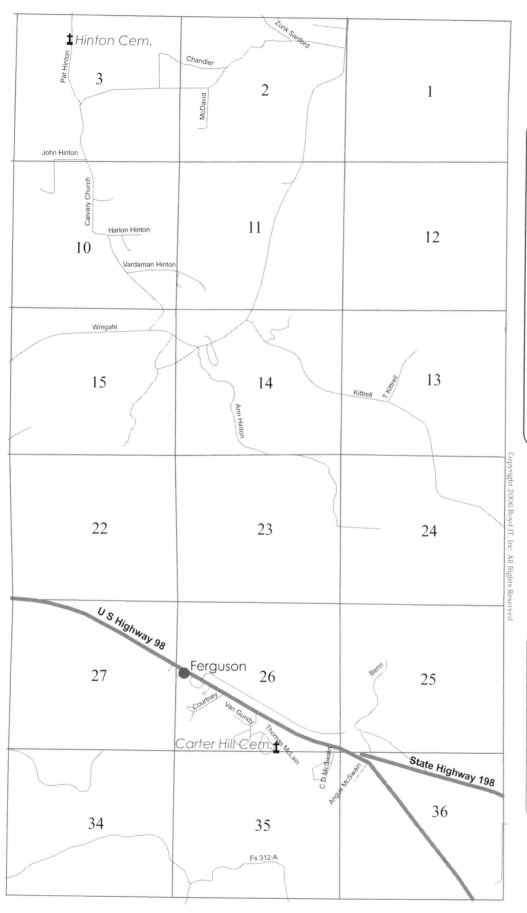

Hinton Cem.

Pat Hinton

3

Zunk Sanford

Chandler

McDavid

2

1

John Hinton

Calvary Church

Harlon Hinton

10

11

12

Vardaman Hinton

Wingate

15

14

Ann Hinton

Kittrell

T Kittrell

13

22

23

24

U S Highway 98

Ferguson

27

26

Benn

25

Courtney

Van Gundy

Thomas McLain

Carter Hill Cem.

C B McSwain

Angus McSwain

State Highway 198

34

35

36

Fs 312-A

Helpful Hints

1. This road map has a number of uses, but primarily it is to help you: a) find the present location of land owned by your ancestors (at least the general area), b) find cemeteries and city-centers, and c) estimate the route/roads used by Census-takers & tax-assessors.

2. If you plan to travel to Perry County to locate cemeteries or land parcels, please pick up a modern travel map for the area before you do. Mapping old land parcels on modern maps is not as exact a science as you might think. Just the slightest variations in public land survey coordinates, estimates of parcel boundaries, or road-map deviations can greatly alter a map's representation of how a road either does or doesn't cross a particular parcel of land.

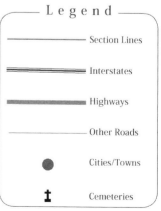

Legend

———	Section Lines
═══	Interstates
▬▬▬	Highways
———	Other Roads
●	Cities/Towns
✝	Cemeteries

Scale: Section = 1 mile X 1 mile
(generally, with some exceptions)

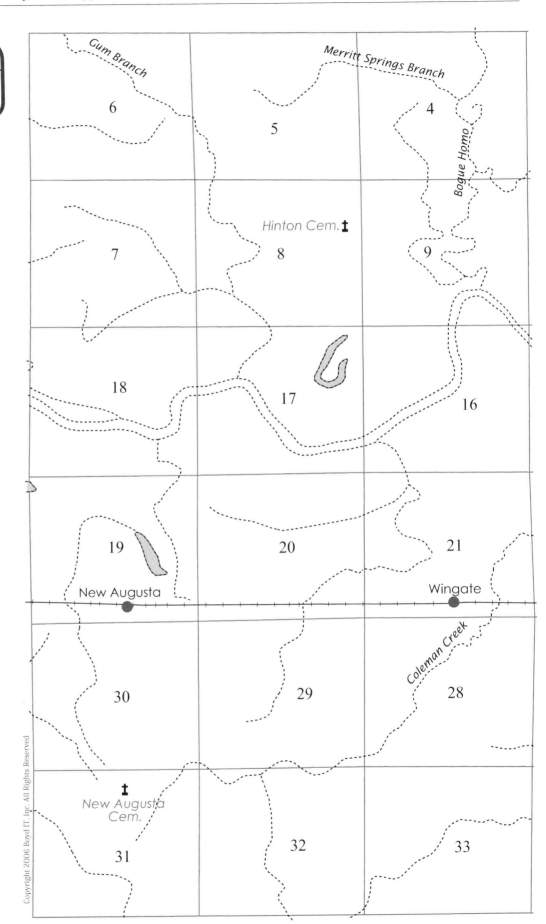

Historical Map

T3-N R10-W
St Stephens Meridian

Map Group 8

Cities & Towns
Ferguson
New Augusta
Wingate

Cemeteries
Carter Hill Cemetery
Hinton Cemetery
Hinton Cemetery
New Augusta Cemetery

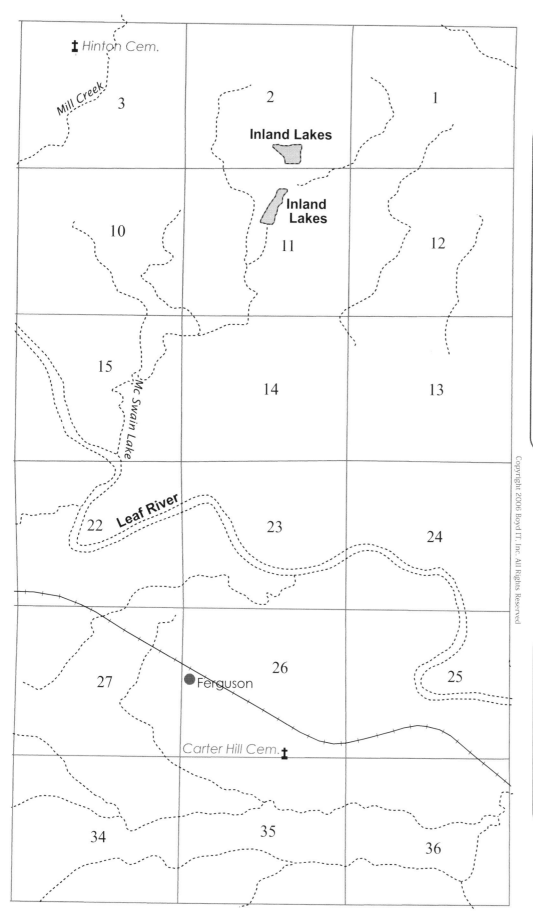

Hinton Cem.

Mill Creek

3

2

Inland Lakes

1

Inland Lakes

10

11

12

15

Mc Swain Lake

14

13

22 **Leaf River**

23

24

27

● Ferguson

26

25

Carter Hill Cem.

34

35

36

Helpful Hints

1. This Map takes a different look at the same Congressional Township displayed in the preceding two maps. It presents features that can help you better envision the historical development of the area: a) Water-bodies (lakes & ponds), b) Water-courses (rivers, streams, etc.), c) Railroads, d) City/town center-points (where they were oftentimes located when first settled), and e) Cemeteries.

2. Using this "Historical" map in tandem with this Township's Patent Map and Road Map, may lead you to some interesting discoveries. You will often find roads, towns, cemeteries, and waterways are named after nearby landowners: sometimes those names will be the ones you are researching. See how many of these research gems you can find here in Perry County.

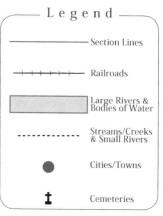

L e g e n d

——————— Section Lines

+++++++ Railroads

▭ Large Rivers & Bodies of Water

- - - - - - Streams/Creeks & Small Rivers

● Cities/Towns

✝ Cemeteries

Scale: Section = 1 mile X 1 mile
(there are some exceptions)

Map Group 9: Index to Land Patents

Township 3-North Range 9-West (St Stephens)

After you locate an individual in this Index, take note of the Section and Section Part then proceed to the Land Patent map on the pages immediately following. You should have no difficulty locating the corresponding parcel of land.

The "For More Info" Column will lead you to more information about the underlying Patents. See the *Legend* at right, and the "How to Use this Book" chapter, for more information.

ID	Individual in Patent	Sec.	Sec. Part	Date Issued	Other Counties	For More Info . . .
1955	ALBRITTON, William H	26	SWNW	1859-05-02		A1
1954	" "	26	NWSW	1859-06-01		A1
1956	" "	26	SWSW	1860-07-02		A1
1853	ANDREWS, Feril	5	SWNE	1906-06-21		A4
1881	BACKSTROM, John F	2	NWSW	1882-12-30		A1
1910	BOULTON, Ras	29	E½3	1910-05-09		A4
1911	" "	29	E½NW	1910-05-09		A4
1855	BRADLEY, George W	11	E½SW	1890-08-16		A4
1856	" "	11	W½SE	1890-08-16		A4
1896	BRADLEY, Margaret	25	SWSW	1879-05-06		A4
1897	" "	26	N½SE	1879-05-06		A4
1898	" "	26	SESE	1879-05-06		A4
1904	BRADLEY, Quincy A	22	E½NW	1860-07-02		A1
1905	" "	22	NE	1860-07-02		A1
1907	" "	23	NWSW	1860-07-02		A1
1908	" "	23	SWNW	1860-07-02		A1
1906	" "	22	NESE	1889-11-29		A1
1924	BRADLEY, Sion	25	NWSW	1859-05-02		A1
1937	BRADLEY, Thomas R	11	E½SE	1905-12-30		A4
1938	" "	11	SENE	1905-12-30		A4
1939	" "	12	SWNW	1905-12-30		A4
1944	BRADLEY, William	32	SW	1898-12-01		A4
1899	BRADLY, Margaret	36	SENW	1859-11-10		A1
1900	" "	36	W½NW	1859-11-10		A1
1925	BRADLY, Sion	25	S½NW	1859-05-02		A1
1926	" "	25	SWNE	1859-05-02		A1
1829	BRELAND, Braxton B	23	N½NW	1901-04-22		A4
1830	" "	23	NWNE	1901-04-22		A4
1831	" "	23	SENW	1901-04-22		A4
1857	BRELAND, George Y	17	N½NE	1894-02-01		A4
1858	" "	17	SWNE	1894-02-01		A4
1859	" "	8	SESE	1894-02-01		A4
1866	BRELAND, Isham H C	21	NESE	1916-06-10		A4
1867	" "	21	S½NE	1916-06-10		A4
1868	" "	22	SWNW	1916-06-10		A4
1887	BYRD, Joseph C	24	SE	1913-05-08		A4
1901	BYRD, Melton S	12	W½SW	1921-08-30		A4
1915	CLARK, Samuel	12	E½SW	1905-03-30		A4
1791	COMPANY, Albert C Danner And	11	NWSW	1882-12-30		A1
1792	" "	11	SWNW	1882-12-30		A1
1913	COX, Robert H	1	SW	1917-08-11		A4
1797	DEVENPORT, Alice	27	NENW	1904-09-28		A4 G28
1798	" "	27	NWNE	1904-09-28		A4 G28
1797	DEVENPORT, William	27	NENW	1904-09-28		A4 G28
1798	" "	27	NWNE	1904-09-28		A4 G28
1888	ELLIOTT, Joshua	36	E½NE	1859-05-02		A1

ID	Individual in Patent	Sec.	Sec. Part	Date Issued	Other Counties	For More Info . . .
1889	ELLIOTT, Joshua (Cont'd)	36	NESE	1859-05-02		A1
1912	FOWLER, Rebecca	36	SW	1859-06-01		A1
1865	FREEMAN, Hughie J	31	SW	1892-05-16		A4
1885	FREEMAN, John W	31	6	1906-06-21		A4
1886	"	31	7	1906-06-21		A4
1909	GILMER, R H	34		1914-06-15		A1 F
1960	HARRIS, William	22	SWSE	1910-04-11		A4
1947	HARVISON, William D	13	NWSW	1911-01-05		A4
1948	" "	13	S½SW	1911-01-05		A4
1949	" "	13	SWSE	1911-01-05		A4
1917	HERRING, Samuel	31	1	1859-05-02		A1
1918	" "	31	2	1859-05-02		A1
1919	" "	31	S½3	1859-05-02		A1
1796	HINTON, Alex	22	SWSW	1905-02-13		A4 G45
1836	HINTON, Colonel C	2	NW	1905-03-30		A4
1837	HINTON, Dan	11	SWNE	1910-03-17		A4
1845	HINTON, Dekalb	7	E½NE	1897-04-02		A4
1846	" "	8	W½NW	1897-04-02		A4
1851	HINTON, Effie	4	NESE	1911-07-20		A4 G48
1796	HINTON, Hannah	22	SWSW	1905-02-13		A4 G45
1869	HINTON, James	1	NENW	1888-04-05		A4
1870	" "	1	S½NW	1888-04-05		A4
1871	" "	2	SENE	1888-04-05		A4
1874	HINTON, Jepthah P	5	N½NW	1889-01-05		A4
1875	" "	5	NWNE	1889-01-05		A4
1876	HINTON, Jimmie	2	SWSE	1916-07-25		A4
1902	HINTON, Nathaniel	11	NWNW	1919-06-26		A4
1903	HINTON, Pompey	4	W½SE	1893-10-19		A4
1920	HINTON, Sandy	12	NWNW	1920-03-02		A4
1842	HOLLINGSWORTH, David P	36	NWSE	1859-11-10		A1
1843	" "	36	W½NE	1860-07-02		A1
1921	HOLLINGSWORTH, Seborn W	25	N½SE	1859-11-10		A1
1844	HOLLINSWORTH, David P	36	S½SE	1859-05-02		A1
1922	HOLLINSWORTH, Seborn W	25	E½SW	1859-05-02		A1
1923	" "	25	SWSE	1859-05-02		A1
1941	HUFF, Viola Lawrence	13	W½NW	1920-03-04		A4
1942	" "	14	E½NE	1920-03-04		A4
1892	HUGGINS, Manlius	22	NWSW	1854-03-15		A1 G55
1893	" "	22	SESW	1854-03-15		A1 G55
1895	" "	23	SENE	1854-03-15		A1 G56
1894	" "	4	SESE	1854-03-15		A1 G55
1793	JORDAN, Albert C	26	NESW	1905-12-30		A4
1794	" "	26	SENW	1905-12-30		A4
1795	" "	26	W½NE	1905-12-30		A4
1861	JORDAN, Henry	26	SENE	1912-04-18		A4
1877	JORDAN, John A	17	N½SE	1915-09-03		A4
1878	" "	17	SWSE	1915-09-03		A4
1961	JORDAN, William J	23	SE	1889-12-19		A4
1892	KIRKLAND, Philemon	22	NWSW	1854-03-15		A1 G55
1893	" "	22	SESW	1854-03-15		A1 G55
1894	" "	4	SESE	1854-03-15		A1 G55
1892	KIRKLAND, Rebecca	22	NWSW	1854-03-15		A1 G55
1893	" "	22	SESW	1854-03-15		A1 G55
1895	" "	23	SENE	1854-03-15		A1 G56
1894	" "	4	SESE	1854-03-15		A1 G55
1783	KITTRELL, Abaslom	12	E½NW	1882-05-10		A1
1784	" "	12	W½SE	1882-05-10		A1
1785	KITTRELL, Absolom	12	E½SE	1882-12-30		A1
1786	" "	19	NENW	1882-12-30		A1
1787	" "	19	NWSE	1882-12-30		A1
1788	" "	19	W½NE	1882-12-30		A1
1789	" "	23	NENE	1884-12-30		A1
1790	" "	26	NENE	1884-12-30		A1
1963	KITTRELL, William R	28	S½5	1901-11-16		A4
1964	" "	29	7	1901-11-16		A4
1965	" "	29	N½6	1901-11-16		A4
1972	LAURWENCE, Willson	23	SWNE	1902-02-12		A4
1973	LAWRENCE, Wilson W	23	NESW	1910-07-05		A4
1872	LEE, James N	36	NENW	1912-09-16		A4
1834	LOTT, Calvin T	23	S½SW	1901-04-22		A4
1835	" "	26	N½NW	1901-04-22		A4
1841	LOTT, Darling	27	S½	1859-05-02		A1 F
1946	LOTT, William C	22	SESE	1882-05-10		A1

ID	Individual in Patent	Sec.	Sec. Part	Date Issued	Other Counties	For More Info . . .
1945	LOTT, William C (Cont'd)	22	NWSE	1882-12-30		A1
1968	LOTT, William R	27	S½NE	1860-04-02		A1
1969	" "	27	S½NW	1860-04-02		A1
1966	" "	27	NENE	1860-07-02		A1
1967	" "	27	NWNW	1860-07-02		A1
1970	" "	28	1	1860-07-02		A1
1971	" "	28	2	1860-07-02		A1
1780	MCDONALD, Aaron	17	SWSW	1902-01-17		A4
1781	" "	20	N½NW	1902-01-17		A4
1782	" "	20	NWNE	1902-01-17		A4
1838	MCDONALD, Daniel	28	N½SW	1892-07-20		A4 G61
1839	" "	28	W½NW	1892-07-20		A4 G61
1851	MCDONALD, Effie	4	NESE	1911-07-20		A4 G48
1838	MCDONALD, Eliza	28	N½SW	1892-07-20		A4 G61
1839	" "	28	W½NW	1892-07-20		A4 G61
1854	MCDONALD, George P	19	SENW	1895-06-27		A4
1864	MCDONALD, Hugh	21	W½NW	1906-08-10		A4
1882	MCDONALD, John	19	E½SW	1859-05-02		A1
1883	" "	19	NWSW	1860-04-02		A1
1884	" "	19	SWSE	1860-04-02		A1
1916	MCDONALD, Samuel H	20	SENW	1910-09-06		A4
1957	MCDONALD, William H	19	E½NE	1888-04-05		A4
1958	" "	19	NESE	1888-04-05		A4
1959	" "	20	SWNW	1888-04-05		A4
1962	MCDONALD, William O	29	NE	1891-06-30		A4
1953	MCKENZIE, William D	28	E½	1859-05-02		A1 F
1950	" "	28	6	1860-04-02		A1
1951	" "	28	7	1860-04-02		A1
1952	" "	28	8	1860-04-02		A1
1914	MERRETT, Robert	17	E½SW	1860-07-02		A1
1840	MERRITT, Daniel	20	S½	1860-04-02		A1
1847	MERRITT, Edmon	13	E½SE	1859-11-10		A1
1848	" "	13	NWSE	1859-11-10		A1
1849	" "	13	SENW	1859-11-10		A1
1850	MERRITT, Edmond	13	NE	1859-05-02		A1
1852	MOORE, Ella	1	NWNW	1919-05-26		A4
1890	PRENTISS, Lizzie	21	N½NE	1916-09-23		A4
1891	" "	22	NWNW	1916-09-23		A4
1927	RICH, Stirling B	1	SE	1882-08-03		A1
1928	" "	12	NE	1882-08-03		A1
1930	" "	14	W½	1882-08-03		A1
1933	" "	15	E½SE	1882-08-03		A1
1934	" "	15	E½SW	1882-08-03		A1
1935	" "	15	N½	1882-08-03		A1
1936	" "	15	W½SE	1882-08-03		A1
1929	" "	14	NESE	1882-10-10		A1
1931	" "	14	W½NE	1882-10-10		A1
1932	" "	14	W½SE	1882-10-10		A1
1860	SOWELL, Hardee	14	SESE	1882-04-20		A1
1826	STAFFORD, Auston	17	SESE	1902-01-17		A4
1827	" "	20	NENE	1902-01-17		A4
1828	" "	20	S½NE	1902-01-17		A4
1832	SYLVESTER, Calvin	25	N½NW	1906-05-01		A4
1833	" "	25	NWNE	1906-05-01		A4
1879	SYLVESTER, John A	26	SESW	1859-11-10		A1
1880	" "	26	SWSE	1859-11-10		A1
1943	SYLVESTER, Wiley	25	SENE	1913-02-10		A4
1862	TANNER, Horrace	30	2	1914-12-03		A4
1863	" "	30	W½1	1914-12-03		A4
1799	WATSON, Amasa B	1	NE	1882-10-10		A1
1800	" "	10		1882-10-10		A1
1801	" "	15	W½SW	1882-10-10		A1
1802	" "	17	NW	1882-10-10		A1
1803	" "	17	NWSW	1882-10-10		A1
1804	" "	17	SENE	1882-10-10		A1
1805	" "	18		1882-10-10		A1
1806	" "	2	S½SW	1882-10-10		A1
1807	" "	24	W½	1882-10-10		A1
1808	" "	3	SE	1882-10-10		A1
1809	" "	3	SENE	1882-10-10		A1
1810	" "	3	W½	1882-10-10		A1
1811	" "	3	W½NE	1882-10-10		A1
1812	" "	4	E½SW	1882-10-10		A1

ID	Individual in Patent	Sec.	Sec. Part	Date Issued	Other Counties	For More Info . . .
1813	WATSON, Amasa B (Cont'd)	4	NE	1882-10-10		A1
1814	" "	5	E½SE	1882-10-10		A1
1815	" "	5	S½NW	1882-10-10		A1
1816	" "	5	SW	1882-10-10		A1
1817	" "	6		1882-10-10		A1
1818	" "	7	SE	1882-10-10		A1
1819	" "	7	W½	1882-10-10		A1
1820	" "	7	W½NE	1882-10-10		A1
1821	" "	8	E½NW	1882-10-10		A1
1822	" "	8	NESE	1882-10-10		A1
1823	" "	8	W½SE	1882-10-10		A1
1824	" "	8	W½SW	1882-10-10		A1
1825	" "	9		1882-10-10		A1
1940	WHITE, Thomas	3	NENE	1882-05-10		A1
1873	WHITTINGTON, James W	33	SWNE	1906-10-15		A4

Patent Map

T3-N R9-W
St Stephens Meridian

Map Group 9

Township Statistics

Parcels Mapped	:	194
Number of Patents	:	111
Number of Individuals	:	91
Patentees Identified	:	86
Number of Surnames	:	45
Multi-Patentee Parcels	:	10
Oldest Patent Date	:	3/15/1854
Most Recent Patent	:	8/30/1921
Block/Lot Parcels	:	16
Parcels Re - Issued	:	0
Parcels that Overlap	:	0
Cities and Towns	:	3
Cemeteries	:	4

Copyright 2006 Boyd IT. Inc. All Rights Reserved

Section 6:
WATSON Amasa B 1882

Section 5:
HINTON Jepthah P 1889
HINTON Jepthah P 1889
WATSON Amasa B 1882
ANDREWS Feril 1906
WATSON Amasa B 1882
WATSON Amasa B 1882

Section 4:
WATSON Amasa B 1882
HINTON Pompey 1893
HINTON [48] Effie 1911
WATSON Amasa B 1882
HUGGINS [55] Manlius 1854

Section 7:
WATSON Amasa B 1882
WATSON Amasa B 1882
HINTON Dekalb 1897
WATSON Amasa B 1882

Section 8:
HINTON Dekalb 1897
WATSON Amasa B 1882
WATSON Amasa B 1882
WATSON Amasa B 1882
WATSON Amasa B 1882
BRELAND George Y 1894

Section 9:
WATSON Amasa B 1882

Section 18:
WATSON Amasa B 1882

Section 17:
WATSON Amasa B 1882
BRELAND George Y 1894
BRELAND George Y 1894
WATSON Amasa B 1882
WATSON Amasa B 1882
JORDAN John A 1915
MCDONALD Aaron 1902
MERRETT Robert 1860
JORDAN John A 1915
STAFFORD Auston 1902

Section 16

Section 19:
KITTRELL Absolom 1882
KITTRELL Absolom 1882
MCDONALD William H 1888
MCDONALD George P 1895
MCDONALD John 1860
KITTRELL Absolom 1882
MCDONALD William H 1888
MCDONALD John 1859
MCDONALD John 1860

Section 20:
MCDONALD Aaron 1902
MCDONALD Aaron 1902
STAFFORD Auston 1902
MCDONALD William H 1888
MCDONALD Samuel H 1910
STAFFORD Auston 1902
MERRITT Daniel 1860

Section 21:
MCDONALD Hugh 1906
PRENTISS Lizzie 1916
BRELAND Isham H C 1916
BRELAND Isham H C 1916

Section 30:
Lots-Sec. 30
----
2 TANNER, Horrace 1914
2 TANNER, Horrace 1914

Section 29:
BOULTON Ras 1910
MCDONALD William O 1891
Lots-Sec. 29
----
7 KITTRELL, William R 1901
7 BOULTON, Ras 1910
7 KITTRELL, William R 1901

Section 28:
MCDONALD [61] Daniel 1892
Lots-Sec. 28
----
1 LOTT, William R 1860
2 LOTT, William R 1860
6 MCKENZIE, William D 1860
7 MCKENZIE, William D 1860
8 MCKENZIE, William D 1860
8 KITTRELL, William R 1901
MCDONALD [61] Daniel 1892
MCKENZIE William D 1859

Section 31:
Lots-Sec. 31
----
1 HERRING, Samuel 1859
2 HERRING, Samuel 1859
6 FREEMAN, John W 1906
7 HERRING, Samuel 1859
7 FREEMAN, John W 1906
FREEMAN Hughie J 1892

Section 32:
BRADLEY William 1898

Section 33:
WHITTINGTON James W 1906

WATSON
Amasa B
1882

WATSON
Amasa B
1882

WHITE
Thomas
1882

WATSON
Amasa B
1882

3

HINTON
Colonel C
1905

MOORE
Ella
1919

HINTON
James
1888

HINTON
James
1888

HINTON
James
1888

WATSON
Amasa B
1882

1

BACKSTROM
John F
1882

2

WATSON
Amasa B
1882

HINTON
Jimmie
1916

COX
Robert H
1917

RICH
Stirling B
1882

HINTON
Nathaniel
1919

HINTON
Sandy
1920

WATSON
Amasa B
1882

COMPANY
Albert C Danner And
1882

HINTON
Dan
1910

BRADLEY
Thomas R
1905

KITTRELL
Abaslom
1882

RICH
Stirling B
1882

10

COMPANY
Albert C Danner And
1882

11

BRADLEY
George W
1890

BYRD
Melton S
1921

12

KITTRELL
Abaslom
1882

BRADLEY
George W
1890

BRADLEY
Thomas R
1905

CLARK
Samuel
1905

KITTRELL
Absolom
1882

RICH
Stirling B
1882

RICH
Stirling B
1882

HUFF
Viola Lawrence
1920

HUFF
Viola Lawrence
1920

MERRITT
Edmond
1859

15

14

MERRITT
Edmon
1859

13

WATSON
Amasa B
1882

RICH
Stirling B
1882

RICH
Stirling B
1882

RICH
Stirling B
1882

RICH
Stirling B
1882

HARVISON
William D
1911

MERRITT
Edmon
1859

RICH
Stirling B
1882

RICH
Stirling B
1882

SOWELL
Hardee
1882

HARVISON
William D
1911

HARVISON
William D
1911

MERRITT
Edmon
1859

PRENTISS
Lizzie
1916

BRADLEY
Quincy A
1860

BRELAND
Braxton B
1901

BRELAND
Braxton B
1901

KITTRELL
Absolom
1884

24

BRELAND
Isham H C
1916

BRADLEY
Quincy A
1860

22

BRADLEY
Quincy A
1860

BRELAND
Braxton B
1901

LAURWENCE
Willson
1902

HUGGINS [56]
Manlius
1854

WATSON
Amasa B
1882

HUGGINS [55]
Manlius
1854

LOTT
William C
1882

BRADLEY
Quincy A
1889

BRADLEY
Quincy A
1860

LAWRENCE
Wilson W
1910

23

BYRD
Joseph C
1913

HINTON [45]
Alex
1905

HUGGINS [55]
Manlius
1854

HARRIS
William
1910

LOTT
William C
1882

LOTT
Calvin T
1901

JORDAN
William J
1889

LOTT
William R
1860

DEVENPORT [28]
Alice
1904

DEVENPORT [28]
Alice
1904

LOTT
William R
1860

LOTT
Calvin T
1901

JORDAN
Albert C
1905

KITTRELL
Absolom
1884

SYLVESTER
Calvin
1906

SYLVESTER
Calvin
1906

LOTT
William R
1860

LOTT
William R
1860

ALBRITTON
William H
1859

JORDAN
Albert C
1905

26

JORDAN
Henry
1912

BRADLY
Sion
1859

BRADLY
Sion
1859

25

SYLVESTER
Wiley
1913

27

ALBRITTON
William H
1859

JORDAN
Albert C
1905

BRADLEY
Margaret
1879

BRADLEY
Sion
1859

HOLLINGSWORTH
Seborn W
1859

LOTT
Darling
1859

ALBRITTON
William H
1860

SYLVESTER
John A
1859

SYLVESTER
John A
1859

BRADLEY
Margaret
1879

BRADLEY
Margaret
1879

HOLLINSWORTH
Seborn W
1859

HOLLINSWORTH
Seborn W
1859

GILMER
R H
1914

34

35

BRADLY
Margaret
1859

LEE
James N
1912

HOLLINGSWORTH
David P
1860

BRADLY
Margaret
1859

36

ELLIOTT
Joshua
1859

HOLLINGSWORTH
David P
1859

ELLIOTT
Joshua
1859

FOWLER
Rebecca
1859

HOLLINSWORTH
David P
1859

Helpful Hints

1. This Map's INDEX can be found on the preceding pages.

2. Refer to Map "C" to see where this Township lies within Perry County, Mississippi.

3. Numbers within square brackets [ ] denote a multi-patentee land parcel (multi-owner). Refer to Appendix "C" for a full list of members in this group.

4. Areas that look to be crowded with Patentees usually indicate multiple sales of the same parcel (Re-issues) or Overlapping parcels. See this Township's Index for an explanation of these and other circumstances that might explain "odd" groupings of Patentees on this map.

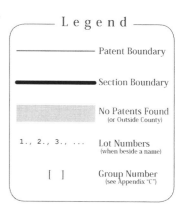

Legend

——————— Patent Boundary

━━━━━━━ Section Boundary

No Patents Found
(or Outside County)

1., 2., 3., ... Lot Numbers
(when beside a name)

[ ] Group Number
(see Appendix "C")

Scale: Section = 1 mile X 1 mile
(generally, with some exceptions)

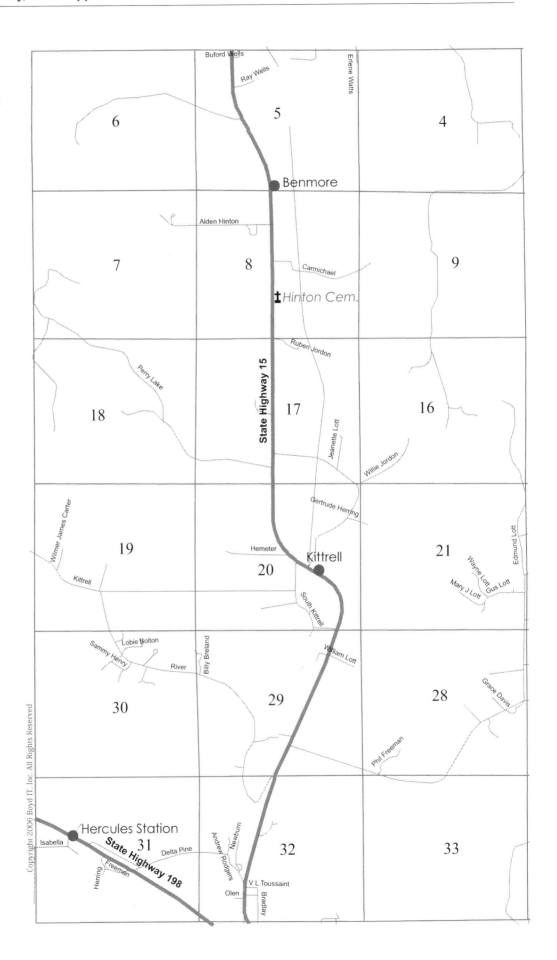

Road Map

T3-N R9-W
St Stephens Meridian

Map Group 9

Cities & Towns
Benmore
Hercules Station
Kittrell

Cemeteries
Hinton Cemetery
Lott Cemetery
Sylvester Cemetery
Sylvester Cemetery

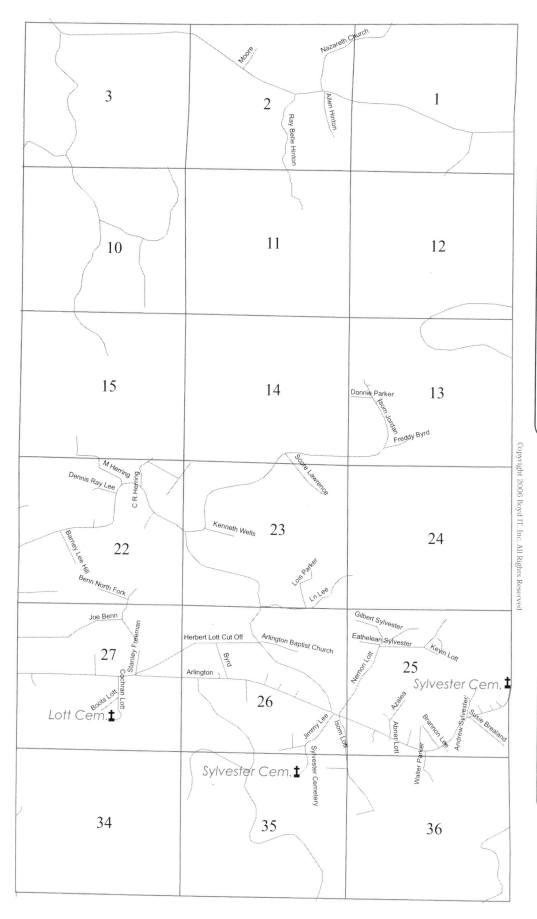

3

2

1

Moore

Nazareth Church

Allen Hinton

Ray Belle Hinton

10

11

12

15

14

13

Donnie Parker

Isom Jordan

Freddy Byrd

M Herring

Dennis Ray Lee

C R Herring

Score Lawrence

Kenneth Wells

22

23

24

Barney Lee Hill

Benn North Fork

Lois Parker

Ln Lee

Joe Benn

Stanley Freeman

Gilbert Sylvester

Eathelean Sylvester

Kevin Lott

27

Herbert Lott Cut Off

Byrd

Arlington Baptist Church

Nemon Lott

25

Arlington

26

Sylvester Cem.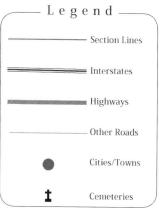

Cochran Lott

Boots Lott

Jimmy Lee

Isom Lott

Azalea

Abner Lott

Brannon Lee

Andrew Sylvester

Susie Brealand

Lott Cem.

Sylvester Cem.

Sylvester Cemetery

Walter Parker

34

35

36

Helpful Hints

1. This road map has a number of uses, but primarily it is to help you: a) find the present location of land owned by your ancestors (at least the general area), b) find cemeteries and city-centers, and c) estimate the route/roads used by Census-takers & tax-assessors.

2. If you plan to travel to Perry County to locate cemeteries or land parcels, please pick up a modern travel map for the area before you do. Mapping old land parcels on modern maps is not as exact a science as you might think. Just the slightest variations in public land survey coordinates, estimates of parcel boundaries, or road-map deviations can greatly alter a map's representation of how a road either does or doesn't cross a particular parcel of land.

Legend

———— Section Lines

═══════ Interstates

▬▬▬▬▬ Highways

———— Other Roads

● Cities/Towns

✝ Cemeteries

Scale: Section = 1 mile X 1 mile
(generally, with some exceptions)

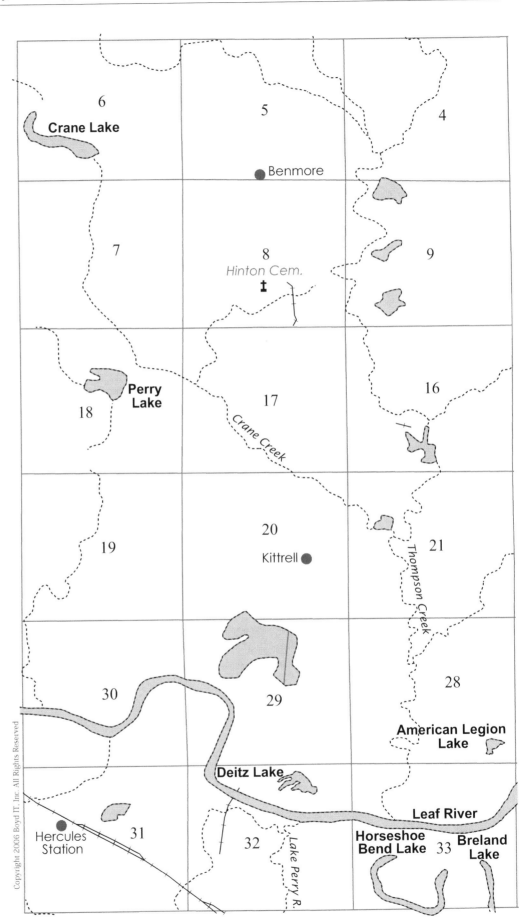

Historical Map

T3-N R9-W
St Stephens Meridian

Map Group 9

Cities & Towns
Benmore
Hercules Station
Kittrell

Cemeteries
Hinton Cemetery
Lott Cemetery
Sylvester Cemetery
Sylvester Cemetery

6

Crane Lake

5

4

● Benmore

7

8

Hinton Cem.

9

18

Perry
Lake

17

Crane Creek

16

19

20

Kittrell ●

21

Thompson Creek

30

29

28

American Legion
Lake

Deitz Lake

Leaf River

Hercules
Station

31

32

Lake Perry R.

Horseshoe
Bend Lake

33

Breland
Lake

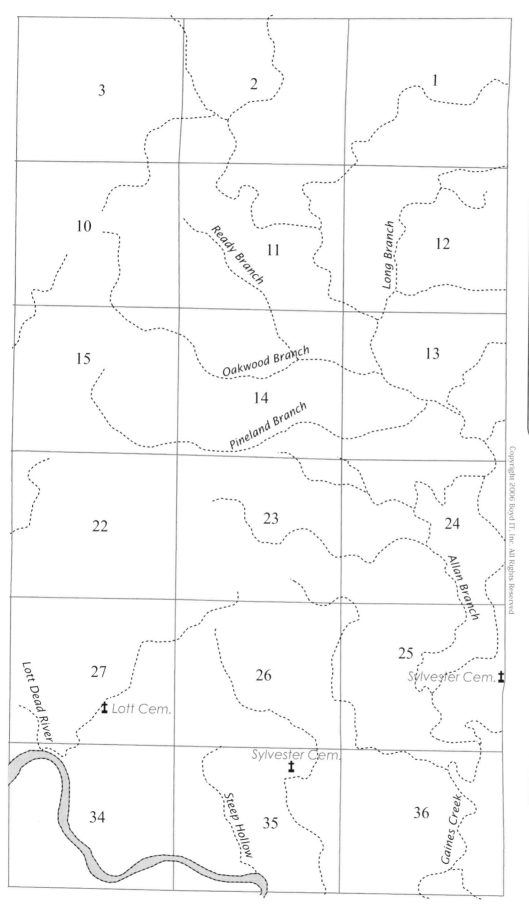

3
2
1
10
11
12
Ready Branch
Long Branch
15
14
13
Oakwood Branch
Pineland Branch
22
23
24
Allan Branch
27
26
25
Lott Dead River
Lott Cem.
Sylvester Cem.
34
35
36
Sylvester Cem.
Steep Hollow
Gaines Creek

Helpful Hints

1. This Map takes a different look at the same Congressional Township displayed in the preceding two maps. It presents features that can help you better envision the historical development of the area: a) Water-bodies (lakes & ponds), b) Water-courses (rivers, streams, etc.), c) Railroads, d) City/town center-points (where they were oftentimes located when first settled), and e) Cemeteries.

2. Using this "Historical" map in tandem with this Township's Patent Map and Road Map, may lead you to some interesting discoveries. You will often find roads, towns, cemeteries, and waterways are named after nearby landowners: sometimes those names will be the ones you are researching. See how many of these research gems you can find here in Perry County.

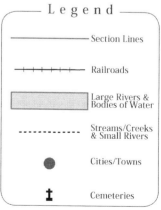

Legend

- Section Lines
- Railroads
- Large Rivers & Bodies of Water
- Streams/Creeks & Small Rivers
- Cities/Towns
- Cemeteries

Scale: Section = 1 mile X 1 mile
(there are some exceptions)

Map Group 10: Index to Land Patents

Township 2-North Range 11-West (St Stephens)

After you locate an individual in this Index, take note of the Section and Section Part then proceed to the Land Patent map on the pages immediately following. You should have no difficulty locating the corresponding parcel of land.

The "For More Info" Column will lead you to more information about the underlying Patents. See the *Legend* at right, and the "How to Use this Book" chapter, for more information.

ID	Individual in Patent	Sec.	Sec. Part	Date Issued	Other Counties	For More Info . . .
2184	ALEXANDER, Nelson	5	NWNW	1906-01-30		A4
2151	CARTER, George	12	SW	1895-10-09		A4
2159	CARTER, Jack	5	E½NW	1906-06-16		A4
2160	" "	5	NWSW	1906-06-16		A4
2161	" "	5	SWNW	1906-06-16		A4
2188	CARTER, Peter H	4	SWNW	1910-03-17		A4
2189	" "	4	W½SW	1910-03-17		A4
2190	CARTER, Sam	1	N½NW	1897-02-15		A4
2191	" "	1	W½NE	1897-02-15		A4
2185	DENHAM, Nelson	12	SENW	1892-05-31		A4
2186	" "	12	SWNE	1892-05-31		A4
2187	" "	12	W½NW	1892-05-31		A4
2162	DURDEN, Jefferson F	7	S½SE	1916-11-28		A4
2163	" "	7	S½SW	1916-11-28		A4
2183	FILLINGAME, Moses	17	NE	1901-06-08		A4
2193	GARAWAY, Solomon T	35	SWNW	1854-03-15		A1
2194	"	35	SWSW	1859-05-02		A1 R2110
2164	GRIFFIN, John A	32	SWSW	1854-03-15		A1
2197	GRIFFIN, Washington	31	SWNE	1854-03-15		A1
2198	GRIFFIN, William E	31	SWSW	1884-12-30		A1 G43
2199	" "	33	S½SE	1884-12-30		A1 G43
2200	" "	34	SWSW	1884-12-30		A1 G43
2201	MARTIN, William I	34	NWSE	1910-03-17		A4
2202	" "	34	S½SE	1910-03-17		A4
2195	MISSISSIPPI, State Of	34	SENE	1911-01-23		A6
2196	" "	35	NWNW	1911-01-23		A6
1974	MIXON, Asa A	1	N½SE	1890-06-25		A4
1975	" "	1	NESW	1890-06-25		A4
1976	" "	1	SENW	1890-06-25		A4
1983	MIXON, Cornelius L	1	S½SE	1885-06-12		A4
1984	" "	1	SESW	1885-06-12		A4
1985	" "	12	NENE	1885-06-12		A4
2152	MIXON, George	19	NESE	1892-05-31		A4
2153	" "	19	SENE	1892-05-31		A4
2154	" "	20	NWSW	1892-05-31		A4
2155	" "	20	SWNW	1892-05-31		A4
2175	MONTAGUE, Luke S	29	N½	1889-11-29		A1
2176	" "	29	SESE	1889-11-29		A1
2178	" "	29	SWSW	1889-11-29		A1
2181	" "	33	N½NW	1889-11-29		A1
2182	" "	33	SWNW	1889-11-29		A1
2174	" "	27	SWNW	1890-07-03		A1
2177	" "	29	SESW	1890-07-03		A1
2179	" "	31	SESW	1890-07-03		A1
2180	" "	31	SWNW	1890-07-03		A1
2156	NEAL, Green L	24	E½SW	1906-05-01		A1

ID	Individual in Patent	Sec.	Sec. Part	Date Issued	Other Counties	For More Info . . .
2157	NEAL, Green L (Cont'd)	25	NENW	1906-05-01		A1
2158	" "	25	NWNE	1906-05-01		A1
2165	PEARCE, John C	14	NWSW	1882-05-10		A1
2166	" "	14	S½SE	1890-06-25		A4
2167	" "	14	S½SW	1890-06-25		A4
2168	PEARCE, John T	14	E½NE	1898-11-11		A4
2169	" "	14	NESE	1898-11-11		A4
2170	" "	14	SWNE	1898-11-11		A4
2198	PERKINS, Benjamin F	31	SWSW	1884-12-30		A1 G43
2199	" "	33	S½SE	1884-12-30		A1 G43
2200	" "	34	SWSW	1884-12-30		A1 G43
1986	RANSDELL, Daniel M	1	NWSW	1884-12-30		A1
1987	" "	1	SWSW	1884-12-30		A1
1988	" "	10	N½SW	1884-12-30		A1
1989	" "	10	NE	1884-12-30		A1
1990	" "	10	NW	1884-12-30		A1
1991	" "	10	NWSE	1884-12-30		A1
1992	" "	10	SESE	1884-12-30		A1
1993	" "	10	SWSW	1884-12-30		A1
1994	" "	11	N½SE	1884-12-30		A1
1995	" "	11	NWNW	1884-12-30		A1
1996	" "	11	S½NW	1884-12-30		A1
1997	" "	11	SW	1884-12-30		A1
1998	" "	12	NENW	1884-12-30		A1
1999	" "	13	N½SW	1884-12-30		A1
2000	" "	13	NWNW	1884-12-30		A1
2001	" "	13	S½SW	1884-12-30		A1
2002	" "	13	SWNW	1884-12-30		A1
2003	" "	13	SWSE	1884-12-30		A1
2004	" "	14	N½NW	1884-12-30		A1
2005	" "	14	NESW	1884-12-30		A1
2006	" "	14	S½NW	1884-12-30		A1
2007	" "	15	NENE	1884-12-30		A1
2008	" "	15	NWNW	1884-12-30		A1
2009	" "	15	NWSW	1884-12-30		A1
2010	" "	15	S½SW	1884-12-30		A1
2011	" "	15	SE	1884-12-30		A1
2012	" "	15	SENE	1884-12-30		A1
2013	" "	15	SWNW	1884-12-30		A1
2014	" "	17	N½NW	1884-12-30		A1
2015	" "	17	NWSW	1884-12-30		A1
2016	" "	17	SWNW	1884-12-30		A1
2017	" "	18	E½NW	1884-12-30		A1
2018	" "	18	N½SW	1884-12-30		A1
2019	" "	18	NE	1884-12-30		A1
2020	" "	18	SE	1884-12-30		A1
2021	" "	18	SWNW	1884-12-30		A1
2022	" "	18	SWSW	1884-12-30		A1
2023	" "	19	NENE	1884-12-30		A1
2024	" "	19	SENW	1884-12-30		A1
2025	" "	19	SESE	1884-12-30		A1
2026	" "	19	SW	1884-12-30		A1
2027	" "	19	SWNE	1884-12-30		A1
2028	" "	19	W½SE	1884-12-30		A1
2029	" "	2	N½	1884-12-30		A1
2030	" "	2	N½SE	1884-12-30		A1
2031	" "	2	N½SW	1884-12-30		A1
2032	" "	2	S½SE	1884-12-30		A1
2033	" "	2	S½SW	1884-12-30		A1
2034	" "	20	N½NW	1884-12-30		A1
2035	" "	20	NENE	1884-12-30		A1
2036	" "	20	SENW	1884-12-30		A1
2037	" "	20	SESE	1884-12-30		A1
2038	" "	20	SWSW	1884-12-30		A1
2039	" "	21	N½SE	1884-12-30		A1
2040	" "	21	NE	1884-12-30		A1
2041	" "	21	NWNW	1884-12-30		A1
2042	" "	21	S½NW	1884-12-30		A1
2043	" "	21	SW	1884-12-30		A1
2044	" "	21	SWSE	1884-12-30		A1
2045	" "	22	N½NE	1884-12-30		A1
2046	" "	22	N½NW	1884-12-30		A1
2047	" "	22	NWSW	1884-12-30		A1

ID	Individual in Patent	Sec.	Sec. Part	Date Issued	Other Counties	For More Info . . .
2048	RANSDELL, Daniel M (Cont'd)	22	SENE	1884-12-30		A1
2049	" "	22	SENW	1884-12-30		A1
2050	" "	22	SESW	1884-12-30		A1
2062	" "	26		1884-12-30		A1
2063	" "	27	E½SW	1884-12-30		A1
2064	" "	27	N½NW	1884-12-30		A1
2065	" "	27	NE	1884-12-30		A1
2067	" "	27	SENW	1884-12-30		A1
2068	" "	27	W½SW	1884-12-30		A1
2069	" "	28	E½SW	1884-12-30		A1
2070	" "	28	N½NE	1884-12-30		A1
2071	" "	28	NESE	1884-12-30		A1
2072	" "	28	SWNE	1884-12-30		A1
2073	" "	28	SWSE	1884-12-30		A1
2074	" "	28	W½NW	1884-12-30		A1
2075	" "	29	N½SW	1884-12-30		A1
2076	" "	29	NESE	1884-12-30		A1
2077	" "	29	W½SE	1884-12-30		A1
2078	" "	3		1884-12-30		A1
2079	" "	30	E½NE	1884-12-30		A1
2080	" "	30	NW	1884-12-30		A1
2081	" "	30	S½	1884-12-30		A1
2082	" "	30	SWNE	1884-12-30		A1
2083	" "	31	E½NE	1884-12-30		A1
2084	" "	31	E½NW	1884-12-30		A1
2085	" "	31	N½SW	1884-12-30		A1
2086	" "	31	NWNE	1884-12-30		A1
2087	" "	31	NWNW	1884-12-30		A1
2088	" "	31	SE	1884-12-30		A1
2089	" "	32	E½NW	1884-12-30		A1
2090	" "	32	N½SW	1884-12-30		A1
2091	" "	32	SESE	1884-12-30		A1
2092	" "	32	SESW	1884-12-30		A1
2093	" "	32	SWNW	1884-12-30		A1
2094	" "	32	W½NE	1884-12-30		A1
2095	" "	32	W½SE	1884-12-30		A1
2096	" "	33	E½SW	1884-12-30		A1
2097	" "	33	N½SE	1884-12-30		A1
2098	" "	33	NE	1884-12-30		A1
2099	" "	33	SENW	1884-12-30		A1
2100	" "	33	SWSW	1884-12-30		A1
2111	" "	36	NWSE	1884-12-30		A1
2112	" "	36	S½SE	1884-12-30		A1
2113	" "	36	SENW	1884-12-30		A1
2114	" "	36	SW	1884-12-30		A1
2115	" "	36	SWNE	1884-12-30		A1
2116	" "	36	W½NW	1884-12-30		A1
2117	" "	4	E½NW	1884-12-30		A1
2118	" "	4	N½SE	1884-12-30		A1
2119	" "	4	NE	1884-12-30		A1
2120	" "	4	NESW	1884-12-30		A1
2121	" "	4	NWNW	1884-12-30		A1
2122	" "	4	S½SE	1884-12-30		A1
2123	" "	4	SESW	1884-12-30		A1
2124	" "	5	E½NE	1884-12-30		A1
2125	" "	5	E½SW	1884-12-30		A1
2126	" "	5	SESE	1884-12-30		A1
2127	" "	5	SWSW	1884-12-30		A1
2128	" "	5	W½NE	1884-12-30		A1
2129	" "	5	W½SE	1884-12-30		A1
2130	" "	6	NESW	1884-12-30		A1
2131	" "	6	NW	1884-12-30		A1
2132	" "	6	S½NE	1884-12-30		A1
2133	" "	6	S½SW	1884-12-30		A1
2134	" "	6	SE	1884-12-30		A1
2135	" "	7	E½NE	1884-12-30		A1
2136	" "	7	N½NW	1884-12-30		A1
2137	" "	7	N½SW	1884-12-30		A1
2138	" "	7	NESE	1884-12-30		A1
2139	" "	8	N½NE	1884-12-30		A1
2140	" "	8	S½SE	1884-12-30		A1
2141	" "	8	S½SW	1884-12-30		A1
2142	" "	8	SENW	1884-12-30		A1

ID	Individual in Patent	Sec.	Sec. Part	Date Issued	Other Counties	For More Info . . .
2143	RANSDELL, Daniel M (Cont'd) (Cont'd)	8	W½NW	1884-12-30		A1
2144	" "	9	N½NE	1884-12-30		A1
2145	" "	9	N½NW	1884-12-30		A1
2146	" "	9	NESW	1884-12-30		A1
2147	" "	9	S½NE	1884-12-30		A1
2148	" "	9	S½SW	1884-12-30		A1
2149	" "	9	SE	1884-12-30		A1
2150	" "	9	SENW	1884-12-30		A1
2051	" "	23		1888-11-30		A1
2052	" "	24	E½	1888-11-30		A1
2053	" "	24	NW	1888-11-30		A1
2054	" "	24	W½SW	1888-11-30		A1
2055	" "	25	E½NE	1888-11-30		A1
2056	" "	25	N½SE	1888-11-30		A1
2057	" "	25	SENW	1888-11-30		A1
2058	" "	25	SW	1888-11-30		A1
2059	" "	25	SWNE	1888-11-30		A1
2060	" "	25	SWSE	1888-11-30		A1
2061	" "	25	W½NW	1888-11-30		A1
2066	" "	27	SE	1888-11-30		A1
2101	" "	34	E½SW	1888-11-30		A1
2102	" "	34	N½NE	1888-11-30		A1
2103	" "	34	NESE	1888-11-30		A1
2104	" "	34	NW	1888-11-30		A1
2105	" "	34	NWSW	1888-11-30		A1
2106	" "	34	SWNE	1888-11-30		A1
2107	" "	35	E½	1888-11-30		A1
2108	" "	35	E½NW	1888-11-30		A1
2109	" "	35	E½SW	1888-11-30		A1
2110	" "	35	SWSW	1888-11-30		A1 R2194
2171	SMITH, Joseph R	19	N½NW	1906-05-01		A4
2172	" "	19	NWNE	1906-05-01		A4
2173	" "	19	SWNW	1906-05-01		A4
1977	TINGLE, Benjaman F	13	E½NW	1901-06-25		A4
1978	" "	13	NWSE	1901-06-25		A4
1979	" "	13	SWNE	1901-06-25		A4
1980	TINGLE, Benjamin F	13	E½SE	1906-03-05		A4
1981	" "	13	SENE	1906-03-05		A4
1982	TINGLE, Charley J	11	NE	1906-06-16		A4
2192	WEST, Sam	12	NWNE	1906-06-30		A4

Patent Map

T2-N R11-W
St Stephens Meridian

Map Group 10

Township Statistics

Parcels Mapped	:	229
Number of Patents	:	62
Number of Individuals	:	28
Patentees Identified	:	27
Number of Surnames	:	18
Multi-Patentee Parcels	:	3
Oldest Patent Date	:	3/15/1854
Most Recent Patent	:	11/28/1916
Block/Lot Parcels	:	0
Parcels Re - Issued	:	1
Parcels that Overlap	:	0
Cities and Towns	:	1
Cemeteries	:	0

Copyright 2006 Boyd IT. Inc. All Rights Reserved

Map

Section 3
RANSDELL
Daniel M
1884
3

Section 2
RANSDELL
Daniel M
1884
2

RANSDELL
Daniel M
1884

RANSDELL
Daniel M
1884

RANSDELL
Daniel M
1884

RANSDELL
Daniel M
1884

Section 1
CARTER
Sam
1897

CARTER
Sam
1897

MIXON
Asa A
1890

1

RANSDELL
Daniel M
1884

MIXON
Asa A
1890

MIXON
Asa A
1890

RANSDELL
Daniel M
1884

MIXON
Cornelius L
1885

MIXON
Cornelius L
1885

Section 10
RANSDELL
Daniel M
1884

RANSDELL
Daniel M
1884

10

RANSDELL
Daniel M
1884

RANSDELL
Daniel M
1884

RANSDELL
Daniel M
1884

RANSDELL
Daniel M
1884

Section 11
RANSDELL
Daniel M
1884

TINGLE
Charley J
1906

RANSDELL
Daniel M
1884

11

RANSDELL
Daniel M
1884

RANSDELL
Daniel M
1884

RANSDELL
Daniel M
1884

Section 12
DENHAM
Nelson
1892

RANSDELL
Daniel M
1884

WEST
Sam
1906

MIXON
Cornelius L
1885

DENHAM
Nelson
1892

DENHAM
Nelson
1892

12

CARTER
George
1895

Section 15
RANSDELL
Daniel M
1884

RANSDELL
Daniel M
1884

RANSDELL
Daniel M
1884

15

RANSDELL
Daniel M
1884

RANSDELL
Daniel M
1884

RANSDELL
Daniel M
1884

RANSDELL
Daniel M
1884

Section 14
RANSDELL
Daniel M
1884

RANSDELL
Daniel M
1884

14

PEARCE
John T
1898

PEARCE
John T
1898

PEARCE
John C
1882

RANSDELL
Daniel M
1884

PEARCE
John T
1898

PEARCE
John C
1890

PEARCE
John C
1890

Section 13
RANSDELL
Daniel M
1884

TINGLE
Benjaman F
1901

RANSDELL
Daniel M
1884

TINGLE
Benjaman F
1901

13

TINGLE
Benjamin F
1906

TINGLE
Benjaman F
1901

RANSDELL
Daniel M
1884

RANSDELL
Daniel M
1884

RANSDELL
Daniel M
1884

TINGLE
Benjamin F
1906

Section 22
RANSDELL
Daniel M
1884

RANSDELL
Daniel M
1884

RANSDELL
Daniel M
1884

RANSDELL
Daniel M
1884

22

RANSDELL
Daniel M
1884

RANSDELL
Daniel M
1884

Section 23
RANSDELL
Daniel M
1888

23

Section 24
RANSDELL
Daniel M
1888

24

RANSDELL
Daniel M
1888

RANSDELL
Daniel M
1888

NEAL
Green L
1906

Section 27
RANSDELL
Daniel M
1884

MONTAGUE
Luke S
1890

RANSDELL
Daniel M
1884

RANSDELL
Daniel M
1884

27

RANSDELL
Daniel M
1884

RANSDELL
Daniel M
1884

RANSDELL
Daniel M
1888

Section 26
RANSDELL
Daniel M
1884

26

Section 25
RANSDELL
Daniel M
1888

NEAL
Green L
1906

NEAL
Green L
1906

RANSDELL
Daniel M
1888

RANSDELL
Daniel M
1888

RANSDELL
Daniel M
1888

25

RANSDELL
Daniel M
1888

RANSDELL
Daniel M
1888

RANSDELL
Daniel M
1888

Section 34
RANSDELL
Daniel M
1888

RANSDELL
Daniel M
1888

34

RANSDELL
Daniel M
1888

RANSDELL
Daniel M
1888

MARTIN
William I
1910

RANSDELL
Daniel M
1888

RANSDELL
Daniel M
1888

GRIFFIN [43]
William E
1884

MARTIN
William I
1910

Section 35
MISSISSIPPI
State Of
1911

MISSISSIPPI
State Of
1911

GARAWAY
Solomon T
1854

RANSDELL
Daniel M
1888

RANSDELL
Daniel M
1888

35

RANSDELL
Daniel M
1888

GARAWAY
Solomon T
1859

RANSDELL
Daniel M
1888

Section 36
RANSDELL
Daniel M
1884

RANSDELL
Daniel M
1884

RANSDELL
Daniel M
1884

RANSDELL
Daniel M
1884

36

RANSDELL
Daniel M
1884

RANSDELL
Daniel M
1884

Helpful Hints

1. This Map's INDEX can be found on the preceding pages.

2. Refer to Map "C" to see where this Township lies within Perry County, Mississippi.

3. Numbers within square brackets [ ] denote a multi-patentee land parcel (multi-owner). Refer to Appendix "C" for a full list of members in this group.

4. Areas that look to be crowded with Patentees usually indicate multiple sales of the same parcel (Re-issues) or Overlapping parcels. See this Township's Index for an explanation of these and other circumstances that might explain "odd" groupings of Patentees on this map.

Legend

——————— Patent Boundary

━━━━━━━ Section Boundary

▨ No Patents Found
(or Outside County)

1., 2., 3., ... Lot Numbers
(when beside a name)

[ ] Group Number
(see Appendix "C")

Scale: Section = 1 mile X 1 mile
(generally, with some exceptions)

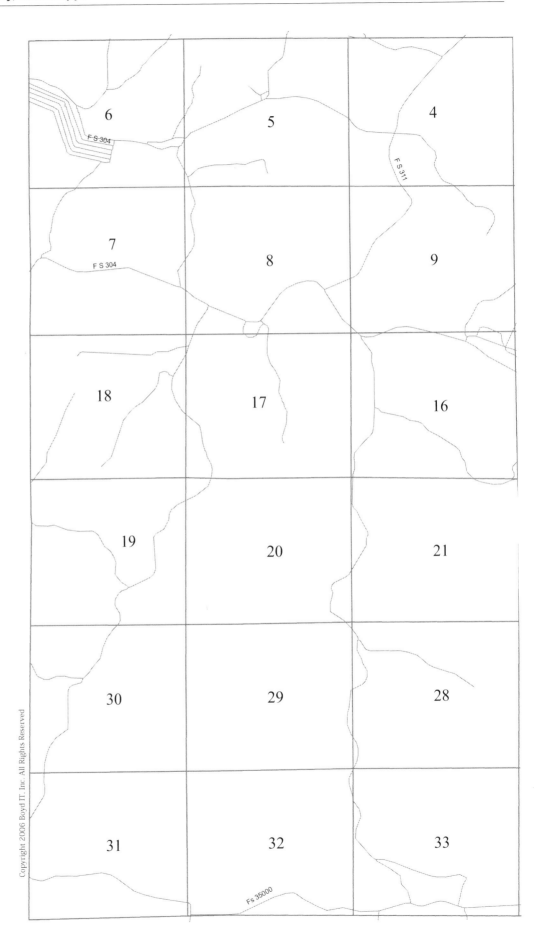

Road Map

T2-N R11-W
St Stephens Meridian

Map Group 10

Cities & Towns

Redhill

Cemeteries

None

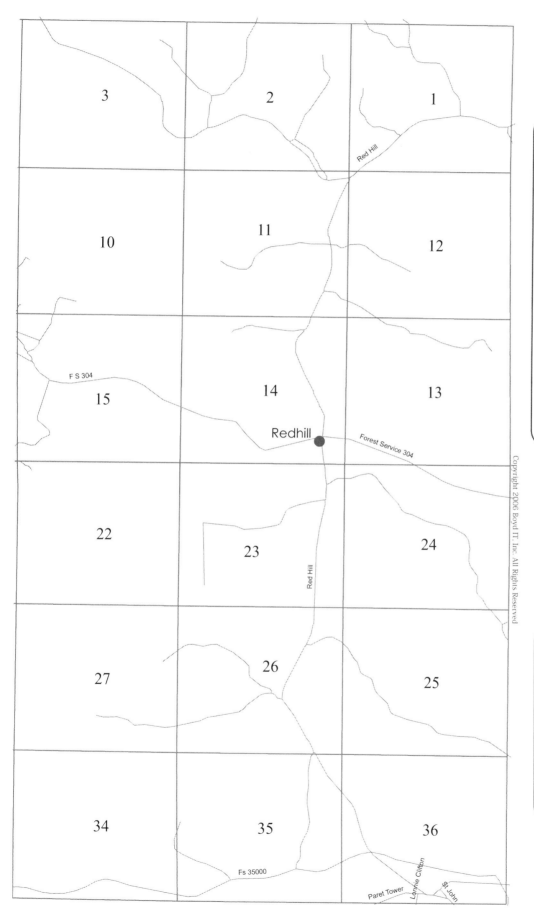

3

2

1

10

11

12

F S 304

15

14

13

Redhill

Forest Service 304

22

23

Red Hill

24

27

26

25

34

35

36

Fs 35000

Paret Tower

Lonnie Clifton

St John

Red Hill

Helpful Hints

1. This road map has a number of uses, but primarily it is to help you: a) find the present location of land owned by your ancestors (at least the general area), b) find cemeteries and city-centers, and c) estimate the route/roads used by Census-takers & tax-assessors.

2. If you plan to travel to Perry County to locate cemeteries or land parcels, please pick up a modern travel map for the area before you do. Mapping old land parcels on modern maps is not as exact a science as you might think. Just the slightest variations in public land survey coordinates, estimates of parcel boundaries, or road-map deviations can greatly alter a map's representation of how a road either does or doesn't cross a particular parcel of land.

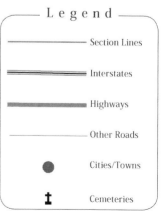

Legend

———— Section Lines

═══ Interstates

━━━ Highways

——— Other Roads

● Cities/Towns

† Cemeteries

Scale: Section = 1 mile X 1 mile
(generally, with some exceptions)

Historical Map

T2-N R11-W
St Stephens Meridian

Map Group 10

<u>Cities & Towns</u>
Redhill

<u>Cemeteries</u>
None

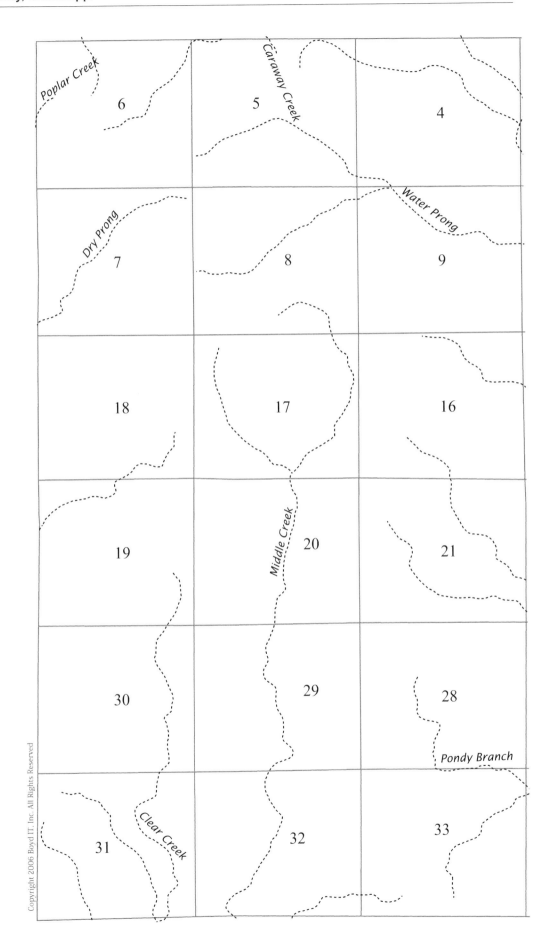

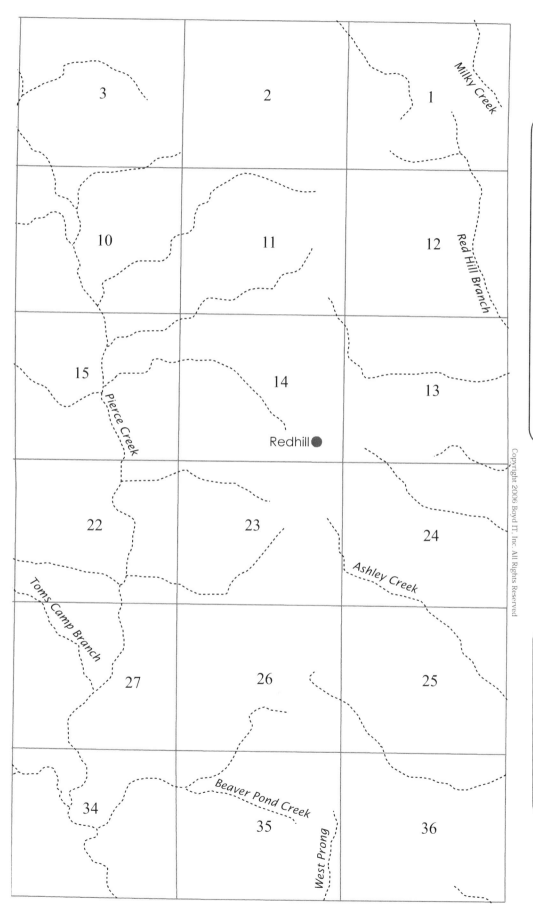

3

2

1

Milky Creek

10

11

12

Red Hill Branch

15

14

13

Pierce Creek

Redhill ●

22

23

24

Ashley Creek

Toms Camp Branch

27

26

25

34

Beaver Pond Creek

35

West Prong

36

Copyright 2006 Boyd IT, Inc. All Rights Reserved

Helpful Hints

1. This Map takes a different look at the same Congressional Township displayed in the preceding two maps. It presents features that can help you better envision the historical development of the area: a) Water-bodies (lakes & ponds), b) Water-courses (rivers, streams, etc.), c) Railroads, d) City/town center-points (where they were oftentimes located when first settled), and e) Cemeteries.

2. Using this "Historical" map in tandem with this Township's Patent Map and Road Map, may lead you to some interesting discoveries. You will often find roads, towns, cemeteries, and waterways are named after nearby landowners: sometimes those names will be the ones you are researching. See how many of these research gems you can find here in Perry County.

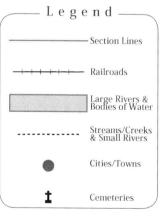

Legend

——————— Section Lines

+++++++ Railroads

▮▮▮▮▮ Large Rivers & Bodies of Water

- - - - - - Streams/Creeks & Small Rivers

● Cities/Towns

✝ Cemeteries

Scale: Section = 1 mile X 1 mile
(there are some exceptions)

143

Map Group 11: Index to Land Patents

Township 2-North Range 10-West (St Stephens)

After you locate an individual in this Index, take note of the Section and Section Part then proceed to the Land Patent map on the pages immediately following. You should have no difficulty locating the corresponding parcel of land.

The "For More Info" Column will lead you to more information about the underlying Patents. See the *Legend* at right, and the "How to Use this Book" chapter, for more information.

```
                         LEGEND
            "For More Info . . . " column
A = Authority (Legislative Act, See Appendix "A")
B = Block or Lot (location in Section unknown)
C = Cancelled Patent
F = Fractional Section
G = Group (Multi-Patentee Patent, see Appendix "C")
V = Overlaps another Parcel
R = Re-Issued (Parcel patented more than once)

(A & G items require you to look in the Appendixes referred
to above. All other Letter-designations followed by a number
require you to locate line-items in this index that possess
the ID number found after the letter).
```

ID	Individual in Patent	Sec.	Sec. Part	Date Issued	Other Counties	For More Info . . .
2351	BIRKETT, Thomas	33	NWSE	1889-11-29		A1
2352	" "	35	SESE	1889-11-29		A1
2353	" "	35	SESW	1889-11-29		A1
2359	BRELAND, Timothy T	17	SESW	1860-07-02		A1
2323	CARPENTER, Georgian I	18	NENW	1906-05-01		A4 G20
2324	" "	18	W½NE	1906-05-01		A4 G20
2325	" "	7	SESW	1906-05-01		A4 G20
2341	CARPENTER, Martha E	6	E½SE	1892-01-18		A4
2342	" "	6	SENE	1892-01-18		A4
2343	" "	6	SWSE	1892-01-18		A4
2208	CARTER, Billy	6	NESW	1897-05-07		A4
2209	" "	6	S½NW	1897-05-07		A4
2210	" "	6	SWNE	1897-05-07		A4
2211	CARTER, Bud	21	NWNW	1906-05-01		A1
2363	CARTER, William	6	NWSW	1841-01-05		A1
2344	COURTNEY, Micajah E	19	SE	1889-12-19		A4
2349	GARAWAY, Solomon T	29	SWNE	1846-09-01		A1
2346	" "	15	SWNW	1854-03-15		A1
2347	" "	21	SWNW	1854-03-15		A1
2348	" "	29	NENE	1854-03-15		A1
2274	HERRING, Charley	34	E½NW	1910-01-20		A4
2275	" "	34	N½NE	1910-01-20		A4
2321	HERRING, Enoch H	35	NW	1892-06-30		A4
2212	HILLS, Charles T	1	N½	1889-11-21		A1
2213	" "	1	NWSE	1889-11-21		A1
2214	" "	1	SW	1889-11-21		A1
2215	" "	10	S½	1889-11-21		A1
2216	" "	10	W½NE	1889-11-21		A1
2217	" "	11		1889-11-21		A1
2218	" "	12	E½NE	1889-11-21		A1
2219	" "	12	NW	1889-11-21		A1
2220	" "	12	S½	1889-11-21		A1
2221	" "	12	SWNE	1889-11-21		A1
2222	" "	13		1889-11-21		A1
2223	" "	14	N½	1889-11-21		A1
2224	" "	14	N½SE	1889-11-21		A1
2225	" "	14	N½SW	1889-11-21		A1
2226	" "	15	E½	1889-11-21		A1
2227	" "	15	E½NW	1889-11-21		A1
2228	" "	15	NWNW	1889-11-21		A1
2229	" "	15	SW	1889-11-21		A1
2230	" "	2		1889-11-21		A1
2231	" "	21	E½	1889-11-21		A1
2232	" "	21	E½NW	1889-11-21		A1
2233	" "	21	E½SW	1889-11-21		A1
2234	" "	22		1889-11-21		A1

ID	Individual in Patent	Sec.	Sec. Part	Date Issued	Other Counties	For More Info . . .
2235	HILLS, Charles T (Cont'd)	23	E½NE	1889-11-21		A1
2236	"	23	S½	1889-11-21		A1
2237	"	23	SENW	1889-11-21		A1
2238	"	23	SWNE	1889-11-21		A1
2239	"	23	W½NW	1889-11-21		A1
2240	"	24		1889-11-21		A1
2241	"	25	N½SE	1889-11-21		A1
2242	"	25	N½SW	1889-11-21		A1
2243	"	25	NENE	1889-11-21		A1
2244	"	25	NW	1889-11-21		A1
2245	"	26	N½	1889-11-21		A1
2246	"	26	N½SE	1889-11-21		A1
2247	"	26	N½SW	1889-11-21		A1
2248	"	27	E½	1889-11-21		A1
2249	"	27	E½NW	1889-11-21		A1
2250	"	27	SW	1889-11-21		A1
2251	"	27	SWNW	1889-11-21		A1
2252	"	28	N½NE	1889-11-21		A1
2253	"	3	E½NW	1889-11-21		A1
2254	"	3	E½SW	1889-11-21		A1
2255	"	3	N½SE	1889-11-21		A1
2256	"	3	NE	1889-11-21		A1
2257	"	3	NWSW	1889-11-21		A1
2258	"	3	SWNW	1889-11-21		A1
2259	"	4	NW	1889-11-21		A1
2260	"	4	NWNE	1889-11-21		A1
2261	"	4	SESW	1889-11-21		A1
2262	"	4	W½SW	1889-11-21		A1
2263	"	5	N½SE	1889-11-21		A1
2264	"	5	S½SW	1889-11-21		A1
2265	"	5	SENE	1889-11-21		A1
2266	"	7	E½	1889-11-21		A1
2267	"	7	NESW	1889-11-21		A1
2268	"	7	SENW	1889-11-21		A1
2269	"	7	W½NW	1889-11-21		A1
2270	"	7	W½SW	1889-11-21		A1
2271	"	8	N½	1889-11-21		A1
2272	"	8	SW	1889-11-21		A1
2273	"	9	N½	1889-11-21		A1
2357	HINTON, Thomas E	23	NENW	1882-12-30		A1
2358	"	23	NWNE	1882-12-30		A1
2355	"	14	SESE	1889-04-20		A1
2354	"	14	S½SW	1894-12-17		A4
2356	"	14	SWSE	1894-12-17		A4
2366	HINTON, William T	33	NESE	1899-06-28		A4
2367	"	34	NWSW	1899-06-28		A4
2326	HOWARD, Henry	31	E½SW	1884-12-30		A4
2327	"	31	W½SE	1884-12-30		A4
2322	LAMBERT, George W	17	NW	1900-10-04		A4
2336	LAMBERT, Hugh	17	N½SW	1889-12-19		A4
2337	"	17	W½SE	1889-12-19		A4
2345	MARTIN, Samuel	33	W½SW	1859-05-02		A1
2203	MCPHERSON, Alexander	32	E½NW	1889-04-23		A1 G62 V2302
2204	"	32	NENE	1889-04-23		A1 G62 R2303
2205	"	32	NESW	1889-04-23		A1 G62 V2361
2206	"	32	SE	1889-04-23		A1 G62 V2364, 2362
2207	"	32	W½NE	1889-04-23		A1 G62
2203	MCPHERSON, Edward G	32	E½NW	1889-04-23		A1 G62 V2302
2204	"	32	NENE	1889-04-23		A1 G62 R2303
2205	"	32	NESW	1889-04-23		A1 G62 V2361
2206	"	32	SE	1889-04-23		A1 G62 V2364, 2362
2207	"	32	W½NE	1889-04-23		A1 G62
2203	MCPHERSON, Martin J	32	E½NW	1889-04-23		A1 G62 V2302
2204	"	32	NENE	1889-04-23		A1 G62 R2303
2205	"	32	NESW	1889-04-23		A1 G62 V2361
2206	"	32	SE	1889-04-23		A1 G62 V2364, 2362
2207	"	32	W½NE	1889-04-23		A1 G62
2203	MCPHERSON, William	32	E½NW	1889-04-23		A1 G62 V2302
2204	"	32	NENE	1889-04-23		A1 G62 R2303
2205	"	32	NESW	1889-04-23		A1 G62 V2361
2206	"	32	SE	1889-04-23		A1 G62 V2364, 2362
2207	"	32	W½NE	1889-04-23		A1 G62
2365	PEARCE, William	33	NESW	1896-10-31		A4

ID	Individual in Patent	Sec.	Sec. Part	Date Issued	Other Counties	For More Info . . .
2364	PEARCE, William (Cont'd)	32	S½SE	1910-06-02		A4 V2206
2360	PEARCE, William C	31	NESE	1914-10-29		A4
2361	" "	32	N½SW	1914-10-29		A4 V2205
2362	" "	32	NWSE	1914-10-29		A4 V2206
2278	RANSDELL, Daniel M	19	NE	1884-12-30		A1
2279	" "	19	NENW	1884-12-30		A1
2280	" "	19	S½NW	1884-12-30		A1
2281	" "	19	SW	1884-12-30		A1
2282	" "	20	SWNW	1884-12-30		A1
2283	" "	20	W½SW	1884-12-30		A1
2284	" "	21	SWSW	1884-12-30		A1
2285	" "	25	S½SW	1884-12-30		A1
2286	" "	25	SESE	1884-12-30		A1
2287	" "	26	S½SE	1884-12-30		A1
2288	" "	26	S½SW	1884-12-30		A1
2289	" "	28	W½NW	1884-12-30		A1
2290	" "	28	W½SW	1884-12-30		A1
2291	" "	29	E½SE	1884-12-30		A1
2292	" "	29	SENE	1884-12-30		A1
2293	" "	29	W½NW	1884-12-30		A1
2294	" "	30	N½	1884-12-30		A1
2296	" "	30	SE	1884-12-30		A1
2297	" "	30	SESW	1884-12-30		A1
2306	" "	33	S½SE	1884-12-30		A1
2307	" "	33	SESW	1884-12-30		A1
2308	" "	34	E½SW	1884-12-30		A1
2309	" "	34	S½NE	1884-12-30		A1
2310	" "	34	SE	1884-12-30		A1
2311	" "	34	SWSW	1884-12-30		A1
2312	" "	35	N½SE	1884-12-30		A1
2313	" "	35	N½SW	1884-12-30		A1
2314	" "	35	NE	1884-12-30		A1
2315	" "	35	SWSE	1884-12-30		A1
2316	" "	35	SWSW	1884-12-30		A1
2276	" "	17	SWSW	1888-11-30		A1
2277	" "	18	S½SE	1888-11-30		A1
2295	" "	30	NESW	1888-11-30		A1
2298	" "	31	N½	1888-11-30		A1
2299	" "	31	NWSW	1888-11-30		A1
2300	" "	31	SESE	1888-11-30		A1
2301	" "	31	SWSW	1888-11-30		A1
2302	" "	32	N½NW	1888-11-30		A1 V2203
2303	" "	32	NENE	1888-11-30		A1 R2204
2304	" "	32	S½SW	1888-11-30		A1
2305	" "	32	SWNW	1888-11-30		A1
2328	SAWYER, Hiram W	3	SWSW	1889-05-06		A1
2329	" "	4	NESW	1889-05-06		A1
2330	" "	4	S½NE	1889-05-06		A1
2331	" "	4	SE	1889-05-06		A1
2332	" "	5	N½NE	1889-05-06		A1
2333	" "	5	N½SW	1889-05-06		A1
2334	" "	5	NW	1889-05-06		A1
2335	" "	5	SWNE	1889-05-06		A1
2323	STAFFORD, Georgian I	18	NENW	1906-05-01		A4 G20
2324	" "	18	W½NE	1906-05-01		A4 G20
2325	" "	7	SESW	1906-05-01		A4 G20
2319	STRICKLAND, Ellis	6	N½NE	1906-06-26		A4
2320	" "	6	N½NW	1906-06-26		A4
2368	THOMAS, William	8	N½SE	1906-05-01		A1
2369	" "	9	NWSW	1906-05-01		A1
2338	WAGAR, Humphrey R	25	SENE	1889-04-09		A1 G75
2339	" "	25	W½NE	1889-04-09		A1 G75
2370	WELDAY, William	28	NESW	1859-11-10		A1
2338	WELLS, Willard B	25	SENE	1889-04-09		A1 G75
2339	" "	25	W½NE	1889-04-09		A1 G75
2317	WHATLEY, David B	28	SESW	1895-11-11		A4
2318	" "	28	W½SE	1895-11-11		A4
2340	WHATLEY, Jackson	27	NWNW	1914-05-28		A4
2350	WHATLEY, Solomon Travis	21	NWSW	1911-02-23		A4
2371	WHATLEY, Wilson R	28	E½SE	1906-11-02		A4
2372	" "	28	S½NE	1906-11-02		A4

Patent Map

T2-N R10-W
St Stephens Meridian

Map Group 11

Township Statistics

Parcels Mapped	:	170
Number of Patents	:	55
Number of Individuals	:	36
Patentees Identified	:	31
Number of Surnames	:	23
Multi-Patentee Parcels	:	10
Oldest Patent Date	:	1/5/1841
Most Recent Patent	:	10/29/1914
Block/Lot Parcels	:	0
Parcels Re - Issued	:	1
Parcels that Overlap	:	7
Cities and Towns	:	0
Cemeteries	:	3

STRICKLAND Ellis 1906
STRICKLAND Ellis 1906
CARTER Billy 1897
CARTER Billy 1897
CARPENTER Martha E 1892
6
SAWYER Hiram W 1889
5
SAWYER Hiram W 1889
SAWYER Hiram W 1889
HILLS Charles T 1889
HILLS Charles T 1889
4
HILLS Charles T 1889
SAWYER Hiram W 1889

CARTER William 1841
CARTER Billy 1897
CARPENTER Martha E 1892
SAWYER Hiram W 1889
HILLS Charles T 1889
HILLS Charles T 1889
SAWYER Hiram W 1889
SAWYER Hiram W 1889

CARPENTER Martha E 1892
HILLS Charles T 1889
HILLS Charles T 1889

HILLS Charles T 1889
HILLS Charles T 1889
7
HILLS Charles T 1889
HILLS Charles T 1889
8
HILLS Charles T 1889
9

HILLS Charles T 1889
HILLS Charles T 1889
HILLS Charles T 1889
THOMAS William 1906
THOMAS William 1906

CARPENTER [20] Georgian I 1906

CARPENTER [20] Georgian I 1906
CARPENTER [20] Georgian I 1906
LAMBERT George W 1900
18
17
16

LAMBERT Hugh 1889
LAMBERT Hugh 1889

RANSDELL Daniel M 1888
RANSDELL Daniel M 1888
BRELAND Timothy T 1860

RANSDELL Daniel M 1884
RANSDELL Daniel M 1884
RANSDELL Daniel M 1884
CARTER Bud 1906

RANSDELL Daniel M 1884
19
20
GARAWAY Solomon T 1854
HILLS Charles T 1889
21
HILLS Charles T 1889

RANSDELL Daniel M 1884
WHATLEY Solomon Travis 1911

RANSDELL Daniel M 1884
COURTNEY Micajah E 1889
RANSDELL Daniel M 1884
HILLS Charles T 1889

RANSDELL Daniel M 1884
GARAWAY Solomon T 1854
RANSDELL Daniel M 1884
HILLS Charles T 1889

RANSDELL Daniel M 1884
30
GARAWAY Solomon T 1846
RANSDELL Daniel M 1884
28
WHATLEY Wilson R 1906

RANSDELL Daniel M 1888
RANSDELL Daniel M 1884
29
RANSDELL Daniel M 1884
WELDAY William 1859
WHATLEY David B 1895

RANSDELL Daniel M 1884
RANSDELL Daniel M 1884
WHATLEY David B 1895
WHATLEY Wilson R 1906

MCPHERSON [62] Alexander 1889

RANSDELL Daniel M 1888
RANSDELL Daniel M 1888

RANSDELL Daniel M 1888
31
RANSDELL Daniel M 1888
MCPHERSON [62] Alexander 1889
MCPHERSON [62] Alexander 1889
33

32

RANSDELL Daniel M 1888
HOWARD Henry 1884
PEARCE William C 1914
MCPHERSON [62] Alexander 1889
PEARCE William C 1914
PEARCE William C 1914
MARTIN Samuel 1859
PEARCE William 1896
BIRKETT Thomas 1889
HINTON William T 1899

RANSDELL Daniel M 1888
HOWARD Henry 1884
RANSDELL Daniel M 1888
RANSDELL Daniel M 1888
MCPHERSON [62] Alexander 1889
PEARCE William 1910
RANSDELL Daniel M 1884
RANSDELL Daniel M 1884

HILLS
Charles T
1889

HILLS
Charles T
1889

HILLS
Charles T
1889

HILLS
Charles T
1889

HILLS
Charles T
1889

3

HILLS
Charles T
1889

2

HILLS
Charles T
1889

1

SAWYER
Hiram W
1889

HILLS
Charles T
1889

HILLS
Charles T
1889

HILLS
Charles T
1889

HILLS
Charles T
1889

HILLS
Charles T
1889

HILLS
Charles T
1889

HILLS
Charles T
1889

10

11

HILLS
Charles T
1889

12

HILLS
Charles T
1889

HILLS
Charles T
1889

HILLS
Charles T
1889

HILLS
Charles T
1889

GARAWAY
Solomon T
1854

HILLS
Charles T
1889

HILLS
Charles T
1889

14

HILLS
Charles T
1889

13

15

HILLS
Charles T
1889

HILLS
Charles T
1889

HILLS
Charles T
1889

HILLS
Charles T
1889

HINTON
Thomas E
1894

HINTON
Thomas E
1894

HINTON
Thomas E
1889

HILLS
Charles T
1889

HINTON
Thomas E
1882

HINTON
Thomas E
1882

HILLS
Charles T
1889

22

HILLS
Charles T
1889

HILLS
Charles T
1889

HILLS
Charles T
1889

24

23

HILLS
Charles T
1889

HILLS
Charles T
1889

WHATLEY
Jackson
1914

WAGAR [75]
Humphrey R
1889

HILLS
Charles T
1889

HILLS
Charles T
1889

HILLS
Charles T
1889

HILLS
Charles T
1889

HILLS
Charles T
1889

WAGAR [75]
Humphrey R
1889

HILLS
Charles T
1889

26

25

27

HILLS
Charles T
1889

HILLS
Charles T
1889

HILLS
Charles T
1889

HILLS
Charles T
1889

HILLS
Charles T
1889

RANSDELL
Daniel M
1884

RANSDELL
Daniel M
1884

RANSDELL
Daniel M
1884

RANSDELL
Daniel M
1884

HERRING
Charley
1910

HERRING
Charley
1910

RANSDELL
Daniel M
1884

HERRING
Enoch H
1892

RANSDELL
Daniel M
1884

36

35

HINTON
William T
1899

34

RANSDELL
Daniel M
1884

RANSDELL
Daniel M
1884

RANSDELL
Daniel M
1884

RANSDELL
Daniel M
1884

RANSDELL
Daniel M
1884

RANSDELL
Daniel M
1884

BIRKETT
Thomas
1889

RANSDELL
Daniel M
1884

BIRKETT
Thomas
1889

Helpful Hints

1. This Map's INDEX can be found on the preceding pages.

2. Refer to Map "C" to see where this Township lies within Perry County, Mississippi.

3. Numbers within square brackets [ ] denote a multi-patentee land parcel (multi-owner). Refer to Appendix "C" for a full list of members in this group.

4. Areas that look to be crowded with Patentees usually indicate multiple sales of the same parcel (Re-issues) or Overlapping parcels. See this Township's Index for an explanation of these and other circumstances that might explain "odd" groupings of Patentees on this map.

Legend

———— Patent Boundary

▬▬▬▬ Section Boundary

░░░░ No Patents Found
(or Outside County)

1., 2., 3., ... Lot Numbers
(when beside a name)

[ ] Group Number
(see Appendix "C")

Scale: Section = 1 mile X 1 mile
(generally, with some exceptions)

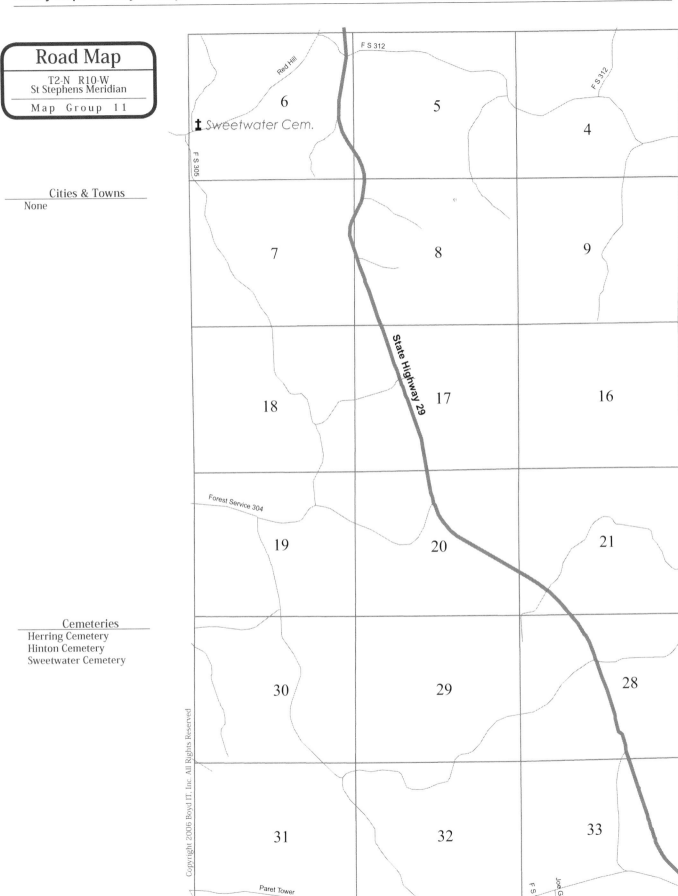

Road Map

T2-N R10-W
St Stephens Meridian

Map Group 11

Cities & Towns
None

Cemeteries
Herring Cemetery
Hinton Cemetery
Sweetwater Cemetery

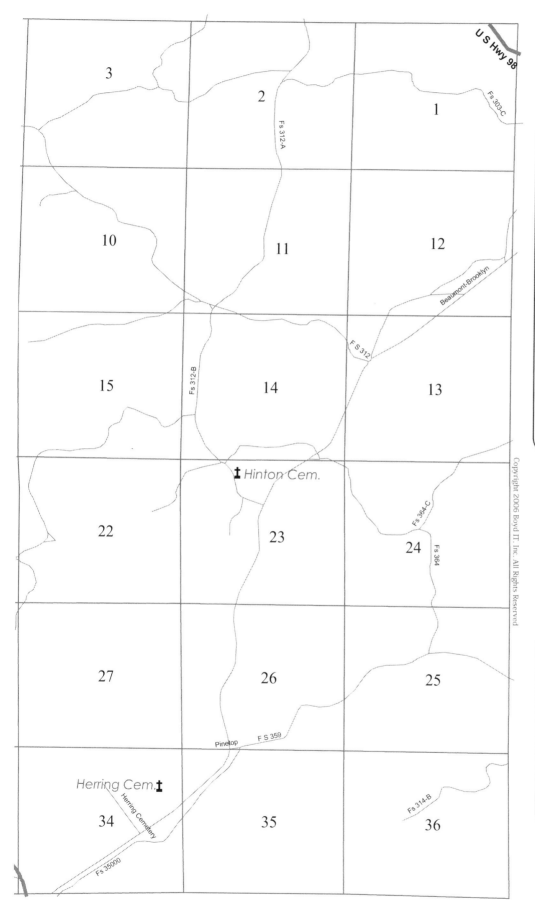

US Hwy 98

3

2

1

Fs 303-C

Fs 312-A

10

11

12

Beaumont-Brooklyn

F S 312

15

Fs 312-B

14

13

‡ Hinton Cem.

22

23

24

Fs 364-C

Fs 364

27

26

25

Pinetop   F S 359

Herring Cem.‡

34

Herring Cemetery

35

36

Fs 314-B

Fs 35000

Helpful Hints

1. This road map has a number of uses, but primarily it is to help you: a) find the present location of land owned by your ancestors (at least the general area), b) find cemeteries and city-centers, and c) estimate the route/roads used by Census-takers & tax-assessors.

2. If you plan to travel to Perry County to locate cemeteries or land parcels, please pick up a modern travel map for the area before you do. Mapping old land parcels on modern maps is not as exact a science as you might think. Just the slightest variations in public land survey coordinates, estimates of parcel boundaries, or road-map deviations can greatly alter a map's representation of how a road either does or doesn't cross a particular parcel of land.

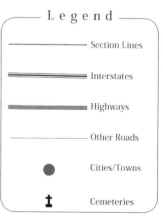

L e g e n d

	Section Lines
	Interstates
	Highways
	Other Roads
●	Cities/Towns
‡	Cemeteries

Scale: Section = 1 mile X 1 mile
(generally, with some exceptions)

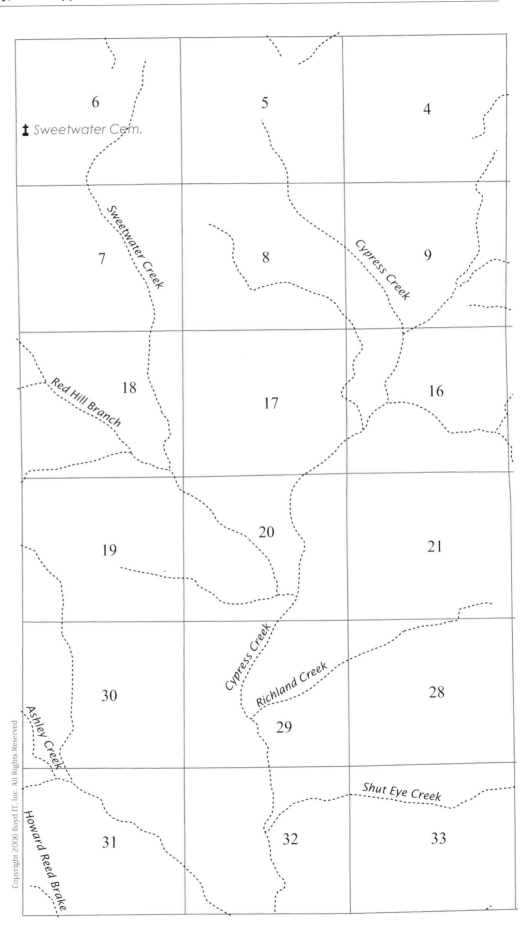

Historical Map

T2-N R10-W
St Stephens Meridian

Map Group 11

<u>Cities & Towns</u>
None

<u>Cemeteries</u>
Herring Cemetery
Hinton Cemetery
Sweetwater Cemetery

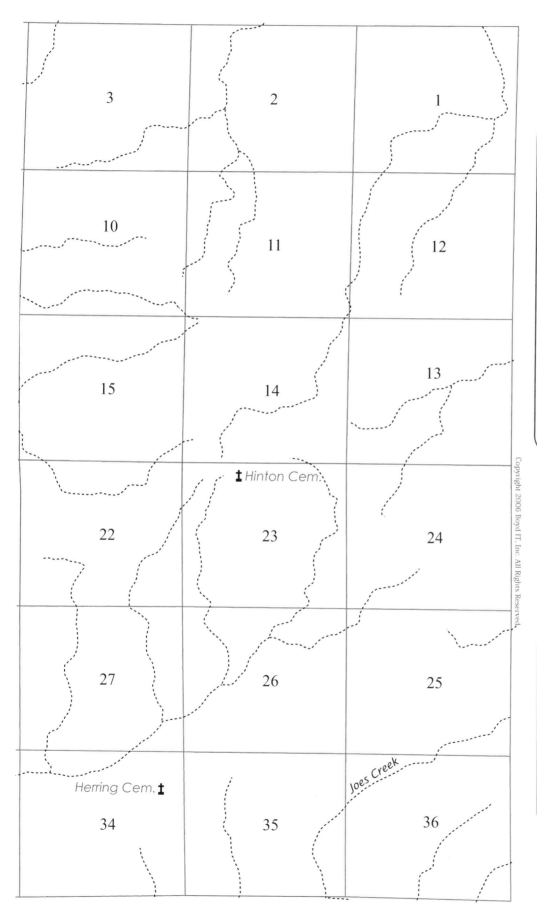

3

2

1

10

11

12

15

14

13

✝ Hinton Cem.

22

23

24

27

26

25

Joes Creek

Herring Cem. ✝

34

35

36

Helpful Hints

1. This Map takes a different look at the same Congressional Township displayed in the preceding two maps. It presents features that can help you better envision the historical development of the area: a) Water-bodies (lakes & ponds), b) Water-courses (rivers, streams, etc.), c) Railroads, d) City/town center-points (where they were oftentimes located when first settled), and e) Cemeteries.

2. Using this "Historical" map in tandem with this Township's Patent Map and Road Map, may lead you to some interesting discoveries. You will often find roads, towns, cemeteries, and waterways are named after nearby landowners: sometimes those names will be the ones you are researching. See how many of these research gems you can find here in Perry County.

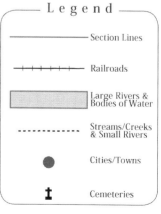

L e g e n d

—————— Section Lines

+++++++ Railroads

Large Rivers & Bodies of Water

- - - - - Streams/Creeks & Small Rivers

● Cities/Towns

✝ Cemeteries

Scale: Section = 1 mile X 1 mile
(there are some exceptions)

153

Map Group 12: Index to Land Patents

Township 2-North Range 9-West (St Stephens)

After you locate an individual in this Index, take note of the Section and Section Part then proceed to the Land Patent map on the pages immediately following. You should have no difficulty locating the corresponding parcel of land.

The "For More Info" Column will lead you to more information about the underlying Patents. See the *Legend* at right, and the "How to Use this Book" chapter, for more information.

```
                                    LEGEND
              "For More Info . . . " column
A = Authority (Legislative Act, See Appendix "A")
B = Block or Lot (location in Section unknown)
C = Cancelled Patent
F = Fractional Section
G = Group  (Multi-Patentee Patent, see Appendix "C")
V = Overlaps another Parcel
R = Re-Issued (Parcel patented more than once)

(A & G items require you to look in the Appendixes referred
to above. All other Letter-designations followed by a number
require you to locate line-items in this index that possess
the ID number found after the letter).
```

ID	Individual in Patent	Sec.	Sec. Part	Date Issued	Other Counties	For More Info . . .
2492	BANG, Fannie	14	E½NE	1897-11-01		A4
2504	BEARDSLEY, Henderson	8	E½NW	1888-04-05		A4
2505	" "	8	W½NE	1888-04-05		A4
2522	BEARDSLEY, Johnson	9	E½SW	1905-02-13		A4
2408	BOLTON, Charles	14	N½SW	1914-06-29		A4
2374	BOULTON, Absolem	22	SENE	1895-02-21		A4
2375	" "	22	W½NE	1895-02-21		A4
2376	" "	23	SWNW	1895-02-21		A4
2373	BOULTON, Absolem A	30	N½NW	1905-02-13		A4
2396	BOULTON, Annie	6	SESW	1905-05-02		A4
2397	" "	6	SWSE	1905-05-02		A4
2398	" "	7	N½NE	1905-05-02		A4
2399	BOULTON, Austin	23	N½NW	1899-04-17		A4
2400	" "	23	SENW	1899-04-17		A4
2401	" "	23	SWNE	1899-04-17		A4
2402	BOULTON, Blake	5	SESW	1882-12-30		A4
2403	" "	5	SWNW	1882-12-30		A4
2404	" "	5	W½SW	1882-12-30		A4
2407	BOULTON, Caroline	17	NW	1896-09-16		A4
2409	BOULTON, Charles	5	NESE	1859-05-02		A1
2467	BOULTON, Charley P	33	NWNE	1906-05-01		A4
2468	" "	33	S½NE	1906-05-01		A4
2469	" "	33	SENW	1906-05-01		A4
2485	BOULTON, Effy	9	NW	1882-03-30		A4
2487	BOULTON, Emaline	22	NESE	1901-08-12		A4
2495	BOULTON, Frank	15	W½NW	1900-11-28		A4
2496	" "	15	W½SW	1900-11-28		A4
2499	BOULTON, Gabe	9	NE	1881-08-20		A4
2500	BOULTON, George	8	SESW	1894-03-12		A4
2513	BOULTON, Jack	8	W½NW	1904-10-27		A4
2514	" "	8	W½SW	1904-10-27		A4
2515	BOULTON, Jacob	15	SE	1888-04-05		A4
2516	BOULTON, Jake	27	S½NE	1904-09-28		A4
2517	BOULTON, James	22	NW	1894-02-28		A4
2526	BOULTON, Keziah	15	NE	1888-04-05		A4
2527	BOULTON, Lee	15	E½NW	1894-02-28		A4
2528	" "	15	E½SW	1894-02-28		A4
2547	BOULTON, Samuel	9	SE	1884-12-30		A4
2552	BOULTON, Thomas A	5	SENE	1859-05-02		A1
2554	" "	5	W½NE	1859-05-02		A1
2550	" "	5	NENW	1860-04-02		A1
2551	" "	5	NESW	1881-05-10		A4
2553	" "	5	SENW	1881-05-10		A4
2555	BOULTON, Wash	7	N½SE	1911-01-05		A4
2556	" "	7	S½NE	1911-01-05		A4
2529	BRADFORD, Leonard J	25	NESE	1882-05-10		A1

ID	Individual in Patent	Sec.	Sec. Part	Date Issued	Other Counties	For More Info . . .
2530	BRADFORD, Leonard J (Cont'd)	25	SENE	1882-05-10		A1
2491	BRELAND, Eugene	33	W½SE	1906-10-15		A4
2501	BRELAND, George	35	E½NE	1902-04-08		A4 G15
2525	BRELAND, Joseph T	6	SESE	1882-12-30		A1
2523	" "	6	NWSE	1901-03-23		A4
2524	" "	6	S½NE	1901-03-23		A4
2501	BRELAND, Margret	35	E½NE	1902-04-08		A4 G15
2541	BRELAND, Riley E	35	E½NW	1894-09-28		A4
2542	"	35	W½NE	1894-09-28		A4
2560	BRELAND, William C	19	NENE	1914-06-27		A1
2561	" "	19	NENW	1914-06-27		A1
2562	" "	19	W½NE	1914-06-27		A1
2563	DANTZLER, William	23	SE	1889-01-05		A4
2521	DAVIS, James L	14	W½NE	1900-11-28		A4
2536	DOSSETT, Moses H	6	NESE	1908-10-29		A1
2497	EPHRAM, Frank	26	N½SE	1901-03-23		A4
2498	" "	26	S½NE	1901-03-23		A4
2534	FACEN, Mary	26	S½NW	1910-09-01		A4 G31
2489	FAIRLY, Enoch	18	N½NE	1902-02-12		A4
2490	" "	7	S½SE	1902-02-12		A4
2503	FREEMAN, George P	6	NW	1891-06-30		A4
2502	GAINES, George D	12		1912-08-08		A1 F
2565	GAINES, Young	1	NW	1912-08-08		A1
2566	" "	2	E½	1912-08-08		A1 F
2567	" "	2	W½	1912-08-08		A1 F
2395	GAVIN, Andrews	10	SESW	1841-01-05		A1
2548	GREEN, Samuel J	36	SESE	1889-04-23		A1
2394	GRIFFIN, Alfred	34	SWNW	1904-10-27		A4
2474	GRIFFIN, Dandy	33	E½SE	1904-11-15		A4
2472	" "	26	N½NE	1906-08-16		A4
2473	" "	26	N½NW	1906-08-16		A4
2538	GRIFFIN, Randall	24	E½SE	1904-09-28		A4
2539	" "	25	NENE	1904-09-28		A4
2379	HARLSFIELD, Adam	25	SESW	1889-05-06		A1
2380	HARTFIELD, Adam	25	NWNE	1882-05-10		A1
2381	"	25	SWNE	1882-05-10		A1
2470	HARTFIELD, Cyrus	24	S½NE	1890-12-31		A4
2471	"	24	W½SE	1890-12-31		A4
2482	HARTFIELD, Dennis D	27	NESW	1906-06-04		A4
2483	" "	27	SENW	1906-06-04		A4
2484	" "	27	W½SE	1906-06-04		A4
2488	HARTFIELD, Emanuel	24	SW	1889-11-23		A4
2537	HARTFIELD, Plummer L	27	SWSW	1907-05-13		A4
2543	HARTFIELD, Riley	24	NENE	1906-05-01		A4
2557	HARTFIELD, Wash	23	N½NE	1905-10-19		A4
2558	HARTFIELD, Washington	23	SENE	1905-12-30		A4
2559	" "	24	SWNW	1905-12-30		A4
2382	HARTSFIELD, Adam	25	NENW	1882-06-01		A1
2383	" "	25	NWSE	1882-10-10		A1
2384	" "	25	SENW	1882-10-10		A1
2405	HEMPHILL, Brickley C	8	NESW	1890-07-03		A1 G44
2406	" "	8	W½SE	1890-07-03		A1 G44
2405	HEMPHILL, Samuel H	8	NESW	1890-07-03		A1 G44
2406	" "	8	W½SE	1890-07-03		A1 G44
2410	HILLS, Charles T	18	W½	1890-07-03		A1
2411	" "	19	S½	1890-07-03		A1
2412	" "	19	SENE	1890-07-03		A1
2413	" "	19	SENW	1890-07-03		A1
2414	" "	20	N½	1890-07-03		A1
2415	" "	20	NWSE	1890-07-03		A1
2416	" "	20	SESE	1890-07-03		A1
2417	" "	20	SW	1890-07-03		A1
2418	" "	21	E½SE	1890-07-03		A1
2419	" "	21	NENE	1890-07-03		A1
2420	" "	21	SENE	1890-07-03		A1
2421	" "	21	SWNW	1890-07-03		A1
2422	" "	21	SWSW	1890-07-03		A1
2423	" "	22	N½SW	1890-07-03		A1
2424	" "	22	NWSE	1890-07-03		A1
2425	" "	25	SWSE	1890-07-03		A1
2426	" "	26	S½SE	1890-07-03		A1
2427	" "	26	SW	1890-07-03		A1
2428	" "	27	E½SE	1890-07-03		A1

ID	Individual in Patent	Sec.	Sec. Part	Date Issued	Other Counties	For More Info . . .
2429	HILLS, Charles T (Cont'd)	27	NWSW	1890-07-03		A1
2430	" "	27	SWNW	1890-07-03		A1
2431	" "	28	E½NE	1890-07-03		A1
2432	" "	28	NESE	1890-07-03		A1
2433	" "	28	SENW	1890-07-03		A1
2434	" "	28	SW	1890-07-03		A1
2435	" "	28	SWSE	1890-07-03		A1
2436	" "	28	W½NW	1890-07-03		A1
2437	" "	29	NENE	1890-07-03		A1
2438	" "	29	NESW	1890-07-03		A1
2439	" "	29	S½NW	1890-07-03		A1
2440	" "	29	SE	1890-07-03		A1
2441	" "	29	SWNE	1890-07-03		A1
2442	" "	29	W½SW	1890-07-03		A1
2443	" "	30	E½	1890-07-03		A1
2444	" "	31	NENE	1890-07-03		A1
2445	" "	32	E½SW	1890-07-03		A1
2446	" "	32	NENE	1890-07-03		A1
2447	" "	32	NWSW	1890-07-03		A1
2448	" "	32	SENW	1890-07-03		A1
2449	" "	32	W½NE	1890-07-03		A1
2450	" "	32	W½NW	1890-07-03		A1
2451	" "	32	W½SE	1890-07-03		A1
2452	" "	33	NENW	1890-07-03		A1
2453	" "	34	NENE	1890-07-03		A1
2454	" "	34	SESW	1890-07-03		A1
2455	" "	34	SWSE	1890-07-03		A1
2456	" "	34	W½SW	1890-07-03		A1
2457	" "	35	NWSW	1890-07-03		A1
2458	" "	35	SESW	1890-07-03		A1
2459	" "	35	W½NW	1890-07-03		A1
2460	" "	36	N½SE	1890-07-03		A1
2461	" "	36	S½NE	1890-07-03		A1
2462	" "	36	SWSE	1890-07-03		A1
2463	" "	36	W½	1890-07-03		A1
2464	" "	6	N½SW	1890-07-03		A1
2465	" "	7	S½NW	1890-07-03		A1
2466	" "	7	SW	1890-07-03		A1
2481	HOLLINSWORTH, David P	1	N½NE	1859-05-02		A1
2531	HOUSLEY, Mary E	24	N½NW	1895-05-11		A4
2532	" "	24	NWNE	1895-05-11		A4
2533	" "	24	SENW	1895-05-11		A4
2519	KILPATRICK, James	18	NESE	1919-07-01		A4
2520	" "	18	SENE	1919-07-01		A4
2377	KITTRELL, Absolom	1	S½NE	1882-05-10		A1
2378	" "	1	SE	1882-05-10		A1
2534	MAMAN, Frank	26	S½NW	1910-09-01		A4 G31
2534	MAMAN, Mary	26	S½NW	1910-09-01		A4 G31
2477	MARTIN, Daniel W	17	E½	1890-07-03		A1
2478	" "	17	E½SW	1890-07-03		A1
2479	" "	17	NWSW	1890-07-03		A1
2480	" "	21	NWNW	1890-07-03		A1
2386	MCKENZIE, Alexander	4	NESW	1859-11-10		A1
2387	" "	4	SESW	1859-11-10		A1
2388	MCPHERSON, Alexander	30	NESW	1889-04-23		A1 G62
2389	" "	30	SENW	1889-04-23		A1 G62
2390	" "	30	W½SW	1889-04-23		A1 G62
2391	" "	31	N½SE	1889-04-23		A1 G62
2392	" "	31	SWNE	1889-04-23		A1 G62
2393	" "	31	W½	1889-04-23		A1 G62
2388	MCPHERSON, Edward G	30	NESW	1889-04-23		A1 G62
2389	" "	30	SENW	1889-04-23		A1 G62
2390	" "	30	W½SW	1889-04-23		A1 G62
2391	" "	31	N½SE	1889-04-23		A1 G62
2392	" "	31	SWNE	1889-04-23		A1 G62
2393	" "	31	W½	1889-04-23		A1 G62
2388	MCPHERSON, Martin J	30	NESW	1889-04-23		A1 G62
2389	" "	30	SENW	1889-04-23		A1 G62
2390	" "	30	W½SW	1889-04-23		A1 G62
2391	" "	31	N½SE	1889-04-23		A1 G62
2392	" "	31	SWNE	1889-04-23		A1 G62
2393	" "	31	W½	1889-04-23		A1 G62
2388	MCPHERSON, William	30	NESW	1889-04-23		A1 G62

ID	Individual in Patent	Sec.	Sec. Part	Date Issued	Other Counties	For More Info . . .
2389	MCPHERSON, William (Cont'd)	30	SENW	1889-04-23		A1 G62
2390	" "	30	W½SW	1889-04-23		A1 G62
2391	" "	31	N½SE	1889-04-23		A1 G62
2392	" "	31	SWNE	1889-04-23		A1 G62
2393	" "	31	W½	1889-04-23		A1 G62
2512	MERRITT, Isaac	14	NW	1859-05-02		A1
2549	MERRITT, Susan	13	SW	1906-05-01		A4
2385	MOODY, Adam	23	SW	1892-03-17		A4
2493	MOODY, Forest	22	S½SW	1890-12-31		A4
2494	" "	27	N½NW	1890-12-31		A4
2540	MOODY, Redick	14	SE	1888-04-05		A4
2564	MOODY, William	14	S½SW	1910-06-02		A4
2544	MORGAN, Rufus	36	NWNE	1919-11-14		A4
2518	PATTERSON, James H	5	NENE	1914-05-28		A4
2475	ROBERTS, Daniel	25	N½SW	1891-05-20		A4
2476	" "	25	W½NW	1891-05-20		A4
2535	SMITH, Mary	10	W½SW	1906-05-01		A4
2545	STAFFORD, Sam	22	S½SE	1891-06-30		A4
2546	" "	27	N½NE	1891-06-30		A4
2506	WAGAR, Humphrey R	30	SESW	1889-04-09		A1 G75
2507	" "	30	SWNW	1889-04-09		A1 G75
2508	" "	31	NWNE	1889-04-09		A1 G75
2509	" "	31	S½SE	1889-04-09		A1 G75
2510	" "	31	SENE	1889-04-09		A1 G75
2511	" "	32	SWSW	1889-04-09		A1 G75
2506	WELLS, Willard B	30	SESW	1889-04-09		A1 G75
2507	" "	30	SWNW	1889-04-09		A1 G75
2508	" "	31	NWNE	1889-04-09		A1 G75
2509	" "	31	S½SE	1889-04-09		A1 G75
2510	" "	31	SENE	1889-04-09		A1 G75
2511	" "	32	SWSW	1889-04-09		A1 G75
2486	WILLIAMS, Elijah E	19	W½NW	1915-04-12		A4

Patent Map

T2-N R9-W
St Stephens Meridian

Map Group 12

Township Statistics

Parcels Mapped	:	195
Number of Patents	:	105
Number of Individuals	:	86
Patentees Identified	:	78
Number of Surnames	:	40
Multi-Patentee Parcels	:	16
Oldest Patent Date	:	1/5/1841
Most Recent Patent	:	11/14/1919
Block/Lot Parcels	:	0
Parcels Re - Issued	:	0
Parcels that Overlap	:	0
Cities and Towns	:	2
Cemeteries	:	1

Section 6
FREEMAN George P 1891
BRELAND Joseph T 1901
HILLS Charles T 1890
BRELAND Joseph T 1901
DOSSETT Moses H 1908
BOULTON Annie 1905
BOULTON Annie 1905
BRELAND Joseph T 1882

Section 5
BOULTON Blake 1882
BOULTON Thomas A 1860
BOULTON Thomas A 1859
PATTERSON James H 1914
BOULTON Blake 1882
BOULTON Thomas A 1881
BOULTON Thomas A 1881
BOULTON Thomas A 1859
BOULTON Thomas A 1881
BOULTON Charles 1859
BOULTON Blake 1882

Section 4
MCKENZIE Alexander 1859
MCKENZIE Alexander 1859

Section 7
BOULTON Annie 1905
HILLS Charles T 1890
BOULTON Wash 1911
HILLS Charles T 1890
BOULTON Wash 1911
FAIRLY Enoch 1902

Section 8
BOULTON Jack 1904
BEARDSLEY Henderson 1888
BEARDSLEY Henderson 1888
BOULTON Jack 1904
HEMPHILL [44] Brickley C 1890
HEMPHILL [44] Brickley C 1890
BOULTON George 1894

Section 9
BOULTON Effy 1882
BOULTON Gabe 1881
BEARDSLEY Johnson 1905
BOULTON Samuel 1884

Section 18
FAIRLY Enoch 1902
HILLS Charles T 1890

Section 17
KILPATRICK James 1919
BOULTON Caroline 1896
KILPATRICK James 1919
MARTIN Daniel W 1890
MARTIN Daniel W 1890
MARTIN Daniel W 1890

Section 16

Section 19
WILLIAMS Elijah E 1915
BRELAND William C 1914
BRELAND William C 1914
BRELAND William C 1914
HILLS Charles T 1890
HILLS Charles T 1890
HILLS Charles T 1890

Section 20
HILLS Charles T 1890
HILLS Charles T 1890
HILLS Charles T 1890

Section 21
MARTIN Daniel W 1890
HILLS Charles T 1890
HILLS Charles T 1890
HILLS Charles T 1890
HILLS Charles T 1890
HILLS Charles T 1890
HILLS Charles T 1890

Section 30
BOULTON Absolem A 1905
MCPHERSON [62] Alexander 1889
WAGAR [75] Humphrey R 1889
MCPHERSON [62] Alexander 1889
MCPHERSON [62] Alexander 1889
HILLS Charles T 1890
WAGAR [75] Humphrey R 1889

Section 29
HILLS Charles T 1890
HILLS Charles T 1890
HILLS Charles T 1890
HILLS Charles T 1890
HILLS Charles T 1890
HILLS Charles T 1890

Section 28
HILLS Charles T 1890
HILLS Charles T 1890
HILLS Charles T 1890
HILLS Charles T 1890
HILLS Charles T 1890
HILLS Charles T 1890
HILLS Charles T 1890

Section 31
WAGAR [75] Humphrey R 1889
HILLS Charles T 1890
MCPHERSON [62] Alexander 1889
WAGAR [75] Humphrey R 1889
MCPHERSON [62] Alexander 1889
MCPHERSON [62] Alexander 1889
WAGAR [75] Humphrey R 1889

Section 32
HILLS Charles T 1890
HILLS Charles T 1890
HILLS Charles T 1890
HILLS Charles T 1890
HILLS Charles T 1890
HILLS Charles T 1890
HILLS Charles T 1890
WAGAR [75] Humphrey R 1889

Section 33
HILLS Charles T 1890
HILLS Charles T 1890
BOULTON Charley P 1906
BOULTON Charley P 1906
BOULTON Charley P 1906
BRELAND Eugene 1906
GRIFFIN Dandy 1904

3	GAINES Young 1912	2	GAINES Young 1912

GAINES Young 1912

HOLLINSWORTH David P 1859

1

KITTRELL Absolom 1882

KITTRELL Absolom 1882

SMITH Mary 1906

10

GAVIN Andrews 1841

11

GAINES George D 1912

12

BOULTON Frank 1900

BOULTON Lee 1894

BOULTON Keziah 1888

MERRITT Isaac 1859

DAVIS James L 1900

14

BANG Fannie 1897

13

BOULTON Frank 1900

15

BOULTON Lee 1894

BOULTON Jacob 1888

BOLTON Charles 1914

MOODY William 1910

MOODY Redick 1888

MERRITT Susan 1906

BOULTON James 1894

BOULTON Absolem 1895

22

BOULTON Absolem 1895

BOULTON Austin 1899

BOULTON Absolem 1895

BOULTON Austin 1899

BOULTON Austin 1899

HARTFIELD Washington 1905

HARTFIELD Wash 1905

HARTFIELD Washington 1905

HOUSLEY Mary E 1895

HOUSLEY Mary E 1895

HOUSLEY Mary E 1895

24

HARTFIELD Riley 1906

HARTFIELD Cyrus 1890

HILLS Charles T 1890

HILLS Charles T 1890

BOULTON Emaline 1901

23

MOODY Adam 1892

DANTZLER William 1889

HARTFIELD Emanuel 1889

HARTFIELD Cyrus 1890

GRIFFIN Randall 1904

MOODY Forest 1890

STAFFORD Sam 1891

MOODY Forest 1890

STAFFORD Sam 1891

GRIFFIN Dandy 1906

GRIFFIN Dandy 1906

ROBERTS Daniel 1891

HARTSFIELD Adam 1882

HARTFIELD Adam 1882

GRIFFIN Randall 1904

HILLS Charles T 1890

HARTFIELD Dennis D 1906

BOULTON Jake 1904

FACEN [31] Mary 1910

EPHRAM Frank 1901

HARTSFIELD Adam 1882

25

HARTFIELD Adam 1882

BRADFORD Leonard J 1882

HILLS Charles T 1890

HARTFIELD Dennis D 1906

27

HILLS Charles T 1890

26

EPHRAM Frank 1901

ROBERTS Daniel 1891

HARTSFIELD Adam 1882

BRADFORD Leonard J 1882

HARTFIELD Plummer L 1907

HARTFIELD Dennis D 1906

HILLS Charles T 1890

HILLS Charles T 1890

HARTSFIELD Adam 1889

HILLS Charles T 1890

GRIFFIN Alfred 1904

34

HILLS Charles T 1890

HILLS Charles T 1890

HILLS Charles T 1890

HILLS Charles T 1890

HILLS Charles T 1890

BRELAND Riley E 1894

BRELAND Riley E 1894

BRELAND [15] George 1902

35

HILLS Charles T 1890

HILLS Charles T 1890

MORGAN Rufus 1919

36

HILLS Charles T 1890

HILLS Charles T 1890

HILLS Charles T 1890

GREEN Samuel J 1889

Helpful Hints

1. This Map's INDEX can be found on the preceding pages.

2. Refer to Map "C" to see where this Township lies within Perry County, Mississippi.

3. Numbers within square brackets [ ] denote a multi-patentee land parcel (multi-owner). Refer to Appendix "C" for a full list of members in this group.

4. Areas that look to be crowded with Patentees usually indicate multiple sales of the same parcel (Re-issues) or Overlapping parcels. See this Township's Index for an explanation of these and other circumstances that might explain "odd" groupings of Patentees on this map.

Legend

———— Patent Boundary

━━━━ Section Boundary

░░░░ No Patents Found (or Outside County)

1., 2., 3., ... Lot Numbers (when beside a name)

[ ] Group Number (see Appendix "C")

Scale: Section = 1 mile X 1 mile (generally, with some exceptions)

159

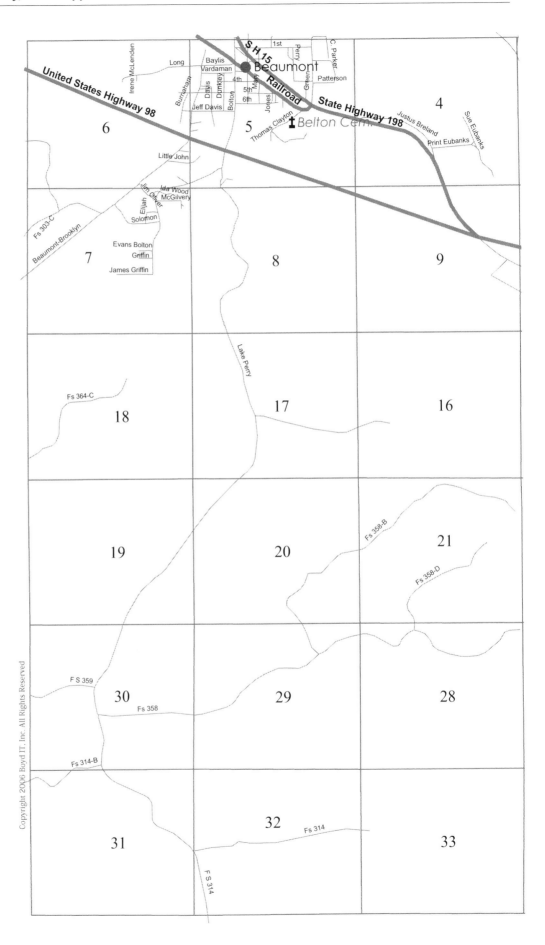

Road Map

T2-N R9-W
St Stephens Meridian

Map Group 12

Cities & Towns
Beaumont
Little Creek

Cemeteries
Belton Cemetery

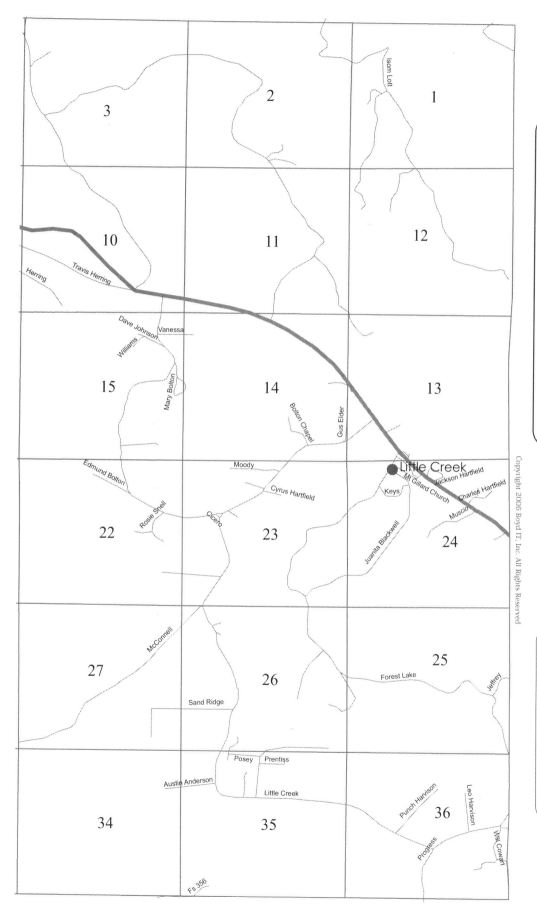

3

2

1

Isom Lott

10

11

12

Travis Herring

Herring

Dave Johnson

Vanessa

Williams

Mary Bolton

15

14

13

Bolton Chapel

Gus Elder

Moody

Little Creek

Mt Gillard Church

Jackson Hartfield

Edmund Bolton

Cyrus Hartfield

Keys

Charles Hartfield

Muscio

Rosie Snell

Cicero

22

23

Juanita Blackwell

24

McConnell

25

26

Forest Lake

Jeffrey

Sand Ridge

Posey

Prentiss

Austin Anderson

Little Creek

Punch Harvison

Leo Harvison

34

35

36

Progress

Whit Cowart

Fs 356

Helpful Hints

1. This road map has a number of uses, but primarily it is to help you: a) find the present location of land owned by your ancestors (at least the general area), b) find cemeteries and city-centers, and c) estimate the route/roads used by Census-takers & tax-assessors.

2. If you plan to travel to Perry County to locate cemeteries or land parcels, please pick up a modern travel map for the area before you do. Mapping old land parcels on modern maps is not as exact a science as you might think. Just the slightest variations in public land survey coordinates, estimates of parcel boundaries, or road-map deviations can greatly alter a map's representation of how a road either does or doesn't cross a particular parcel of land.

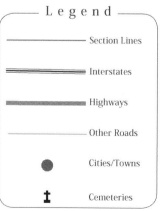

Legend

———	Section Lines
═══	Interstates
▓▓▓	Highways
———	Other Roads
●	Cities/Towns
✝	Cemeteries

Scale: Section = 1 mile X 1 mile
(generally, with some exceptions)

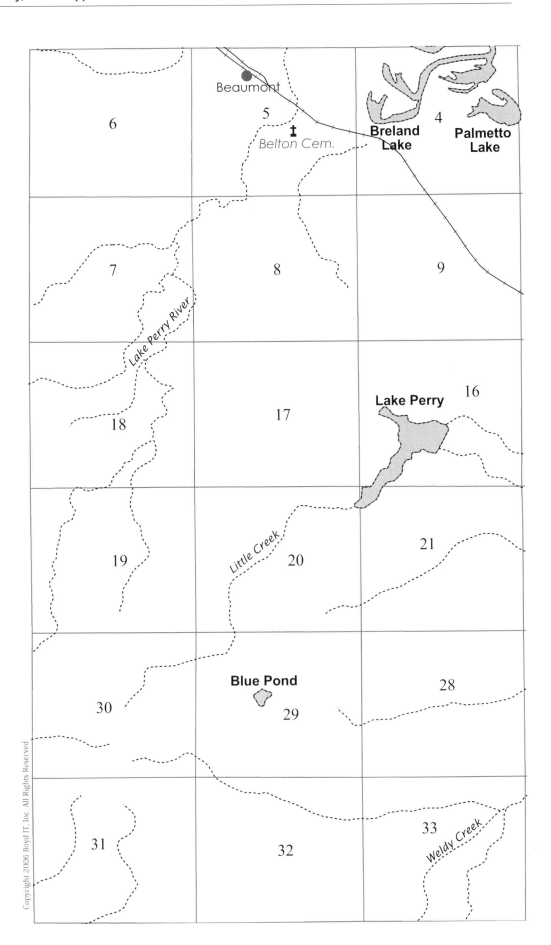

Historical Map

T2-N R9-W
St Stephens Meridian

Map Group 12

Cities & Towns
Beaumont
Little Creek

Cemeteries
Belton Cemetery

Beaumont

6

5

Belton Cem.

4

Breland Lake

Palmetto Lake

7

8

9

Lake Perry River

18

17

Lake Perry

16

19

Little Creek

20

21

30

Blue Pond

29

28

31

32

33

Weldy Creek

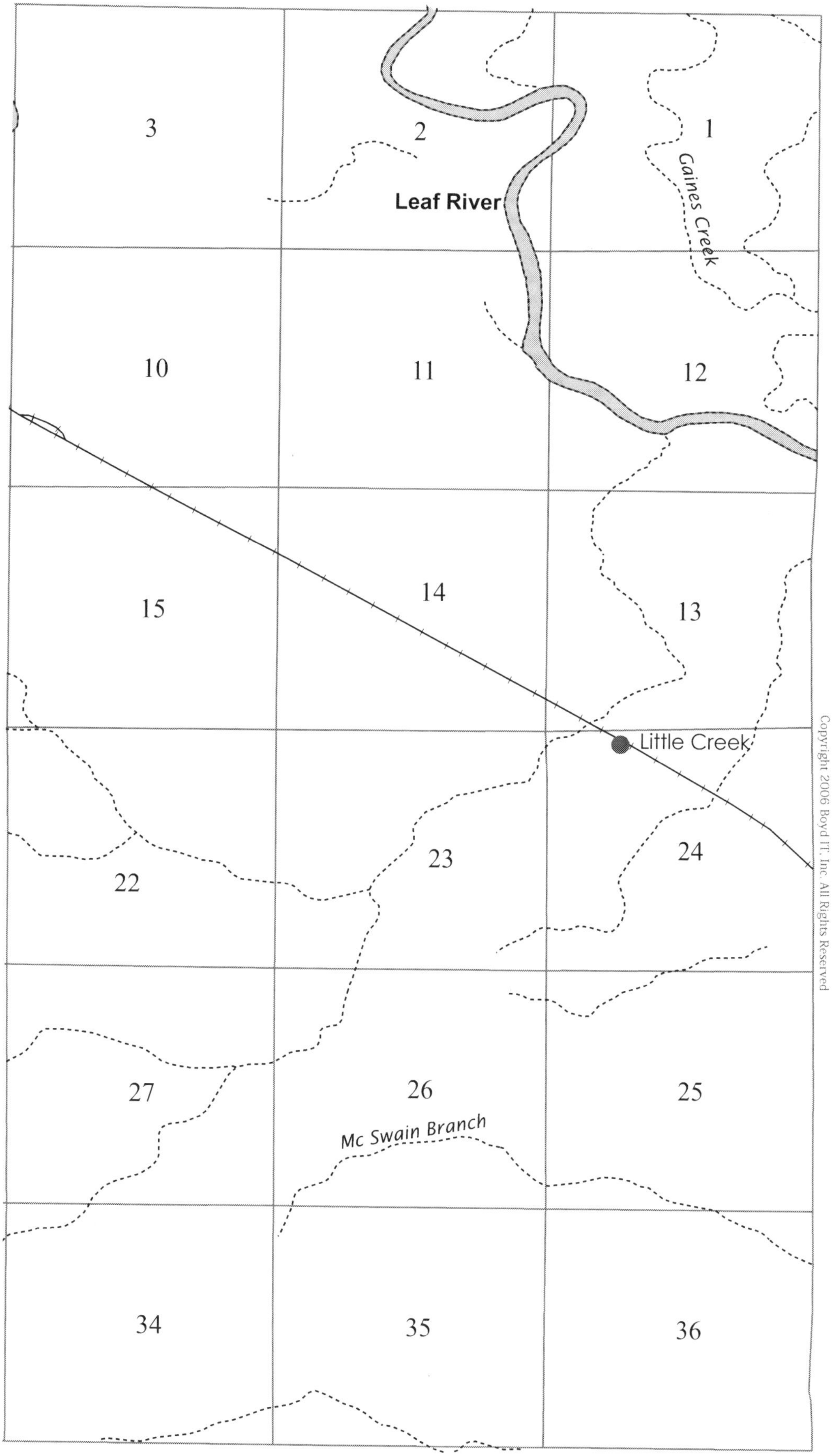
3
2
1
Leaf River
Gaines Creek
10
11
12
15
14
13
Little Creek
22
23
24
27
26
25
Mc Swain Branch
34
35
36
Copyright 2006 Boyd IT, Inc. All Rights Reserved

Helpful Hints

1. This Map takes a different look at the same Congressional Township displayed in the preceding two maps. It presents features that can help you better envision the historical development of the area: a) Water-bodies (lakes & ponds), b) Water-courses (rivers, streams, etc.), c) Railroads, d) City/town center-points (where they were oftentimes located when first settled), and e) Cemeteries.

2. Using this "Historical" map in tandem with this Township's Patent Map and Road Map, may lead you to some interesting discoveries. You will often find roads, towns, cemeteries, and waterways are named after nearby landowners: sometimes those names will be the ones you are researching. See how many of these research gems you can find here in Perry County.

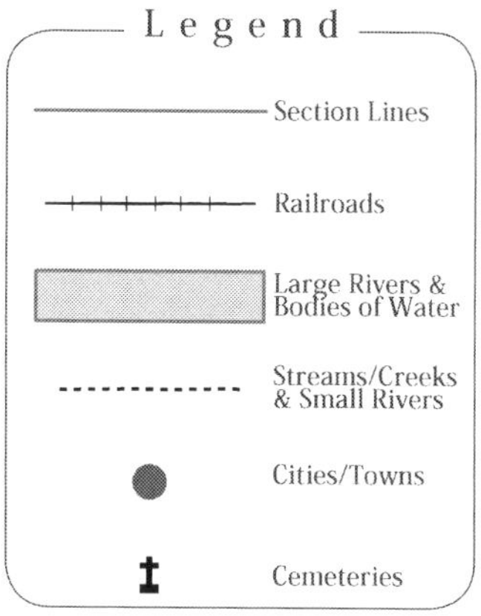
Legend
Section Lines
Railroads
Large Rivers & Bodies of Water
Streams/Creeks & Small Rivers
Cities/Towns
Cemeteries

Scale: Section = 1 mile X 1 mile
(there are some exceptions)

Map Group 13: Index to Land Patents

Township 1-North Range 11-West (St Stephens)

After you locate an individual in this Index, take note of the Section and Section Part then proceed to the Land Patent map on the pages immediately following. You should have no difficulty locating the corresponding parcel of land.

The "For More Info" Column will lead you to more information about the underlying Patents. See the *Legend* at right, and the "How to Use this Book" chapter, for more information.

```
                            LEGEND
                  "For More Info . . . " column
A = Authority (Legislative Act, See Appendix "A")
B = Block or Lot (location in Section unknown)
C = Cancelled Patent
F = Fractional Section
G = Group  (Multi-Patentee Patent, see Appendix "C")
V = Overlaps another Parcel
R = Re-Issued (Parcel patented more than once)

(A & G items require you to look in the Appendixes referred
to above. All other Letter-designations followed by a number
require you to locate line-items in this index that possess
the ID number found after the letter).
```

ID	Individual in Patent	Sec.	Sec. Part	Date Issued	Other Counties	For More Info . . .
2654	ALDRIDGE, Gordon	27	NESE	1914-10-08		A1
2684	ALFRED, Jesse	18	NWSW	1917-08-11		A4
2668	ANDERSON, James	7	SWNE	1859-11-10		A1
2779	ANDREW, Prentiss	34	2	1891-06-30		A4
2780	" "	34	6	1891-06-30		A4
2781	" "	34	7	1891-06-30		A4
2782	" "	34	8	1891-06-30		A4
2794	ANDREW, Samuel	29	E½NW	1890-08-16		A4
2795	" "	29	NESW	1890-08-16		A4
2796	" "	29	NWSE	1890-08-16		A4
2659	ANDREWS, Henry	35	10	1910-05-09		A4
2660	" "	35	9	1910-05-09		A4
2807	ANDREWS, Solomon L	29	SWNW	1904-08-30		A4
2820	ANDREWS, Tillis	28	NENW	1916-11-01		A4
2568	BENJAMIN, Albert	28	E½SW	1888-04-05		A4
2569	" "	28	SENW	1888-04-05		A4
2570	" "	33	3	1888-04-05		A4
2584	BIVINS, Arthur M	36	NENW	1909-01-28		A4
2585	" "	36	NWNE	1909-01-28		A4
2586	" "	36	SENW	1909-01-28		A4
2688	BOOTH, Joe B	25	N½NW	1906-03-05		A4
2689	" "	25	SWNW	1906-03-05		A4
2725	BOOTH, Lawyer	9	S½SE	1919-05-26		A4
2582	BOULTON, Annie	17	NWSW	1893-12-18		A1 G10
2583	" "	17	S½SW	1893-12-18		A1 G10
2571	BRELAND, Alex	23	N½SE	1906-10-15		A4 V2702
2572	" "	23	W½NE	1906-10-15		A4
2576	BRELAND, Andrew J	24	NENE	1912-12-13		A1
2595	BRELAND, Bully	21	N½NE	1910-04-11		A4
2596	" "	22	W½NW	1910-04-11		A4
2603	BRELAND, Dan B	15	N½SE	1906-06-21		A4
2604	" "	15	SWSE	1910-11-28		A4
2605	BRELAND, Daniel	24	NW	1889-01-12		A4
2646	BRELAND, Gabriel L	22	E½NE	1904-11-15		A4
2647	" "	22	SENW	1904-11-15		A4
2648	" "	22	SWNE	1904-11-15		A4
2658	BRELAND, Harry	14	SE	1917-04-30		A4
2669	BRELAND, James M	11	SWSE	1890-08-16		A4
2670	" "	14	SENW	1890-08-16		A4
2671	" "	14	W½NE	1890-08-16		A4
2745	BRELAND, Lugene	11	SESE	1898-11-11		A4
2746	" "	12	SWSW	1898-11-11		A4
2747	BRELAND, Lula	34	1	1911-06-29		A4 G16
2748	" "	35	3	1911-06-29		A4 G16
2749	" "	35	4	1911-06-29		A4 G16
2826	BROADUS, Will	7	NWSE	1916-03-20		A4

ID	Individual in Patent	Sec.	Sec. Part	Date Issued	Other Counties	For More Info . . .
2785	BROWN, Rosa	32	8	1909-01-11		A4 G18
2763	BUCKHALTER, Martha M	18	SESW	1884-12-30		A1
2764	" "	18	SWSE	1884-12-30		A1
2765	" "	19	NENW	1884-12-30		A1
2766	" "	19	NWNE	1884-12-30		A1
2888	BYRD, William W	24	N½SE	1897-05-20		A4
2889	" "	24	S½NE	1897-05-20		A4
2787	CESAR, Sabra	28	SWNW	1885-05-25		A4
2788	" "	28	W½SW	1885-05-25		A4
2789	" "	29	SESE	1885-05-25		A4
2640	CROSBY, Elisha J	23	S½SE	1906-05-01		A1
2641	" "	24	SWSW	1906-05-01		A1
2723	DANTZLER, Julia	32	10	1893-08-23		A4
2724	" "	32	11	1893-08-23		A4
2735	DANTZLER, Lorenzo N	12	N½SE	1883-09-15		A1 G27
2737	" "	12	SESW	1883-09-15		A1 G27
2738	" "	12	SWSE	1883-09-15		A1 G27
2733	" "	1	S½SE	1884-12-30		A1 G27
2734	" "	12	E½NE	1884-12-30		A1 G27
2736	" "	12	SESE	1884-12-30		A1 G27
2739	" "	12	W½NE	1884-12-30		A1 G27
2740	" "	13	NWNW	1884-12-30		A1 G27
2731	" "	15	SWSW	1885-06-12		A1
2732	" "	25	NENE	1890-07-03		A1
2637	DAVIS, Edwin	15	E½SW	1889-11-23		A4
2638	" "	22	NENW	1889-11-23		A4
2639	" "	22	NWNE	1889-11-23		A4
2677	DAVIS, James W	25	E½SE	1915-04-12		A4
2678	" "	36	1	1915-04-12		A4
2726	DEAKEL, Lee	7	NESE	1897-05-07		A4
2727	" "	7	S½SE	1897-05-07		A4
2643	FAIRLEY, Evander	3	NESW	1891-05-20		A4
2644	" "	3	SENW	1891-05-20		A4
2645	" "	3	W½SW	1891-05-20		A4
2714	FAIRLEY, John W	25	NWNE	1882-12-30		A1
2716	" "	35	5	1882-12-30		A1
2713	" "	15	SENW	1884-12-30		A1
2715	" "	28	SWSE	1884-12-30		A1
2753	FAIRLEY, Mack	19	S½NE	1902-02-12		A4
2754	" "	19	S½NW	1902-02-12		A4
2798	FAIRLEY, Sarah	33	1	1889-01-05		A4 G36
2799	" "	33	2	1889-01-05		A4 G36
2800	" "	33	7	1889-01-05		A4 G36
2804	FAIRLEY, Simon	34	3	1882-12-30		A1
2805	" "	34	4	1882-12-30		A1
2801	" "	27	W½SW	1884-12-30		A1
2802	" "	28	NWNW	1884-12-30		A1
2803	" "	28	SESE	1884-12-30		A1
2750	FILINGIM, Luther	10	NENE	1910-01-20		A4
2751	" "	10	SENW	1910-01-20		A4
2752	" "	10	W½NE	1910-01-20		A4
2685	FILLINGINE, Jesse D	10	NENW	1911-10-09		A4
2686	" "	3	SESW	1911-10-09		A4
2687	" "	3	SWSE	1911-10-09		A4
2591	GAMMILL, Benjamin F	8	S½NE	1899-04-17		A4
2705	GARAWAY, John	15	SESE	1859-05-02		A1
2704	" "	14	SWSW	1859-06-01		A1
2808	GARAWAY, Solomon T	11	NENW	1854-03-15		A1
2810	" "	14	NENW	1854-03-15		A1
2811	" "	2	NESW	1854-03-15		A1
2812	" "	2	SESW	1854-03-15		A1
2813	" "	8	NESE	1854-03-15		A1
2809	" "	11	SESW	1859-05-02		A1
2601	GARRAWAY, Charley M	24	SESE	1896-12-14		A4
2814	GARRAWAY, Solomon T	10	SWSW	1882-05-10		A1
2815	" "	15	NWNW	1882-08-03		A1
2816	" "	9	NWSE	1882-08-03		A1
2882	GARRAWAY, William	36	4	1859-11-10		A1
2580	GRIFFIN, Andy	34	11	1881-09-17		A4
2581	" "	34	12	1881-09-17		A4
2655	GRIFFIN, Harrison	27	SWNW	1884-12-30		A4
2656	" "	28	N½SE	1884-12-30		A4
2657	" "	28	SENE	1884-12-30		A4

ID	Individual in Patent	Sec.	Sec. Part	Date Issued	Other Counties	For More Info . . .
2664	GRIFFIN, Jackson	34	10	1885-05-20		A4
2665	" "	34	9	1885-05-20		A4
2666	" "	35	11	1885-05-20		A4
2667	" "	35	12	1885-05-20		A4
2681	GRIFFIN, James W	1	SENW	1883-02-03		A1
2679	" "	1	N½SE	1884-12-30		A1
2680	" "	1	S½NE	1884-12-30		A1
2690	GRIFFIN, John A	7	NWNE	1854-03-15		A1
2691	" "	8	NWNW	1854-03-15		A1
2709	GRIFFIN, John P	32	12	1890-08-16		A4 C R2710
2711	" "	6	N½NE	1890-08-16		A4 C
2710	" "	32	12	1922-10-30		A4 R2709
2758	GRIFFIN, Margaret	29	SESW	1894-12-17		A4
2759	" "	29	SWSE	1894-12-17		A4
2760	" "	32	1	1894-12-17		A4
2761	" "	32	2	1894-12-17		A4
2790	GRIFFIN, Sam	33	11	1892-07-20		A4
2791	" "	33	4	1892-07-20		A4
2792	" "	33	5	1892-07-20		A4
2793	" "	33	6	1892-07-20		A4
2825	GRIFFIN, Washington	7	SENW	1854-03-15		A1
2884	GRIFFIN, William	31	12	1846-09-01		A1 F
2883	" "	31	10	1895-05-11		A4
2885	" "	31	2	1895-05-11		A4
2886	" "	31	7	1895-05-11		A4
2887	" "	31	9	1895-05-11		A4
2836	GRIFFIN, William C	29	S½NE	1882-10-10		A1
2839	" "	30	N½NE	1882-10-10		A1
2827	" "	18	SWSW	1883-09-15		A1
2828	" "	19	NENE	1884-12-30		A1
2829	" "	19	SESE	1884-12-30		A1
2830	" "	19	SESW	1884-12-30		A1
2831	" "	19	W½SW	1884-12-30		A1
2832	" "	29	NENE	1884-12-30		A1
2834	" "	29	NWNW	1884-12-30		A1
2837	" "	29	SWSW	1884-12-30		A1
2838	" "	30	E½SW	1884-12-30		A1
2840	" "	30	NENW	1884-12-30		A1
2841	" "	30	NWSE	1884-12-30		A1
2842	" "	30	SENE	1884-12-30		A1
2843	" "	30	SENW	1884-12-30		A1
2844	" "	30	SESE	1884-12-30		A1
2845	" "	30	SWNE	1884-12-30		A1
2846	" "	31	1	1884-12-30		A1
2847	" "	32	3	1884-12-30		A1
2848	" "	32	5	1884-12-30		A1
2849	" "	32	6	1884-12-30		A1
2850	" "	32	9	1884-12-30		A1
2833	" "	29	NWNE	1889-11-29		A1
2835	" "	29	NWSW	1889-11-29		A1
2856	GRIFFIN, William E	6	SESE	1881-06-23		A1
2858	" "	6	SWSE	1881-06-30		A1
2852	" "	13	SWSW	1882-05-10		A1
2855	" "	5	SWSW	1882-05-10		A1
2857	" "	6	SESW	1882-05-10		A1
2859	" "	7	NENE	1882-05-10		A1
2860	" "	8	NENW	1882-05-10		A1
2870	" "	4	SWSE	1882-08-03		A1 G43
2872	" "	5	S½SE	1882-08-03		A1 G43
2876	" "	8	NWNE	1882-08-03		A1 G43
2878	" "	9	NWNE	1882-08-03		A1 G43
2879	" "	9	SENE	1882-08-03		A1 G43
2851	" "	13	E½SW	1882-10-10		A1
2862	" "	23	NENE	1882-10-10		A1 G43
2865	" "	3	N½NW	1882-10-10		A1 G43
2866	" "	3	SWNW	1882-10-10		A1 G43
2874	" "	5	SESW	1882-10-10		A1 G43
2880	" "	9	SWNE	1882-10-10		A1 G43
2735	" "	12	N½SE	1883-09-15		A1 G27
2737	" "	12	SESW	1883-09-15		A1 G27
2738	" "	12	SWSE	1883-09-15		A1 G27
2853	" "	14	E½NE	1883-09-15		A1
2877	" "	9	NESW	1883-09-15		A1 G43

ID	Individual in Patent	Sec.	Sec. Part	Date Issued	Other Counties	For More Info . . .
2733	GRIFFIN, William E (Cont'd)	1	S½SE	1884-12-30		A1 G27
2734	"	12	E½NE	1884-12-30		A1 G27
2736	"	12	SESE	1884-12-30		A1 G27
2739	"	12	W½NE	1884-12-30		A1 G27
2740	"	13	NWNW	1884-12-30		A1 G27
2861	"	13	NWSW	1884-12-30		A1 G43
2863	"	23	SENE	1884-12-30		A1 G43
2854	"	28	SWNE	1884-12-30		A1
2864	"	29	NESE	1884-12-30		A1 G43
2867	"	4	N½NE	1884-12-30		A1 G43
2868	"	4	NWSW	1884-12-30		A1 G43
2869	"	4	SWNE	1884-12-30		A1 G43
2871	"	5	N½SE	1884-12-30		A1 G43
2873	"	5	SENE	1884-12-30		A1 G43
2875	"	6	W½NW	1884-12-30		A1 G43
2587	HARRIS, Augustus W	36	10	1913-05-21		A4
2588	"	36	7	1913-05-21		A4
2589	"	36	8	1913-05-21		A4
2590	"	36	9	1913-05-21		A4
2747	HARTFIELD, Lula	34	1	1911-06-29		A4 G16
2748	"	35	3	1911-06-29		A4 G16
2749	"	35	4	1911-06-29		A4 G16
2786	HERRING, Rufus Q	25	SW	1882-12-30		A1
2597	HOGAN, C E	10	N½SW	1883-04-30		A4
2598	"	10	W½NW	1883-04-30		A4
2720	HOGAN, Josiah L	4	NESW	1895-10-09		A4
2721	"	4	S½NW	1895-10-09		A4
2722	"	9	NWNW	1906-05-01		A4
2770	HOGAN, Mary M	15	N½NE	1904-08-26		A4 G52
2771	"	15	NENW	1904-08-26		A4 G52
2772	"	15	SWNE	1904-08-26		A4 G52
2577	HOLDER, Andrew J	7	SENE	1884-12-30		A4
2578	"	8	NWSW	1884-12-30		A4
2579	"	8	S½NW	1884-12-30		A4
2573	HOTIN, Alfred	33	12	1905-02-13		A4
2582	HOTON, Annie	17	NWSW	1893-12-18		A1 G10
2583	"	17	S½SW	1893-12-18		A1 G10
2762	JACKSON, Marion J	26	NE	1914-05-13		A4
2741	JAMES, Lucretia	31	3	1902-07-03		A4 G57
2742	"	31	4	1902-07-03		A4 G57
2743	"	31	5	1902-07-03		A4 G57
2744	"	31	6	1902-07-03		A4 G57
2663	JONES, Jack	25	SENE	1913-02-14		A4
2649	KENNEDY, George M	13	NENE	1889-11-29		A1
2650	"	13	W½SE	1889-11-29		A1
2674	LAMBERT, James S	4	E½SE	1884-11-20		A4
2675	"	4	NWSE	1884-11-20		A4
2676	"	9	NENE	1884-11-20		A4
2821	LEWIS, Vincent	33	10	1885-04-04		A4
2822	"	33	8	1885-04-04		A4
2823	"	33	9	1885-04-04		A4
2824	"	34	5	1885-04-04		A4
2634	MARTIN, Edward	2	NWNW	1891-05-20		A4
2635	"	3	N½NE	1891-05-20		A4
2636	"	3	SENE	1891-05-20		A4
2672	MARTIN, James	2	E½NW	1891-05-20		A4
2673	"	2	W½NE	1891-05-20		A4
2881	MARTIN, William F	8	SWSW	1910-05-09		A4
2707	MAXWELL, John L	4	SESW	1884-12-30		A1
2708	"	9	SESW	1884-12-30		A1
2706	"	31	11	1885-04-04		A4
2599	MCCARDLE, Charley J	23	E½SW	1905-12-13		A4
2600	"	23	SENW	1905-12-13		A4
2701	MCCARDLE, John F	23	N½NW	1904-11-15		A4
2702	"	23	NWSE	1904-11-15		A4 V2571
2703	"	23	SWNW	1904-11-15		A4
2741	MCINNIS, Albert	31	3	1902-07-03		A4 G57
2742	"	31	4	1902-07-03		A4 G57
2743	"	31	5	1902-07-03		A4 G57
2744	"	31	6	1902-07-03		A4 G57
2741	MCINNIS, Lucretia	31	3	1902-07-03		A4 G57
2742	"	31	4	1902-07-03		A4 G57
2743	"	31	5	1902-07-03		A4 G57

ID	Individual in Patent	Sec.	Sec. Part	Date Issued	Other Counties	For More Info . . .
2744	MCINNIS, Lucretia (Cont'd)	31	6	1902-07-03		A4 G57
2661	MCLOUD, Ida	15	NWSW	1906-06-04		A4
2662	" "	15	SWNW	1906-06-04		A4
2817	MISSISSIPPI, State Of	19	NWNW	1911-01-23		A6
2755	MIXON, Mack	17	NENE	1914-05-06		A4
2770	MIXON, Mary M	15	N½NE	1904-08-26		A4 G52
2771	" "	15	NENW	1904-08-26		A4 G52
2772	" "	15	SWNE	1904-08-26		A4 G52
2767	MOODY, Martin S	24	E½SW	1888-04-05		A4
2768	" "	24	NWSW	1888-04-05		A4
2769	" "	24	SWSE	1888-04-05		A4
2642	NIXON, Eran	10	SESW	1908-08-17		A4 G68
2574	PEARCE, Alfred	11	N½SW	1890-08-16		A4
2575	" "	11	W½NW	1890-08-16		A4
2712	PEARCE, John	8	SESW	1859-11-10		A1
2696	PEARCE, John C	11	SWSW	1882-05-10		A1
2699	" "	9	NESE	1882-05-10		A1
2697	" "	8	NENE	1882-06-01		A1
2698	" "	9	E½NW	1882-08-03		A1
2695	" "	11	SENW	1884-12-30		A1
2700	" "	9	SWNW	1889-04-20		A1
2718	PEARCE, Joseph	8	S½SE	1885-04-04		A4
2719	" "	9	W½SW	1885-04-04		A4
2728	PEARCE, Leona	11	NWSE	1923-01-04		A4 G69
2729	PEARCE, Levi	6	W½SW	1889-01-12		A4
2730	" "	7	N½NW	1889-01-12		A4
2818	PEARCE, Thomas	10	SESE	1859-05-02		A1
2819	" "	10	SWSE	1859-05-02		A1
2870	PERKINS, Benjamin F	4	SWSE	1882-08-03		A1 G43
2872	" "	5	S½SE	1882-08-03		A1 G43
2876	" "	8	NWNE	1882-08-03		A1 G43
2878	" "	9	NWNE	1882-08-03		A1 G43
2879	" "	9	SENE	1882-08-03		A1 G43
2862	" "	23	NENE	1882-10-10		A1 G43
2865	" "	3	N½NW	1882-10-10		A1 G43
2866	" "	3	SWNW	1882-10-10		A1 G43
2874	" "	5	SESW	1882-10-10		A1 G43
2880	" "	9	SWNE	1882-10-10		A1 G43
2877	" "	9	NESW	1883-09-15		A1 G43
2861	" "	13	NWSW	1884-12-30		A1 G43
2863	" "	23	SENE	1884-12-30		A1 G43
2864	" "	29	NESE	1884-12-30		A1 G43
2867	" "	4	N½NE	1884-12-30		A1 G43
2868	" "	4	NWSW	1884-12-30		A1 G43
2869	" "	4	SWNE	1884-12-30		A1 G43
2871	" "	5	N½SE	1884-12-30		A1 G43
2873	" "	5	SENE	1884-12-30		A1 G43
2875	" "	6	W½NW	1884-12-30		A1 G43
2592	" "	5	N½SW	1889-05-06		A1
2593	" "	5	S½NW	1889-05-06		A1
2594	" "	5	SWNE	1889-11-29		A1
2797	PERKINS, Samuel	17	NESW	1846-09-01		A1
2806	PERKINS, Solomon E	31	8	1890-07-03		A1
2778	RAMSEY, Plummer	15	SENE	1911-11-20		A4
2606	RANSDELL, Daniel M	1	N½NE	1884-12-30		A1
2607	" "	1	N½NW	1884-12-30		A1
2608	" "	1	SW	1884-12-30		A1
2609	" "	10	NESE	1884-12-30		A1
2610	" "	10	SENE	1884-12-30		A1
2611	" "	11	E½NE	1884-12-30		A1
2612	" "	11	NESE	1884-12-30		A1
2613	" "	12	N½SW	1884-12-30		A1
2614	" "	12	NW	1884-12-30		A1
2617	" "	2	E½SE	1884-12-30		A1
2618	" "	2	NENE	1884-12-30		A1
2623	" "	4	N½NW	1884-12-30		A1
2624	" "	5	N½NE	1884-12-30		A1
2625	" "	5	N½NW	1884-12-30		A1
2626	" "	6	E½NE	1884-12-30		A1
2627	" "	6	N½SE	1884-12-30		A1
2628	" "	6	NENW	1884-12-30		A1
2629	" "	6	NESW	1884-12-30		A1
2630	" "	6	SWNE	1884-12-30		A1

ID	Individual in Patent	Sec.	Sec. Part	Date Issued	Other Counties	For More Info . . .
2615	RANSDELL, Daniel M (Cont'd)	19	NESE	1888-11-30		A1
2616	" "	19	W½SE	1888-11-30		A1
2619	" "	30	NESE	1888-11-30		A1
2620	" "	30	NWSW	1888-11-30		A1
2621	" "	30	SWSE	1888-11-30		A1
2622	" "	30	W½NW	1888-11-30		A1
2798	RAYBORN, Sarah	33	1	1889-01-05		A4 G36
2799	" "	33	2	1889-01-05		A4 G36
2800	" "	33	7	1889-01-05		A4 G36
2783	SHATTLES, Raynor	2	SWNW	1912-02-01		A4
2784	SHATTLES, Raynor W	2	SENE	1920-06-25		A1
2756	SIMMONS, Malinda	11	W½NE	1895-11-13		A4
2757	" "	2	W½SE	1895-11-13		A4
2642	SINGLEY, Eran	10	SESW	1908-08-17		A4 G68
2728	SINGLEY, Leona	11	NWSE	1923-01-04		A4 G69
2785	SLOAN, Rosa	32	8	1909-01-11		A4 G18
2651	SMITH, George	18	N½SE	1891-05-20		A4
2652	" "	18	NESW	1891-05-20		A4
2653	" "	18	SESE	1891-05-20		A4
2717	SMITH, Johnie C	2	SWSW	1912-09-19		A1
2631	STAFFORD, Edward B	25	SENW	1861-02-01		A1
2632	" "	25	SWNE	1861-02-01		A1
2633	" "	25	W½SE	1861-02-01		A1
2692	STAFFORD, John A	2	NWSW	1897-01-12		A4
2693	" "	3	N½SE	1897-01-12		A4
2694	" "	3	SESE	1897-01-12		A4
2775	STAFFORD, Newton J	14	E½SW	1895-11-11		A4
2776	" "	14	NWSW	1895-11-11		A4
2777	" "	14	SWNW	1895-11-11		A4
2682	WEST, James W	27	E½SW	1889-12-19		A4
2683	" "	27	W½SE	1889-12-19		A4
2602	WHITE, Charley	13	SWNW	1916-03-09		A4 G76
2602	WHITE, Sarah	13	SWNW	1916-03-09		A4 G76
2773	WILLIAMSON, Mary	13	E½NW	1895-11-11		A4
2774	" "	13	W½NE	1895-11-11		A4

Patent Map

T1-N R11-W
St Stephens Meridian

Map Group 13

Township Statistics

Parcels Mapped	:	322
Number of Patents	:	167
Number of Individuals	:	116
Patentees Identified	:	108
Number of Surnames	:	62
Multi-Patentee Parcels	:	47
Oldest Patent Date	:	9/1/1846
Most Recent Patent	:	1/4/1923
Block/Lot Parcels	:	60
Parcels Re - Issued	:	1
Parcels that Overlap	:	2
Cities and Towns	:	0
Cemeteries	:	1

Section 6
RANSDELL Daniel M 1884
GRIFFIN John P 1890
GRIFFIN [43] William E 1884
RANSDELL Daniel M 1884
RANSDELL Daniel M 1884
PEARCE Levi 1889
RANSDELL Daniel M 1884
RANSDELL Daniel M 1884
GRIFFIN William E 1882
GRIFFIN William E 1881
GRIFFIN William E 1881

Section 5
RANSDELL Daniel M 1884
RANSDELL Daniel M 1884
PERKINS Benjamin F 1889
PERKINS Benjamin F 1889
GRIFFIN [43] William E 1884
PERKINS Benjamin F 1889
GRIFFIN [43] William E 1884
GRIFFIN William E 1882
GRIFFIN [43] William E 1882
GRIFFIN [43] William E 1882

Section 4
RANSDELL Daniel M 1884
GRIFFIN [43] William E 1884
HOGAN Josiah L 1895
GRIFFIN [43] William E 1884
GRIFFIN [43] William E 1884
HOGAN Josiah L 1895
LAMBERT James S 1884
LAMBERT James S 1884
MAXWELL John L 1884
GRIFFIN [43] William E 1882

Section 7
PEARCE Levi 1889
GRIFFIN John A 1854
GRIFFIN William E 1882
GRIFFIN Washington 1854
ANDERSON James 1859
HOLDER Andrew J 1884
BROADUS Will 1916
DEAKEL Lee 1897
DEAKEL Lee 1897

Section 8
GRIFFIN John A 1854
GRIFFIN William E 1882
GRIFFIN [43] William E 1882
PEARCE John C 1882
HOLDER Andrew J 1884
GAMMILL Benjamin F 1899
HOLDER Andrew J 1884
GARAWAY Solomon T 1854
MARTIN William F 1910
PEARCE John 1859
PEARCE Joseph 1885

Section 9
HOGAN Josiah L 1906
GRIFFIN [43] William E 1882
PEARCE John C 1882
LAMBERT James S 1884
PEARCE John C 1889
GRIFFIN [43] William E 1882
GRIFFIN [43] William E 1882
PEARCE Joseph 1885
GRIFFIN [43] William E 1883
GARRAWAY Solomon T 1882
PEARCE John C 1882
MAXWELL John L 1884
BOOTH Lawyer 1919

Section 18
ALFRED Jesse 1917
SMITH George 1891
SMITH George 1891
GRIFFIN William C 1883
BUCKHALTER Martha M 1884
BUCKHALTER Martha M 1884
SMITH George 1891

Section 17
MIXON Mack 1914
BOULTON [10] Annie 1893
PERKINS Samuel 1846
BOULTON [10] Annie 1893

Section 16

Section 19
MISSISSIPPI State Of 1911
BUCKHALTER Martha M 1884
GRIFFIN William E 1884
BUCKHALTER Martha M 1884
FAIRLEY Mack 1902
FAIRLEY Mack 1902
GRIFFIN William C 1884
RANSDELL Daniel M 1888
RANSDELL Daniel M 1888
GRIFFIN William C 1884
GRIFFIN William C 1884

Section 20

Section 21
BRELAND Bully 1910

Section 30
RANSDELL Daniel M 1888
GRIFFIN William C 1884
GRIFFIN William C 1882
GRIFFIN William C 1884
GRIFFIN William C 1884
RANSDELL Daniel M 1888
GRIFFIN William C 1884
RANSDELL Daniel M 1888
GRIFFIN William C 1884

Section 29
GRIFFIN William C 1884
GRIFFIN William C 1889
GRIFFIN William C 1884
ANDREWS Solomon L 1904
ANDREW Samuel 1890
GRIFFIN William C 1882
GRIFFIN William C 1889
ANDREW Samuel 1890
ANDREW Samuel 1890
GRIFFIN [43] William E 1884
GRIFFIN William C 1884
GRIFFIN Margaret 1894
CESAR Sabra 1885

Section 28
FAIRLEY Simon 1884
ANDREWS Tillis 1916
CESAR Sabra 1885
BENJAMIN Albert 1888
GRIFFIN William E 1884
GRIFFIN Harrison 1884
CESAR Sabra 1885
GRIFFIN Harrison 1884
BENJAMIN Albert 1888
FAIRLEY John W 1884
FAIRLEY Simon 1884

Lots-Sec. 31

1	GRIFFIN, William C	1884	
2	GRIFFIN, William	1895	
3	JAMES, Lucretia [57]	1902	
4	JAMES, Lucretia [57]	1902	
5	JAMES, Lucretia [57]	1902	
6	JAMES, Lucretia [57]	1902	
7	GRIFFIN, William	1895	
8	PERKINS, Solomon E	1890	
9	GRIFFIN, William	1895	
10	GRIFFIN, William	1895	
11	MAXWELL, John L	1885	
12	GRIFFIN, William	1846	

Lots-Sec. 32

1	GRIFFIN, Margaret	1894	
2	GRIFFIN, Margaret	1894	
3	GRIFFIN, William C	1884	
4	GRIFFIN, William C	1884	
5	GRIFFIN, William C	1884	
6	GRIFFIN, William C	1884	
8	BROWN, Rosa	[18]	1909
9	GRIFFIN, William C	1884	
10	DANTZLER, Julia	1893	
11	DANTZLER, Julia	1893	
12	GRIFFIN, John P	1922	
12	GRIFFIN, John P	1890	

Lots-Sec. 33

1	FAIRLEY, Sarah [36]	1889	
10	LEWIS, Vincent	1885	
11	GRIFFIN, Sam	1892	
12	HOTIN, Alfred	1905	
2	FAIRLEY, Sarah [36]	1889	
3	BENJAMIN, Albert	1888	
4	GRIFFIN, Sam	1892	
5	GRIFFIN, Sam	1892	
6	GRIFFIN, Sam	1892	
7	FAIRLEY, Sarah [36]	1889	
8	LEWIS, Vincent	1885	
9	LEWIS, Vincent	1885	

Section 3

GRIFFIN [43] William E 1882

MARTIN Edward 1891

GRIFFIN [43] William E 1882

FAIRLEY Evander 1891

3

MARTIN Edward 1891

FAIRLEY Evander 1891

FAIRLEY Evander 1891

STAFFORD John A 1897

STAFFORD John A 1897

FILLINGIM Jesse D 1911

STAFFORD John A 1897

Section 2

MARTIN Edward 1891

MARTIN James 1891

SHATTLES Raynor 1912

MARTIN James 1891

2

STAFFORD John A 1897

GARAWAY Solomon T 1854

SIMMONS Malinda 1895

SMITH Johnie C 1912

GARAWAY Solomon T 1854

Section 1

RANSDELL Daniel M 1884

SHATTLES Raynor W 1920

GRIFFIN James W 1883

RANSDELL Daniel M 1884

RANSDELL Daniel M 1884

GRIFFIN James W 1884

RANSDELL Daniel M 1884

GRIFFIN James W 1884

RANSDELL Daniel M 1884

DANTZLER [27] Lorenzo N 1884

Section 10

HOGAN C E 1883

FILLINGIM Jesse D 1911

FILINGIM Luther 1910

FILINGIM Luther 1910

FILINGIM Luther 1910

RANSDELL Daniel M 1884

HOGAN C E 1883

10

RANSDELL Daniel M 1884

Section 11

PEARCE Alfred 1890

GARAWAY Solomon T 1854

SIMMONS Malinda 1895

PEARCE John C 1884

11

PEARCE Alfred 1890

PEARCE [69] Leona 1923

PEARCE John C 1882

PEARCE Thomas 1859

GARAWAY Solomon T 1859

BRELAND James M 1890

Section 12

DANTZLER [27] Lorenzo N 1884

RANSDELL Daniel M 1884

DANTZLER [27] Lorenzo N 1884

12

RANSDELL Daniel M 1884

DANTZLER [27] Lorenzo N 1883

RANSDELL Daniel M 1884

BRELAND Lugene 1898

DANTZLER [27] Lorenzo N 1883

DANTZLER [27] Lorenzo N 1883

DANTZLER [27] Lorenzo N 1884

Section 15

GARRAWAY Solomon T 1882

NIXON [68] Eran 1908

PEARCE Thomas 1859

PEARCE Thomas 1859

MCLOUD Ida 1906

HOGAN [52] Mary M 1904

HOGAN [52] Mary M 1904

MCLOUD Ida 1906

FAIRLEY John W 1884

HOGAN [52] Mary M 1904

RAMSEY Plummer 1911

15

DAVIS Edwin 1889

BRELAND Dan B 1906

DANTZLER Lorenzo N 1885

BRELAND Dan B 1910

GARRAWAY John 1859

Section 14

GARRAWAY Solomon T 1882

HOGAN [52] Mary M 1904

GARAWAY Solomon T 1854

BRELAND James M 1890

STAFFORD Newton J 1895

BRELAND James M 1890

GRIFFIN William E 1883

14

STAFFORD Newton J 1895

STAFFORD Newton J 1895

BRELAND Harry 1917

GARAWAY John 1859

Section 13

DANTZLER [27] Lorenzo N 1884

WHITE [76] Charley 1916

WILLIAMSON Mary 1895

WILLIAMSON Mary 1895

KENNEDY George M 1889

GRIFFIN [43] William E 1884

13

KENNEDY George M 1889

GRIFFIN William E 1882

GRIFFIN William E 1882

Section 22

BRELAND Bully 1910

DAVIS Edwin 1889

DAVIS Edwin 1889

BRELAND Gabriel L 1904

BRELAND Gabriel L 1904

BRELAND Gabriel L 1904

22

Section 23

MCCARDLE John F 1904

BRELAND Alex 1906

MCCARDLE John F 1904

MCCARDLE Charley J 1905

23

MCCARDLE John F 1904

MCCARDLE Charley J 1905

BRELAND Alex 1906

CROSBY Elisha J 1906

GRIFFIN [43] William E 1882

GRIFFIN [43] William E 1884

Section 24

BRELAND Daniel 1889

BRELAND Andrew J 1912

BYRD William W 1897

MOODY Martin S 1888

24

BYRD William W 1897

CROSBY Elisha J 1906

MOODY Martin S 1888

MOODY Martin S 1888

GARRAWAY Charley M 1896

Section 27

GRIFFIN Harrison 1884

27

FAIRLEY Simon 1884

WEST James W 1889

ALDRIDGE Gordon 1914

WEST James W 1889

Section 26

JACKSON Marion J 1914

26

Section 25

BOOTH Joe B 1906

FAIRLEY John W 1882

DANTZLER Lorenzo N 1890

BOOTH Joe B 1906

STAFFORD Edward B 1861

STAFFORD Edward B 1861

JONES Jack 1913

25

STAFFORD Edward B 1861

HERRING Rufus Q 1882

DAVIS James W 1915

Section 36

BIVINS Arthur M 1909

BIVINS Arthur M 1909

BIVINS Arthur M 1909

36

Lots-Sec. 34

1 BRELAND, Lula [16] 1911
2 ANDREW, Prentiss 1891
3 FAIRLEY, Simon 1882
4 FAIRLEY, Simon 1882
5 LEWIS, Vincent 1885
6 ANDREW, Prentiss 1891
7 ANDREW, Prentiss 1891
8 ANDREW, Prentiss 1891
9 GRIFFIN, Jackson 1885
10 GRIFFIN, Jackson 1885
11 GRIFFIN, Andy 1881
12 GRIFFIN, Andy 1881

34

Lots-Sec. 35

3 BRELAND, Lula [16] 1911
4 BRELAND, Lula [16] 1911
5 FAIRLEY, John W 1882
9 ANDREWS, Henry 1910
10 ANDREWS, Henry 1910
11 GRIFFIN, Jackson 1885
12 GRIFFIN, Jackson 1885

35

Lots-Sec. 36

1 DAVIS, James W 1915
4 GARRAWAY, William 1859
3 HARRIS, Augustus W 1913
8 HARRIS, Augustus W 1913
9 HARRIS, Augustus W 1913
10 HARRIS, Augustus W 1913

Helpful Hints

1. This Map's INDEX can be found on the preceding pages.

2. Refer to Map "C" to see where this Township lies within Perry County, Mississippi.

3. Numbers within square brackets [ ] denote a multi-patentee land parcel (multi-owner). Refer to Appendix "C" for a full list of members in this group.

4. Areas that look to be crowded with Patentees usually indicate multiple sales of the same parcel (Re-issues) or Overlapping parcels. See this Township's Index for an explanation of these and other circumstances that might explain "odd" groupings of Patentees on this map.

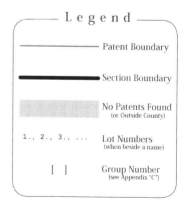

Legend

———— Patent Boundary

━━━ Section Boundary

▦ No Patents Found (or Outside County)

1., 2., 3., ... Lot Numbers (when beside a name)

[ ] Group Number (see Appendix "C")

Scale: Section = 1 mile X 1 mile (generally, with some exceptions)

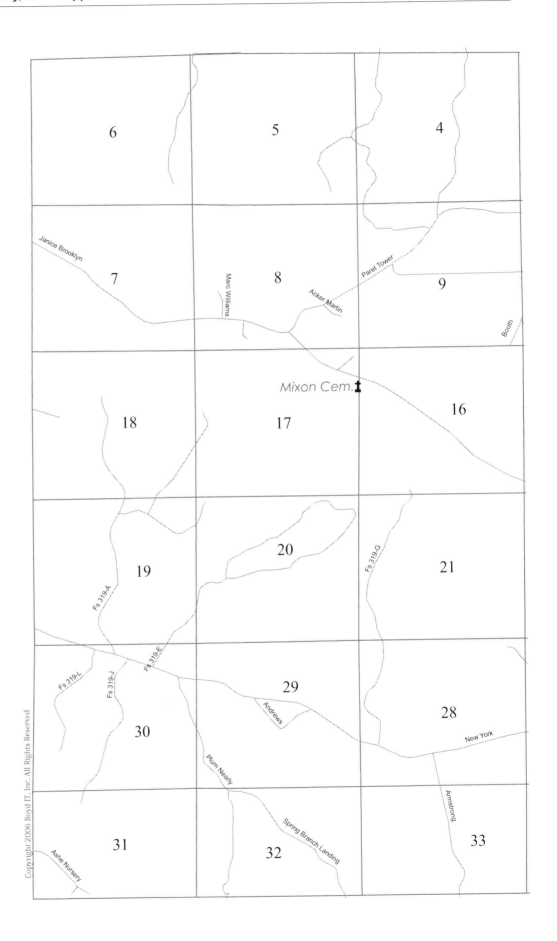

Road Map

T1-N R11-W
St Stephens Meridian

Map Group 13

Cities & Towns

None

Cemeteries

Mixon Cemetery

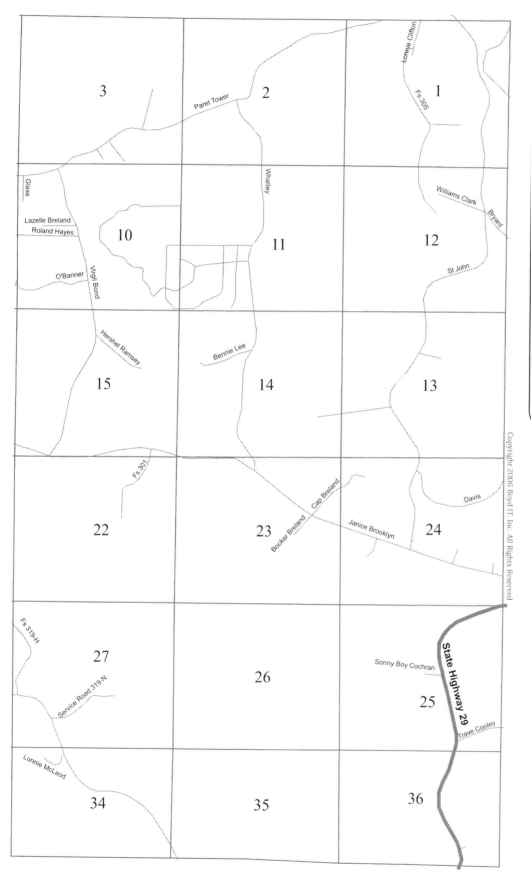

Helpful Hints

1. This road map has a number of uses, but primarily it is to help you: a) find the present location of land owned by your ancestors (at least the general area), b) find cemeteries and city-centers, and c) estimate the route/roads used by Census-takers & tax-assessors.

2. If you plan to travel to Perry County to locate cemeteries or land parcels, please pick up a modern travel map for the area before you do. Mapping old land parcels on modern maps is not as exact a science as you might think. Just the slightest variations in public land survey coordinates, estimates of parcel boundaries, or road-map deviations can greatly alter a map's representation of how a road either does or doesn't cross a particular parcel of land.

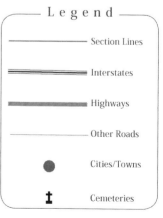

Legend

Section Lines

Interstates

Highways

Other Roads

● Cities/Towns

✝ Cemeteries

Scale: Section = 1 mile X 1 mile
(generally, with some exceptions)

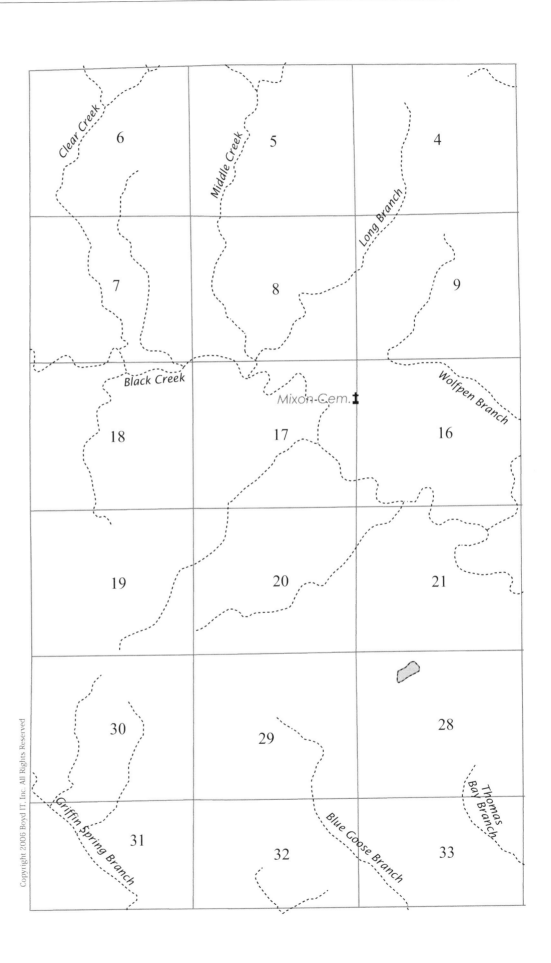

Historical Map

T1-N R11-W
St Stephens Meridian

Map Group 13

Cities & Towns
None

Cemeteries
Mixon Cemetery

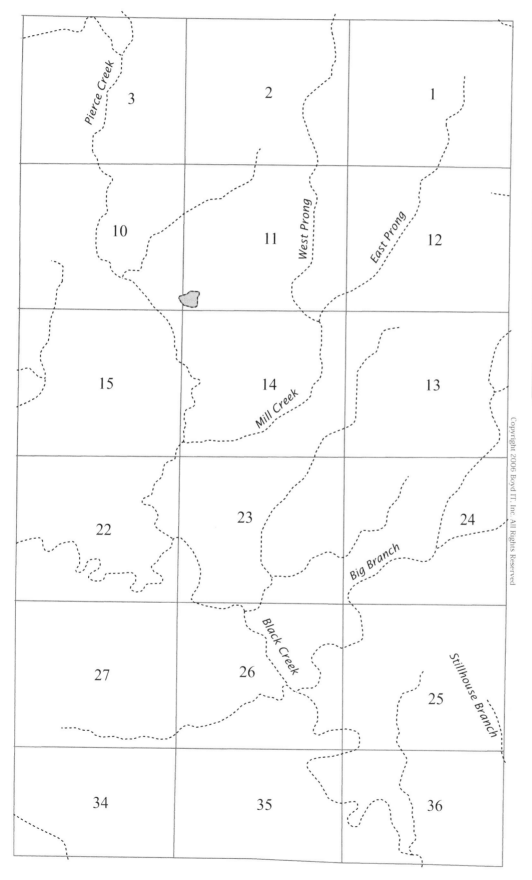

Helpful Hints

1. This Map takes a different look at the same Congressional Township displayed in the preceding two maps. It presents features that can help you better envision the historical development of the area: a) Water-bodies (lakes & ponds), b) Water-courses (rivers, streams, etc.), c) Railroads, d) City/town center-points (where they were oftentimes located when first settled), and e) Cemeteries.

2. Using this "Historical" map in tandem with this Township's Patent Map and Road Map, may lead you to some interesting discoveries. You will often find roads, towns, cemeteries, and waterways are named after nearby landowners: sometimes those names will be the ones you are researching. See how many of these research gems you can find here in Perry County.

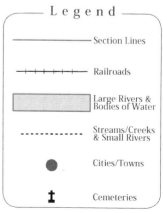

L e g e n d

————————	Section Lines
+++++++++	Railroads
�	Large Rivers & Bodies of Water
- - - - - - - -	Streams/Creeks & Small Rivers
●	Cities/Towns
✝	Cemeteries

Scale: Section = 1 mile X 1 mile
(there are some exceptions)

Map Group 14: Index to Land Patents

Township 1-North Range 10-West (St Stephens)

After you locate an individual in this Index, take note of the Section and Section Part then proceed to the Land Patent map on the pages immediately following. You should have no difficulty locating the corresponding parcel of land.

The "For More Info" Column will lead you to more information about the underlying Patents. See the *Legend* at right, and the "How to Use this Book" chapter, for more information.

<table>
<tr><td colspan="3" align="center">LEGEND</td></tr>
<tr><td colspan="3" align="center">"For More Info . . . " column</td></tr>
<tr><td colspan="3">A = Authority (Legislative Act, See Appendix "A")</td></tr>
<tr><td colspan="3">B = Block or Lot (location in Section unknown)</td></tr>
<tr><td colspan="3">C = Cancelled Patent</td></tr>
<tr><td colspan="3">F = Fractional Section</td></tr>
<tr><td colspan="3">G = Group (Multi-Patentee Patent, see Appendix "C")</td></tr>
<tr><td colspan="3">V = Overlaps another Parcel</td></tr>
<tr><td colspan="3">R = Re-Issued (Parcel patented more than once)</td></tr>
</table>

(A & G items require you to look in the Appendixes referred to above. All other Letter-designations followed by a number require you to locate line-items in this index that possess the ID number found after the letter).

ID	Individual in Patent	Sec.	Sec. Part	Date Issued	Other Counties	For More Info . . .
3068	ALFRED, John W	18	SW	1890-12-31		A4
3101	BIRKETT, Thomas	1	NWNW	1889-11-29		A1
3102	" "	1	NWSE	1889-11-29		A1
3103	" "	10	W½SW	1889-11-29		A1
3104	" "	11	NWNE	1889-11-29		A1
3105	" "	11	NWNW	1889-11-29		A1
3106	" "	13	N½NE	1889-11-29		A1
3107	" "	13	NWSE	1889-11-29		A1
3108	" "	14	NENW	1889-11-29		A1
3109	" "	2	NENE	1889-11-29		A1
3110	" "	2	SWSW	1889-11-29		A1
3111	" "	9	S½NE	1889-11-29		A1
3112	" "	9	S½NW	1889-11-29		A1
3113	" "	9	S½SE	1889-11-29		A1
3114	BOYKIN, Thomas	29	NENE	1919-08-21		A4
3074	BREELAND, Joseph T	15	N½NE	1859-05-02		A1
3075	" "	15	NENW	1859-05-02		A1
3079	BREELAND, Josiah	20	SENE	1881-08-20		A4
3080	" "	21	S½NW	1881-08-20		A4
3081	" "	21	SWNE	1881-08-20		A4
2916	BRELAND, Calvin	23	SESW	1906-05-01		A4
2917	" "	26	E½NW	1906-05-01		A4
2918	" "	36	3	1911-06-29		A4
2919	BRELAND, Cerena	25	N½SW	1906-05-01		A4
2920	" "	25	NWSE	1906-05-01		A4
2925	BRELAND, Cicero	21	N½SE	1906-06-21		A4
2926	" "	21	NESW	1906-06-21		A4
2927	" "	21	SENE	1906-06-21		A4
3023	BRELAND, Emer A	8	SWSE	1910-03-17		A4
3076	BRELAND, Joseph T	10	E½SE	1859-05-02		A1
3077	" "	11	W½SW	1859-05-02		A1 V3038
3078	" "	14	NWNW	1859-05-02		A1
3083	BRELAND, Leven L	36	N½8	1906-09-14		A4
3154	BRELAND, William P	22	NENE	1895-02-21		A4
3155	" "	23	NWNW	1895-02-21		A4
3125	BRIGHTMAN, Will M	21	NENW	1918-06-17		A4
3126	" "	21	NWNE	1918-06-17		A4
3158	BYRD, William W	17	SWSW	1882-04-20		A1
3096	CARTER, Samuel	17	NE	1907-05-13		A4
3124	CARTER, Wesley	18	W½SE	1901-12-17		A4
2915	COLLINS, Bryant P	17	E½W½	1923-06-25		A4
3115	COOLEY, Trave	31	4	1916-01-21		A4
3116	" "	31	N½5	1916-01-21		A4
3082	COURTNEY, Lenorah P	19	SWSE	1914-06-19		A4
3087	DANTZLER, Lorenzo N	7	NW	1884-12-30		A1 G27
3088	" "	7	NWSW	1884-12-30		A1 G27

ID	Individual in Patent	Sec.	Sec. Part	Date Issued	Other Counties	For More Info . . .
3086	DANTZLER, Lorenzo N (Cont'd)	17	SWNW	1890-07-03		A1
3027	DAVIS, George	18	NWNE	1914-10-13		A4
2893	FAIRLEY, Alexander S	35	1	1885-04-04		A4
2894	"	35	8	1885-04-04		A4
3032	FAIRLEY, Harriet A	8	NWSW	1897-05-20		A4 G33
3033	"	8	S½SW	1897-05-20		A4 G33
3034	"	8	SWNW	1897-05-20		A4 G33
3089	FAIRLEY, Melissa A	34	1	1881-09-17		A4
3090	"	34	2	1881-09-17		A4
3122	FAIRLEY, Watson	29	NWSE	1905-12-06		A1
3123	"	29	SWNE	1905-12-06		A1
2921	GARAWAY, Charles M	20	NENW	1883-09-15		A1
3059	GARAWAY, John	30	N½SE	1860-04-02		A1
2922	GARRAWAY, Charles M	29	NWNW	1882-04-20		A1
2923	GARRAWAY, Charley M	19	NWSW	1896-12-14		A4
2924	"	19	S½SW	1896-12-14		A4
3060	GARRAWAY, John	29	W½SW	1860-04-02		A1
3061	"	30	S½NE	1860-04-02		A1
3062	"	30	S½SE	1860-04-02		A1
3069	GARRAWAY, John W	31	1	1888-04-05		A4
3070	"	32	4	1888-04-05		A4
3097	GARRAWAY, Solomon T	9	NWNE	1882-08-03		A1
3042	GRIFFIN, James W	5	W½SW	1884-12-30		A1
3043	"	6	E½SW	1884-12-30		A1
3044	"	6	NWSW	1884-12-30		A1
3045	"	6	S½NE	1884-12-30		A1
3046	"	6	SE	1884-12-30		A1
3047	"	6	SENW	1884-12-30		A1
3048	"	6	SWSW	1884-12-30		A1
3049	"	7	NENE	1884-12-30		A1
3050	"	7	W½NE	1884-12-30		A1
3051	"	19	W½NW	1889-11-29		A1 G41
3052	"	31	3	1889-11-29		A1 G41
3053	"	7	NESE	1889-11-29		A1 G41
3054	"	7	SENE	1889-11-29		A1 G41
3071	GRIFFIN, John W	36	6	1890-07-03		A1 G42
3072	"	36	N½7	1890-07-03		A1 G42
3073	GRIFFIN, Joseph C	29	SESW	1889-04-20		A1
3120	GRIFFIN, Washington	19	NESW	1854-03-15		A1
3121	"	32	N½5	1854-03-15		A1
3142	GRIFFIN, William E	6	3	1882-05-10		A1
3143	"	6	NWNE	1882-05-10		A1
3144	"	6	S½6	1882-05-10		A1
3131	"	19	NENE	1882-05-20		A1
3127	"	17	NWSW	1882-08-03		A1
3128	"	18	E½SE	1882-08-03		A1
3129	"	18	NENE	1882-08-03		A1
3134	"	19	SENE	1882-08-03		A1
3139	"	31	S½8	1882-08-03		A1
3141	"	32	N½6	1882-08-03		A1
3145	"	7	SESE	1882-08-03		A1
3146	"	8	E½SE	1882-08-03		A1
3147	"	9	W½SW	1882-08-03		A1
3140	"	32	2	1882-10-10		A1
3137	"	20	W½NW	1882-12-30		A1
3138	"	20	W½SW	1882-12-30		A1
3148	"	21	NWNW	1882-12-30		A1 G43
3135	"	19	SESE	1883-02-03		A1
3130	"	19	E½NW	1884-12-30		A1
3132	"	19	NESE	1884-12-30		A1
3133	"	19	NWSE	1884-12-30		A1
3136	"	19	W½NE	1884-12-30		A1
3149	"	31	N½7	1884-12-30		A1 G43
3150	"	31	N½8	1884-12-30		A1 G43
3151	"	33	N½7	1884-12-30		A1 G43
3152	"	33	N½8	1884-12-30		A1 G43
3087	"	7	NW	1884-12-30		A1 G27
3088	"	7	NWSW	1884-12-30		A1 G27
3038	HARTFIELD, Jack J	11	NWSW	1914-06-29		A4 V3077
3055	HINTON, Jesse A	10	NWNE	1906-03-05		A1
3091	HINTON, Morgain M	10	SENE	1906-08-10		A4
3032	HOLLIMON, Harriet A	8	NWSW	1897-05-20		A4 G33
3033	"	8	S½SW	1897-05-20		A4 G33

ID	Individual in Patent	Sec.	Sec. Part	Date Issued	Other Counties	For More Info . . .
3034	HOLLIMON, Harriet A (Cont'd)	8	SWNW	1897-05-20		A4 G33
3051	HOWZE, George H	19	W½NW	1889-11-29		A1 G41
3052	" "	31	3	1889-11-29		A1 G41
3053	" "	7	NESE	1889-11-29		A1 G41
3054	" "	7	SENE	1889-11-29		A1 G41
3071	" "	36	6	1890-07-03		A1 G42
3072	" "	36	N½7	1890-07-03		A1 G42
3039	JONES, Jack	30	SWNW	1913-02-14		A4
3028	KENNEDY, George	29	SWNW	1884-12-30		A1
3029	" "	30	NENE	1884-12-30		A1
3153	LANTRIP, William	18	SWNE	1859-05-02		A1
3025	MATHESON, Gavin R	35	2	1884-12-30		A1
3026	" "	35	3	1884-12-30		A1
3092	MCLEOD, Nancy A	34	8	1898-02-24		A4
3093	" " "	35	5	1898-02-24		A4
3056	MERRITT, John B	34	3	1900-11-28		A4
3057	" "	34	4	1900-11-28		A4
3098	MISSISSIPPI, State Of	11	NWSE	1910-12-27		A6
2908	PATTERSON, Archibald A	8	NESW	1909-06-17		A4
2909	" "	8	NWSE	1909-06-17		A4
2910	" "	8	SENW	1909-06-17		A4
2911	" "	8	SWNE	1909-06-17		A4
3058	PEARCE, John C	35	7	1883-02-03		A1
3157	PEARCE, William	8	E½NE	1882-08-03		A1
3156	" "	5	NWNE	1910-06-02		A4
3148	PERKINS, Benjamin F	21	NWNW	1882-12-30		A1 G43
3149	" "	31	N½7	1884-12-30		A1 G43
3150	" "	31	N½8	1884-12-30		A1 G43
3151	" "	33	N½7	1884-12-30		A1 G43
3152	" "	33	N½8	1884-12-30		A1 G43
2928	RANSDELL, Daniel M	1	NE	1884-12-30		A1
2929	" "	1	NENW	1884-12-30		A1
2930	" "	1	NESE	1884-12-30		A1
2931	" "	1	S½NW	1884-12-30		A1
2932	" "	1	S½SE	1884-12-30		A1
2933	" "	1	SW	1884-12-30		A1
2941	" "	12		1884-12-30		A1
2942	" "	13	E½SE	1884-12-30		A1
2943	" "	13	E½SW	1884-12-30		A1
2944	" "	13	N½NW	1884-12-30		A1
2945	" "	13	NWSW	1884-12-30		A1
2946	" "	13	S½NE	1884-12-30		A1
2947	" "	13	SENW	1884-12-30		A1
2948	" "	13	SWNW	1884-12-30		A1
2949	" "	13	SWSE	1884-12-30		A1
2962	" "	2	E½SW	1884-12-30		A1
2963	" "	2	NWNE	1884-12-30		A1
2964	" "	2	S½NE	1884-12-30		A1
2965	" "	2	SE	1884-12-30		A1
2966	" "	21	NENE	1884-12-30		A1
2967	" "	21	S½SE	1884-12-30		A1
2968	" "	21	SESW	1884-12-30		A1
2969	" "	22	NENW	1884-12-30		A1
2970	" "	22	NWNE	1884-12-30		A1
2971	" "	22	S½	1884-12-30		A1
2972	" "	22	S½NE	1884-12-30		A1
2973	" "	22	S½NW	1884-12-30		A1
2974	" "	23	N½SW	1884-12-30		A1
2975	" "	23	NENW	1884-12-30		A1
2976	" "	23	NWNE	1884-12-30		A1
2977	" "	23	S½NW	1884-12-30		A1
2978	" "	23	SE	1884-12-30		A1
2979	" "	23	SWNE	1884-12-30		A1
2980	" "	23	SWSW	1884-12-30		A1
2981	" "	24	E½	1884-12-30		A1
2982	" "	24	E½NW	1884-12-30		A1
2983	" "	24	SW	1884-12-30		A1
2984	" "	25	E½SE	1884-12-30		A1
2985	" "	25	N½	1884-12-30		A1
2986	" "	25	S½SW	1884-12-30		A1
2987	" "	25	SWSE	1884-12-30		A1
2988	" "	26	NE	1884-12-30		A1
2989	" "	26	S½	1884-12-30		A1

ID	Individual in Patent	Sec.	Sec. Part	Date Issued	Other Counties	For More Info . . .
2990	RANSDELL, Daniel M (Cont'd)	26	W½NW	1884-12-30		A1
2991	"	27	E½SE	1884-12-30		A1
2992	"	27	N½	1884-12-30		A1
2993	"	27	NWSE	1884-12-30		A1
2994	"	27	SW	1884-12-30		A1
2995	"	28	NE	1884-12-30		A1
2996	"	28	NENW	1884-12-30		A1
2997	"	3	N½	1884-12-30		A1
2998	"	3	N½SE	1884-12-30		A1
2999	"	3	SW	1884-12-30		A1
3000	"	33	1	1884-12-30		A1
3001	"	34	5	1884-12-30		A1
3002	"	34	6	1884-12-30		A1
3003	"	36	1	1884-12-30		A1
3004	"	36	2	1884-12-30		A1
3005	"	36	4	1884-12-30		A1
3006	"	4		1884-12-30		A1
3007	"	5	E½SW	1884-12-30		A1
3008	"	5	NENE	1884-12-30		A1
3009	"	5	NW	1884-12-30		A1
3010	"	5	S½NE	1884-12-30		A1
3011	"	5	SE	1884-12-30		A1
3012	"	6	NENE	1884-12-30		A1
3013	"	6	NENW	1884-12-30		A1
3014	"	6	W½NW	1884-12-30		A1
3015	"	7	E½SW	1884-12-30		A1
3016	"	7	SWSW	1884-12-30		A1
3017	"	7	W½SE	1884-12-30		A1
3018	"	8	N½NW	1884-12-30		A1
3019	"	8	NWNE	1884-12-30		A1
3020	"	9	N½NW	1884-12-30		A1
3021	"	9	NENE	1884-12-30		A1
2934	"	11	E½NW	1888-11-30		A1
2935	"	11	E½SE	1888-11-30		A1
2936	"	11	NENE	1888-11-30		A1
2937	"	11	NESW	1888-11-30		A1
2938	"	11	S½NE	1888-11-30		A1
2939	"	11	SWNW	1888-11-30		A1
2940	"	11	SWSE	1888-11-30		A1
2950	"	14	E½SW	1888-11-30		A1
2951	"	14	NE	1888-11-30		A1
2952	"	14	S½NW	1888-11-30		A1
2953	"	14	SWSW	1888-11-30		A1
2954	"	14	W½SE	1888-11-30		A1
2955	"	15	N½SW	1888-11-30		A1
2956	"	15	NWNW	1888-11-30		A1
2957	"	15	S½NE	1888-11-30		A1
2958	"	15	S½NW	1888-11-30		A1
2959	"	15	SESE	1888-11-30		A1
2960	"	15	SESW	1888-11-30		A1
2961	"	15	W½SE	1888-11-30		A1
3030	RILEY, George W	23	E½NE	1901-03-23		A4
3031	"	24	SWNW	1901-03-23		A4
3067	SAMUEL, John	18	NW	1890-08-16		A4
3117	SELLIVAN, Vander	17	N½SE	1906-06-30		A1
3118	"	17	SESE	1906-06-30		A1
3119	"	20	NENE	1906-06-30		A1
2912	SMITH, Arthur Vernon	32	7	1922-08-15		A4
3063	SMITH, John P	17	NWNW	1889-04-20		A1
3064	"	30	N½NW	1897-04-19		A4
3065	"	30	NWNE	1897-04-19		A4
3066	"	30	SENW	1897-04-19		A4
3094	STAFFORD, Nancy	30	SW	1896-10-31		A4
2913	SULLIVAN, Ben F	29	SESE	1920-04-20		A4
2914	"	29	SWSE	1920-04-20		A4
3024	SULLIVAN, Fed	10	SWNW	1907-06-05		A1
2904	THOMAS, Andrew J	35	N½6	1882-04-20		A1
2899	"	28	W½NW	1882-05-10		A1
2906	"	36	N½5	1882-10-10		A1
2907	"	36	S½5	1882-10-10		A1
2897	"	28	NWSW	1883-09-15		A1
2898	"	28	SENW	1883-09-15		A1
2895	"	28	NESE	1884-12-30		A1

ID	Individual in Patent	Sec.	Sec. Part	Date Issued	Other Counties	For More Info . . .
2896	THOMAS, Andrew J (Cont'd)	28	NESW	1884-12-30		A1
2900	" "	28	W½SE	1884-12-30		A1
2901	" "	33	2	1884-12-30		A1
2905	" "	35	S½6	1884-12-30		A1
2902	" "	33	S½7	1889-11-29		A1
2903	" "	33	S½8	1889-11-29		A1
3095	THOMAS, Reuben W	10	SESW	1917-08-11		A4
3022	TILLIS, Dollie	17	SWSE	1905-11-03		A1
2890	TISDALE, A Wayne	29	E½NW	1919-06-30		A4 G73
2891	" "	29	NESW	1919-06-30		A4 G73
2892	" "	29	NWNE	1919-06-30		A4 G73
3035	TISDALE, J Amos	20	E½SW	1914-10-13		A4
3036	" "	20	SENW	1914-10-13		A4
3037	" "	20	SWSE	1914-10-13		A4
2890	TISDALE, Norma	29	E½NW	1919-06-30		A4 G73
2891	" "	29	NESW	1919-06-30		A4 G73
2892	" "	29	NWNE	1919-06-30		A4 G73
3099	TURK, Stewart	15	SWSW	1918-04-11		A4
3100	" "	22	NWNW	1918-04-11		A4
3159	WOODS, Willis	27	SWSE	1905-11-24		A4
3040	YOUNG, James M	33	5	1918-04-17		A1
3041	" "	33	6	1918-04-17		A1
3084	YOUNG, Lewis D	20	E½SE	1920-01-08		A4
3085	" "	21	W½SW	1920-01-08		A4

Patent Map

T1-N R10-W
St Stephens Meridian

Map Group 14

Township Statistics

Parcels Mapped	:	270
Number of Patents	:	118
Number of Individuals	:	72
Patentees Identified	:	71
Number of Surnames	:	44
Multi-Patentee Parcels	:	19
Oldest Patent Date	:	3/15/1854
Most Recent Patent	:	6/25/1923
Block/Lot Parcels	:	46
Parcels Re-Issued	:	0
Parcels that Overlap	:	2
Cities and Towns	:	2
Cemeteries	:	1

Section 6
RANSDELL Daniel M 1884
RANSDELL Daniel M 1884
GRIFFIN William E 1882
RANSDELL Daniel M 1884
GRIFFIN James W 1884
GRIFFIN James W 1884
GRIFFIN James W 1884
Lots-Sec. 6
3 GRIFFIN, William E 1882
3 GRIFFIN, William E 1882
GRIFFIN James W 1884
GRIFFIN James W 1884
GRIFFIN James W 1884

Section 5
PEARCE William 1910
RANSDELL Daniel M 1884
RANSDELL Daniel M 1884
RANSDELL Daniel M 1884
GRIFFIN James W 1884
RANSDELL Daniel M 1884
RANSDELL Daniel M 1884

Section 4
RANSDELL Daniel M 1884

Section 7
DANTZLER [27] Lorenzo N 1884
GRIFFIN James W 1884
GRIFFIN James W 1884
GRIFFIN [41] James W 1889
DANTZLER [27] Lorenzo N 1884
RANSDELL Daniel M 1884
GRIFFIN [41] James W 1889
RANSDELL Daniel M 1884
GRIFFIN William E 1882

Section 8
RANSDELL Daniel M 1884
RANSDELL Daniel M 1884
PATTERSON Archibald A 1909
PATTERSON Archibald A 1909
FAIRLEY [33] Harriet A 1897
PEARCE William 1882
FAIRLEY [33] Harriet A 1897
PATTERSON Archibald A 1909
PATTERSON Archibald A 1909
FAIRLEY [33] Harriet A 1897
BRELAND Emer A 1910
GRIFFIN William E 1882

Section 9
RANSDELL Daniel M 1884
GARRAWAY Solomon T 1882
RANSDELL Daniel M 1884
BIRKETT Thomas 1889
BIRKETT Thomas 1889
GRIFFIN William E 1882
BIRKETT Thomas 1889

Section 18
SAMUEL John 1890
DAVIS George 1914
GRIFFIN William E 1882
LANTRIP William 1859
ALFRED John W 1890
CARTER Wesley 1901
GRIFFIN William E 1882

Section 17
SMITH John P 1889
DANTZLER Lorenzo N 1890
COLLINS Bryant P 1923
GRIFFIN William E 1882
BYRD William W 1882
CARTER Samuel 1907
SELLIVAN Vander 1906
TILLIS Dollie 1905
SELLIVAN Vander 1906

Section 16

Section 19
GRIFFIN [41] James W 1889
GRIFFIN William E 1884
GARRAWAY Charley M 1896
GRIFFIN Washington 1854
GRIFFIN William E 1884
GRIFFIN William E 1882
GRIFFIN William E 1882
GRIFFIN William E 1884
GRIFFIN William E 1882
GARRAWAY Charley M 1896
COURTNEY Lenorah P 1914
GRIFFIN William E 1883

Section 20
GRIFFIN William E 1882
GARAWAY Charles M 1883
TISDALE J Amos 1914
GRIFFIN William E 1882
TISDALE J Amos 1914
TISDALE J Amos 1914
SELLIVAN Vander 1906
BREELAND Josiah 1881
YOUNG Lewis D 1920

Section 21
GRIFFIN [43] William E 1882
BRIGHTMAN Will M 1918
BRIGHTMAN Will M 1918
RANSDELL Daniel M 1884
BREELAND Josiah 1881
BREELAND Josiah 1881
BRELAND Cicero 1906
YOUNG Lewis D 1920
BRELAND Cicero 1906
BRELAND Cicero 1906
RANSDELL Daniel M 1884
RANSDELL Daniel M 1884

Section 30
SMITH John P 1897
SMITH John P 1897
KENNEDY George 1884
JONES Jack 1913
SMITH John P 1897
GARRAWAY John 1860
STAFFORD Nancy 1896
GARAWAY John 1860
GARRAWAY John 1860

Section 29
GARRAWAY Charles M 1882
TISDALE [73] A Wayne 1919
TISDALE [73] A Wayne 1919
KENNEDY George 1884
FAIRLEY Watson 1905
TISDALE [73] A Wayne 1919
FAIRLEY Watson 1905
GARRAWAY John 1860
GRIFFIN Joseph C 1889
SULLIVAN Ben F 1920
SULLIVAN Ben F 1920

Section 28
BOYKIN Thomas 1919
THOMAS Andrew J 1882
RANSDELL Daniel M 1884
THOMAS Andrew J 1883
RANSDELL Daniel M 1884
THOMAS Andrew J 1883
THOMAS Andrew J 1884
THOMAS Andrew J 1884
THOMAS Andrew J 1884

Section 31
Lots-Sec. 31
----
1 GARRAWAY, John W 1888
3 GRIFFIN, James W[41] 1889
4 COOLEY, Trave 1916
4 COOLEY, Trave 1916
4 GRIFFIN, William[43] 1884
4 GRIFFIN, William[43] 1884
4 GRIFFIN, William E 1882

Section 32
Lots-Sec. 32
----
2 GRIFFIN, William E 1882
4 GARRAWAY, John W 1888
4 GRIFFIN, William E 1882
7 SMITH, Arthur Vernon 1922
7 GRIFFIN, Washington 1854

Section 33
Lots-Sec. 33
----
1 RANSDELL, Daniel M 1884
2 THOMAS, Andrew J 1884
5 YOUNG, James M 1918
6 THOMAS, Andrew J 1889
6 YOUNG, James M 1918
6 GRIFFIN, William[43] 1884
6 GRIFFIN, William[43] 1884
6 THOMAS, Andrew J 1889

Section 3 / 2 / 1 (top row)

RANSDELL Daniel M 1884

RANSDELL Daniel M 1884

BIRKETT Thomas 1889

BIRKETT Thomas 1889

RANSDELL Daniel M 1884

RANSDELL Daniel M 1884

3

RANSDELL Daniel M 1884

2

RANSDELL Daniel M 1884

RANSDELL Daniel M 1884

RANSDELL Daniel M 1884

1

RANSDELL Daniel M 1884

BIRKETT Thomas 1889

RANSDELL Daniel M 1884

BIRKETT Thomas 1889

RANSDELL Daniel M 1884

RANSDELL Daniel M 1884

RANSDELL Daniel M 1884

Section 10 / 11 / 12

HINTON Jesse A 1906

BIRKETT Thomas 1889

BIRKETT Thomas 1889

RANSDELL Daniel M 1888

SULLIVAN Fed 1907

HINTON Morgain M 1906

RANSDELL Daniel M 1888

RANSDELL Daniel M 1888

10

11

BIRKETT Thomas 1889

HARTFIELD Jack J 1914

RANSDELL Daniel M 1888

MISSISSIPPI State Of 1910

12

RANSDELL Daniel M 1884

THOMAS Reuben W 1917

BRELAND Joseph T 1859

BRELAND Joseph T 1859

RANSDELL Daniel M 1888

RANSDELL Daniel M 1888

Section 15 / 14 / 13

RANSDELL Daniel M 1888

BREELAND Joseph T 1859

BREELAND Joseph T 1859

BRELAND Joseph T 1859

BIRKETT Thomas 1889

RANSDELL Daniel M 1888

RANSDELL Daniel M 1884

BIRKETT Thomas 1889

RANSDELL Daniel M 1888

RANSDELL Daniel M 1888

RANSDELL Daniel M 1888

RANSDELL Daniel M 1884

RANSDELL Daniel M 1884

RANSDELL Daniel M 1884

15

14

RANSDELL Daniel M 1888

13

RANSDELL Daniel M 1888

RANSDELL Daniel M 1888

RANSDELL Daniel M 1888

RANSDELL Daniel M 1884

BIRKETT Thomas 1889

TURK Stewart 1918

RANSDELL Daniel M 1888

RANSDELL Daniel M 1888

RANSDELL Daniel M 1884

RANSDELL Daniel M 1884

RANSDELL Daniel M 1884

Section 22 / 23 / 24

TURK Stewart 1918

RANSDELL Daniel M 1884

RANSDELL Daniel M 1884

BRELAND William P 1895

BRELAND William P 1895

RANSDELL Daniel M 1884

RANSDELL Daniel M 1884

RANSDELL Daniel M 1884

RANSDELL Daniel M 1884

22

RANSDELL Daniel M 1884

RANSDELL Daniel M 1884

RANSDELL Daniel M 1884

RILEY George W 1901

RILEY George W 1901

24

RANSDELL Daniel M 1884

23

RANSDELL Daniel M 1884

RANSDELL Daniel M 1884

RANSDELL Daniel M 1884

RANSDELL Daniel M 1884

RANSDELL Daniel M 1884

BRELAND Calvin 1906

Section 27 / 26 / 25

RANSDELL Daniel M 1884

RANSDELL Daniel M 1884

RANSDELL Daniel M 1884

RANSDELL Daniel M 1884

BRELAND Calvin 1906

27

25

RANSDELL Daniel M 1884

RANSDELL Daniel M 1884

26

BRELAND Cerena 1906

BRELAND Cerena 1906

RANSDELL Daniel M 1884

WOODS Willis 1905

RANSDELL Daniel M 1884

RANSDELL Daniel M 1884

RANSDELL Daniel M 1884

RANSDELL Daniel M 1884

Section 34 / 35 / 36

34

35

36

Lots-Sec. 34

1	FAIRLEY, Melissa A	1881
2	FAIRLEY, Melissa A	1881
3	MERRITT, John B	1900
4	MERRITT, John B	1900
5	RANSDELL, Daniel M	1884
6	RANSDELL, Daniel M	1884
8	MCLEOD, Nancy A	1898

Lots-Sec. 35

1	FAIRLEY, Alexander S	1885
2	MATHESON, Gavin R	1884
3	MATHESON, Gavin R	1884
5	MCLEOD, Nancy A	1898
7	PEARCE, John C	1883
8	THOMAS, Andrew J	1884
8	FAIRLEY, Alexander S	1885
8	THOMAS, Andrew J	1882

Lots-Sec. 36

1	RANSDELL, Daniel M	1884
2	RANSDELL, Daniel M	1884
3	BRELAND, Calvin	1911
4	RANSDELL, Daniel M	1884
6	THOMAS, Andrew J	1882
6	GRIFFIN, John W [42]	1890
6	THOMAS, Andrew J	1882
6	GRIFFIN, John W [42]	1890
6	BRELAND, Leven L	1906

Helpful Hints

1. This Map's INDEX can be found on the preceding pages.

2. Refer to Map "C" to see where this Township lies within Perry County, Mississippi.

3. Numbers within square brackets [ ] denote a multi-patentee land parcel (multi-owner). Refer to Appendix "C" for a full list of members in this group.

4. Areas that look to be crowded with Patentees usually indicate multiple sales of the same parcel (Re-issues) or Overlapping parcels. See this Township's Index for an explanation of these and other circumstances that might explain "odd" groupings of Patentees on this map.

Legend

— Patent Boundary

━ Section Boundary

▦ No Patents Found (or Outside County)

1., 2., 3., ... Lot Numbers (when beside a name)

[ ] Group Number (see Appendix "C")

Scale: Section = 1 mile X 1 mile (generally, with some exceptions)

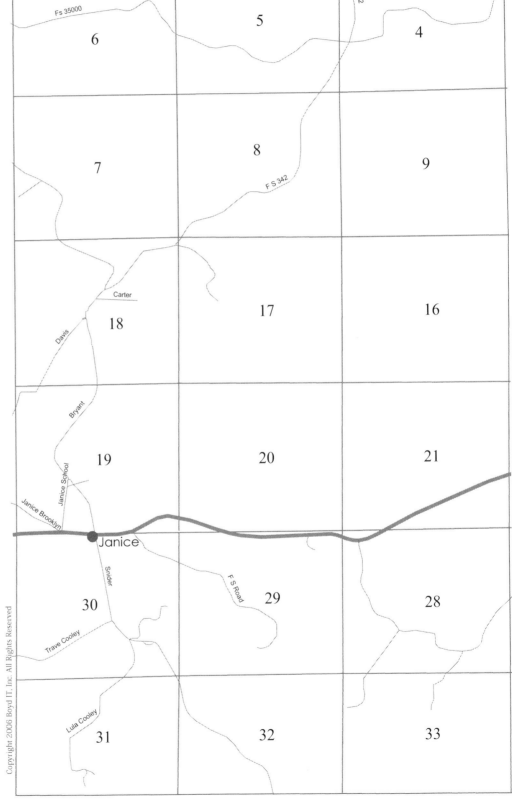

Road Map

T1-N R10-W
St Stephens Meridian

Map Group 14

Cities & Towns
Janice
Oak Grove

Cemeteries
Breland Cemetery

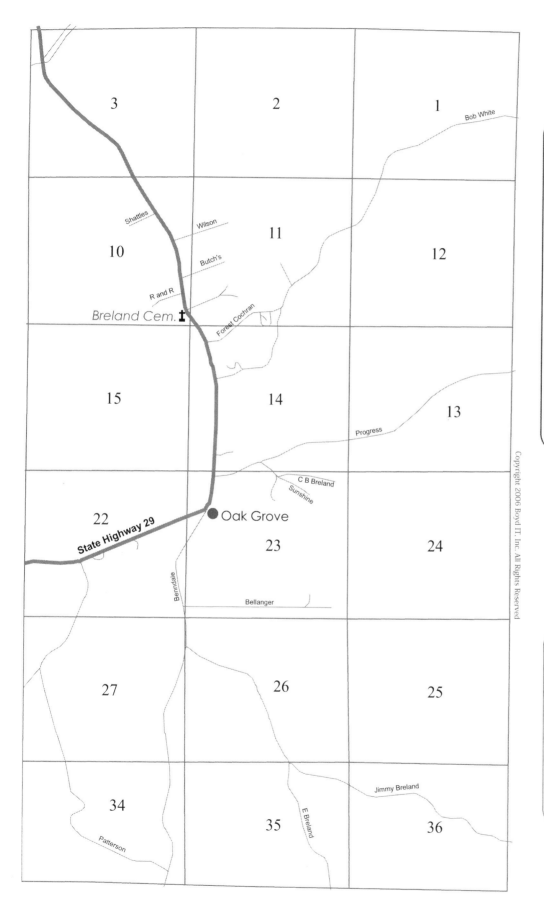

Helpful Hints

1. This road map has a number of uses, but primarily it is to help you: a) find the present location of land owned by your ancestors (at least the general area), b) find cemeteries and city-centers, and c) estimate the route/roads used by Census-takers & tax-assessors.

2. If you plan to travel to Perry County to locate cemeteries or land parcels, please pick up a modern travel map for the area before you do. Mapping old land parcels on modern maps is not as exact a science as you might think. Just the slightest variations in public land survey coordinates, estimates of parcel boundaries, or road-map deviations can greatly alter a map's representation of how a road either does or doesn't cross a particular parcel of land.

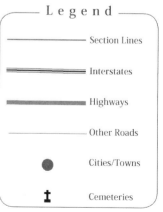

Legend

- Section Lines
- Interstates
- Highways
- Other Roads
- ● Cities/Towns
- ✝ Cemeteries

Scale: Section = 1 mile X 1 mile
(generally, with some exceptions)

185

Historical Map

T1-N R10-W
St Stephens Meridian

Map Group 14

Cities & Towns
- Janice
- Oak Grove

Cemeteries
- Breland Cemetery

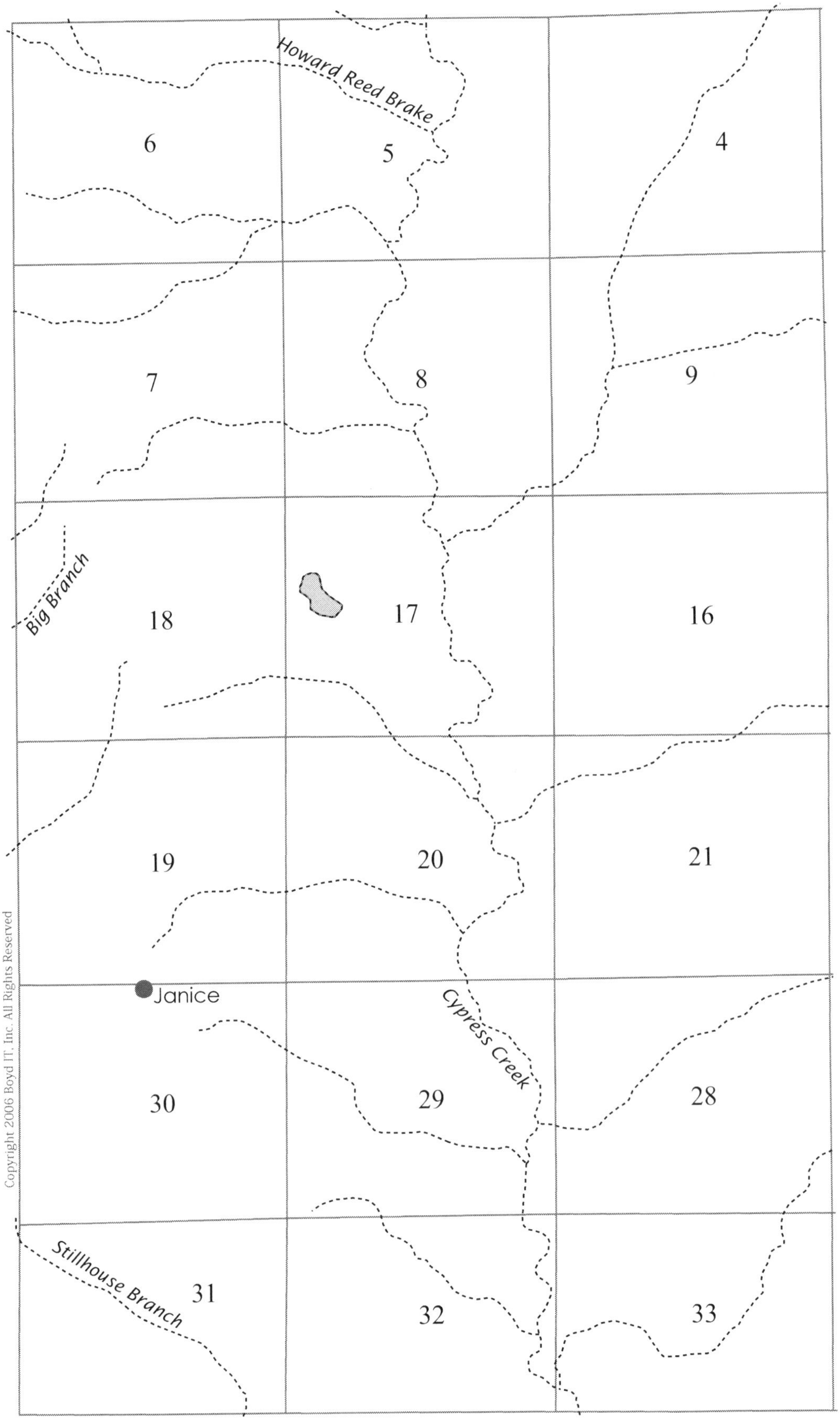

Howard Reed Brake
6
5
4
7
8
9
Big Branch
18
17
16
19
20
21
Janice
Cypress Creek
30
29
28
Stillhouse Branch
31
32
33
Copyright 2006 Boyd IT, Inc. All Rights Reserved

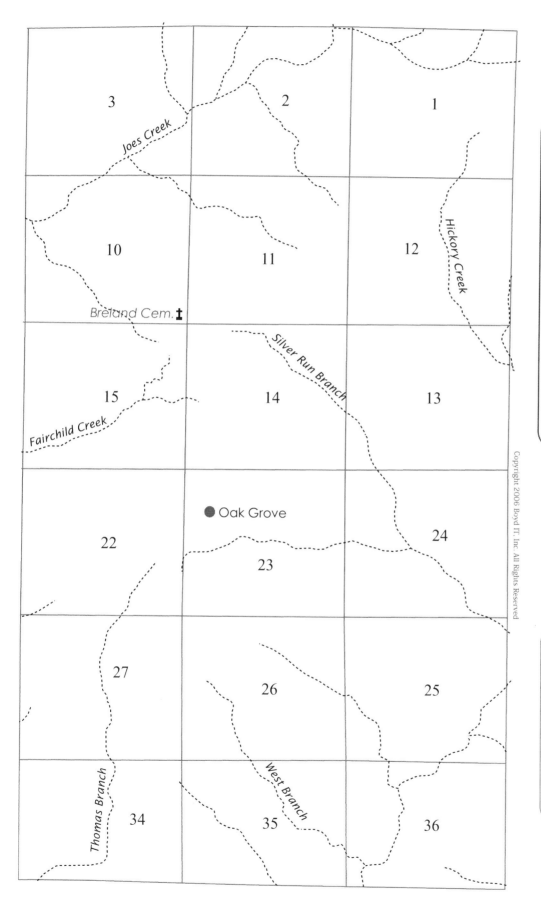

3

2

1

Joes Creek

10

11

12

Hickory Creek

Breland Cem. ☦

15

14

13

Silver Run Branch

Fairchild Creek

● Oak Grove

22

23

24

27

26

25

Thomas Branch

34

West Branch

35

36

Helpful Hints

1. This Map takes a different look at the same Congressional Township displayed in the preceding two maps. It presents features that can help you better envision the historical development of the area: a) Water-bodies (lakes & ponds), b) Water-courses (rivers, streams, etc.), c) Railroads, d) City/town center-points (where they were oftentimes located when first settled), and e) Cemeteries.

2. Using this "Historical" map in tandem with this Township's Patent Map and Road Map, may lead you to some interesting discoveries. You will often find roads, towns, cemeteries, and waterways are named after nearby landowners: sometimes those names will be the ones you are researching. See how many of these research gems you can find here in Perry County.

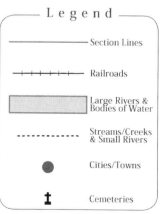

Legend

————————	Section Lines
+++++++++	Railroads
▭	Large Rivers & Bodies of Water
- - - - - -	Streams/Creeks & Small Rivers
●	Cities/Towns
☦	Cemeteries

Scale: Section = 1 mile X 1 mile
(there are some exceptions)

Map Group 15: Index to Land Patents

Township 1-North Range 9-West (St Stephens)

After you locate an individual in this Index, take note of the Section and Section Part then proceed to the Land Patent map on the pages immediately following. You should have no difficulty locating the corresponding parcel of land.

The "For More Info" Column will lead you to more information about the underlying Patents. See the *Legend* at right, and the "How to Use this Book" chapter, for more information.

```
                        LEGEND
              "For More Info . . . " column
A = Authority (Legislative Act, See Appendix "A")
B = Block or Lot (location in Section unknown)
C = Cancelled Patent
F = Fractional Section
G = Group  (Multi-Patentee Patent, see Appendix "C")
V = Overlaps another Parcel
R = Re-Issued (Parcel patented more than once)

(A & G items require you to look in the Appendixes referred
to above. All other Letter-designations followed by a number
require you to locate line-items in this index that possess
the ID number found after the letter).
```

ID	Individual in Patent	Sec.	Sec. Part	Date Issued	Other Counties	For More Info . . .
3219	BRELAND, Ellis	31	NWSE	1914-06-18		A4
3220	"	31	SWNE	1914-06-18		A4
3274	BRELAND, Leven L	31	NWSW	1906-09-14		A4
3218	CARTER, Daniel D	29	NWSW	1908-11-23		A1
3276	COWART, Newit	9	NENE	1882-12-30		A1
3275	"	4	SWSW	1889-05-06		A1
3277	"	9	NWNW	1889-05-06		A1
3272	FAIRLY, Katie	18	NWSE	1904-08-30		A4 G38
3273	"	18	SWNE	1904-08-30		A4 G38
3281	GREEN, Samuel I	1	NE	1886-04-10		A4
3279	HERRING, Rufus Q	6	S½NE	1897-02-15		A4
3280	"	6	SENW	1897-02-15		A4
3163	HILLS, Charles T	1	NW	1889-11-21		A1
3164	"	1	SE	1889-11-21		A1
3165	"	1	SESW	1889-11-21		A1
3166	"	10		1889-11-21		A1
3167	"	11		1889-11-21		A1
3168	"	12	E½NW	1889-11-21		A1
3169	"	12	NE	1889-11-21		A1
3170	"	12	S½	1889-11-21		A1
3171	"	12	SWNW	1889-11-21		A1
3172	"	13		1889-11-21		A1
3173	"	14		1889-11-21		A1
3174	"	15		1889-11-21		A1
3175	"	2	N½	1889-11-21		A1
3176	"	2	SW	1889-11-21		A1
3177	"	21		1889-11-21		A1
3178	"	22		1889-11-21		A1
3179	"	23		1889-11-21		A1
3180	"	24		1889-11-21		A1
3181	"	25		1889-11-21		A1
3182	"	26	E½SW	1889-11-21		A1
3183	"	26	N½	1889-11-21		A1
3184	"	26	NWSW	1889-11-21		A1
3185	"	26	SE	1889-11-21		A1
3186	"	27	N½	1889-11-21		A1
3187	"	27	SESE	1889-11-21		A1
3188	"	27	SW	1889-11-21		A1
3189	"	27	W½SE	1889-11-21		A1
3190	"	28		1889-11-21		A1
3191	"	3	E½	1889-11-21		A1
3192	"	3	SENW	1889-11-21		A1
3193	"	3	SW	1889-11-21		A1
3194	"	3	W½NW	1889-11-21		A1
3195	"	32		1889-11-21		A1
3196	"	33		1889-11-21		A1

ID	Individual in Patent	Sec.	Sec. Part	Date Issued	Other Counties	For More Info . . .
3197	HILLS, Charles T (Cont'd)	34		1889-11-21		A1
3198	"	35		1889-11-21		A1
3199	"	36		1889-11-21		A1
3200	"	4	E½SW	1889-11-21		A1
3201	"	4	N½	1889-11-21		A1
3202	"	4	NWSW	1889-11-21		A1
3203	"	4	SE	1889-11-21		A1
3204	"	5	E½	1889-11-21		A1
3205	"	5	E½NW	1889-11-21		A1
3206	"	5	NWNW	1889-11-21		A1
3207	"	5	SW	1889-11-21		A1
3208	"	8	E½	1889-11-21		A1
3209	"	8	E½NW	1889-11-21		A1
3210	"	8	SW	1889-11-21		A1
3211	"	8	SWNW	1889-11-21		A1
3212	"	9	E½NW	1889-11-21		A1
3213	"	9	S½	1889-11-21		A1
3214	"	9	SENE	1889-11-21		A1
3215	"	9	W½NE	1889-11-21		A1
3284	HOGAN, William	18	SW	1905-03-11		A1
3271	MAINOR, Judson	18	SWNW	1924-03-26		A4
3272	MCDOWELL, Katie	18	NWSE	1904-08-30		A4 G38
3273	"	18	SWNE	1904-08-30		A4 G38
3278	MERRITT, Nowel	2	SE	1896-03-04		A4
3270	MORROW, Joe	6	SESE	1919-06-26		A4
3216	PATTERSON, Daniel B	17	W½SW	1906-06-21		A4
3217	"	18	E½SE	1906-06-21		A4
3282	PATTERSON, William H	7	W½NW	1901-12-17		A4
3283	"	7	W½SW	1901-12-17		A4
3160	RILEY, Alexander M	20	SWSE	1904-12-31		A4
3161	"	29	N½NE	1904-12-31		A4
3162	THOMAS, Andrew J	5	SWNW	1884-12-30		A1
3224	WAGAR, Humphrey R	17	N½	1889-04-09		A1 G75
3225	"	17	NESW	1889-04-09		A1 G75
3226	"	17	SE	1889-04-09		A1 G75
3227	"	18	N½NE	1889-04-09		A1 G75
3228	"	18	N½NW	1889-04-09		A1 G75
3229	"	18	SENE	1889-04-09		A1 G75
3230	"	18	SENW	1889-04-09		A1 G75
3258	"	6	N½NE	1889-04-09		A1 G75
3259	"	6	N½NW	1889-04-09		A1 G75
3260	"	6	N½SE	1889-04-09		A1 G75
3261	"	6	NWSW	1889-04-09		A1 G75
3262	"	6	S½SW	1889-04-09		A1 G75
3263	"	6	SWNW	1889-04-09		A1 G75
3264	"	6	SWSE	1889-04-09		A1 G75
3265	"	7	E½SW	1889-04-09		A1 G75
3266	"	7	N½SE	1889-04-09		A1 G75
3267	"	7	NE	1889-04-09		A1 G75
3268	"	7	SENW	1889-04-09		A1 G75
3269	"	8	NWNW	1889-04-09		A1 G75
3232	"	19		1889-04-10		A1 G75
3233	"	20	E½NW	1889-04-10		A1 G75
3234	"	20	E½SW	1889-04-10		A1 G75
3235	"	20	NE	1889-04-10		A1 G75
3236	"	20	NWNW	1889-04-10		A1 G75
3237	"	20	NWSE	1889-04-10		A1 G75
3238	"	20	SESE	1889-04-10		A1 G75
3239	"	20	SWSW	1889-04-10		A1 G75
3240	"	29	E½SE	1889-04-10		A1 G75
3241	"	29	NESW	1889-04-10		A1 G75
3242	"	29	NW	1889-04-10		A1 G75
3243	"	29	S½NE	1889-04-10		A1 G75
3244	"	29	SWSW	1889-04-10		A1 G75
3245	"	30	E½NW	1889-04-10		A1 G75
3246	"	30	E½SW	1889-04-10		A1 G75
3247	"	30	NWSW	1889-04-10		A1 G75
3248	"	30	SE	1889-04-10		A1 G75
3249	"	30	SENE	1889-04-10		A1 G75
3250	"	30	SWNW	1889-04-10		A1 G75
3251	"	30	W½NE	1889-04-10		A1 G75
3252	"	31	E½NE	1889-04-10		A1 G75
3253	"	31	E½SE	1889-04-10		A1 G75

ID	Individual in Patent	Sec.	Sec. Part	Date Issued	Other Counties	For More Info . . .
3254	WAGAR, Humphrey R (Cont'd)	31	E½SW	1889-04-10		A1 G75
3255	" "	31	NW	1889-04-10		A1 G75
3256	" "	31	NWNE	1889-04-10		A1 G75
3257	" "	31	SWSE	1889-04-10		A1 G75
3231	" "	18	SWSE	1889-05-06		A1 G75
3224	WELLS, Willard B	17	N½	1889-04-09		A1 G75
3225	" "	17	NESW	1889-04-09		A1 G75
3226	" "	17	SE	1889-04-09		A1 G75
3227	" "	18	N½NE	1889-04-09		A1 G75
3228	" "	18	N½NW	1889-04-09		A1 G75
3229	" "	18	SENE	1889-04-09		A1 G75
3230	" "	18	SENW	1889-04-09		A1 G75
3258	" "	6	N½NE	1889-04-09		A1 G75
3259	" "	6	N½NW	1889-04-09		A1 G75
3260	" "	6	N½SE	1889-04-09		A1 G75
3261	" "	6	NWSW	1889-04-09		A1 G75
3262	" "	6	S½SW	1889-04-09		A1 G75
3263	" "	6	SWNW	1889-04-09		A1 G75
3264	" "	6	SWSE	1889-04-09		A1 G75
3265	" "	7	E½SW	1889-04-09		A1 G75
3266	" "	7	N½SE	1889-04-09		A1 G75
3267	" "	7	NE	1889-04-09		A1 G75
3268	" "	7	SENW	1889-04-09		A1 G75
3269	" "	8	NWNW	1889-04-09		A1 G75
3232	" "	19		1889-04-10		A1 G75
3233	" "	20	E½NW	1889-04-10		A1 G75
3234	" "	20	E½SW	1889-04-10		A1 G75
3235	" "	20	NE	1889-04-10		A1 G75
3236	" "	20	NWNW	1889-04-10		A1 G75
3237	" "	20	NWSE	1889-04-10		A1 G75
3238	" "	20	SESE	1889-04-10		A1 G75
3239	" "	20	SWSW	1889-04-10		A1 G75
3240	" "	29	E½SE	1889-04-10		A1 G75
3241	" "	29	NESW	1889-04-10		A1 G75
3242	" "	29	NW	1889-04-10		A1 G75
3243	" "	29	S½NE	1889-04-10		A1 G75
3244	" "	29	SWSW	1889-04-10		A1 G75
3245	" "	30	E½NW	1889-04-10		A1 G75
3246	" "	30	E½SW	1889-04-10		A1 G75
3247	" "	30	NWSW	1889-04-10		A1 G75
3248	" "	30	SE	1889-04-10		A1 G75
3249	" "	30	SENE	1889-04-10		A1 G75
3250	" "	30	SWNW	1889-04-10		A1 G75
3251	" "	30	W½NE	1889-04-10		A1 G75
3252	" "	31	E½NE	1889-04-10		A1 G75
3253	" "	31	E½SE	1889-04-10		A1 G75
3254	" "	31	E½SW	1889-04-10		A1 G75
3255	" "	31	NW	1889-04-10		A1 G75
3256	" "	31	NWNE	1889-04-10		A1 G75
3257	" "	31	SWSE	1889-04-10		A1 G75
3231	" "	18	SWSE	1889-05-06		A1 G75
3221	WILLIAMSON, Elum C	1	N½SW	1894-09-28		A4
3222	" "	1	SWSW	1894-09-28		A4
3223	" "	12	NWNW	1894-09-28		A4

Patent Map

T1-N R9-W
St Stephens Meridian

Map Group 15

Township Statistics

Parcels Mapped	:	125
Number of Patents	:	39
Number of Individuals	:	20
Patentees Identified	:	18
Number of Surnames	:	18
Multi-Patentee Parcels	:	48
Oldest Patent Date	:	12/30/1882
Most Recent Patent	:	3/26/1924
Block/Lot Parcels	:	0
Parcels Re - Issued	:	0
Parcels that Overlap	:	0
Cities and Towns	:	1
Cemeteries	:	1

HILLS
Charles T
1889

HILLS
Charles T
1889

HILLS
Charles T
1889

3

HILLS
Charles T
1889

HILLS
Charles T
1889

2

HILLS
Charles T
1889

MERRITT
Nowel
1896

HILLS
Charles T
1889

1

GREEN
Samuel I
1886

WILLIAMSON
Elum C
1894

WILLIAMSON
Elum C
1894

HILLS
Charles T
1889

HILLS
Charles T
1889

WILLIAMSON
Elum C
1894

HILLS
Charles T
1889

HILLS
Charles T
1889

HILLS
Charles T
1889

10

HILLS
Charles T
1889

11

HILLS
Charles T
1889

12

HILLS
Charles T
1889

15

HILLS
Charles T
1889

14

HILLS
Charles T
1889

13

HILLS
Charles T
1889

22

HILLS
Charles T
1889

23

HILLS
Charles T
1889

24

HILLS
Charles T
1889

HILLS
Charles T
1889

27

HILLS
Charles T
1889

HILLS
Charles T
1889

HILLS
Charles T
1889

HILLS
Charles T
1889

26

HILLS
Charles T
1889

HILLS
Charles T
1889

25

HILLS
Charles T
1889

34

HILLS
Charles T
1889

35

HILLS
Charles T
1889

36

HILLS
Charles T
1889

Copyright 2006 Boyd IT, Inc. All Rights Reserved

Helpful Hints

1. This Map's INDEX can be found on the preceding pages.

2. Refer to Map "C" to see where this Township lies within Perry County, Mississippi.

3. Numbers within square brackets [ ] denote a multi-patentee land parcel (multi-owner). Refer to Appendix "C" for a full list of members in this group.

4. Areas that look to be crowded with Patentees usually indicate multiple sales of the same parcel (Re-issues) or Overlapping parcels. See this Township's Index for an explanation of these and other circumstances that might explain "odd" groupings of Patentees on this map.

Legend

———— Patent Boundary

━━━━ Section Boundary

No Patents Found
(or Outside County)

1., 2., 3., ...   Lot Numbers
(when beside a name)

[ ]   Group Number
(see Appendix "C")

Scale: Section = 1 mile X 1 mile
(generally, with some exceptions)

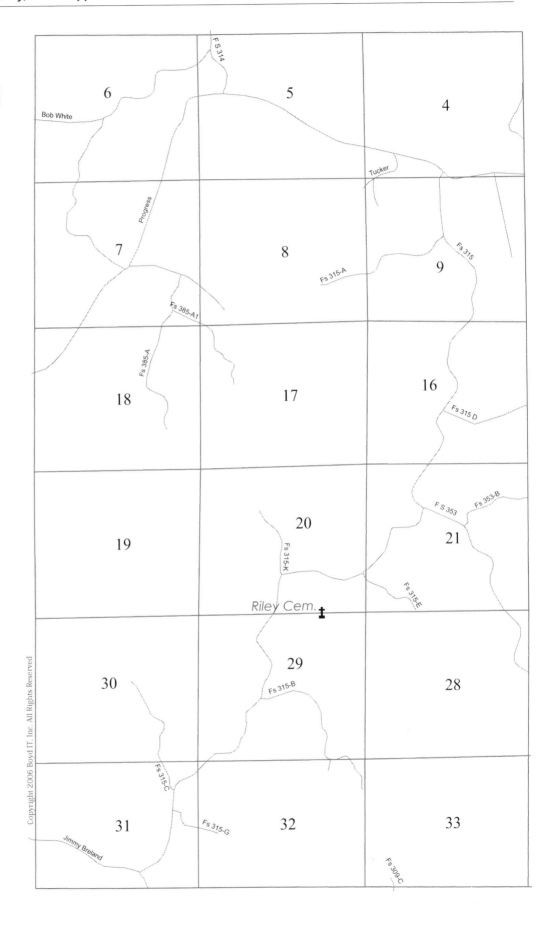

Road Map

T1-N R9-W
St Stephens Meridian

Map Group 15

Cities & Towns

Progress

Cemeteries

Riley Cemetery

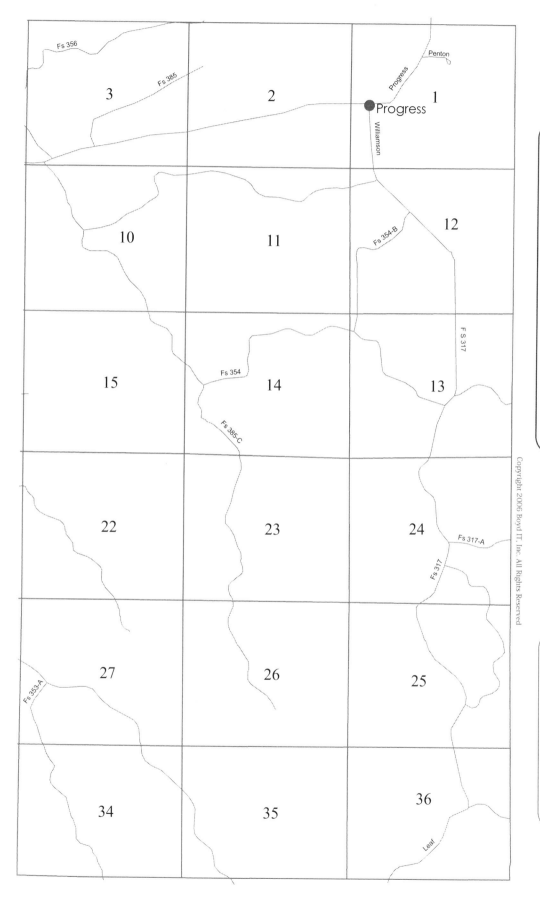

Fs 356

Fs 385

Penton

Progress

3

2

Progress

Williamson

1

10

Fs 354-B

11

12

F s 317

15

Fs 354

14

Fs 385-C

13

22

23

24

Fs 317-A

Fs 317

27

Fs 353-A

26

25

34

35

36

Leaf

Copyright 2006 Boyd IT, Inc. All Rights Reserved

Helpful Hints

1. This road map has a number of uses, but primarily it is to help you: a) find the present location of land owned by your ancestors (at least the general area), b) find cemeteries and city-centers, and c) estimate the route/roads used by Census-takers & tax-assessors.

2. If you plan to travel to Perry County to locate cemeteries or land parcels, please pick up a modern travel map for the area before you do. Mapping old land parcels on modern maps is not as exact a science as you might think. Just the slightest variations in public land survey coordinates, estimates of parcel boundaries, or road-map deviations can greatly alter a map's representation of how a road either does or doesn't cross a particular parcel of land.

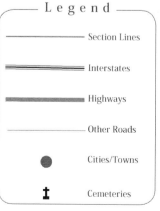

Legend

———— Section Lines

════ Interstates

▬▬▬ Highways

———— Other Roads

● Cities/Towns

✝ Cemeteries

Scale: Section = 1 mile X 1 mile
(generally, with some exceptions)

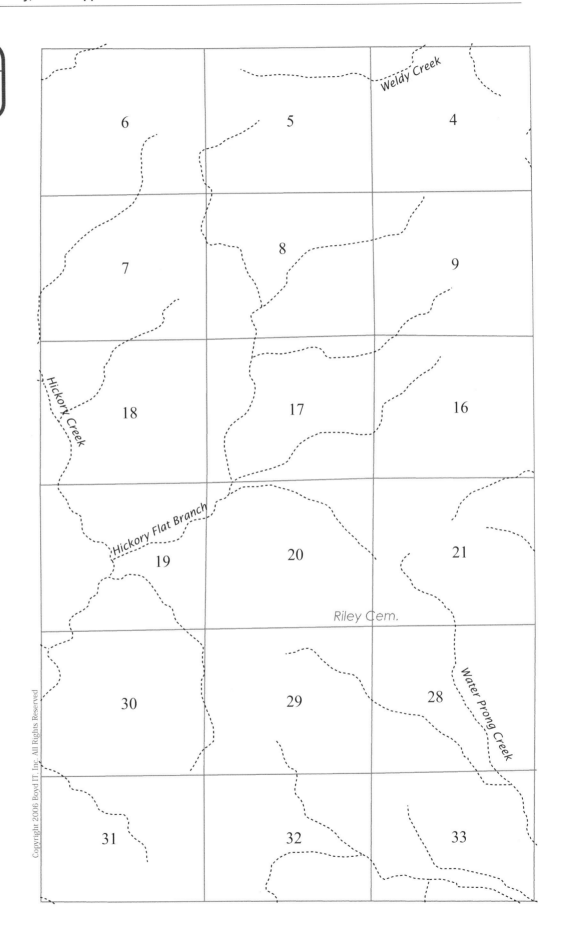

Historical Map

T1-N R9-W
St Stephens Meridian

Map Group 15

Cities & Towns
Progress

Cemeteries
Riley Cemetery

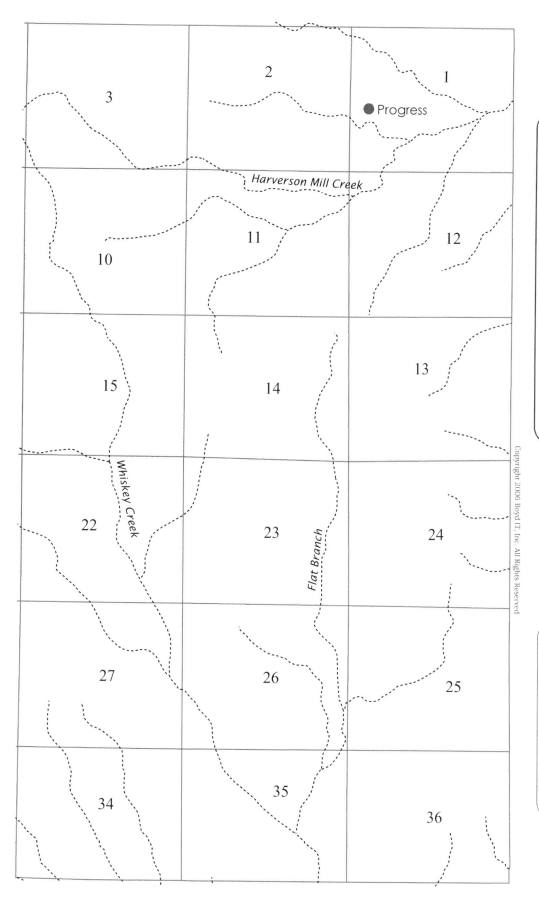

● Progress

Harverson Mill Creek

3

2

1

10

11

12

15

14

13

Whiskey Creek

22

23

Flat Branch

24

27

26

25

34

35

36

Helpful Hints

1. This Map takes a different look at the same Congressional Township displayed in the preceding two maps. It presents features that can help you better envision the historical development of the area: a) Water-bodies (lakes & ponds), b) Water-courses (rivers, streams, etc.), c) Railroads, d) City/town center-points (where they were oftentimes located when first settled), and e) Cemeteries.

2. Using this "Historical" map in tandem with this Township's Patent Map and Road Map, may lead you to some interesting discoveries. You will often find roads, towns, cemeteries, and waterways are named after nearby landowners: sometimes those names will be the ones you are researching. See how many of these research gems you can find here in Perry County.

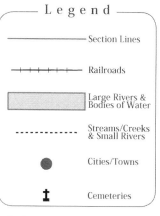

L e g e n d

———————— Section Lines

+++++++ Railroads

[ ] Large Rivers & Bodies of Water

- - - - - - Streams/Creeks & Small Rivers

● Cities/Towns

✝ Cemeteries

Scale: Section = 1 mile X 1 mile
(there are some exceptions)

197

Map Group 16: Index to Land Patents

Township 1-South Range 11-West (St Stephens)

After you locate an individual in this Index, take note of the Section and Section Part then proceed to the Land Patent map on the pages immediately following. You should have no difficulty locating the corresponding parcel of land.

The "For More Info" Column will lead you to more information about the underlying Patents. See the *Legend* at right, and the "How to Use this Book" chapter, for more information.

ID	Individual in Patent	Sec.	Sec. Part	Date Issued	Other Counties	For More Info . . .
3378	ALFRED, Ed	13	SWSW	1908-10-26		A4
3490	ANDREW, Mary J	4	E½NE	1897-05-07		A4 G2
3491	"	4	SWNE	1897-05-07		A4 G2
3500	ANDREWS, Nancy	3	NWSE	1912-12-07		A4 G3
3301	BATSON, Calvin A	5	N½SW	1884-12-30		A1
3302	"	6	NESE	1884-12-30		A1
3298	BENJAMIN, Anna	4	NWNE	1914-06-29		A4 G5
3399	BOULTON, Hattie	26	E½SE	1894-11-22		A4 G11
3400	"	26	S½NE	1894-11-22		A4 G11
3456	BOULTON, Levi	8	N½SE	1895-07-18		A1
3457	"	8	NESW	1895-07-18		A1
3458	"	8	SENE	1895-07-18		A1
3384	BREELAND, Emanuel	26	SWSE	1896-10-31		A4
3385	"	35	NWNE	1896-10-31		A4
3288	BRELAND, Abram	3	SENE	1889-01-05		A4
3289	"	3	W½NE	1889-01-05		A4
3295	BRELAND, Andrew	4	SWSW	1905-12-30		A4
3296	"	5	S½SE	1905-12-30		A4
3298	BRELAND, Anna	4	NWNE	1914-06-29		A4 G5
3300	BRELAND, Betsy	15	NENE	1909-01-25		A4
3382	BRELAND, Elizabeth	24	W½SW	1888-04-05		A4
3383	"	25	N½NW	1888-04-05		A4
3386	BRELAND, Enoch	11	NWSW	1897-02-15		A4
3387	"	11	S½SW	1897-02-15		A4
3388	"	14	NWNW	1897-02-15		A4
3404	BRELAND, Israel	14	N½SE	1892-03-23		A4
3405	"	14	N½SW	1892-03-23		A4
3420	BRELAND, John	13	N½NW	1906-06-16		A4
3421	"	13	SWNW	1906-06-16		A4
3454	BRELAND, Julia A	10	S½N½	1906-09-19		A4
3481	BRELAND, Margaret	23	S½SE	1897-04-10		A4
3482	"	23	SESW	1897-04-10		A4
3483	"	26	NENE	1897-04-10		A4
3479	"	10	N½NE	1906-05-01		A4
3480	"	10	NENW	1906-05-01		A4
3484	BRELAND, Mariah	36	N½NW	1898-01-19		A4
3485	"	36	SENW	1898-01-19		A4
3486	"	36	SWNE	1898-01-19		A4
3501	BRELAND, Nathaniel	9	NW	1904-11-15		A4
3504	BRELAND, Paul	5	E½NE	1905-10-10		A4
3505	BRELAND, Richard	11	N½SE	1906-09-14		A4
3506	"	11	S½NE	1906-09-14		A4
3507	BRELAND, Robert	10	NWNW	1879-05-06		A4
3508	"	3	S½SW	1879-05-06		A4
3543	BRELAND, Zelphey	10	W½SW	1895-02-21		A4
3544	"	9	E½SE	1895-02-21		A4

ID	Individual in Patent	Sec.	Sec. Part	Date Issued	Other Counties	For More Info . . .
3434	BROWN, John P	28	SESE	1859-06-01		A1
3436	BUNN, John S	29	NWSW	1901-08-12		A4
3437	" "	29	S½NW	1901-08-12		A4
3389	CARTER, Fannie	25	S½NW	1895-05-11		A4
3390	" "	25	W½NE	1895-05-11		A4
3422	COACHMAN, John	11	NWNW	1905-07-18		A1
3423	" "	2	SWSW	1905-07-18		A1
3500	CROSBY, Nancy	3	NWSE	1912-12-07		A4 G3
3460	DANTZLER, Lorenzo N	7	NESE	1884-12-30		A1 G26
3461	" "	8	S½SE	1884-12-30		A1 G26
3462	" "	9	W½SW	1884-12-30		A1 G26
3459	" "	3	NENW	1889-11-29		A1
3540	DEARMAN, William R	36	E½SW	1892-08-01		A1
3541	" "	36	NWSE	1892-08-01		A1
3542	" "	36	SWSW	1892-08-01		A1
3290	DENHAM, Alex	13	NE	1890-08-16		A4
3499	DENHAM, Mitchel	9	NE	1906-01-30		A4
3521	DUNLAP, Shirley E	31	SWSW	1924-06-06		A1
3446	FAIRLEY, John W	3	NESW	1882-12-30		A1
3441	" "	23	NENE	1883-02-03		A1
3440	" "	14	SESE	1883-09-15		A1
3449	" "	5	NENW	1883-09-15		A1
3439	" "	13	SENW	1884-12-30		A1
3442	" "	23	SENE	1884-12-30		A1
3443	" "	24	W½NW	1884-12-30		A1
3445	" "	29	SENE	1884-12-30		A1
3447	" "	3	SENW	1884-12-30		A1
3450	" "	5	SWNE	1884-12-30		A1
3444	" "	25	E½SE	1903-03-28		A4
3448	" "	36	N½NE	1903-03-28		A4
3512	FAIRLEY, Robert	13	NESE	1905-11-24		A4
3522	FAIRLEY, Simon	3	NWNW	1883-09-15		A1
3523	FAIRLEY, Washington	15	NENW	1890-04-25		A1
3524	" "	15	NWNE	1890-04-25		A1
3525	" "	15	S½NE	1890-04-25		A1
3285	GIBSON, Abner	17	NESW	1905-11-03		A1
3497	GIBSON, Minerva	17	N½SE	1899-09-30		A4 G40
3498	" "	17	S½NE	1899-09-30		A4 G40
3497	GIBSON, Uriah M	17	N½SE	1899-09-30		A4 G40
3498	" "	17	S½NE	1899-09-30		A4 G40
3455	GODFREY, Lawrence	15	NWSW	1911-10-09		A4
3401	GRIFFIN, Isham	3	NWSW	1894-02-17		A4
3402	" "	3	SWNW	1894-02-17		A4
3403	" "	4	NESE	1894-02-17		A4
3460	GRIFFIN, James W	7	NESE	1884-12-30		A1 G26
3461	" "	8	S½SE	1884-12-30		A1 G26
3462	" "	9	W½SW	1884-12-30		A1 G26
3412	GRIFFIN, John A	23	NESE	1854-03-15		A1
3413	" "	24	SENW	1854-03-15		A1
3414	" "	25	SWSW	1854-03-15		A1 R3415
3416	" "	26	NWNE	1854-03-15		A1
3417	" "	26	SENW	1854-03-15		A1
3415	" "	25	SWSW	1862-04-10		A1 R3414
3435	GRIFFIN, John P	6	N½NE	1922-10-30		A4
3451	GRIFFIN, Joseph C	15	S½NW	1889-11-29		A1
3513	GRIFFIN, Robert M	5	NESE	1884-12-30		A1
3531	GRIFFIN, William C	5	NWSE	1883-09-15		A1
3532	" "	5	S½NW	1883-09-15		A1
3538	" "	9	NESW	1883-09-15		A1
3539	" "	9	NWSE	1883-09-15		A1
3533	" "	6	NESW	1884-12-30		A1
3534	" "	6	NWSW	1884-12-30		A1
3535	" "	6	SENW	1884-12-30		A1
3536	" "	6	SWNE	1884-12-30		A1
3537	" "	6	W½SE	1884-12-30		A1
3530	" "	5	NWNE	1889-11-29		A1
3406	HOLLIMON, James	22	SESE	1897-11-22		A4
3407	" "	23	SWSW	1897-11-22		A4
3408	" "	26	N½NW	1897-11-22		A4
3299	HOTEN, Benjamin	6	NENW	1897-05-20		A4
3379	HOUSLEY, Eli	35	E½NE	1891-05-20		A4
3380	" "	35	NESE	1891-05-20		A4
3381	" "	36	NWSW	1891-05-20		A4

ID	Individual in Patent	Sec.	Sec. Part	Date Issued	Other Counties	For More Info . . .
3452	JACKSON, Joshua	3	E½SE	1906-01-30		A4
3453	" "	3	SWSE	1906-01-30		A4
3391	JOHNSON, Franklin W	7	NENW	1906-06-30		A4
3392	" "	7	NWSE	1906-06-30		A4
3393	" "	7	W½NE	1906-06-30		A4
3526	JOHNSON, Washington	27	W½SW	1899-06-28		A4
3293	KNIGHT, Allen T	24	E½SE	1892-04-29		A4
3294	" "	24	S½NE	1892-04-29		A4
3490	KNIGHT, Mary J	4	E½NE	1897-05-07		A4 G2
3491	" "	4	SWNE	1897-05-07		A4 G2
3509	LOTT, Robert C	27	NWSE	1894-03-23		A4
3510	" "	27	S½SE	1894-03-23		A4
3511	" "	27	SWNE	1894-03-23		A4
3428	MAXWELL, John L	7	SENE	1884-12-30		A1
3429	" "	8	SWNW	1884-12-30		A1
3430	" "	9	SESW	1884-12-30		A1
3431	" "	9	SWSE	1884-12-30		A1
3427	" "	6	NWNW	1885-04-04		A4
3409	MCDOWELL, Jerry	11	NENW	1891-05-20		A4
3410	" "	11	NWNE	1891-05-20		A4
3411	" "	11	S½NW	1891-05-20		A4
3433	MCDOWELL, John	11	NENE	1906-05-01		A4
3492	MCDOWELL, Mary	4	NESW	1905-12-13		A4
3493	" "	4	NWSE	1905-12-13		A4
3494	" "	4	SENW	1905-12-13		A4
3396	MCLEOD, Handy	13	N½SW	1889-12-19		A4
3397	" "	13	NWSE	1889-12-19		A4
3398	" "	13	SESW	1889-12-19		A4
3463	MONTAGUE, Luke S	19	SESW	1889-11-29		A1
3464	" "	25	E½NE	1889-11-29		A1
3465	" "	25	E½SW	1889-11-29		A1
3466	" "	25	NWSW	1889-11-29		A1
3467	" "	25	W½SE	1889-11-29		A1
3468	" "	27	E½SW	1889-11-29		A1
3469	" "	27	N½NE	1889-11-29		A1
3470	" "	27	NW	1889-11-29		A1
3471	" "	29	N½NE	1889-11-29		A1
3472	" "	29	N½NW	1889-11-29		A1
3473	" "	29	S½SW	1889-11-29		A1
3474	" "	29	SE	1889-11-29		A1
3475	" "	29	SWNE	1889-11-29		A1
3476	" "	35	NWSE	1889-11-29		A1
3477	" "	35	SESE	1889-11-29		A1
3478	" "	35	SWNE	1889-11-29		A1
3495	MORGAN, Millie	24	E½SW	1893-12-28		A4
3496	" "	24	W½SE	1893-12-28		A4
3399	OWENS, Hattie	26	E½SE	1894-11-22		A4 G11
3400	" "	26	S½NE	1894-11-22		A4 G11
3527	PAYTON, Washington	26	N½SW	1895-06-19		A4
3528	" "	26	NWSE	1895-06-19		A4
3529	" "	26	SWNW	1895-06-19		A4
3514	PORTER, S Goss	7	SESE	1911-01-05		A4
3303	RANSDELL, Daniel M	13	SESE	1884-12-30		A1
3304	" "	14	S½SW	1884-12-30		A1
3305	" "	14	SWSE	1884-12-30		A1
3306	" "	15	NESW	1884-12-30		A1
3307	" "	15	NWNW	1884-12-30		A1
3308	" "	15	NWSE	1884-12-30		A1
3309	" "	15	S½SE	1884-12-30		A1
3310	" "	15	S½SW	1884-12-30		A1
3311	" "	17	N½NE	1884-12-30		A1
3312	" "	17	NENW	1884-12-30		A1
3313	" "	17	NWSW	1884-12-30		A1
3314	" "	17	S½SE	1884-12-30		A1
3315	" "	17	S½SW	1884-12-30		A1
3316	" "	17	SWNW	1884-12-30		A1
3317	" "	18	E½SE	1884-12-30		A1
3318	" "	18	N½NW	1884-12-30		A1
3319	" "	18	NWSE	1884-12-30		A1
3320	" "	19	N½SW	1884-12-30		A1
3321	" "	19	NENE	1884-12-30		A1
3322	" "	19	S½NW	1884-12-30		A1
3323	" "	19	SWNE	1884-12-30		A1

ID	Individual in Patent	Sec.	Sec. Part	Date Issued	Other Counties	For More Info . . .
3324	RANSDELL, Daniel M (Cont'd)	19	SWSW	1884-12-30		A1
3325	" "	19	W½SE	1884-12-30		A1
3326	" "	20	E½SE	1884-12-30		A1
3327	" "	20	N½NE	1884-12-30		A1
3328	" "	20	NENW	1884-12-30		A1
3329	" "	20	SWSW	1884-12-30		A1
3330	" "	21	N½SE	1884-12-30		A1
3331	" "	21	N½SW	1884-12-30		A1
3332	" "	21	NENE	1884-12-30		A1
3333	" "	21	NWNW	1884-12-30		A1
3334	" "	21	S½NE	1884-12-30		A1
3335	" "	21	S½NW	1884-12-30		A1
3336	" "	22	N½NE	1884-12-30		A1
3337	" "	22	N½SE	1884-12-30		A1
3338	" "	22	N½SW	1884-12-30		A1
3339	" "	22	NENW	1884-12-30		A1
3340	" "	22	SENE	1884-12-30		A1
3341	" "	22	SWNW	1884-12-30		A1
3342	" "	23	N½SW	1884-12-30		A1
3343	" "	23	NW	1884-12-30		A1
3344	" "	23	NWSE	1884-12-30		A1
3345	" "	23	W½NE	1884-12-30		A1
3346	" "	27	NESE	1884-12-30		A1
3347	" "	27	SENE	1884-12-30		A1
3348	" "	30	S½SE	1884-12-30		A1
3349	" "	30	SENW	1884-12-30		A1
3350	" "	30	W½NW	1884-12-30		A1
3351	" "	31	E½SW	1884-12-30		A1
3352	" "	31	N½NE	1884-12-30		A1
3353	" "	31	NW	1884-12-30		A1
3354	" "	31	NWSE	1884-12-30		A1
3355	" "	31	SESE	1884-12-30		A1
3356	" "	32	NESW	1884-12-30		A1
3357	" "	32	S½NE	1884-12-30		A1
3358	" "	32	S½SE	1884-12-30		A1
3359	" "	32	S½SW	1884-12-30		A1
3360	" "	33	N½SE	1884-12-30		A1
3361	" "	33	N½SW	1884-12-30		A1
3362	" "	33	SENE	1884-12-30		A1
3363	" "	33	SESW	1884-12-30		A1
3364	" "	33	SWNW	1884-12-30		A1
3365	" "	33	SWSE	1884-12-30		A1
3366	" "	5	NWNW	1884-12-30		A1
3367	" "	6	SENE	1884-12-30		A1
3368	" "	6	SWSW	1884-12-30		A1
3369	" "	7	E½SW	1884-12-30		A1
3370	" "	7	NENE	1884-12-30		A1
3371	" "	7	SENW	1884-12-30		A1
3372	" "	7	SWSE	1884-12-30		A1
3373	" "	7	SWSW	1884-12-30		A1
3374	" "	7	W½NW	1884-12-30		A1
3375	" "	8	SESW	1884-12-30		A1
3286	RAYBORN, Abner	4	NWSW	1889-12-19		A4
3287	" "	4	W½NW	1889-12-19		A4
3502	RAYBURN, Oliver	36	E½SE	1890-08-16		A4
3503	" "	36	SENE	1890-08-16		A4
3432	SCARBOROUGH, John L	15	NESE	1912-12-21		A4
3487	SEAL, Martha	21	SWSW	1897-04-10		A4
3488	" "	28	N½NW	1897-04-10		A4
3489	" "	28	SENW	1897-04-10		A4
3519	SIMMS, Sarah E	21	S½SE	1905-10-02		A1
3520	" "	28	N½NE	1905-10-02		A1
3394	SIMS, George W	28	N½SE	1884-12-30		A4
3395	" "	28	S½NE	1884-12-30		A4
3515	SMITH, Samuel Z	19	NESE	1890-08-16		A4
3516	" "	19	SENE	1890-08-16		A4
3517	" "	20	NWSW	1890-08-16		A4
3518	" "	20	SWNW	1890-08-16		A4
3376	TAYLOR, Daniel	20	E½SW	1896-10-31		A4
3377	" "	20	W½SE	1896-10-31		A4
3418	TAYLOR, John A	21	NENW	1905-11-03		A1
3419	" "	21	NWNE	1905-11-03		A1
3424	TAYLOR, John J	33	SESE	1890-08-16		A4

ID	Individual in Patent	Sec.	Sec. Part	Date Issued	Other Counties	For More Info . . .
3425	TAYLOR, John J (Cont'd)	34	NESW	1890-08-16		A4
3426	" "	34	S½SW	1890-08-16		A4
3297	THOMAS, Andrew J	11	S½SE	1876-12-01		A4
3438	THOMAS, John	4	NENW	1841-01-05		A1
3291	WALKER, Alexander B	26	S½SW	1895-01-17		A4
3292	" "	35	N½NW	1895-01-17		A4

Patent Map

T1-S R11-W
St Stephens Meridian

Map Group 16

Township Statistics

Parcels Mapped	:	260
Number of Patents	:	114
Number of Individuals	:	82
Patentees Identified	:	77
Number of Surnames	:	47
Multi-Patentee Parcels	:	11
Oldest Patent Date	:	1/5/1841
Most Recent Patent	:	6/6/1924
Block/Lot Parcels	:	0
Parcels Re - Issued	:	1
Parcels that Overlap	:	0
Cities and Towns	:	0
Cemeteries	:	3

Map (Township 1-S Range 11-W, St Stephens)

Section 3
- FAIRLEY Simon 1883
- DANTZLER Lorenzo N 1889
- BRELAND Abram 1889
- GRIFFIN Isham 1894
- FAIRLEY John W 1884
- BRELAND Abram 1889
- GRIFFIN Isham 1894
- FAIRLEY John W 1882
- ANDREWS [3] Nancy 1912
- JACKSON Joshua 1906
- BRELAND Robert 1879
- JACKSON Joshua 1906
- COACHMAN John 1905

Section 2

Section 1

Section 10
- BRELAND Robert 1879
- BRELAND Margaret 1906
- BRELAND Margaret 1906
- BRELAND Julia A 1906
- BRELAND Zelphey 1895

Section 11
- COACHMAN John 1905
- MCDOWELL Jerry 1891
- MCDOWELL Jerry 1891
- MCDOWELL John 1906
- MCDOWELL Jerry 1891
- BRELAND Richard 1906
- BRELAND Enoch 1897
- BRELAND Richard 1906
- BRELAND Enoch 1897
- THOMAS Andrew J 1876

Section 12

Section 15
- RANSDELL Daniel M 1884
- FAIRLEY Washington 1890
- FAIRLEY Washington 1890
- BRELAND Betsy 1909
- GRIFFIN Joseph C 1889
- FAIRLEY Washington 1890
- GODFREY Lawrence 1911
- RANSDELL Daniel M 1884
- RANSDELL Daniel M 1884
- SCARBOROUGH John L 1912
- RANSDELL Daniel M 1884
- RANSDELL Daniel M 1884

Section 14
- BRELAND Enoch 1897
- BRELAND Israel 1892
- BRELAND Israel 1892
- RANSDELL Daniel M 1884
- RANSDELL Daniel M 1884
- FAIRLEY John W 1883

Section 13
- BRELAND John 1906
- DENHAM Alex 1890
- BRELAND John 1906
- FAIRLEY John W 1884
- MCLEOD Handy 1889
- MCLEOD Handy 1889
- FAIRLEY Robert 1905
- ALFRED Ed 1908
- MCLEOD Handy 1889
- RANSDELL Daniel M 1884

Section 22
- RANSDELL Daniel M 1884
- RANSDELL Daniel M 1884
- RANSDELL Daniel M 1884
- RANSDELL Daniel M 1884
- RANSDELL Daniel M 1884
- RANSDELL Daniel M 1884
- HOLLIMON James 1897

Section 23
- RANSDELL Daniel M 1884
- FAIRLEY John W 1883
- FAIRLEY John W 1884
- RANSDELL Daniel M 1884
- RANSDELL Daniel M 1884
- RANSDELL Daniel M 1884
- GRIFFIN John A 1854
- HOLLIMON James 1897
- BRELAND Margaret 1897
- BRELAND Margaret 1897

Section 24
- FAIRLEY John W 1884
- GRIFFIN John A 1854
- KNIGHT Allen T 1892
- BRELAND Elizabeth 1888
- MORGAN Millie 1893
- MORGAN Millie 1893
- KNIGHT Allen T 1892

Section 27
- MONTAGUE Luke S 1889
- MONTAGUE Luke S 1889
- LOTT Robert C 1894
- RANSDELL Daniel M 1884
- LOTT Robert C 1894
- RANSDELL Daniel M 1884
- JOHNSON Washington 1899
- MONTAGUE Luke S 1889
- LOTT Robert C 1894

Section 26
- HOLLIMON James 1897
- GRIFFIN John A 1854
- BRELAND Margaret 1897
- PAYTON Washington 1895
- GRIFFIN John A 1854
- BOULTON [11] Hattie 1894
- PAYTON Washington 1895
- PAYTON Washington 1895
- BOULTON [11] Hattie 1894
- WALKER Alexander B 1895
- BREELAND Emanuel 1896

Section 25
- BRELAND Elizabeth 1888
- CARTER Fannie 1895
- CARTER Fannie 1895
- MONTAGUE Luke S 1889
- MONTAGUE Luke S 1889
- MONTAGUE Luke S 1889
- GRIFFIN John A 1862
- GRIFFIN John A 1854
- FAIRLEY John W 1903

Section 34
- TAYLOR John J 1890
- TAYLOR John J 1890

Section 35
- WALKER Alexander B 1895
- BREELAND Emanuel 1896
- HOUSLEY Eli 1891
- MONTAGUE Luke S 1889
- MONTAGUE Luke S 1889
- HOUSLEY Eli 1891
- MONTAGUE Luke S 1889

Section 36
- BRELAND Mariah 1898
- FAIRLEY John W 1903
- BRELAND Mariah 1898
- BRELAND Mariah 1898
- RAYBURN Oliver 1890
- HOUSLEY Eli 1891
- DEARMAN William R 1892
- DEARMAN William R 1892
- DEARMAN William R 1892
- RAYBURN Oliver 1890

Helpful Hints

1. This Map's INDEX can be found on the preceding pages.

2. Refer to Map "C" to see where this Township lies within Perry County, Mississippi.

3. Numbers within square brackets [ ] denote a multi-patentee land parcel (multi-owner). Refer to Appendix "C" for a full list of members in this group.

4. Areas that look to be crowded with Patentees usually indicate multiple sales of the same parcel (Re-issues) or Overlapping parcels. See this Township's Index for an explanation of these and other circumstances that might explain "odd" groupings of Patentees on this map.

Legend

— Patent Boundary

— Section Boundary

No Patents Found (or Outside County)

1., 2., 3., ... Lot Numbers (when beside a name)

[ ] Group Number (see Appendix "C")

Scale: Section = 1 mile X 1 mile (generally, with some exceptions)

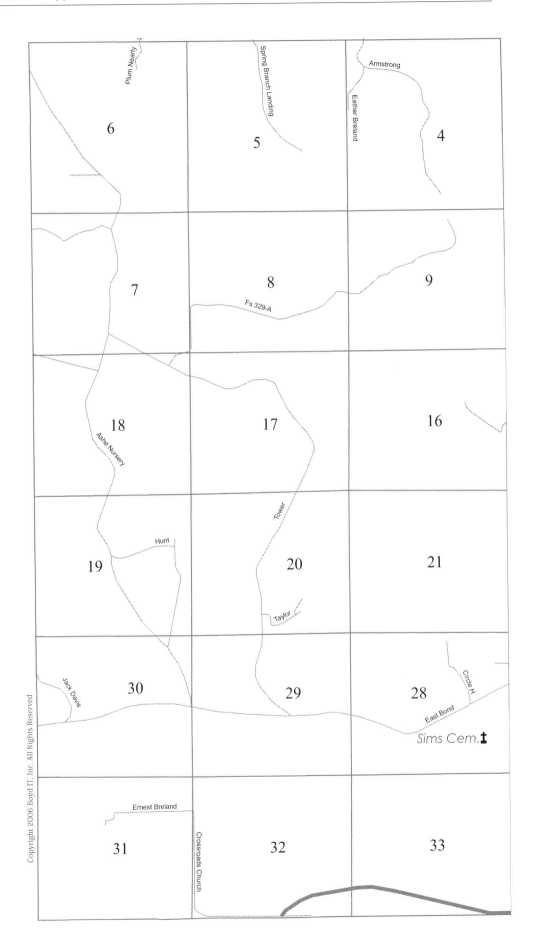

Road Map

T1-S R11-W
St Stephens Meridian

Map Group 16

Cities & Towns
None

Cemeteries
New York Cemetery
Sims Cemetery
Taylor Cemetery

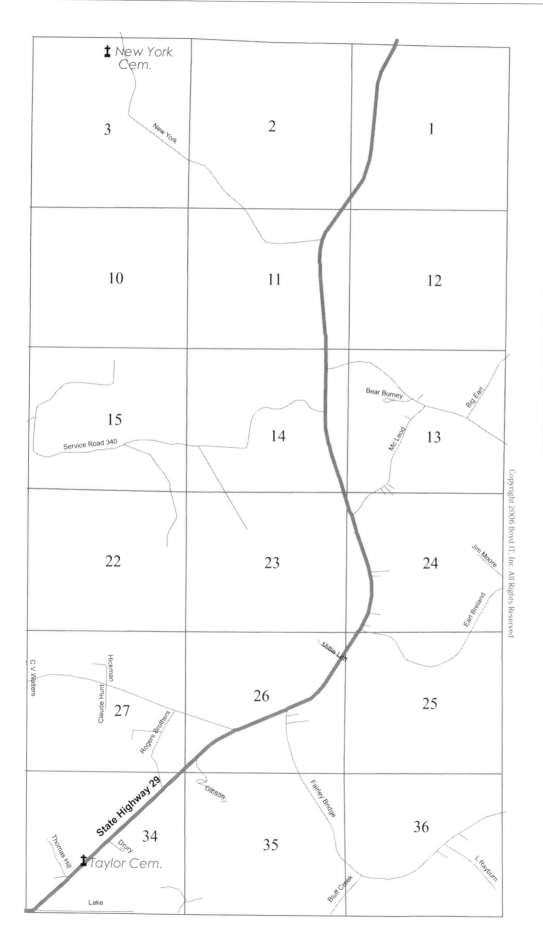

3

2

1

New York Cem.

New York

10

11

12

15

14

13

Bear Burney

Big Earl

Mc Leod

Service Road 340

22

23

24

Jim Moore

Earl Breland

Mittie Lott

27

26

25

C V Walters

Hickman

Claude Hunt

Rogers Brothers

State Highway 29

Gibson

Fairley Bridge

34

35

36

Thomas Hill

Drury

Taylor Cem.

Bluff Creek

L Rayburn

Lake

Helpful Hints

1. This road map has a number of uses, but primarily it is to help you: a) find the present location of land owned by your ancestors (at least the general area), b) find cemeteries and city-centers, and c) estimate the route/roads used by Census-takers & tax-assessors.

2. If you plan to travel to Perry County to locate cemeteries or land parcels, please pick up a modern travel map for the area before you do. Mapping old land parcels on modern maps is not as exact a science as you might think. Just the slightest variations in public land survey coordinates, estimates of parcel boundaries, or road-map deviations can greatly alter a map's representation of how a road either does or doesn't cross a particular parcel of land.

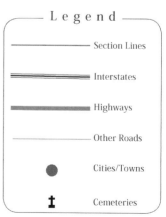

Legend

————	Section Lines
━━━━	Interstates
▬▬▬▬	Highways
————	Other Roads
●	Cities/Towns
✝	Cemeteries

Scale: Section = 1 mile X 1 mile
(generally, with some exceptions)

Historical Map

T1-S R11-W
St Stephens Meridian

Map Group 16

Cities & Towns
None

Cemeteries
New York Cemetery
Sims Cemetery
Taylor Cemetery

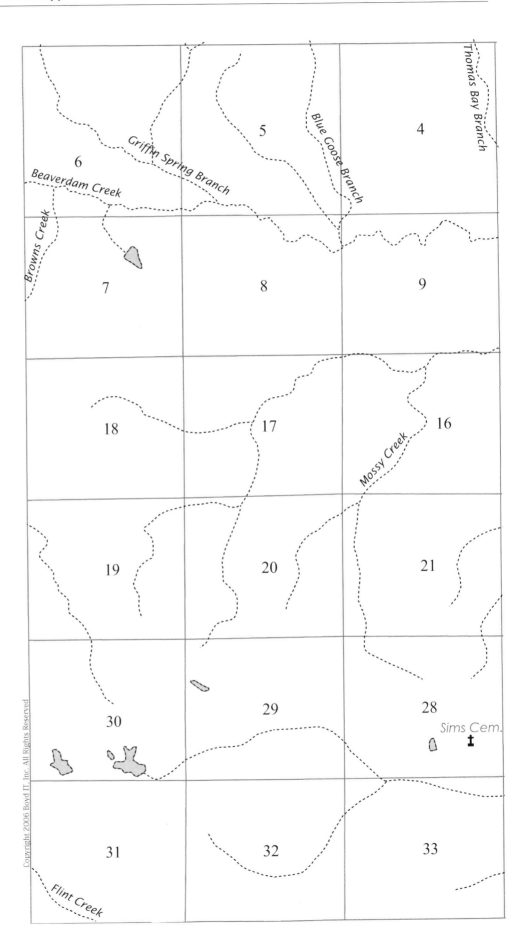

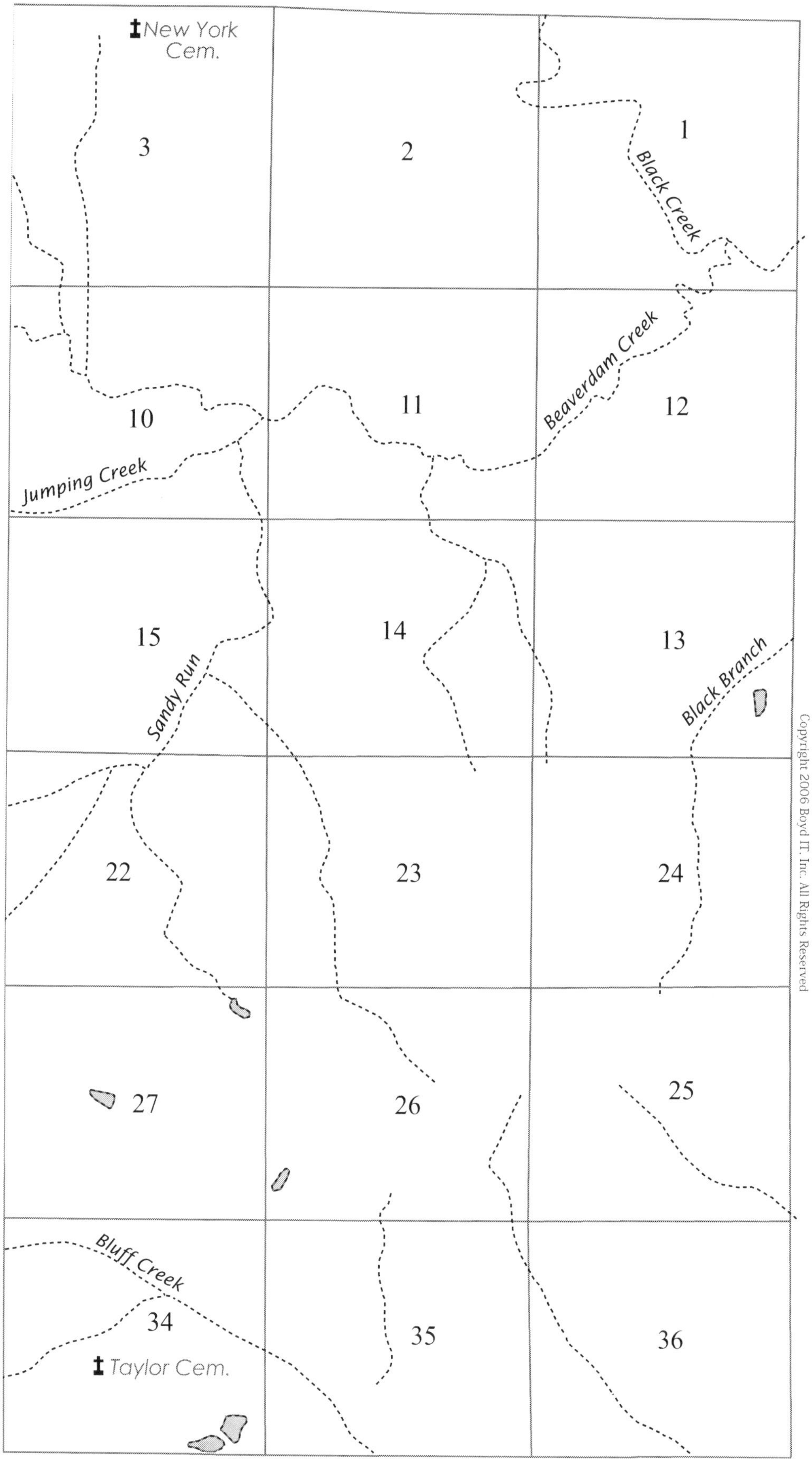
New York Cem.
3
2
1
Black Creek
Beaverdam Creek
10
11
12
Jumping Creek
15
14
13
Sandy Run
Black Branch
22
23
24
27
26
25
Bluff Creek
34
35
36
Taylor Cem.

Helpful Hints

1. This Map takes a different look at the same Congressional Township displayed in the preceding two maps. It presents features that can help you better envision the historical development of the area: a) Water-bodies (lakes & ponds), b) Water-courses (rivers, streams, etc.), c) Railroads, d) City/town center-points (where they were oftentimes located when first settled), and e) Cemeteries.
2. Using this "Historical" map in tandem with this Township's Patent Map and Road Map, may lead you to some interesting discoveries. You will often find roads, towns, cemeteries, and waterways are named after nearby landowners: sometimes those names will be the ones you are researching. See how many of these research gems you can find here in Perry County.

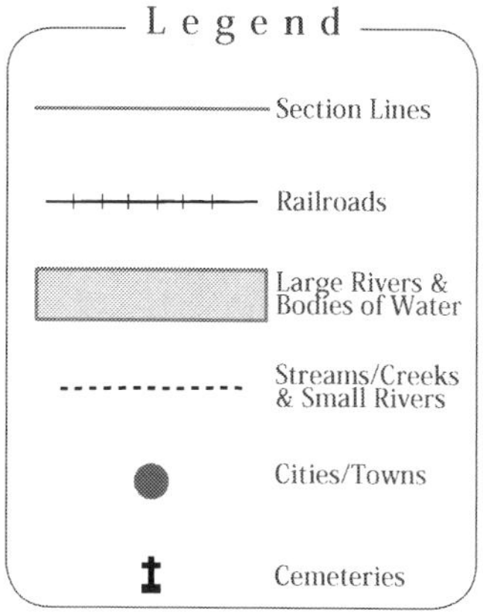
Legend
Section Lines
Railroads
Large Rivers & Bodies of Water
Streams/Creeks & Small Rivers
Cities/Towns
Cemeteries

Scale: Section = 1 mile X 1 mile
(there are some exceptions)

Map Group 17: Index to Land Patents

Township 1-South Range 10-West (St Stephens)

After you locate an individual in this Index, take note of the Section and Section Part then proceed to the Land Patent map on the pages immediately following. You should have no difficulty locating the corresponding parcel of land.

The "For More Info" Column will lead you to more information about the underlying Patents. See the *Legend* at right, and the "How to Use this Book" chapter, for more information.

```
                        LEGEND
              "For More Info . . . " column
A = Authority (Legislative Act, See Appendix "A")
B = Block or Lot (location in Section unknown)
C = Cancelled Patent
F = Fractional Section
G = Group  (Multi-Patentee Patent, see Appendix "C")
V = Overlaps another Parcel
R = Re-Issued (Parcel patented more than once)

(A & G items require you to look in the Appendixes referred
to above. All other Letter-designations followed by a number
require you to locate line-items in this index that possess
the ID number found after the letter).
```

ID	Individual in Patent	Sec.	Sec. Part	Date Issued	Other Counties	For More Info . . .
3577	BATTE, Charles C	10	E½SW	1920-04-20		A4
3682	BENNETT, Louisa	4	SESE	1920-12-04		A4 G6
3682	BENNETT, William	4	SESE	1920-12-04		A4 G6
3747	BILBO, Sebe H	13	NESW	1889-11-29		A1
3748	" "	13	SENW	1889-11-29		A1
3749	" "	25	NWSW	1889-11-29		A1
3571	BOND, Annie	12	NENE	1904-11-15		A4
3603	BOND, Gilbert	25	E½NE	1892-05-16		A4
3604	" "	25	NESE	1892-05-16		A4
3605	" "	25	SWNE	1892-05-16		A4
3545	BRELAND, Adam	20	NE	1891-11-03		A4
3579	BRELAND, Columbus	13	SWNW	1889-11-29		A1
3608	BRELAND, Isaac	20	N½SE	1884-12-30		A4
3609	" "	21	NWSW	1884-12-30		A4
3610	" "	21	SWNW	1884-12-30		A4
3615	BRELAND, Isiah	20	S½SE	1889-12-19		A4
3616	" "	20	S½SW	1889-12-19		A4
3756	BRELAND, Vesta A	17	E½SE	1884-12-30		A4
3757	" "	17	NWSE	1884-12-30		A4
3761	BRELAND, William	19	SESW	1906-08-16		A1
3774	BRELAND, Zerra D	25	SWSW	1905-05-02		A4
3775	" "	35	NENE	1905-05-02		A4
3776	" "	36	W½NW	1905-05-02		A4
3550	COCHRAN, Amaziah	36	SWNE	1883-02-03		A1
3549	" "	36	S½SE	1891-06-30		A4
3618	COCHRAN, James A	36	N½SW	1902-07-03		A4
3619	" "	36	NWSE	1902-07-03		A4
3620	" "	36	SWSW	1902-07-03		A4
3701	CONKLIN, Oscar F	1	E½NE	1890-07-03		A1
3702	" "	1	E½NW	1890-07-03		A1
3703	" "	1	E½SE	1890-07-03		A1
3704	" "	1	NWNE	1890-07-03		A1
3705	" "	11	S½SW	1890-07-03		A1
3706	" "	11	SESE	1890-07-03		A1
3707	" "	12	S½NE	1890-07-03		A1
3708	" "	12	S½NW	1890-07-03		A1
3709	" "	12	S½SE	1890-07-03		A1
3710	" "	12	S½SW	1890-07-03		A1
3711	" "	13	N½NW	1890-07-03		A1
3712	" "	13	S½SW	1890-07-03		A1
3713	" "	13	SE	1890-07-03		A1
3714	" "	13	SENE	1890-07-03		A1
3715	" "	14	N½NE	1890-07-03		A1
3716	" "	14	SESE	1890-07-03		A1
3717	" "	2	NENE	1890-07-03		A1
3718	" "	2	NWSE	1890-07-03		A1

ID	Individual in Patent	Sec.	Sec. Part	Date Issued	Other Counties	For More Info . . .
3719	CONKLIN, Oscar F (Cont'd)	2	SESW	1890-07-03		A1
3720	" "	2	W½NE	1890-07-03		A1
3721	" "	23	NE	1890-07-03		A1
3722	" "	23	S½NW	1890-07-03		A1
3723	" "	23	SW	1890-07-03		A1
3724	" "	24	N½	1890-07-03		A1
3725	" "	24	NESE	1890-07-03		A1
3726	" "	24	SESW	1890-07-03		A1
3727	" "	24	SWSE	1890-07-03		A1
3728	" "	25	NENW	1890-07-03		A1
3729	" "	25	NWNE	1890-07-03		A1
3730	" "	25	SESE	1890-07-03		A1
3731	" "	29	E½NE	1890-07-03		A1
3732	" "	29	N½SE	1890-07-03		A1
3733	" "	33	NENE	1890-07-03		A1
3734	" "	33	SWNE	1890-07-03		A1
3735	" "	33	W½NW	1890-07-03		A1
3736	" "	36	E½NE	1890-07-03		A1
3737	" "	36	NESE	1890-07-03		A1
3606	CONN, Henry C	5	NESE	1919-08-21		A4
3675	CRONK, Lindsey Arnold	5	NWSW	1923-10-15		A4
3679	DANTZLER, Lorenzo N	10	SENW	1890-08-13		A1
3680	" "	25	NWNW	1890-08-13		A1
3681	" "	9	NESE	1890-08-13		A1
3574	FAIRLEY, Archey A	24	NESW	1904-09-28		A4
3575	" "	24	NWSE	1904-09-28		A4
3576	" "	24	W½SW	1904-09-28		A4
3582	FAIRLEY, David T	13	NWSW	1884-12-30		A1 G32
3583	" "	14	NESE	1884-12-30		A1 G32
3621	FAIRLEY, James	18	SESW	1900-10-04		A4
3622	" "	19	E½NW	1900-10-04		A4
3623	" "	19	SWNE	1900-10-04		A4
3644	FAIRLEY, John	17	SWSE	1859-05-02		A1
3645	" "	22	NESE	1859-05-02		A1
3639	FAIRLEY, John C	26	NWSW	1906-05-01		A4
3640	" "	26	S½NW	1906-05-01		A4
3641	" "	26	SWNE	1906-05-01		A4
3650	FAIRLEY, John S	26	N½NW	1895-12-14		A4
3651	" "	27	N½NE	1895-12-14		A4
3656	FAIRLEY, John W	18	SWSW	1882-05-10		A1
3652	" "	10	NENW	1884-12-30		A1
3653	" "	11	SWNE	1884-12-30		A1
3654	" "	14	S½NE	1884-12-30		A1
3655	" "	18	NENW	1884-12-30		A1
3657	" "	19	NWSW	1884-12-30		A1
3658	" "	19	W½NW	1884-12-30		A1
3659	" "	22	SENW	1884-12-30		A1
3660	" "	26	SESW	1884-12-30		A1
3661	" "	28	SWSW	1884-12-30		A1
3662	" "	33	NWNE	1884-12-30		A1
3665	" "	9	SENE	1884-12-30		A1
3666	" "	9	SWNE	1884-12-30		A1
3664	" "	33	SESW	1889-11-29		A1
3663	" "	33	NWSE	1890-07-03		A1
3582	FAIRLEY, Joseph A	13	NWSW	1884-12-30		A1 G32
3583	" "	14	NESE	1884-12-30		A1 G32
3676	FAIRLEY, London	30	E½NE	1894-04-10		A4
3677	" "	30	NENW	1894-04-10		A4
3678	" "	30	NWNE	1894-04-10		A4
3693	FAIRLEY, Malcom	29	E½NW	1890-08-16		A4
3694	" "	29	W½NE	1890-08-16		A4
3695	FAIRLEY, Margaret M	27	E½NW	1896-01-25		A4 G34
3696	" "	27	S½NE	1896-01-25		A4 G34
3738	FAIRLEY, Rachel	5	SESE	1906-06-26		A4 G35
3739	" "	5	W½SE	1906-06-26		A4 G35
3740	FAIRLEY, Robert	7	N½SW	1891-06-30		A4
3741	" "	7	SESW	1891-06-30		A4
3742	FAIRLEY, Sarah A	12	N½SE	1904-03-19		A4
3743	" "	12	N½SW	1904-03-19		A4
3762	FAIRLEY, William E	26	SWSE	1916-11-16		A4
3763	" "	35	SENE	1916-11-16		A4
3764	" "	35	W½NE	1916-11-16		A4
3588	FAIRLY, David T	14	SWSW	1881-06-30		A1 G37

ID	Individual in Patent	Sec.	Sec. Part	Date Issued	Other Counties	For More Info . . .
3584	FAIRLY, David T (Cont'd)	10	W½NE	1882-12-30		A1 G37
3585	" "	14	NW	1882-12-30		A1 G37
3586	" "	14	NWSW	1882-12-30		A1 G37
3587	" "	14	SESW	1882-12-30		A1 G37
3589	" "	14	W½SE	1882-12-30		A1 G37
3590	" "	15	SE	1882-12-30		A1 G37
3591	" "	22	N½NE	1882-12-30		A1 G37
3593	" "	23	N½NW	1882-12-30		A1 G37
3594	" "	25	SWNW	1882-12-30		A1 G37
3592	" "	22	NENW	1884-12-30		A1 G37
3649	FAIRLY, John	20	SWNW	1851-10-01		A1
3646	" "	13	NWNE	1859-05-02		A1
3647	" "	20	NESW	1859-05-02		A1
3648	" "	20	SENW	1859-05-02		A1
3642	FAIRLY, John C	10	W½SW	1901-03-23		A4
3643	" "	9	SESE	1901-03-23		A4
3588	FAIRLY, Joseph A	14	SWSW	1881-06-30		A1 G37
3584	" "	10	W½NE	1882-12-30		A1 G37
3585	" "	14	NW	1882-12-30		A1 G37
3586	" "	14	NWSW	1882-12-30		A1 G37
3587	" "	14	SESW	1882-12-30		A1 G37
3589	" "	14	W½SE	1882-12-30		A1 G37
3590	" "	15	SE	1882-12-30		A1 G37
3591	" "	22	N½NE	1882-12-30		A1 G37
3593	" "	23	N½NW	1882-12-30		A1 G37
3594	" "	25	SWNW	1882-12-30		A1 G37
3592	" "	22	NENW	1884-12-30		A1 G37
3670	FAIRLY, Liddie	32	E½SE	1893-09-08		A4
3671	" "	32	SESW	1893-09-08		A4
3672	" "	32	SWSE	1893-09-08		A4
3753	FAIRLY, Solomon	19	NESE	1905-11-08		A4
3754	" "	19	S½SE	1905-11-08		A4
3755	" "	20	NWSW	1905-11-08		A4
3627	GRIFFIN, James W	30	S½	1884-12-30		A1
3628	" "	30	SWNE	1884-12-30		A1
3629	" "	32	NESW	1884-12-30		A1
3630	" "	32	NW	1884-12-30		A1
3631	" "	32	NWSE	1884-12-30		A1
3632	" "	32	SWNE	1884-12-30		A1
3633	" "	1	SESW	1890-04-25		A1 G41
3634	" "	1	SWSE	1890-04-25		A1 G41
3635	" "	11	NESW	1890-04-25		A1 G41
3636	" "	12	N½NW	1890-04-25		A1 G41
3637	" "	12	NWNE	1890-04-25		A1 G41
3638	GRIFFIN, John A	7	SENE	1854-03-15		A1
3758	GRIFFIN, Washington	10	NWNW	1854-03-15		A1
3759	" "	3	NWSE	1854-03-15		A1
3765	GRIFFIN, William E	6	NENE	1882-08-03		A1
3766	" "	13	NENE	1882-12-30		A1 G43
3767	" "	13	SWNE	1882-12-30		A1 G43
3769	" "	6	NENW	1883-09-15		A1 G43
3768	" "	25	W½SE	1884-12-30		A1 G43
3770	" "	7	SWSW	1884-12-30		A1 G43
3611	HARTFIELD, Isaac	2	NWSW	1899-06-28		A4
3612	" "	2	SWNW	1899-06-28		A4
3614	" "	3	SENE	1899-06-28		A4
3613	" "	3	NESE	1909-12-20		A4
3667	HARTFIELD, Lawrence	9	NENW	1918-04-17		A1
3668	" "	9	S½NW	1918-04-17		A1
3673	HOLLIMON, Lillie	5	NESW	1916-01-26		A4
3674	" "	5	S½SW	1916-01-26		A4
3633	HOWZE, George H	1	SESW	1890-04-25		A1 G41
3634	" "	1	SWSE	1890-04-25		A1 G41
3635	" "	11	NESW	1890-04-25		A1 G41
3636	" "	12	N½NW	1890-04-25		A1 G41
3637	" "	12	NWNE	1890-04-25		A1 G41
3578	JOHNSON, Chester A	9	W½SE	1916-01-21		A4
3744	JONES, Saul	2	SWSW	1919-07-01		A4
3624	LANTRIP, James	6	SESE	1854-03-15		A1
3602	MATHESON, Gavin R	27	NWNW	1883-02-03		A1
3599	" "	1	N½SW	1884-12-30		A1
3600	" "	1	NWSE	1884-12-30		A1
3601	" "	1	SWNW	1884-12-30		A1

ID	Individual in Patent	Sec.	Sec. Part	Date Issued	Other Counties	For More Info . . .
3750	MCINNIS, Simeon	33	NESW	1894-09-28		A4
3751	" "	33	SENW	1894-09-28		A4
3752	" "	33	W½SW	1894-09-28		A4
3581	MCQUAGGE, Daniel G	15	NW	1906-10-29		A1
3607	MILES, Hezekiah	25	SESW	1882-10-10		A1
3617	MILES, Isiah	25	NESW	1882-10-10		A1
3760	MILES, Wesley	25	SENW	1882-10-10		A1
3771	MILES, William	36	NENW	1882-10-10		A1
3772	" "	36	NWNE	1882-10-10		A1
3683	MONTAGUE, Luke S	19	NESW	1889-11-29		A1
3684	" "	19	NWSE	1889-11-29		A1
3685	" "	19	SWSW	1889-11-29		A1
3686	" "	29	S½SE	1889-11-29		A1
3687	" "	29	SW	1889-11-29		A1
3688	" "	29	W½NW	1889-11-29		A1
3689	" "	31	E½	1889-11-29		A1
3690	" "	31	E½SW	1889-11-29		A1
3691	" "	31	NW	1889-11-29		A1
3692	" "	31	NWSW	1889-11-29		A1
3580	MOORE, Daniel C	23	SE	1901-08-12		A4
3572	PAYNE, Arby	21	E½SW	1920-04-20		A4
3573	" "	21	SWSW	1920-04-20		A4
3625	PEARCE, James	19	E½NE	1881-08-20		A4
3626	" "	20	NWNW	1881-08-20		A4
3766	PERKINS, Benjamin F	13	NENE	1882-12-30		A1 G43
3767	" "	13	SWNE	1882-12-30		A1 G43
3769	" "	6	NENW	1883-09-15		A1 G43
3768	" "	25	W½SE	1884-12-30		A1 G43
3770	" "	7	SWSW	1884-12-30		A1 G43
3700	RAYBURN, Oliver	31	SWSW	1890-08-16		A4
3695	RILEY, Margaret M	27	E½NW	1896-01-25		A4 G34
3696	" "	27	S½NE	1896-01-25		A4 G34
3738	SAMUEL, Rachel	5	SESE	1906-06-26		A4 G35
3739	" "	5	W½SE	1906-06-26		A4 G35
3570	THOMAS, Andrew	3	NW	1884-12-30		A1
3554	THOMAS, Andrew J	11	NWNE	1882-04-20		A1
3557	" "	2	NWNW	1882-05-10		A1
3561	" "	3	NENE	1882-05-10		A1
3553	" "	10	SWNW	1882-08-03		A1
3569	" "	4	NWSE	1882-08-03		A1
3555	" "	2	NENW	1882-10-10		A1
3556	" "	2	NESE	1882-10-10		A1
3560	" "	2	SWSE	1882-10-10		A1
3562	" "	3	NESW	1882-10-10		A1
3565	" "	3	SWNE	1882-10-10		A1
3558	" "	2	SENE	1883-09-15		A1
3559	" "	2	SESE	1883-09-15		A1
3551	" "	1	NWNW	1884-12-30		A1
3552	" "	1	SWNE	1884-12-30		A1
3563	" "	3	NWNE	1884-12-30		A1
3564	" "	3	SESW	1884-12-30		A1
3566	" "	3	W½SW	1884-12-30		A1
3567	" "	4	E½NW	1884-12-30		A1
3568	" "	4	NESE	1884-12-30		A1
3669	THOMAS, Lawson	35	SE	1893-09-28		A4
3697	THOMAS, Melissa	4	SESW	1892-04-16		A1
3698	" "	4	SWSE	1892-04-16		A1
3699	" "	9	N½NE	1892-04-16		A1
3773	THOMAS, William	4	NE	1898-03-15		A4
3745	WOOD, Schofield	2	NESW	1909-12-06		A4
3746	" "	2	SENW	1909-12-06		A4
3546	WOODS, Alexander	11	N½SE	1900-11-28		A4
3547	" "	11	SENE	1900-11-28		A4
3548	" "	11	SWSE	1900-11-28		A4
3595	YELVERTON, Elizabeth	18	NESW	1879-05-06		A4
3596	" "	18	NWSE	1879-05-06		A4
3597	" "	18	SENW	1879-05-06		A4
3598	" "	18	SWNE	1879-05-06		A4

Patent Map

T1-S R10-W
St Stephens Meridian

Map Group 17

Township Statistics

Parcels Mapped	:	232
Number of Patents	:	116
Number of Individuals	:	74
Patentees Identified	:	69
Number of Surnames	:	35
Multi-Patentee Parcels	:	28
Oldest Patent Date	:	10/1/1851
Most Recent Patent	:	10/15/1923
Block/Lot Parcels	:	0
Parcels Re-Issued	:	0
Parcels that Overlap	:	0
Cities and Towns	:	2
Cemeteries	:	4

6

GRIFFIN [43]
William E
1883

GRIFFIN
William E
1882

5

CRONK
Lindsey Arnold
1923

HOLLIMON
Lillie
1916

FAIRLEY [35]
Rachel
1906

CONN
Henry C
1919

LANTRIP
James
1854

HOLLIMON
Lillie
1916

FAIRLEY [35]
Rachel
1906

4

THOMAS
Andrew J
1884

THOMAS
William
1898

THOMAS
Andrew J
1882

THOMAS
Andrew J
1884

THOMAS
Melissa
1892

THOMAS
Melissa
1892

BENNETT [6]
Louisa
1920

7

GRIFFIN
John A
1854

FAIRLEY
Robert
1891

GRIFFIN [43]
William E
1884

FAIRLEY
Robert
1891

8

9

HARTFIELD
Lawrence
1918

THOMAS
Melissa
1892

HARTFIELD
Lawrence
1918

FAIRLEY
John W
1884

FAIRLEY
John W
1884

JOHNSON
Chester A
1916

DANTZLER
Lorenzo N
1890

FAIRLY
John C
1901

18

FAIRLEY
John W
1884

YELVERTON
Elizabeth
1879

YELVERTON
Elizabeth
1879

YELVERTON
Elizabeth
1879

YELVERTON
Elizabeth
1879

FAIRLEY
John W
1882

FAIRLEY
James
1900

17

BRELAND
Vesta A
1884

FAIRLEY
John
1859

BRELAND
Vesta A
1884

16

19

FAIRLEY
John W
1884

FAIRLEY
James
1900

FAIRLEY
James
1900

PEARCE
James
1881

FAIRLEY
John W
1884

MONTAGUE
Luke S
1889

MONTAGUE
Luke S
1889

FAIRLY
Solomon
1905

MONTAGUE
Luke S
1889

BRELAND
William
1906

FAIRLY
Solomon
1905

PEARCE
James
1881

FAIRLY
John
1851

FAIRLY
Solomon
1905

FAIRLY
John
1859

20

PEARCE
James
1881

BRELAND
Adam
1891

FAIRLY
John
1859

BRELAND
Isaac
1884

BRELAND
Isiah
1889

BRELAND
Isiah
1889

BRELAND
Isaac
1884

BRELAND
Isaac
1884

PAYNE
Arby
1920

21

PAYNE
Arby
1920

30

FAIRLEY
London
1894

FAIRLEY
London
1894

GRIFFIN
James W
1884

FAIRLEY
London
1894

GRIFFIN
James W
1884

MONTAGUE
Luke S
1889

29

FAIRLEY
Malcom
1890

FAIRLEY
Malcom
1890

CONKLIN
Oscar F
1890

MONTAGUE
Luke S
1889

CONKLIN
Oscar F
1890

MONTAGUE
Luke S
1889

FAIRLEY
John W
1884

28

31

MONTAGUE
Luke S
1889

MONTAGUE
Luke S
1889

MONTAGUE
Luke S
1889

MONTAGUE
Luke S
1889

RAYBURN
Oliver
1890

32

GRIFFIN
James W
1884

GRIFFIN
James W
1884

GRIFFIN
James W
1884

GRIFFIN
James W
1884

FAIRLY
Liddie
1893

FAIRLY
Liddie
1893

FAIRLY
Liddie
1893

33

CONKLIN
Oscar F
1890

FAIRLEY
John W
1884

CONKLIN
Oscar F
1890

MCINNIS
Simeon
1894

CONKLIN
Oscar F
1890

MCINNIS
Simeon
1894

MCINNIS
Simeon
1894

FAIRLEY
John W
1890

FAIRLEY
John W
1889

Helpful Hints

1. This Map's INDEX can be found on the preceding pages.

2. Refer to Map "C" to see where this Township lies within Perry County, Mississippi.

3. Numbers within square brackets [ ] denote a multi-patentee land parcel (multi-owner). Refer to Appendix "C" for a full list of members in this group.

4. Areas that look to be crowded with Patentees usually indicate multiple sales of the same parcel (Re-issues) or Overlapping parcels. See this Township's Index for an explanation of these and other circumstances that might explain "odd" groupings of Patentees on this map.

Legend

— Patent Boundary

— Section Boundary

No Patents Found (or Outside County)

1., 2., 3., ... Lot Numbers (when beside a name)

[ ] Group Number (see Appendix "C")

Scale: Section = 1 mile X 1 mile (generally, with some exceptions)

Road Map

T1-S R10-W
St Stephens Meridian

Map Group 17

Cities & Towns
Barbara
Batt Place

Cemeteries
Cochran Cemetery
Fairley Cemetery
Howard-Breland Cemetery
Thomas Cemetery

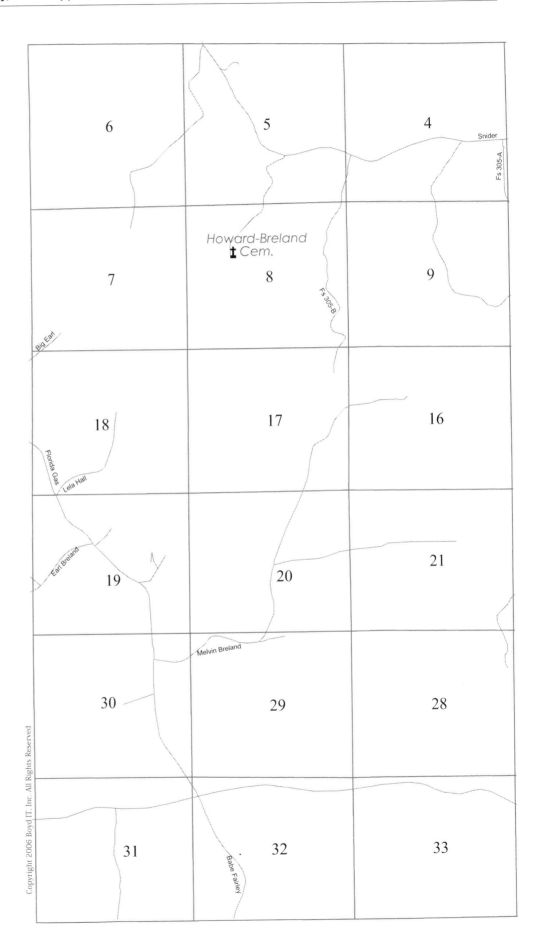

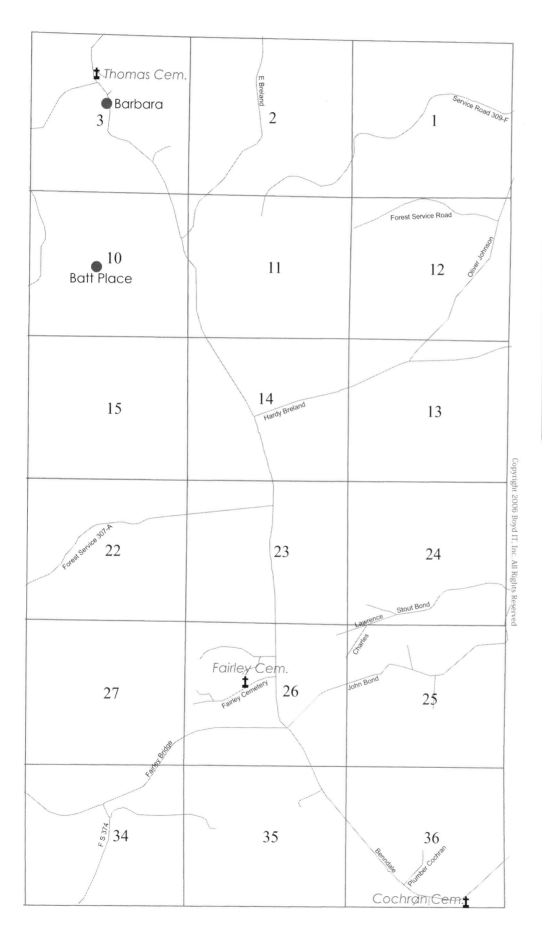

Thomas Cem.

Barbara

3

2

E Breland

1

Service Road 309-F

Forest Service Road

10

Batt Place

11

12

Oliver Johnson

15

14

Hardy Breland

13

Forest Service 307-A

22

23

24

Stout Bond

Lawrence

Charles

Fairley Cem.

Fairley Cemetery

26

John Bond

25

27

Fairley Bridge

F S 374

34

35

36

Benndale

Plumber Cochran

Cochran Cem.

Copyright 2006 Boyd IT, Inc. All Rights Reserved

Helpful Hints

1. This road map has a number of uses, but primarily it is to help you: a) find the present location of land owned by your ancestors (at least the general area), b) find cemeteries and city-centers, and c) estimate the route/roads used by Census-takers & tax-assessors.

2. If you plan to travel to Perry County to locate cemeteries or land parcels, please pick up a modern travel map for the area before you do. Mapping old land parcels on modern maps is not as exact a science as you might think. Just the slightest variations in public land survey coordinates, estimates of parcel boundaries, or road-map deviations can greatly alter a map's representation of how a road either does or doesn't cross a particular parcel of land.

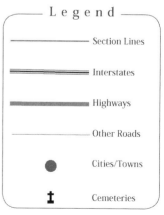

L e g e n d

————	Section Lines
═══════	Interstates
▬▬▬▬▬	Highways
————	Other Roads
●	Cities/Towns
✝	Cemeteries

Scale: Section = 1 mile X 1 mile
(generally, with some exceptions)

217

Historical Map

T1-S R10-W
St Stephens Meridian

Map Group 17

Cities & Towns
Barbara
Batt Place

Cemeteries
Cochran Cemetery
Fairley Cemetery
Howard-Breland Cemetery
Thomas Cemetery

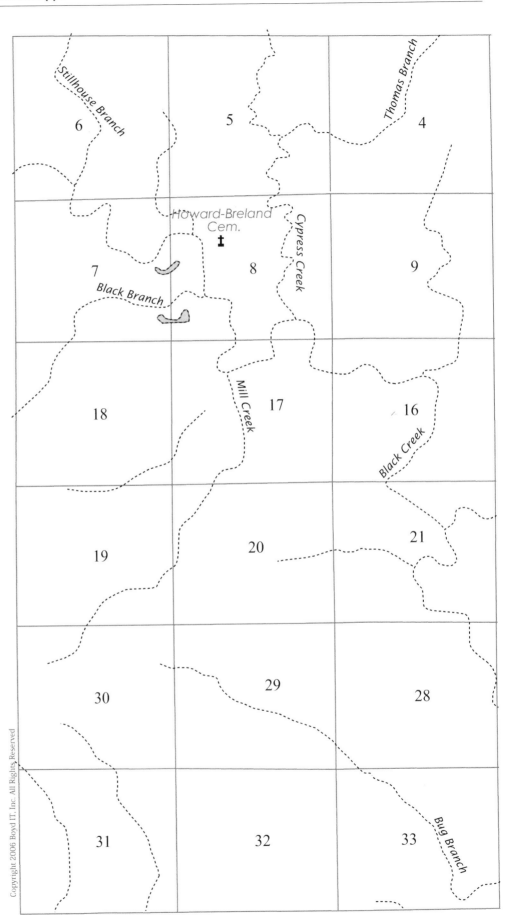

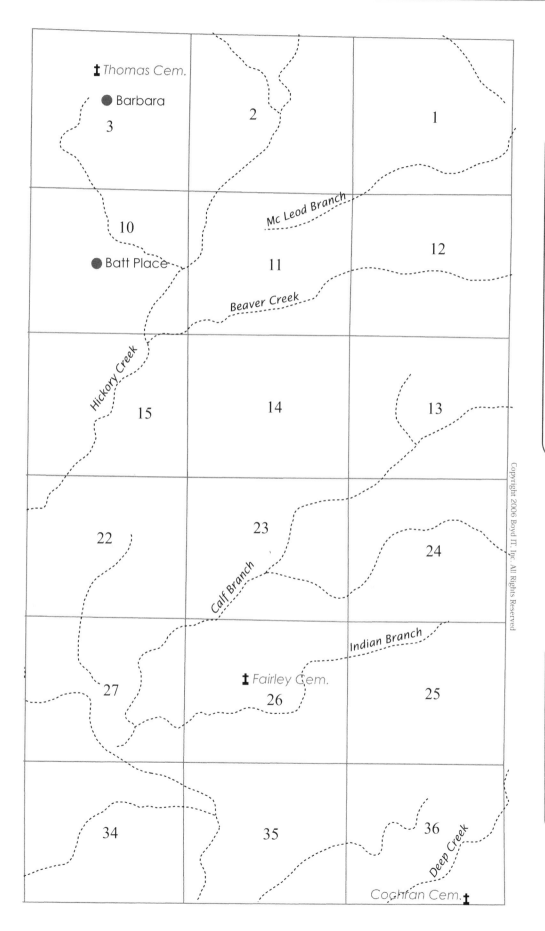

3

Thomas Cem.

Barbara

2

1

10

Mc Leod Branch

Batt Place

11

12

Beaver Creek

Hickory Creek

15

14

13

22

23

24

Calf Branch

Indian Branch

Fairley Cem.

27

26

25

34

35

36

Deep Creek

Cochran Cem.

Helpful Hints

1. This Map takes a different look at the same Congressional Township displayed in the preceding two maps. It presents features that can help you better envision the historical development of the area: a) Water-bodies (lakes & ponds), b) Water-courses (rivers, streams, etc.), c) Railroads, d) City/town center-points (where they were oftentimes located when first settled), and e) Cemeteries.

2. Using this "Historical" map in tandem with this Township's Patent Map and Road Map, may lead you to some interesting discoveries. You will often find roads, towns, cemeteries, and waterways are named after nearby landowners: sometimes those names will be the ones you are researching. See how many of these research gems you can find here in Perry County.

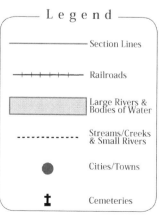

L e g e n d

————————	Section Lines
+++++++	Railroads
▬▬▬	Large Rivers & Bodies of Water
- - - - - -	Streams/Creeks & Small Rivers
●	Cities/Towns
†	Cemeteries

Scale: Section = 1 mile X 1 mile
(there are some exceptions)

Map Group 18: Index to Land Patents

Township 1-South Range 9-West (St Stephens)

After you locate an individual in this Index, take note of the Section and Section Part then proceed to the Land Patent map on the pages immediately following. You should have no difficulty locating the corresponding parcel of land.

The "For More Info" Column will lead you to more information about the underlying Patents. See the *Legend* at right, and the "How to Use this Book" chapter, for more information.

ID	Individual in Patent	Sec.	Sec. Part	Date Issued	Other Counties	For More Info . . .
3777	BOND, Aaron	6	E½SW	1907-05-13		A4
3778	" "	7	NENW	1907-05-13		A4
3781	BOND, Annie	6	SWSW	1904-11-15		A4
3782	" "	7	NWNW	1904-11-15		A4
3906	BREELAND, Loami	18	W½NW	1892-05-26		A4
3907	" "	7	SWSW	1892-05-26		A4
3897	BRELAND, Josiah	29	SWSE	1890-06-25		A4
3898	" "	32	NENW	1890-06-25		A4
3899	" "	32	W½NE	1890-06-25		A4
3845	CONWAY, Edith F	8	E½SE	1894-03-30		A4
3846	" "	8	SESW	1894-03-30		A4
3847	" "	8	SWSE	1894-03-30		A4
3779	FAIRLEY, Angus R	21	NWSE	1854-03-15		A1
3780	" "	36	NESE	1854-03-15		A1
3842	FAIRLEY, Daniel	35	NESE	1890-06-25		A4
3843	" "	36	N½SW	1890-06-25		A4
3844	" "	36	NWSE	1890-06-25		A4
3910	FAIRLEY, Nepsy	35	E½SW	1899-07-15		A4
3894	FAIRLY, John	18	SWSW	1859-05-02		A1
3895	FAIRLY, Joseph A	17	E½NE	1891-08-19		A4
3896	" "	17	E½SE	1891-08-19		A4
3783	HILLS, Charles T	1		1889-11-21		A1
3784	" "	11	S½	1889-11-21		A1
3785	" "	12	E½	1889-11-21		A1
3786	" "	12	E½NW	1889-11-21		A1
3787	" "	14	N½NE	1889-11-21		A1
3788	" "	14	N½NW	1889-11-21		A1
3789	" "	17	SWSE	1889-11-21		A1
3790	" "	18	E½NW	1889-11-21		A1
3791	" "	18	E½SW	1889-11-21		A1
3792	" "	18	NENE	1889-11-21		A1
3793	" "	18	NWSW	1889-11-21		A1
3794	" "	18	SE	1889-11-21		A1
3795	" "	18	W½NE	1889-11-21		A1
3796	" "	19		1889-11-21		A1
3797	" "	2	N½	1889-11-21		A1
3798	" "	2	NESE	1889-11-21		A1
3799	" "	21	E½SE	1889-11-21		A1
3800	" "	21	NENE	1889-11-21		A1
3801	" "	21	NWSW	1889-11-21		A1
3802	" "	21	SWNW	1889-11-21		A1
3803	" "	21	SWSE	1889-11-21		A1
3804	" "	21	W½NE	1889-11-21		A1
3805	" "	22	E½	1889-11-21		A1
3806	" "	22	NW	1889-11-21		A1
3807	" "	23		1889-11-21		A1

ID	Individual in Patent	Sec.	Sec. Part	Date Issued	Other Counties	For More Info . . .
3808	HILLS, Charles T (Cont'd)	24	S½SW	1889-11-21		A1
3809	" "	24	SE	1889-11-21		A1
3810	" "	26	N½	1889-11-21		A1
3811	" "	26	NWSE	1889-11-21		A1
3812	" "	27	SESE	1889-11-21		A1
3813	" "	27	SW	1889-11-21		A1
3814	" "	27	W½SE	1889-11-21		A1
3815	" "	28	SE	1889-11-21		A1
3816	" "	29	N½SE	1889-11-21		A1
3817	" "	29	N½SW	1889-11-21		A1
3818	" "	29	SWNW	1889-11-21		A1
3819	" "	30	NESW	1889-11-21		A1
3820	" "	30	NW	1889-11-21		A1
3821	" "	30	W½SW	1889-11-21		A1
3822	" "	31	NE	1889-11-21		A1
3823	" "	32	S½NW	1889-11-21		A1
3824	" "	33	E½NW	1889-11-21		A1
3825	" "	34	NWNE	1889-11-21		A1
3826	" "	34	SENE	1889-11-21		A1
3827	" "	6	NWSW	1889-11-21		A1
3828	" "	6	SENE	1889-11-21		A1
3829	" "	6	SWNW	1889-11-21		A1
3830	" "	7	E½SW	1889-11-21		A1
3831	" "	7	NWSW	1889-11-21		A1
3832	" "	7	S½NW	1889-11-21		A1
3833	" "	7	SE	1889-11-21		A1
3834	" "	7	W½NE	1889-11-21		A1
3835	" "	8	N½SW	1889-11-21		A1
3836	" "	8	NWSE	1889-11-21		A1
3837	" "	8	S½NE	1889-11-21		A1
3838	" "	8	SENW	1889-11-21		A1
3839	" "	9	E½	1889-11-21		A1
3840	" "	9	S½NW	1889-11-21		A1
3841	" "	9	SW	1889-11-21		A1
3900	JONES, Julia	36	S½SE	1890-06-25		A4
3901	" "	36	S½SW	1890-06-25		A4
3902	LEATHERBURY, Kate S	26	NESE	1889-04-23		A1
3903	" "	26	NESW	1889-04-23		A1
3904	" "	26	S½SE	1889-04-23		A1
3905	" "	36	N½	1889-04-23		A1
3908	ONEAL, Major	31	SESW	1882-12-30		A1
3909	" "	31	SWSE	1882-12-30		A1
3848	SAWYER, Hiram W	4	N½SW	1889-05-06		A1
3849	" "	4	NW	1889-05-06		A1
3850	" "	4	NWSE	1889-05-06		A1
3851	" "	4	SWSW	1889-05-06		A1
3852	" "	4	W½NE	1889-05-06		A1
3853	" "	5	NE	1889-05-06		A1
3854	" "	5	S½	1889-05-06		A1
3855	" "	5	S½NW	1889-05-06		A1
3856	" "	6	S½SE	1889-05-06		A1
3857	" "	7	NENE	1889-05-06		A1
3858	" "	8	N½NE	1889-05-06		A1
3859	" "	8	N½NW	1889-05-06		A1
3860	" "	9	NWNW	1889-05-06		A1
3888	WAGAR, Humphrey R	5	N½NW	1889-04-09		A1 G75
3889	" "	6	N½NE	1889-04-09		A1 G75
3890	" "	6	N½NW	1889-04-09		A1 G75
3891	" "	6	N½SE	1889-04-09		A1 G75
3892	" "	6	SENW	1889-04-09		A1 G75
3893	" "	6	SWNE	1889-04-09		A1 G75
3861	" "	17	NWSE	1889-05-06		A1 G75
3862	" "	17	W½	1889-05-06		A1 G75
3863	" "	17	W½NE	1889-05-06		A1 G75
3864	" "	20	E½	1889-05-06		A1 G75
3865	" "	21	E½NW	1889-05-06		A1 G75
3866	" "	21	E½SW	1889-05-06		A1 G75
3867	" "	21	NWNW	1889-05-06		A1 G75
3868	" "	21	SWSW	1889-05-06		A1 G75
3869	" "	28	E½SW	1889-05-06		A1 G75
3870	" "	28	NW	1889-05-06		A1 G75
3871	" "	28	NWSE	1889-05-06		A1 G75
3872	" "	28	S½NE	1889-05-06		A1 G75

ID	Individual in Patent	Sec.	Sec. Part	Date Issued	Other Counties	For More Info . . .
3873	WAGAR, Humphrey R (Cont'd)	29	E½NW	1889-05-06		A1 G75
3874	" "	29	NE	1889-05-06		A1 G75
3875	" "	29	NWNW	1889-05-06		A1 G75
3876	" "	31	N½SE	1889-05-06		A1 G75
3877	" "	31	N½SW	1889-05-06		A1 G75
3878	" "	32	N½SW	1889-05-06		A1 G75
3879	" "	32	SE	1889-05-06		A1 G75
3880	" "	32	SWSW	1889-05-06		A1 G75
3881	" "	33	N½SW	1889-05-06		A1 G75
3882	" "	33	NE	1889-05-06		A1 G75
3883	" "	33	NWSE	1889-05-06		A1 G75
3884	" "	34	NENW	1889-05-06		A1 G75 V3886
3885	" "	34	SWNE	1889-05-06		A1 G75
3886	" "	34	W½	1889-05-06		A1 G75
3887	" "	34	W½SE	1889-05-06		A1 G75
3888	WELLS, Willard B	5	N½NW	1889-04-09		A1 G75
3889	" "	6	N½NE	1889-04-09		A1 G75
3890	" "	6	N½NW	1889-04-09		A1 G75
3891	" "	6	N½SE	1889-04-09		A1 G75
3892	" "	6	SENW	1889-04-09		A1 G75
3893	" "	6	SWNE	1889-04-09		A1 G75
3861	" "	17	NWSE	1889-05-06		A1 G75
3862	" "	17	W½	1889-05-06		A1 G75
3863	" "	17	W½NE	1889-05-06		A1 G75
3864	" "	20	E½	1889-05-06		A1 G75
3865	" "	21	E½NW	1889-05-06		A1 G75
3866	" "	21	E½SW	1889-05-06		A1 G75
3867	" "	21	NWNW	1889-05-06		A1 G75
3868	" "	21	SWSW	1889-05-06		A1 G75
3869	" "	28	E½SW	1889-05-06		A1 G75
3870	" "	28	NW	1889-05-06		A1 G75
3871	" "	28	NWSW	1889-05-06		A1 G75
3872	" "	28	S½NE	1889-05-06		A1 G75
3873	" "	29	E½NW	1889-05-06		A1 G75
3874	" "	29	NE	1889-05-06		A1 G75
3875	" "	29	NWNW	1889-05-06		A1 G75
3876	" "	31	N½SE	1889-05-06		A1 G75
3877	" "	31	N½SW	1889-05-06		A1 G75
3878	" "	32	N½SW	1889-05-06		A1 G75
3879	" "	32	SE	1889-05-06		A1 G75
3880	" "	32	SWSW	1889-05-06		A1 G75
3881	" "	33	N½SW	1889-05-06		A1 G75
3882	" "	33	NE	1889-05-06		A1 G75
3883	" "	33	NWSE	1889-05-06		A1 G75
3884	" "	34	NENW	1889-05-06		A1 G75 V3886
3885	" "	34	SWNE	1889-05-06		A1 G75
3886	" "	34	W½	1889-05-06		A1 G75
3887	" "	34	W½SE	1889-05-06		A1 G75

Patent Map

T1-S R9-W
St Stephens Meridian

Map Group 18

Township Statistics

Parcels Mapped	:	134
Number of Patents	:	36
Number of Individuals	:	17
Patentees Identified	:	16
Number of Surnames	:	13
Multi-Patentee Parcels	:	33
Oldest Patent Date	:	3/15/1854
Most Recent Patent	:	5/13/1907
Block/Lot Parcels	:	0
Parcels Re-Issued	:	0
Parcels that Overlap	:	1
Cities and Towns	:	1
Cemeteries	:	0

3	HILLS Charles T 1889		1
	2	HILLS Charles T 1889	HILLS Charles T 1889

10	11	HILLS Charles T 1889	HILLS Charles T 1889
	HILLS Charles T 1889	12	HILLS Charles T 1889

15	HILLS Charles T 1889	HILLS Charles T 1889	13
	14		

HILLS Charles T 1889	HILLS Charles T 1889	23	24
22		HILLS Charles T 1889	HILLS Charles T 1889
		HILLS Charles T 1889	

27	HILLS Charles T 1889	26	25
HILLS Charles T 1889	HILLS Charles T 1889	LEATHERBURY Kate S 1889	LEATHERBURY Kate S 1889
	HILLS Charles T 1889	HILLS Charles T 1889	
		LEATHERBURY Kate S 1889	

WAGAR [75] Humphrey R 1889	HILLS Charles T 1889	35	LEATHERBURY Kate S 1889
34	WAGAR [75] Humphrey R 1889	HILLS Charles T 1889	36
WAGAR [75] Humphrey R 1889	WAGAR [75] Humphrey R 1889	FAIRLEY Nepsy 1899	FAIRLEY Daniel 1890
			FAIRLEY Daniel 1890
			FAIRLEY Daniel 1890
			FAIRLEY Angus R 1854
			JONES Julia 1890
			JONES Julia 1890

Copyright 2006 Boyd IT, Inc All Rights Reserved

Helpful Hints

1. This Map's INDEX can be found on the preceding pages.

2. Refer to Map "C" to see where this Township lies within Perry County, Mississippi.

3. Numbers within square brackets [ ] denote a multi-patentee land parcel (multi-owner). Refer to Appendix "C" for a full list of members in this group.

4. Areas that look to be crowded with Patentees usually indicate multiple sales of the same parcel (Re-issues) or Overlapping parcels. See this Township's Index for an explanation of these and other circumstances that might explain "odd" groupings of Patentees on this map.

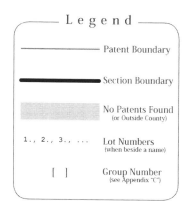

Legend

———————	Patent Boundary
▬▬▬▬▬▬▬	Section Boundary
▓▓▓	No Patents Found (or Outside County)
1., 2., 3., ...	Lot Numbers (when beside a name)
[ ]	Group Number (see Appendix "C")

Scale: Section = 1 mile X 1 mile (generally, with some exceptions)

Road Map

T1-S R9-W
St Stephens Meridian

Map Group 18

Cities & Towns

Deep Creek

Cemeteries

None

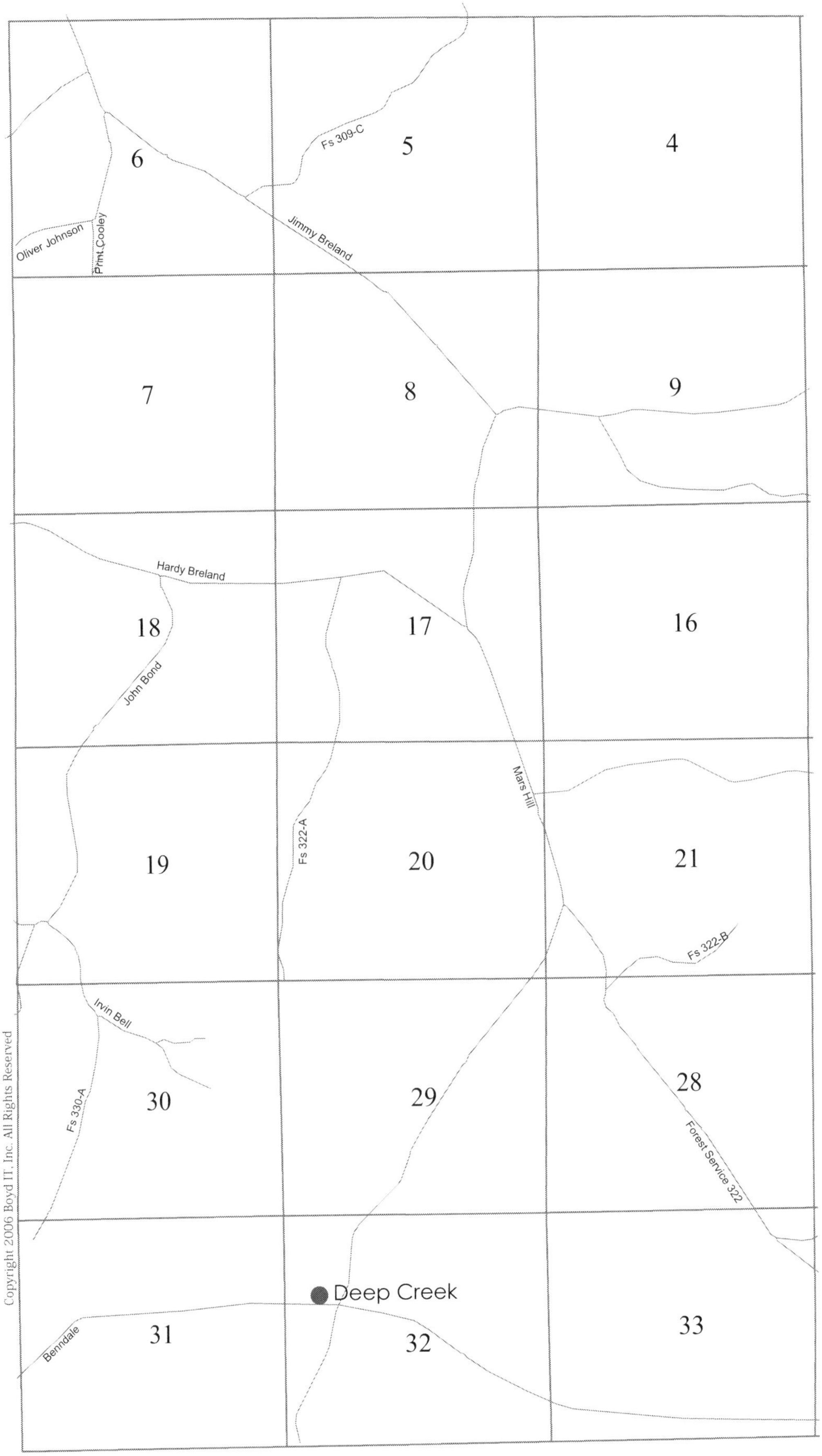

6

Fs 309-C 5

4

Oliver Johnson

Prmt.Cooley

Jimmy Breland

7

8

9

Hardy Breland

18

17

16

John Bond

Mars Hill

Fs 322-A

19

20

21

Fs 322-B

Irvin Bell

Fs 330-A

30

29

28

Forest Service 322

Benndale

Deep Creek

31

32

33

Copyright 2006 Boyd IT Inc. All Rights Reserved

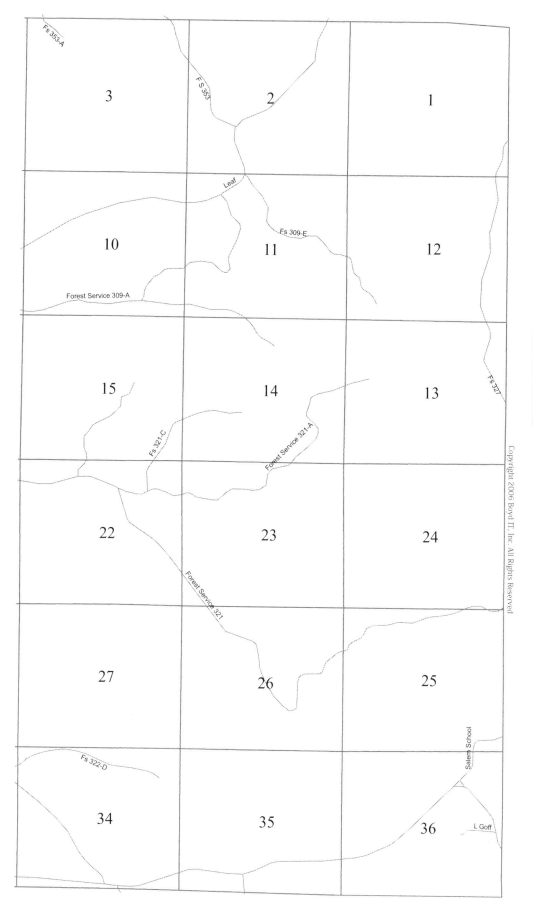

3

2

1

FS 353-A

FS 353

Leaf

Fs 309-E

10

11

12

Forest Service 309-A

15

14

13

Fs 321-C

Forest Service 321-A

Fs 321

22

23

24

Forest Service 321

27

26

25

Salem School

Fs 322-D

34

35

36

L Goff

Helpful Hints

1. This road map has a number of uses, but primarily it is to help you: a) find the present location of land owned by your ancestors (at least the general area), b) find cemeteries and city-centers, and c) estimate the route/roads used by Census-takers & tax-assessors.

2. If you plan to travel to Perry County to locate cemeteries or land parcels, please pick up a modern travel map for the area before you do. Mapping old land parcels on modern maps is not as exact a science as you might think. Just the slightest variations in public land survey coordinates, estimates of parcel boundaries, or road-map deviations can greatly alter a map's representation of how a road either does or doesn't cross a particular parcel of land.

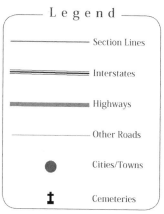

Legend

————	Section Lines
═══════	Interstates
━━━━━━	Highways
————	Other Roads
●	Cities/Towns
✝	Cemeteries

Scale: Section = 1 mile X 1 mile
(generally, with some exceptions)

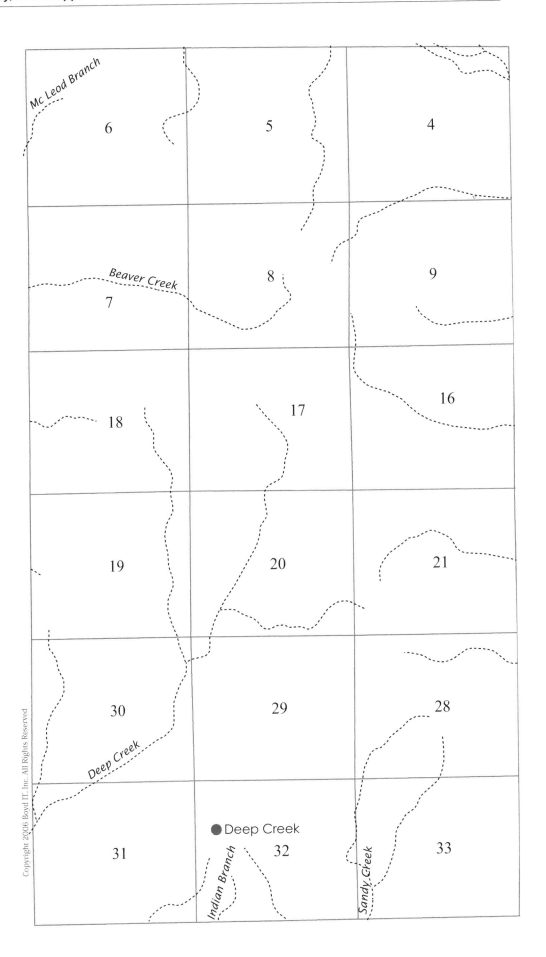

Historical Map

T1-S R9-W
St Stephens Meridian

Map Group 18

Cities & Towns
Deep Creek

Cemeteries
None

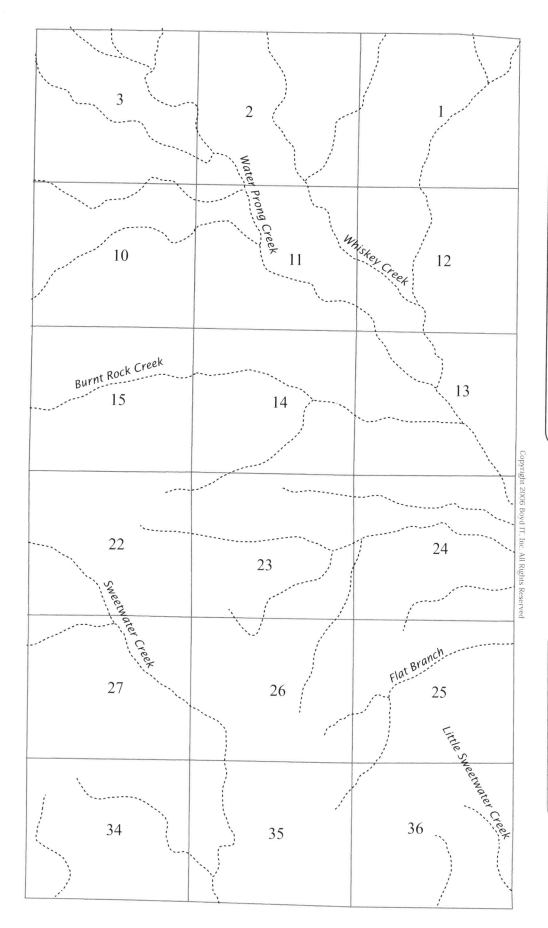

3

2

1

Water Prong Creek

Whiskey Creek

10

11

12

Burnt Rock Creek

15

14

13

22

23

24

Sweetwater Creek

27

26

Flat Branch

25

34

35

Little Sweetwater Creek

36

Helpful Hints

1. This Map takes a different look at the same Congressional Township displayed in the preceding two maps. It presents features that can help you better envision the historical development of the area: a) Water-bodies (lakes & ponds), b) Water-courses (rivers, streams, etc.), c) Railroads, d) City/town center-points (where they were oftentimes located when first settled), and e) Cemeteries.

2. Using this "Historical" map in tandem with this Township's Patent Map and Road Map, may lead you to some interesting discoveries. You will often find roads, towns, cemeteries, and waterways are named after nearby landowners: sometimes those names will be the ones you are researching. See how many of these research gems you can find here in Perry County.

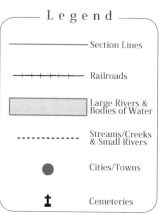

L e g e n d

———— Section Lines

+++++ Railroads

Large Rivers & Bodies of Water

- - - - Streams/Creeks & Small Rivers

● Cities/Towns

✝ Cemeteries

Scale: Section = 1 mile X 1 mile
(there are some exceptions)

Appendices

Appendix A - Acts of Congress Authorizing the Patents Contained in this Book

The following Acts of Congress are referred to throughout the Indexes in this book. The text of the Federal Statutes referred to below can usually be found on the web. For more information on such laws, check out the publishers's web-site at *www.arphax.com*, go to the "Research" page, and click on the "Land-Law" link.

Ref. No.	Date and Act of Congress	Number of Parcels of Land
1	April 24, 1820: Sale-Cash Entry (3 Stat. 566)	2306
2	March 2, 1899: Exchange-Natl Forest (lieu) (30 Stat. 993)	1
3	March 3, 1855: ScripWarrant Act of 1855 (10 Stat. 701)	3
4	May 20, 1862: Homestead EntryOriginal (12 Stat. 392)	1595
5	September 28, 1850: ScripWarrant Act of 1850 (9 Stat. 520)	1
6	September 28, 1850: Swamp Land Grant-Patent (9 Stat. 519)	4

Appendix B - Section Parts (Aliquot Parts)

The following represent the various abbreviations we have found thus far in describing the parts of a Public Land Section. Some of these are very obscure and rarely used, but we wanted to list them for just that reason. A full section is 1 square mile or 640 acres.

Section Part	Description	Acres
\<none\>	Full Acre (if no Section Part is listed, presumed a full Section)	640
\<1-??\>	A number represents a Lot Number and can be of various sizes	?
E½	East Half-Section	320
E½E½	East Half of East Half-Section	160
E½E½SE	East Half of East Half of Southeast Quarter-Section	40
E½N½	East Half of North Half-Section	160
E½NE	East Half of Northeast Quarter-Section	80
E½NENE	East Half of Northeast Quarter of Northeast Quarter-Section	20
E½NENW	East Half of Northeast Quarter of Northwest Quarter-Section	20
E½NESE	East Half of Northeast Quarter of Southeast Quarter-Section	20
E½NESW	East Half of Northeast Quarter of Southwest Quarter-Section	20
E½NW	East Half of Northwest Quarter-Section	80
E½NWNE	East Half of Northwest Quarter of Northeast Quarter-Section	20
E½NWNW	East Half of Northwest Quarter of Northwest Quarter-Section	20
E½NWSE	East Half of Northwest Quarter of Southeast Quarter-Section	20
E½NWSW	East Half of Northwest Quarter of Southwest Quarter-Section	20
E½S½	East Half of South Half-Section	160
E½SE	East Half of Southeast Quarter-Section	80
E½SENE	East Half of Southeast Quarter of Northeast Quarter-Section	20
E½SENW	East Half of Southeast Quarter of Northwest Quarter-Section	20
E½SESE	East Half of Southeast Quarter of Southeast Quarter-Section	20
E½SESW	East Half of Southeast Quarter of Southwest Quarter-Section	20
E½SW	East Half of Southwest Quarter-Section	80
E½SWNE	East Half of Southwest Quarter of Northeast Quarter-Section	20
E½SWNW	East Half of Southwest Quarter of Northwest Quarter-Section	20
E½SWSE	East Half of Southwest Quarter of Southeast Quarter-Section	20
E½SWSW	East Half of Southwest Quarter of Southwest Quarter-Section	20
E½W½	East Half of West Half-Section	160
N½	North Half-Section	320
N½E½NE	North Half of East Half of Northeast Quarter-Section	40
N½E½NW	North Half of East Half of Northwest Quarter-Section	40
N½E½SE	North Half of East Half of Southeast Quarter-Section	40
N½E½SW	North Half of East Half of Southwest Quarter-Section	40
N½N½	North Half of North Half-Section	160
N½NE	North Half of Northeast Quarter-Section	80
N½NENE	North Half of Northeast Quarter of Northeast Quarter-Section	20
N½NENW	North Half of Northeast Quarter of Northwest Quarter-Section	20
N½NESE	North Half of Northeast Quarter of Southeast Quarter-Section	20
N½NESW	North Half of Northeast Quarter of Southwest Quarter-Section	20
N½NW	North Half of Northwest Quarter-Section	80
N½NWNE	North Half of Northwest Quarter of Northeast Quarter-Section	20
N½NWNW	North Half of Northwest Quarter of Northwest Quarter-Section	20
N½NWSE	North Half of Northwest Quarter of Southeast Quarter-Section	20
N½NWSW	North Half of Northwest Quarter of Southwest Quarter-Section	20
N½S½	North Half of South Half-Section	160
N½SE	North Half of Southeast Quarter-Section	80
N½SENE	North Half of Southeast Quarter of Northeast Quarter-Section	20
N½SENW	North Half of Southeast Quarter of Northwest Quarter-Section	20
N½SESE	North Half of Southeast Quarter of Southeast Quarter-Section	20

Section Part	Description	Acres
N½SESW	North Half of Southeast Quarter of Southwest Quarter-Section	20
N½SESW	North Half of Southeast Quarter of Southwest Quarter-Section	20
N½SW	North Half of Southwest Quarter-Section	80
N½SWNE	North Half of Southwest Quarter of Northeast Quarter-Section	20
N½SWNW	North Half of Southwest Quarter of Northwest Quarter-Section	20
N½SWSE	North Half of Southwest Quarter of Southeast Quarter-Section	20
N½SWSE	North Half of Southwest Quarter of Southeast Quarter-Section	20
N½SWSW	North Half of Southwest Quarter of Southwest Quarter-Section	20
N½W½NW	North Half of West Half of Northwest Quarter-Section	40
N½W½SE	North Half of West Half of Southeast Quarter-Section	40
N½W½SW	North Half of West Half of Southwest Quarter-Section	40
NE	Northeast Quarter-Section	160
NEN½	Northeast Quarter of North Half-Section	80
NENE	Northeast Quarter of Northeast Quarter-Section	40
NENENE	Northeast Quarter of Northeast Quarter of Northeast Quarter	10
NENENW	Northeast Quarter of Northeast Quarter of Northwest Quarter	10
NENESE	Northeast Quarter of Northeast Quarter of Southeast Quarter	10
NENESW	Northeast Quarter of Northeast Quarter of Southwest Quarter	10
NENW	Northeast Quarter of Northwest Quarter-Section	40
NENWNE	Northeast Quarter of Northwest Quarter of Northeast Quarter	10
NENWNW	Northeast Quarter of Northwest Quarter of Northwest Quarter	10
NENWSE	Northeast Quarter of Northwest Quarter of Southeast Quarter	10
NENWSW	Northeast Quarter of Northwest Quarter of Southwest Quarter	10
NESE	Northeast Quarter of Southeast Quarter-Section	40
NESENE	Northeast Quarter of Southeast Quarter of Northeast Quarter	10
NESENW	Northeast Quarter of Southeast Quarter of Northwest Quarter	10
NESESE	Northeast Quarter of Southeast Quarter of Southeast Quarter	10
NESESW	Northeast Quarter of Southeast Quarter of Southwest Quarter	10
NESW	Northeast Quarter of Southwest Quarter-Section	40
NESWNE	Northeast Quarter of Southwest Quarter of Northeast Quarter	10
NESWNW	Northeast Quarter of Southwest Quarter of Northwest Quarter	10
NESWSE	Northeast Quarter of Southwest Quarter of Southeast Quarter	10
NESWSW	Northeast Quarter of Southwest Quarter of Southwest Quarter	10
NW	Northwest Quarter-Section	160
NWE½	Northwest Quarter of Eastern Half-Section	80
NWN½	Northwest Quarter of North Half-Section	80
NWNE	Northwest Quarter of Northeast Quarter-Section	40
NWNENE	Northwest Quarter of Northeast Quarter of Northeast Quarter	10
NWNENW	Northwest Quarter of Northeast Quarter of Northwest Quarter	10
NWNESE	Northwest Quarter of Northeast Quarter of Southeast Quarter	10
NWNESW	Northwest Quarter of Northeast Quarter of Southwest Quarter	10
NWNW	Northwest Quarter of Northwest Quarter-Section	40
NWNWNE	Northwest Quarter of Northwest Quarter of Northeast Quarter	10
NWNWNW	Northwest Quarter of Northwest Quarter of Northwest Quarter	10
NWNWSE	Northwest Quarter of Northwest Quarter of Southeast Quarter	10
NWNWSW	Northwest Quarter of Northwest Quarter of Southwest Quarter	10
NWSE	Northwest Quarter of Southeast Quarter-Section	40
NWSENE	Northwest Quarter of Southeast Quarter of Northeast Quarter	10
NWSENW	Northwest Quarter of Southeast Quarter of Northwest Quarter	10
NWSESE	Northwest Quarter of Southeast Quarter of Southeast Quarter	10
NWSESW	Northwest Quarter of Southeast Quarter of Southwest Quarter	10
NWSW	Northwest Quarter of Southwest Quarter-Section	40
NWSWNE	Northwest Quarter of Southwest Quarter of Northeast Quarter	10
NWSWNW	Northwest Quarter of Southwest Quarter of Northwest Quarter	10
NWSWSE	Northwest Quarter of Southwest Quarter of Southeast Quarter	10
NWSWSW	Northwest Quarter of Southwest Quarter of Southwest Quarter	10
S½	South Half-Section	320
S½E½NE	South Half of East Half of Northeast Quarter-Section	40
S½E½NW	South Half of East Half of Northwest Quarter-Section	40
S½E½SE	South Half of East Half of Southeast Quarter-Section	40

Section Part	Description	Acres
S½E½SW	South Half of East Half of Southwest Quarter-Section	40
S½N½	South Half of North Half-Section	160
S½NE	South Half of Northeast Quarter-Section	80
S½NENE	South Half of Northeast Quarter of Northeast Quarter-Section	20
S½NENW	South Half of Northeast Quarter of Northwest Quarter-Section	20
S½NESE	South Half of Northeast Quarter of Southeast Quarter-Section	20
S½NESW	South Half of Northeast Quarter of Southwest Quarter-Section	20
S½NW	South Half of Northwest Quarter-Section	80
S½NWNE	South Half of Northwest Quarter of Northeast Quarter-Section	20
S½NWNW	South Half of Northwest Quarter of Northwest Quarter-Section	20
S½NWSE	South Half of Northwest Quarter of Southeast Quarter-Section	20
S½NWSW	South Half of Northwest Quarter of Southwest Quarter-Section	20
S½S½	South Half of South Half-Section	160
S½SE	South Half of Southeast Quarter-Section	80
S½SENE	South Half of Southeast Quarter of Northeast Quarter-Section	20
S½SENW	South Half of Southeast Quarter of Northwest Quarter-Section	20
S½SESE	South Half of Southeast Quarter of Southeast Quarter-Section	20
S½SESW	South Half of Southeast Quarter of Southwest Quarter-Section	20
S½SESW	South Half of Southeast Quarter of Southwest Quarter-Section	20
S½SW	South Half of Southwest Quarter-Section	80
S½SWNE	South Half of Southwest Quarter of Northeast Quarter-Section	20
S½SWNW	South Half of Southwest Quarter of Northwest Quarter-Section	20
S½SWSE	South Half of Southwest Quarter of Southeast Quarter-Section	20
S½SWSE	South Half of Southwest Quarter of Southeast Quarter-Section	20
S½SWSW	South Half of Southwest Quarter of Southwest Quarter-Section	20
S½W½NE	South Half of West Half of Northeast Quarter-Section	40
S½W½NW	South Half of West Half of Northwest Quarter-Section	40
S½W½SE	South Half of West Half of Southeast Quarter-Section	40
S½W½SW	South Half of West Half of Southwest Quarter-Section	40
SE	Southeast Quarter Section	160
SEN½	Southeast Quarter of North Half-Section	80
SENE	Southeast Quarter of Northeast Quarter-Section	40
SENENE	Southeast Quarter of Northeast Quarter of Northeast Quarter	10
SENENW	Southeast Quarter of Northeast Quarter of Northwest Quarter	10
SENESE	Southeast Quarter of Northeast Quarter of Southeast Quarter	10
SENESW	Southeast Quarter of Northeast Quarter of Southwest Quarter	10
SENW	Southeast Quarter of Northwest Quarter-Section	40
SENWNE	Southeast Quarter of Northwest Quarter of Northeast Quarter	10
SENWNW	Southeast Quarter of Northwest Quarter of Northwest Quarter	10
SENWSE	Souteast Quarter of Northwest Quarter of Southeast Quarter	10
SENWSW	Southeast Quarter of Northwest Quarter of Southwest Quarter	10
SESE	Southeast Quarter of Southeast Quarter-Section	40
SESENE	SoutheastQuarter of Southeast Quarter of Northeast Quarter	10
SESENW	Southeast Quarter of Southeast Quarter of Northwest Quarter	10
SESESE	Southeast Quarter of Southeast Quarter of Southeast Quarter	10
SESESW	Southeast Quarter of Southeast Quarter of Southwest Quarter	10
SESW	Southeast Quarter of Southwest Quarter-Section	40
SESWNE	Southeast Quarter of Southwest Quarter of Northeast Quarter	10
SESWNW	Southeast Quarter of Southwest Quarter of Northwest Quarter	10
SESWSE	Southeast Quarter of Southwest Quarter of Southeast Quarter	10
SESWSW	Southeast Quarter of Southwest Quarter of Southwest Quarter	10
SW	Southwest Quarter-Section	160
SWNE	Southwest Quarter of Northeast Quarter-Section	40
SWNENE	Southwest Quarter of Northeast Quarter of Northeast Quarter	10
SWNENW	Southwest Quarter of Northeast Quarter of Northwest Quarter	10
SWNESE	Southwest Quarter of Northeast Quarter of Southeast Quarter	10
SWNESW	Southwest Quarter of Northeast Quarter of Southwest Quarter	10
SWNW	Southwest Quarter of Northwest Quarter-Section	40
SWNWNE	Southwest Quarter of Northwest Quarter of Northeast Quarter	10
SWNWNW	Southwest Quarter of Northwest Quarter of Northwest Quarter	10

Section Part	Description	Acres
SWNWSE	Southwest Quarter of Northwest Quarter of Southeast Quarter	10
SWNWSW	Southwest Quarter of Northwest Quarter of Southwest Quarter	10
SWSE	Southwest Quarter of Southeast Quarter-Section	40
SWSENE	Southwest Quarter of Southeast Quarter of Northeast Quarter	10
SWSENW	Southwest Quarter of Southeast Quarter of Northwest Quarter	10
SWSESE	Southwest Quarter of Southeast Quarter of Southeast Quarter	10
SWSESW	Southwest Quarter of Southeast Quarter of Southwest Quarter	10
SWSW	Southwest Quarter of Southwest Quarter-Section	40
SWSWNE	Southwest Quarter of Southwest Quarter of Northeast Quarter	10
SWSWNW	Southwest Quarter of Southwest Quarter of Northwest Quarter	10
SWSWSE	Southwest Quarter of Southwest Quarter of Southeast Quarter	10
SWSWSW	Southwest Quarter of Southwest Quarter of Southwest Quarter	10
W½	West Half-Section	320
W½E½	West Half of East Half-Section	160
W½N½	West Half of North Half-Section (same as NW)	160
W½NE	West Half of Northeast Quarter	80
W½NENE	West Half of Northeast Quarter of Northeast Quarter-Section	20
W½NENW	West Half of Northeast Quarter of Northwest Quarter-Section	20
W½NESE	West Half of Northeast Quarter of Southeast Quarter-Section	20
W½NESW	West Half of Northeast Quarter of Southwest Quarter-Section	20
W½NW	West Half of Northwest Quarter-Section	80
W½NWNE	West Half of Northwest Quarter of Northeast Quarter-Section	20
W½NWNW	West Half of Northwest Quarter of Northwest Quarter-Section	20
W½NWSE	West Half of Northwest Quarter of Southeast Quarter-Section	20
W½NWSW	West Half of Northwest Quarter of Southwest Quarter-Section	20
W½S½	West Half of South Half-Section	160
W½SE	West Half of Southeast Quarter-Section	80
W½SENE	West Half of Southeast Quarter of Northeast Quarter-Section	20
W½SENW	West Half of Southeast Quarter of Northwest Quarter-Section	20
W½SESE	West Half of Southeast Quarter of Southeast Quarter-Section	20
W½SESW	West Half of Southeast Quarter of Southwest Quarter-Section	20
W½SW	West Half of Southwest Quarter-Section	80
W½SWNE	West Half of Southwest Quarter of Northeast Quarter-Section	20
W½SWNW	West Half of Southwest Quarter of Northwest Quarter-Section	20
W½SWSE	West Half of Southwest Quarter of Southeast Quarter-Section	20
W½SWSW	West Half of Southwest Quarter of Southwest Quarter-Section	20
W½W½	West Half of West Half-Section	160

Appendix C - Multi-Patentee Groups

The following index presents groups of people who jointly received patents in Perry County, Mississippi. The Group Numbers are used in the Patent Maps and their Indexes so that you may then turn to this Appendix in order to identify all the members of the each buying group.

Group Number 1
ALEXANDER, Nancy; SCOTT, Nancy

Group Number 2
ANDREW, Mary J; KNIGHT, Mary J

Group Number 3
ANDREWS, Nancy; CROSBY, Nancy

Group Number 4
BEARDSLEY, Hellen; HINTON, Hellen

Group Number 5
BENJAMIN, Anna; BRELAND, Anna

Group Number 6
BENNETT, Louisa; BENNETT, William

Group Number 7
BIRKETT, Thomas; MCPHERSON, Alexander;
MCPHERSON, Edward; MCPHERSON, Martin;
MCPHERSON, William

Group Number 8
BIRKETT, Thomas; MCPHERSON, Alexander;
MCPHERSON, Martin; MCPHERSON, William

Group Number 9
BONNER, Eran; PRYOR, Eran

Group Number 10
BOULTON, Annie; HOTON, Annie

Group Number 11
BOULTON, Hattie; OWENS, Hattie

Group Number 12
BRADLEY, Caladonia S; EZELL, Caladonia S

Group Number 13
BRADLEY, Flora C; BRADLEY, Leonedes C

Group Number 14
BRADLEY, Rufus P; HINTON, Singleton

Group Number 15
BRELAND, George; BRELAND, Margret

Group Number 16
BRELAND, Lula; HARTFIELD, Lula

Group Number 17
BROWN, Joe B; BROWN, Letha

Group Number 18
BROWN, Rosa; SLOAN, Rosa

Group Number 19
BULLOCK, Jane; BULLOCK, Joshua

Group Number 20
CARPENTER, Georgian I; STAFFORD, Georgian I

Group Number 21
CLARK, Sallie; DOUGLASS, Sallie

Group Number 22
COLEMAN, Samuel; NEWELL, James

Group Number 23
COURTWRIGHT, Dora A; WHITTLE, Dora A

Group Number 24
CREEL, Daniel; CREEL, John

Group Number 25
CREEL, John; CREEL, Thomas

Group Number 26
DANTZLER, Lorenzo N; GRIFFIN, James W

Group Number 27
DANTZLER, Lorenzo N; GRIFFIN, William E

Group Number 28
DEVENPORT, Alice; DEVENPORT, William

Group Number 29
DRAUGHN, Rufus; MYERS, John W; MYERS, Levi;
STEVENS, William

Group Number 30
ELLSWORTH, John C; MCPHERSON, Hugh A

Group Number 31
FACEN, Mary; MAMAN, Frank; MAMAN, Mary

Group Number 32
FAIRLEY, David T; FAIRLEY, Joseph A

Group Number 33
FAIRLEY, Harriet A; HOLLIMON, Harriet A

Group Number 34
FAIRLEY, Margaret M; RILEY, Margaret M

Group Number 35
FAIRLEY, Rachel; SAMUEL, Rachel

Group Number 36
FAIRLEY, Sarah; RAYBORN, Sarah

Group Number 37
FAIRLY, David T; FAIRLY, Joseph A

Group Number 38
FAIRLY, Katie; MCDOWELL, Katie

Group Number 39
GARRAWAY, Sollomon T; HOLDER, Willis

Group Number 40
GIBSON, Minerva; GIBSON, Uriah M

Group Number 41
GRIFFIN, James W; HOWZE, George H

Group Number 42
GRIFFIN, John W; HOWZE, George H

Group Number 43
GRIFFIN, William E; PERKINS, Benjamin F

Group Number 44
HEMPHILL, Brickley C; HEMPHILL, Samuel H

Group Number 45
HINTON, Alex; HINTON, Hannah

Group Number 46
HINTON, Allen; HINTON, Catherine

Group Number 47
HINTON, Clarisa; PRIER, Clarisa

Group Number 48
HINTON, Effie; MCDONALD, Effie

Group Number 49
HINTON, Mary; HINTON, Sam A

Group Number 50
HINTON, Pheriba; MCSWAIN, Pheriba

Group Number 51
HINTON, Queen V; MCDONALD, Queen V

Group Number 52
HOGAN, Mary M; MIXON, Mary M

Group Number 53
HOLLIMAN, Theodosia; MCGILVARY, Theodosia

Group Number 54
HOLLIMON, John; MCGAHA, Tabitha

Group Number 55
HUGGINS, Manlius; KIRKLAND, Philemon;
KIRKLAND, Rebecca

Group Number 56
HUGGINS, Manlius; KIRKLAND, Rebecca

Group Number 57
JAMES, Lucretia; MCINNIS, Albert; MCINNIS, Lucretia

Group Number 58
JOHNSON, William E; VAUGHAN, Coleman C

Group Number 59
LANDRUM, Mary; LOPER, Isaac

Group Number 60
MCCALLUM, Eliza; MCCALLUM, Malcolm

Group Number 61
MCDONALD, Daniel; MCDONALD, Eliza

Group Number 62
MCPHERSON, Alexander; MCPHERSON, Edward G;
MCPHERSON, Martin J; MCPHERSON, William

Group Number 63
MCPHERSON, William; SMITH, Frederick A;
WAGNER, Jacob K

Group Number 64
MCSWAIN, Patsey; WEST, Patsey

Group Number 65
MYERS, John W; MYERS, Levi; STEVENS, William

Group Number 66
MYERS, Levi S; NICHOLS, Daniel R

Group Number 67
MYRICK, Henry; TOUCHSTONE, Jesse

Group Number 68
NIXON, Eran; SINGLEY, Eran

Group Number 69
PEARCE, Leona; SINGLEY, Leona

Group Number 70
RICH, Ida; RICH, John

Group Number 71
RUNNELS, Jesse; RUNNELS, Lewis

Group Number 72
SMITH, Ervin A; SMITH, John

Group Number 73
TISDALE, A Wayne; TISDALE, Norma

Group Number 74
TOUCHSTONE, Daniel; TOUCHSTONE, Jesse

Group Number 75
WAGAR, Humphrey R; WELLS, Willard B

Group Number 76
WHITE, Charley; WHITE, Sarah

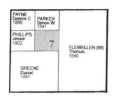

Extra! Extra! (about our Indexes)

We purposefully do not have an all-name index in the back of this volume so that our readers do not miss one of the best uses of this book: finding misspelled names among more specialized indexes.

Without repeating the text of our "How-to" chapter, we have nonetheless tried to assist our more anxious researchers by delivering a short-cut to the two county-wide Surname Indexes, the second of which will lead you to all-name indexes for each Congressional Township mapped in this volume :

For your convenience, the "How To Use this Book" Chart on page 2 is repeated on the reverse of this page.

We should be releasing new titles every week for the foreseeable future. We urge you to write, fax, call, or email us any time for a current list of titles. Of course, our web-page will always have the most current information about current and upcoming books.

Arphax Publishing Co.
2210 Research Park Blvd.
Norman, Oklahoma 73069
(800) 681-5298 toll-free
(405) 366-6181 local
(405) 366-8184 fax
info@arphax.com

www.arphax.com

How to Use This Book - A Graphical Summary

Part I

"The Big Picture"

Map A ▸ *Counties in the State*
Map B ▸ *Surrounding Counties*
Map C ▸ *Congressional Townships (Map Groups) in the County*
Map D ▸ *Cities & Towns in the County*
Map E ▸ *Cemeteries in the County*
Surnames in the County ▸ *Number of Land-Parcels for Each Surname*
Surname/Township Index ▸ Directs you to Township Map Groups in Part II

The Surname/Township Index can direct you to any number of **Township Map Groups**

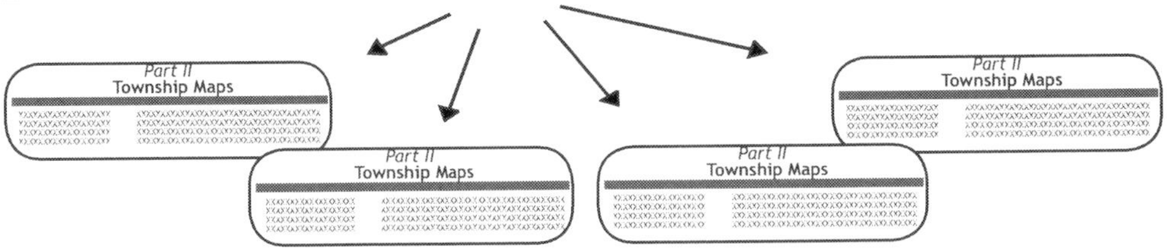

Part II

Township Map Groups

(1 for each Township in the County)

Each Township Map Group contains all four of of the following tools . . .

Land Patent Index ▸ *Every-name Index of Patents Mapped in this Township*
Land Patent Map ▸ *Map of Patents as listed in above Index*
Road Map ▸ *Map of Roads, City-centers, and Cemeteries in the Township*
Historical Map ▸ *Map of Railroads, Lakes, Rivers, Creeks, City-Centers, and Cemeteries*

Appendices

Appendix A ▸ *Congressional Authority enabling Patents within our Maps*
Appendix B ▸ *Section-Parts / Aliquot Parts (a comprehensive list)*
Appendix C ▸ *Multi-patentee Groups (Individuals within Buying Groups)*

(This page is a repeat of page 2 in the text)

Made in the USA
Columbia, SC
26 November 2024

47690372R00137